Pension Planning

Pensions, Profit-Sharing, and Other Deferred Compensation Plans

The Irwin Series in Financial Planning and Insurance
Jerry S. Rosenbloom, *Consulting Editor*

Pension Planning

Pensions, Profit-Sharing, and Other Deferred Compensation Plans

Everett T. Allen, Jr., L.L.B.
Retired Vice President and Principal
Towers, Perrin, Forster & Crosby Inc.

Joseph J. Melone, Ph.D., CLU, ChFC, CPCU
President
The Prudential Insurance Company of America

Jerry S. Rosenbloom, Ph.D., CLU, CPCU
Professor of Insurance and Academic Director
Certified Employee Benefit Specialists Program
Wharton School, University of Pennsylvania

Jack L. VanDerhei, Ph.D., CEBS
Assistant Professor
Wharton School, University of Pennsylvania

This Edition Printed
Exclusively for
The College for Financial Planning®

Sixth Edition

IRWIN
Homewood, IL 60430
Boston, MA 02116

This edition printed
exclusively for the
College for Financial Planning ®

© Richard D. Irwin, Inc., 1966, 1972, 1976, 1981, 1984, and 1988

Editor: Tony Frankos
Project editor: Joan A. Hopkins
Production manager: Diane Palmer
Compositor: Beacon Graphics Corp.
Typeface: 10/12 Caledonia
Printer: Arcata Graphics/Kingsport

ISBN 0-256-09455-1

Printed in the United States of America.

1 2 3 4 5 6 7 8 9 0 K 7 6 5 4 3 2 1 0

Preface

O ur fifth edition was barely in print when a flood of new legislation was enacted, affecting almost all aspects of retirement and capital accumulation plans. This sixth edition reflects the myriad changes brought about by the Omnibus Budget Reconciliation Act of 1987, the Tax Reform Act of 1986 (TRA '86), the Consolidated Omnibus Budget Reconciliation Act of 1985 (COBRA), the Single Employer Pension Plan Amendments Act of 1986 (SEPPA), and the Age Discrimination in Employment Amendments of 1986. Moreover, other legislative and regulatory changes have been incorporated throughout the text. We have also made a good many structural changes in this edition of the text. These changes have been made because of comments received by students, teachers, and others over the years and because of major changes in the field. The changes include a new chapter on Accounting for Pension Plans and two new chapters on Investing Pension Plan Assets. In addition, other chapters have been consolidated and the order of certain chapters has been changed to provide a better flow of material. For the first time questions for review and discussion questions are provided at the end of each chapter. Also for the first time an instructor's manual is available for the text. We believe these changes substantially strengthen this edition of the text.

Another major change in this edition is the addition of another name to the masthead, that of Dr. Jack L. VanDerhei, Assistant Professor of Insurance at the Wharton School of the University of Pennsylvania. Dr.

VanDerhei brings a fresh, new perspective to this text and has contributed a good deal of insight based on his expertise in the employee benefits area and his teaching experience in the retirement plan and capital accumulation area. We are pleased to have him join us in this sixth edition.

We want to express our appreciation once again to the many individuals who assisted us in prior editions of the text. Many of their contributions survived in this sixth edition. We are also very much indebted to the individuals in the insurance, financial, and consulting professions who have reviewed portions of this text and made many valuable suggestions, and to the many teachers and students who over the years have given us extremely constructive comments and have enabled us to improve the readability and quality of the text. Special thanks are also due representatives of The American College, the College for Financial Planning, the International Foundation of Employee Benefit Plans, the Society of Actuaries, and the Life Office Management Association for their very useful reviews and comments over the years.

We do wish to acknowledge specifically the contributions of Donald R. Fleischer, FSA, Vice President and Principal of Towers, Perrin, Forster & Crosby, who made, in this and earlier editions, material contributions to the rewriting of the chapters on funding and actuarial considerations, and to Mary Doane, Principal of Towers, Perrin, Forster & Crosby, who did the same for the chapter on administration and disclosure requirements. Specific thanks are also due to Charles W. Bevis of New England Mutual Life Insurance Company; Robert E. Carlson, Senior Vice President, and Virgil Renne of Northwestern Mutual Life Insurance Company; and Steven N. LaValle, CPC, Associate Director of Technical Operations at Massachusetts Mutual Life Insurance Company, for their review and comments on the insured funding instruments chapter; and Richard Shafer, Assistant Advisory officer, TIAA-CREF, for his work on the tax-deferred annuities chapter.

The reader should be aware that there are many rules, regulations, and interpretations of the recent legislation still to come that could affect some of the material in this text.

Everett T. Allen, Jr.
Joseph J. Melone
Jerry S. Rosenbloom
Jack L. VanDerhei

Contents

1

Development of Private Pension Plans

Individuals constantly seek means to enhance their economic security. One cause of economic insecurity is the probable reduction of an individual's earning power at an advanced age. In this country, this risk is met through one or more of the following means: personal savings (including individual insurance and annuities), private pensions, and government-sponsored programs. When these three elements are combined, they produce a multifaceted approach to economic security often referred to as the "tripod of economic security," the "three-legged stool of economic security," or the "pillars of economic security." The dramatic growth of private plans since the 1940s has focused considerable interest on this form of income maintenance.[1]

GROWTH OF PRIVATE PLANS

The beginnings of industrial pension plans in the United States date back to the establishment of the American Express Company plan in 1875.[2] The second formal plan was established in 1880 by the Baltimore and Ohio Railroad Company. During the next half century, approximately 400 plans

---

[1]*Private plans*, as used in this text, refers to plans established by private agencies, including commercial, industrial, labor, and service organizations, and nonprofit religious, educational, and charitable institutions. Social security and public plans for governmental employees are covered in this text only when they affect private plans.

[2]Murray Webb Latimer, *Industrial Pension Systems* (New York: Industrial Relations Counselors, Inc., 1932), p. 21.

1

were established. These early pension plans were generally found in the railroad, banking, and public utility fields. The development of pensions in manufacturing companies was somewhat slower, largely because most manufacturing companies were still relatively young and therefore not confronted with the superannuation problems of the railroads and public utilities.

Insurance companies entered the pension business with the issuance of the first group annuity contract by the Metropolitan Life Insurance Company in 1921.[3] The second contract was issued by the Metropolitan in 1924 to an employer who already had a retirement plan on a "pay-as-you-go" basis.[4] In 1924, The Equitable Life Assurance Society of the United States announced its intention of offering a group pension service, thus becoming the second company to enter the field.[5]

Although the beginnings of private pensions date back to the 1800s, the significant growth in these programs has come since the 1940s. In 1985, there were more than 39 million households with one or more workers covered by an employer- or union-provided pension plan.[6] The assets of pension funds currently exceed $1 trillion and are growing by over $150 billion a year.

ECONOMIC PROBLEMS OF OLD AGE

Longevity is a source of economic insecurity in that individuals may outlive their financial capacities to maintain themselves and their dependents. The extent to which an aged person will have the financial capacity to meet self-maintenance costs and those of dependents relies upon the standard of living desired during retirement years, employment opportunities, and the prior provisions made to meet this contingency.

Standard of Living after Retirement

The assumption usually is made that the financial needs of an individual decrease after retirement. To some extent, this assumption is valid. The retired individual may have no dependent children, and a home and its furnishings generally have been acquired by retirement age. However, the actual aggregate reduction in the financial needs of a person upon retirement has probably been overstated. Social pressures discourage any drastic

[3]Kenneth Black Jr., *Group Annuities* (Philadelphia: University of Pennsylvania Press, 1955), p. 9.

[4]Ibid., p. 11.

[5]Black, *Group Annuities*, p.11.

[6]Households with one or more persons covered by a pension plan at work represented about 44 percent of all households and 58 percent of households with a working member in 1985. *Receipt of Selected Noncash Benefits: 1985*, Series P-60 (Washington, D.C.: U.S. Government Printing Office, 1985).

change in one's standard of living upon retirement, and an increasing tendency exists for retired persons to remain fairly active, particularly in terms of civic, social, travel, and other recreational activities. Furthermore, urbanization and its corollary, apartment living, minimize the prospect of retired parents moving in with their children.

The authors are not suggesting that retired workers require income benefits equal to their earnings levels immediately preceding retirement, nor even the level of preretirement take-home pay. Presumably, at least at the higher income levels, these individuals were allocating a portion of their take-home pay to individual savings. However, it is suggested that the reduction in standard of living after retirement is not very great; and, more importantly, the trend in social thinking seems to be in the direction of not expecting retired workers to have to take much of a reduction in standard of living after retirement. The effect of inflation in recent years also has militated against a lower standard of living. Therefore, it is questionable whether one should assume any significant decrease in basic financial needs upon retirement, at least for individuals in the low- and middle-income categories.

Employment Opportunities

The proportion of persons 65 and over with some income from active employment is currently about 10 percent,[7] and this percentage has been declining in recent years. Obviously, many reasons account for the withdrawal of the aged from the labor force. A large number of older workers voluntarily retire. If workers have the necessary financial resources, they may wish to withdraw from active employment and live out their remaining years at a more leisurely pace. Others find it necessary for reasons of health to withdraw from the labor force at an advanced age. The aging process takes its toll, and many individuals are physically unable to operate at the level of efficiency attainable at the younger ages. Disabilities at the older ages tend to be more frequent and of longer duration.

Voluntary retirement and the physical inability to continue employment are undoubtedly important reasons for the decrease in the percentage of older persons participating in the labor force. However, these are probably not the most important factors affecting employment opportunities for the aged. The effects of industrialization and the development of the federal Old-Age, Survivors, Disability, and Health Insurance (OASDHI) program, private pensions, and other employee benefit programs probably have had a more significant impact on this problem.

The rapid pace and dynamic evolution of industrial employment operate to the disadvantage of older persons. Automation and the mass-production assembly lines put a premium on physical dexterity and mental alertness.

---

[7]This figure is based on estimates prepared by the staff of the Joint Committee on Taxation using information from the IRS Statistics of Income and the 1984 Current Population Survey.

Employers generally are of the opinion, justifiable or not, that the younger workers are better suited to the demands of industrial employment. In an agricultural economy the able-bodied older person could continue to work, at least on a part-time basis.

The OASDHI program and private pension plans, although created to alleviate the financial risk associated with excessive longevity, have actually aggravated the problem. These programs have tended to institutionalize age 65 as the normal retirement age, although the 1986 amendments to the Age Discrimination in Employment Act (ADEA) banned mandatory retirement (at any age) for most employees. The 1983 amendments to The Social Security Act will gradually raise the normal retirement age for social security benefits to age 67 by the year 2027. Also, some employers may hesitate to hire older workers on the assumption that these employees would increase pension and other employee benefit plan costs. It is difficult to generalize as to the impact of the older worker on employee benefit plan costs. Nevertheless, it must be recognized that an employer's attitude toward the hiring of older workers may be influenced by the assumption, justified or not, that employee benefit costs will be adversely affected.

Self-employed members of the labor force have greater control as to the timing of their retirement from active employment. For example, physicians and lawyers frequently continue in practice, at least on a part-time basis, until advanced ages. Owners of businesses also continue to be active in the firm until relatively old ages. The fact remains, however, that employment opportunities for the majority of older workers are becoming more limited.

Individual Savings of the Aged

If employment opportunities for the aged are decreasing and financial needs are still substantial at advanced ages, the need for savings becomes quite apparent. Relatively little information is available on the extent of savings among the aged. The little data available today indicate clearly that other than equity in a home, the average assets of persons age 65 and over are relatively small.

However, the value of home ownership for the economic security of the aged should not be underestimated. Studies indicate that a substantial proportion of the homes owned by the aged are clear of any mortgage. Home ownership reduces the income needs of the aged insofar as normal maintenance costs and taxes are less than the amount of rent required for comparable housing accommodations. It has been estimated that the maintenance costs for an unencumbered home are about one third to 40 percent less than the costs of renting comparable facilities. Furthermore, there is the possibility that the home can be used in part as an income-producing asset or that a home equity loan can be used to provide additional cash. There is growing interest in the concept of a so-called reverse annuity.[8] Under this approach, the homeowner receives a lifetime monthly income in exchange for the title to the home at the homeowner's death. The amount of the monthly annuity payment depends on the equity in the home and the life expectancy of the homeowner. Also, in any evaluation of the economic status of the aged, resources available in time of need from both the immediate and extended family (i.e., children away from home and relatives) cannot be ignored.

Personal savings rates have been running at historically low levels in recent years. The distribution of savings by savings media has changed considerably over the years. The change that is most pertinent to this discussion is the relative increase in private pension reserves in relation to purely individual forms of saving. Annual contributions to private pension funds now amount to about $65 billion, and the net contributions to pension funds have averaged over 16 percent of personal savings in recent years.[9] The tremendous increases in disposable income over the last quarter century, therefore, have not resulted in any increase in the proportion of personal savings. There have been many forces at work that have restricted the growth of savings. Advertising, installment credit, and the media of mass communications encourage individuals to set their sights on a constantly increasing standard of living. This competition from consumption goods for current income dollars results in a lower priority being placed on the need for accumulating savings for old age. Also, the high levels of federal income tax rates reduce an income earner's capacity to save. In recent decades, inflation has been an additional deterrent to increased levels of saving. Inflation is a particularly serious threat to the adequacy of savings programs of persons who already are retired. For employed persons, increases in the cost of living may be offset, in part or in whole, by increases in current earnings; however, inflation protection is likely to be less comprehensive for most aged persons.[10] Therefore, the aged are faced with the alternatives of accepting a lower standard of living or more rapidly liquidating their accumulated savings.

The proportion of individual (as opposed to group) savings, then, is decreasing at a time when the pattern of living of the aged is becoming increasingly more costly. There has also been increasing concern about the financing and adequacy of the social security system. Under such circumstances, the tremendous importance of pension programs in meeting the economic risk of old age is obvious.

---

[8]Henry Bartel, Michael Daly, and Peter Wrage, "Reverse Mortgages: Supplementary Retirement Income from Homeownership," *Journal of Risk and Insurance* (September 1980), pp. 477–90.

[9]U.S. Department of Commerce, Bureau of Economic Analysis, *Survey of Current Business* 63 (July 1983), Tables 6.8 and 6.15.

[10]Chapter 7 describes the inflation protection inherent in social security payments as well as the techniques used by many private plan sponsors to provide automatic or ad hoc relief.

Increasing Longevity

Still another dimension to the overall economic problem of old age is the number of aged in the population. The fact that life expectancy has been increasing is well recognized. However, that this increase in longevity is a recent and quite dramatic development often is not appreciated. Since 1900 the life expectancy at birth has increased from 47 years to approximately 74.3 years. The rates of mortality at the earlier ages are now so low that further improvements in mortality at these ages would have little impact on further extensions of the average length of life. If additional improvements in longevity are to be realized, reductions in mortality at the older ages are required. This impediment to further extensions in life expectancy may be overcome if medical advances result from the current concentration of research in the areas of the chronic and degenerative diseases.

One effect of the improvements in longevity in the 20th century has been an absolute and relative increase in the population of persons age 65 and over. In 1900, there were approximately 3 million persons age 65 and over, whereas there were about 25 million such persons in 1980. By the year 2000, it is estimated that persons age 65 and over will number about 32 million.[11] The proportion of the U.S. population age 65 and over currently is about 11.5 percent, whereas the proportion of the population in these age brackets in 1900 was about 4 percent.

Another important dimension in the analysis of the changing demography of the elderly — those age 65 and over — is their age distribution. A generation ago, 68 percent of the elderly were 65 to 74 years old, 27 percent were 75 to 84, and only 5 percent were 85 or older. However, today's elderly population reflects a shift toward the upper end of the age scale: approximately 10 percent are over 85, nearly a third are 75 to 84, and less than 60 percent are 65 to 74.[12]

The problem of old-age economic security, therefore, is of concern to an increasing number and percentage of the U.S. population.

REASONS FOR GROWTH OF PRIVATE PENSIONS

From the above discussion it can be seen that the problem of economic security for the aged is a serious and increasingly important one. However, the mere existence of the problem does not explain the phenomenal growth of private pensions. In other words, given the existence of the old-

---

[11]Bureau of the Census, U.S. Department of Commerce, "Estimates and Projections of the Population: 1977–2050," Current Population Reports, Series P-25, no. 704, July 1977.

[12]Peter K. Francese, "Demographic Trends Reshaping Retirement Security," in *Search for a National Retirement Income Policy*, ed. Jack L. VanDerhei (Homewood, Ill.: Richard D. Irwin, 1987).

age economic problem, why did employers and employees choose to meet the need, at least in part, through the vehicle of private pension programs? In a broad sense, the major reason is the fact that private pensions offer substantial advantages to both employers and employees. Without this foundation of mutual benefit, the private pension movement could not have achieved the prolonged and substantial growth it has enjoyed. In addition, for several decades, government officials recognized the social desirability of pension programs and acted to encourage the growth of these plans through favorable treatment under the tax system and by other means. Recently, however, it appears that this attitude has changed and many commentators have speculated that the resulting tax law modifications may curb the growth of these arrangements.

The specific factors generally considered as having influenced the growth of private pensions are discussed below. It must be recognized that the reasons giving rise to the establishment of one plan might be quite different from those in the case of another plan.

Increased Productivity

A systematic method of meeting the problem of superannuated employees can be easily justified on sound management grounds. Practically every employee eventually reaches a point where, because of advanced age, he or she is a liability rather than an asset to the employer. That is, at some advanced age, an employee's contribution to the productivity of the firm is less than the compensation he or she is receiving.

The employer has several courses of action when an employee reaches this point. One, the employee can be terminated without any further compensation or any retirement benefits as soon as the value of the employee's services is less than the salary being paid. For obvious reasons, this course of action is seldom followed by employers. Two, the employer can retain the superannuated employee in the employee's current position and at current level of compensation. The difference between the employee's productivity and salary is absorbed by the employer as a cost of doing business. This alternative is also undesirable. Such an approach would undoubtedly prove to be the most costly method of meeting the problem of superannuated employees. Furthermore, the longer range indirect costs that would be incurred from the resultant inefficiencies and poor employee morale among the younger workers would be significant. Three, the employer could retain the superannuated worker, but transfer the employee to a less demanding job at the same or a reduced level of compensation. In the former case, the direct costs would be similar to alternative two, but the indirect costs would be reduced in that a younger and more capable person would now be staffing the more demanding position. If the employee's salary is reduced, the direct costs of superannuation also would be reduced.

Most employers who do not have a pension plan generally handle the problem of the older worker in the latter manner. The effectiveness of this approach to the problem has certain important limitations. First, a firm usually has only a limited number of positions to which aged workers can be transferred. For a large or even medium-sized firm, only a fraction of the superannuated employees can be efficiently employed. With automation and the increasingly higher levels of skill required in most jobs, the limitations of this solution are apparent. Furthermore, the superannuated employee is generally still overpaid in the less demanding jobs since, for practical purposes, reductions comparable to the decrease in employee productivity are seldom made. Lastly, this approach does not solve the problem of superannuation; it merely defers it, since a point will be reached where the employee's productivity is considerably below even a minimum level of wage.

The fourth alternative available to the employer in meeting the problem of superannuation is to establish a formal pension plan. A pension plan permits employers to provide superannuated employees with an acceptable alternative to continued employment in a humanitarian and nondiscriminatory manner, and the inefficiencies associated with retaining employees beyond their productive years are reduced. Furthermore, the sense of security derived from the knowledge that provision is made, at least in part, for their retirement income needs should increase the morale and productivity of employees. Also, systematic retirement of older workers will keep the channels of promotion open, thereby offering opportunity and incentive to the young, ambitious employees — particularly those aspiring to executive positions. Therefore, a pension plan should permit an employer to attract and keep a better caliber of employee.

The problem of superannuation, then, exists in all business firms. Any solution, except the unlikely alternative of arbitrary termination of older workers without any retirement benefit, results in some cost, direct or indirect, to the employer. Unfortunately, some employers assume that the pension plan solution is the only approach that carries a price tag. The hidden costs of the other alternatives must be recognized. The decision, therefore, is which solution is best suited to the needs and financial position of the employer. For a large number of employers, the formal pension plan approach has proved to be the superior solution.

Tax Considerations

The bulk of the growth in private pension plans has occurred since 1940. One reason for the growth of these plans during the World War II and Korean War periods was that normal and excess profits tax rates imposed on corporations during these years were extremely high. Since the employer's contributions to a *qualified* pension plan are deductible (within limits) for federal income tax purposes, a portion of the plan's liabilities could be funded with very little effective cost to the firm. Furthermore, the investment income earned on pension trust assets is exempt from federal income taxation until distributed.[13]

The tax advantages of qualified pension plans are attractive from the standpoint of employees covered under the plan; for example, the employer's contributions to a pension fund do not constitute taxable income to the employee in the year in which contributions are made. The pension benefits derived from employer contributions are taxed when distributed to the employee. In addition, under limited circumstances, distributions from a pension plan may be taxed on a favorable basis.

Therefore, qualified pension plans offer significant tax advantages to participants generally, and, prior to 1988, employees in high income tax brackets received greater advantages.[14] Since the high-salaried senior officers of corporations often make the decision regarding the establishment and design of employee benefit plans, their role as participants under the plan may have influenced their decisions on these matters. However, in the case of large corporations, cost and other considerations minimized or eliminated the personal tax situations of key employees as factors influencing the establishment or design of a pension plan. In the case of a small, closely held corporation, on the other hand, one can readily see how the tax implications for stockholder-employees might have been a decisive factor in the establishment and design of a pension plan. Lastly, tax considerations are certainly one reason, although not the most important, why some labor leaders negotiate for establishment and liberalization of employee benefit programs in lieu of further wage increases.

Although it is too early to know the full implications of the Tax Reform Act of 1986, benefits available to highly compensated employees will be substantially restricted, perhaps to the point where alternative forms of compensation (such as cash or nonqualified retirement arrangements) will be more desirable. Management of smaller organizations might be tempted to terminate existing plans and use the money to compensate executives in some other way.

Wage Stabilization

The second wartime development that helped to stimulate the growth of pensions was the creation of a wage stabilization program as part of a general price control scheme. Employers, in competing for labor, could not offer the inducement of higher wages. Under these conditions, union leaders found it difficult to prove to their membership the merits of unionism.

---

[13]For a complete discussion of the tax aspects of qualified pension plans, see Chapters 4 and 22.

[14]As recently as 1986, the federal income tax law had 14 progressive tax brackets and a maximum rate of 50 percent. The Tax Reform Act of 1986 reduced the number of tax brackets to two (15 percent and 28 percent), effective in 1988.

Therefore, the War Labor Board attempted to relieve the pressure on management and labor for higher wage rates by permitting the establishment of fringe benefit programs, including pensions. This policy further stimulated the growth of pension plans during the period.

Union Demands

Labor leaders have had mixed emotions over the years regarding the desirability of employer-financed pension plans. In the 1920s, labor generally did not favor such plans for its membership. It held the view that pensions represented an additional form of employer paternalism and were instituted to encourage loyalty to the firm. Labor leaders felt that the need would be best met through the establishment of a government-sponsored universal social security system; in the absence of that solution, unions should establish their own pension plans for their members. The former objective was achieved with the passage of The Social Security Act of 1935. By the 1930s, several unions had established their own plans. However, many of these plans were financed inadequately, a condition that became quite apparent during the depression years. Recognition of the financial burden of a pension program and enactment of wage controls led some labor leaders, in the early 1940s, to favor establishment of employer-supported pension plans.

From 1945 to 1949, the rate of growth of new plans fell off markedly. During this postwar period, employee interest centered upon cash wage increases in an attempt to recover the lost ground suffered during the period of wage stabilization. In the latter part of the 1940s, union leaders once again began expressing an interest in the negotiation of pension programs. The renewal of interest in pensions probably came about because of two factors. First, there was increasing antagonism on the part of the public toward what were viewed by many persons as excessive union demands for cash wage increases. The negotiation of fringe benefits was one way of possibly reducing pressures from this quarter. Second, some union leaders argued that social security benefits were inadequate, and a supplement in the form of private pension benefits was considered to be necessary. Also, certain labor officials believed the negotiation of employer-supported pensions would weaken the resistance of the latter toward liberalizations of social security benefit levels. Thus, pension demands became a central issue in the labor negotiations in the coal, automobile, and steel industries in the late 40s. Although unions had negotiated pension benefits prior to this period, it was not until the late 40s that a major segment of labor made a concerted effort to bargain for private pensions.

Labor's drive for pension benefits was facilitated by a National Labor Relations Board ruling in 1948 that employers had a legal obligation to bargain over the terms of pension plans. Until that time, there was some question whether employee benefit programs fell within the traditional subject areas for collective bargaining; that is, wages, hours, and other conditions of employment. The issue was resolved when the National Labor Relations Board held that pension benefits constitute wages and the provisions of these plans affect conditions of employment.[15] Upon appeal, the court upheld the NLRB decision, although it questioned the assumption that such benefits are wages.[16] The result of these decisions was that an employer cannot install, terminate, or alter the terms of a pension plan covering organized workers without the approval of the authorized bargaining agent for those employees. Furthermore, management has this obligation regardless of whether the plan is contributory or noncontributory, voluntary or compulsory, and regardless of whether the plan was established before or after the certification of the bargaining unit.

Labor was quick to respond to these decisions, and the 1950s were marked by union demands for the establishment of new pension plans, liberalization of existing plans, and the supplanting of employer-sponsored programs with negotiated plans. Undoubtedly, labor's interest in private pensions has been an important factor in the tremendous growth in plans since 1949.

Business Necessity

Employers hire employees in a free, competitive labor market. Therefore, as the number of plans increases, employees come to expect a pension benefit as part of the employment relationship. Employers who do not have such a plan are at a competitive disadvantage in attracting and holding personnel. Therefore, some employers feel they must install a plan even if they are not convinced that the advantages generally associated with a pension plan outweigh the cost of the benefit. Admittedly, this is a negative reason for instituting a plan. In other words, these employers feel that little evidence exists that pension plans truly result in improved morale and efficiency among their work force; but they feel that there would clearly be an adverse employee reaction if they did not offer a pension. Also, in contrast to situations where a plan is established in response to labor demands, an employer may offer a pension plan as part of an employee relations objective aimed at keeping a union out of the firm.

Reward for Service

There is a tendency to argue that employers never provide any increase in employee benefits unless they can expect an economic return in some form. Although this philosophy may generally prevail in a capitalistic system, the fact remains that many employers have established plans out of a

[15]*Inland Steel Company* v. *United Steelworkers of America*, 77 NLRB 4 (1948).
[16]*Inland Steel Company* v. *National Labor Relations Board*, 170 F.(2d) 247, 251 (1949).

sincere desire to reward employees who have served the firm well over a long period of service. Also, some employers may feel a moral responsibility to make some provision for the economic welfare of retired employees.

Efficiency of Approach

Part of the growth of private pensions must be attributed to the belief that a formal group savings approach has certain inherent advantages. The advantages are not such that they eliminate the need for individual savings; but the merits of private pensions as a supplement to social security benefits and individual savings programs are indeed significant. First, the economic risk of old age derives from the fact that a point is reached when an employee is unable or unwilling to continue in active employment. A formal plan as an integral part of compensation arrangements and employment relationships, therefore, is quite logical. There is no additional wage cost to the employer to the extent that pension benefits are provided in lieu of other forms of compensation. If pension benefits are provided in addition to prevailing wage rates, the employer's extra wage costs resulting from the pension plan may be able to be passed on to the consuming public in the form of higher prices.

It has been argued that from a broad social point of view, the private pension system is the lowest cost method of providing economic security for the aged. In addition to the administrative efficiency of group saving arrangements, it is argued that the small increase in consumer prices that might be required to provide pension benefits is a relatively painless method of meeting the risk. In other words, the burden of retirement security is spread over a large number of people and over a long period of time. Still another aspect to the argument is the assumption that private pensions increase consumption levels among the aged, which in turn helps to maintain a high level of economic activity.

Lastly, private pensions constitute a form of forced savings. This advantage is extremely important in view of the apparent desire of many people to maintain a relatively high standard of living during their active employment years. Thus, it may be argued that it is economically more efficient if at least part of the risk is met through a forced saving private pension scheme.

Sales Efforts of Funding Agencies

For all the previously mentioned reasons, there has been a considerable demand over the years for private pensions. However, in many instances, the advantages of these programs had to be called to the attention of specific employers. This function of creating effective demand for the pension product has been aggressively performed by those parties interested in providing services in this area. Insurance companies, through agents, brokers, and salaried representatives, were undoubtedly instrumental in the growth of pensions, particularly in the decades of the 20s and 30s. The trust departments of banks also are equipped to handle pension funds, and many corporate trustees and asset managers have been actively soliciting pension business, particularly since the early 1950s.

RATIONALE OF PRIVATE PENSIONS

The growth of private pensions is attributable, as seen above, to a variety of reasons. It is difficult to determine the extent to which each factor contributed. Indeed, it seems reasonable to conclude that the dominant reasons leading to the establishment of specific plans vary depending on the circumstances surrounding each case. In other words, productivity considerations were dominant forces leading to the creation of some plans, while labor pressures, tax considerations, or other factors encouraged establishment of still other plans. With such variety of motivation, it is difficult to characterize private pensions in terms of a single philosophy or rationale. Nevertheless, attempts have been made over the years to explain private pensions in terms of an underlying concept or philosophy.[17]

Early industrial pension plans were viewed as gratuities or rewards to employees for long and loyal service to the employer. Closely related to this view is the concept that private pensions constitute a systematic and socially desirable method of releasing employees who are no longer productive members of the employer's labor force. Regardless of the view taken, it is clear that these early plans were largely discretionary, and management made it quite evident that employees had no contractual rights to benefits under the plans. Continuation of the pension plan was dependent upon competitive conditions and management policy. Furthermore, management reserved the right to terminate benefit payments to pensioners for misconduct on the part of the beneficiary or for any other reasons justifying such action in the opinion of the employer.

Thus, the growth of early pensions might be best categorized by a single concept: *business expediency*. Business expediency, by the very nature of the concept, implies that the establishment of a plan is a management prerogative and that the primary motivation for the creation of such plans was the economic benefit, direct or indirect, that accrued to the employer. But as the economy became more and more industrialized and pension plans became more prevalent, there was increasing interest in the view that employers had a moral obligation to provide for the economic security of retired workers. This point of view was expressed as early as 1912 by Lee Welling Squier, as follows: "From the standpoint of the whole system of

---

[17]For an excellent discussion of pension philosophies, see Jonas E. Mittelman, "The Vesting of Private Pensions" (Ph.D. dissertation, University of Pennsylvania, 1959), Chapter 2.

social economy, no employer has a right to engage men in any occupation that exhausts the individual's industrial life in 10, 20, or 40 years; and then leave the remnant floating on society at large as a derelict at sea."[18]

This rationale of private pensions has come to be known as the *human depreciation concept*. It was the point of view taken by the United Mine Workers of America in their 1946 drive to establish a welfare fund:

> The United Mine Workers of America has assumed the position over the years that the cost of caring for the human equity in the coal industry is inherently as valid as the cost of the replacement of mining machinery, or the cost of paying taxes, or the cost of paying interest indebtedness, or any other factor incident to the production of a ton of coal for consumers' bins. . . . [The agreement establishing the Welfare Fund] recognized in principle the fact that the industry owed an obligation to those employees, and the coal miners could no longer be used up, crippled beyond repair, and turned out to live or die subject to the charity of the community or the minimum contributions of the state.[19]

This analogy between human labor and industrial machines also was made in the report of the president's fact-finding board in the 1949 steelworkers' labor dispute in support of its conclusion that management had a responsibility to provide for the security of its workers: "We think that all industry, in the absence of adequate Government programs, owes an obligation to workers to provide for maintenance of the human body in the form of medical and similar benefits and full depreciation in the form of old-age retirement—in the same way as it does now for plant and machinery."[20] The report continues as follows: "What does that mean in terms of steelworkers? It should mean the use of earnings to insure against the full depreciation of the human body—say at age 65—in the form of a pension or retirement allowance."[21]

The validity of the human depreciation concept of private pensions has been challenged by many pension experts.[22] The process of aging is physiological and is not attributable to the employment relationship. Admittedly, the hazards of certain occupations undoubtedly shorten the life span of the employees involved. In those instances, the employer can logically be held responsible only for the increase in the rate of aging due to the hazards of the occupation. More importantly, the analogy between humans and

---

[18]Lee Welling Squier, *Old Age Dependency in the United States* (New York: Macmillan, 1912), p. 272.

[19]United Mine Workers of America Welfare and Retirement Fund, *Pensions for Coal Miners* (Washington, D.C., n.d.), p. 4.

[20]Steel Industry Board, *Report to the President of the United States on the Labor Dispute in the Basic Steel Industry* (Washington, D.C.: U.S. Government Printing Office, September 10, 1949), p. 55.

[21]Ibid., p. 65.

[22]For example, see Dan M. McGill, *Fundamentals of Private Pensions*, 5th ed. (Homewood, Ill.: Richard D. Irwin, 1984), pp. 18–19. See also Charles L. Dearing, *Industrial Pensions* (Washington, D.C.: Brookings Institution, 1954), pp. 62–63 and 241–43; and Mittelman, "Vesting of Private Pensions," pp. 28–34.

machines is inherently unsound. A machine is an asset owned by the employer, and depreciation is merely an accounting technique for allocating the costs of equipment to various accounting periods. Employees, on the other hand, are free agents and sell their services to employers for a specified wage rate. An employee, unlike a machine, is free to move from one employer to another. The differences between humans and machines are so great that one must question the value of the analogy as a basis for a rationale of private pensions. As Dearing notes: "Any economic or moral responsibility that is imposed on the employer for the welfare of workers after termination of the labor contract should be grounded on firmer reasoning than is supplied by the machine-worker analogy."[23]

In recent years, a view of private pensions that has achieved broader acceptance is the *deferred wage concept*. This concept views a pension benefit as part of a wage package that is composed of cash wages and other employee fringe benefits. The deferred wage concept has particular appeal with reference to negotiated pension plans. The assumption is made that labor and management negotiators think in terms of total labor costs. Therefore, if labor negotiates a pension benefit, the funds available for increases in cash wages are reduced accordingly. This theory of private pensions was expressed as early as 1913:

> In order to get a full understanding of old-age and service pensions, they should be considered as a part of the real wages of a workman. There is a tendency to speak of these pensions as being paid by the company, or, in cases where the employee contributes a portion, as being paid partly by the employer and partly by the employee. In a certain sense, of course, this may be correct, but it leads to confusion. A pension system considered as part of the real wages of an employee is really paid by the employee, not perhaps in money, but in the forgoing of an increase in wages which he might obtain except for the establishment of a pension system.[24]

The deferred wage concept also has been challenged on several grounds. First, it is noted that some employers who pay the prevailing cash wage rate for the particular industry also provide a pension benefit. Thus, it can be argued that in these cases the pension benefit is offered in addition to, rather than in lieu of, a cash wage increase. Second, the deferred wage concept ignores the possible argument that the employer is willing to accept a lower profit margin to provide a pension plan for employees. Third, it is sometimes argued that if pension benefits are a form of wage, then terminated employees should be entitled to the part of the retirement benefit that has been earned to the date of termination. In practice, one finds that only a small proportion of the plans provides for the full and immediate vesting of all benefits. However, it can be argued that the

---

[23]Dearing, *Industrial Pensions*, p. 243.

[24]Albert de Roode, "Pensions as Wages," *American Economic Review* III, no. 2 (June 1913), p. 287.

deferred wage concept does not necessarily require the full and immediate vesting of benefits. Proponents of this concept view pension benefits as a wage the receipt of which is conditioned upon the employee's remaining in the service of the employer for a specified number of years. This view of the pension benefit is similar, conceptually, to the pure endowment, the consideration of the employee being the reduction in cash wages accepted in lieu of the pension benefit.

In spite of the appeal of the deferred wage theory, it is questionable whether the private pension movement can be explained solely in terms of this concept. Indeed, there is probably no one rationale or theory that fully explains the "reason for being" of private pensions. This conclusion is not surprising in view of the fact that these plans are *private*, and the demands or reasons that give rise to one plan may be quite different from those leading to the introduction of another plan.

RECENT LEGISLATION

Employee benefits in general and pension plans in particular have been the subject of substantial legislative activity in recent years.

After many years of discussion and debate concerning reform of the private pension system, the Employee Retirement Income Security Act of 1974 (ERISA) became law on September 2, 1974. ERISA effected some of the most significant changes ever enacted in the private pension movement. These changes affected virtually all aspects of corporate and self-employed pension plans from a legal, tax, investment, and actuarial viewpoint. In addition, ERISA established new reporting, disclosure, and fiduciary requirements as well as a program of plan termination insurance. Another major feature of ERISA was the establishment of the individual retirement account (IRA) concept, which was initially designed for individuals not covered under a qualified retirement plan.

The Economic Recovery Tax Act of 1981 (ERTA) was one of the biggest tax reduction acts in history. It also included several provisions that affected retirement plans. Most notable were the provisions that greatly expanded IRA opportunities to anyone with personal service income, allowed for voluntary contributions to qualified plans, and increased contribution and deduction limits for both simplified employee pension (SEP) programs and Keogh (H.R. 10) plans. ERTA also made changes that affected stock ownership plans and executive compensation arrangements.

Following on the heels of ERTA came another massive act, the Tax Equity and Fiscal Responsibility Act of 1982 (TEFRA), considered by some to be the biggest revenue-raising bill in history. TEFRA probably touched everyone in some manner and affected retirement plans in many ways. It reduced the maximum limits of pension plan benefits and contributions; brought about parity between corporate plans and plans for self-employed persons; introduced special restrictions on plans that are considered "top heavy," that is, plans that appear to be heavily weighted toward key employees; and provided for federal income tax withholding on pension and annuity payments.

After a one-year hiatus, in 1984 Congress passed two acts with significant implications for qualified retirement plans. The Deficit Reduction Act of 1984 (DEFRA) contained several provisions that substantially modified savings incentives. Cost-of-living adjustments for contribution and benefit limits were frozen for a second time. Estate tax exclusions for distributions from qualified plans and IRAs were repealed. Rules for cash-or-deferred plans, also known as 401(k) plans, were tightened. The Retirement Equity Act of 1984 (REACT) represented an attempt on the part of Congress to provide what was perceived by some as a more equitable distribution of retirement benefits from qualified plans. Young employees and nonworking spouses were the chief benefactors, as REACT required a reduction in the minimum age for mandatory participation, changed the survivor benefit requirements, and allowed for the assignment or alienation of qualified plan benefits in divorce proceedings.

In the most pervasive changes since ERISA, the Tax Reform Act of 1986 imposed new coverage tests and accelerated vesting requirements for qualified plans, changed the rules under which qualified plans can be integrated with social security, lowered limits for retirement benefits that begin before age 65, changed the timing and taxation of plan distributions, and terminated IRA deductions for many qualified plan participants. Substantial changes were also made with respect to employee stock ownership plans and executive compensation. Following the Tax Reform Act of 1986, Congress passed the Omnibus Budget Reconciliation Act of 1987 which made significant changes with respect to (1) minimum funding and maximum tax deductions for qualified plans, and (2) plan termination obligations for defined benefit plans.

Many changes, rulings, and regulations relating to these various pieces of legislation have occurred since their enactment. The legislation and the changes, as well as their impact on retirement plans, will be discussed throughout this book.

QUESTIONS FOR REVIEW

1. Describe the basic economic problems facing the aged.
2. Why have private pension plans grown so rapidly in the last four decades?
3. Explain the alternatives that exist for an employer dealing with superannuated employees. What are the limitations of these alternatives?
4. Briefly describe the principal tax advantages of qualified pension plans.
5. Describe how wage stabilization during World War II affected private pension plans.
6. Explain the role played by the National Labor Relations Board (NLRB) in the development of pension plans.

7. Describe the merits of private pensions as a supplement to social security benefits and individual savings programs.

8. Briefly describe the impact of recent legislation on the design process for private pension plans.

QUESTIONS FOR DISCUSSION

1. Economists have often argued that pension benefits are a form of deferred compensation accepted by employees in lieu of higher present wages. Assume that the employees of a firm ask you how much the pension benefit they earned this year is actually worth in current dollars. In general terms, how would you perform this valuation? What types of assumptions would you need to make? If the employees told you that they would forfeit the entire pension attributable to employer contributions if they were terminated within five years of the time they were originally hired, how would you factor this information into your analysis?

2. For several years it has been argued that one of the primary advantages of a pension plan for employees was that it allowed them to avoid taxation on a portion of their total compensation during the time they were in a high tax bracket and postpone the receipt, and as a consequence the taxation, of this money until after they retire. If, as was usually the case prior to the Tax Reform Act of 1986, the employee expected to be in a lower tax bracket after retirement, the tax savings inherent in this deferral could be substantial. Beginning in 1987, however, it appears the federal income tax system is evolving into a modified form of a flat tax system in which many taxpayers may expect to be taxed at the same rate, regardless of when their money is received. Does this necessarily imply that the tax advantages of private pension plans have ceased to be an important advantage for employees? (Hint: Even if all money received from a pension plan is taxed at the same rate, does the fact that money can accumulate at a before-tax rate of return, instead of an after-tax rate of return, affect the eventual amount of money received by the employee?)

3. The text suggests that a private pension plan allows the burden of retirement security to be spread over a long period of time. Discuss how this specifically applies in the case of investment risk. Assume that there are only two forms of investments for retirement: a risk-free asset with a known rate of return, and a risky asset with a higher expected rate of return. Unfortunately, the risky asset may experience large decreases as well as increases in any particular year. If employees were to invest for their retirement on an individual basis, why might they be willing to choose the risk-free asset, knowing their expected accumulation at retirement will be smaller? In contrast, if employees allowed the employer to invest for their retirement through a defined benefit pension plan (in which the employee's retirement benefit is guaranteed regardless of the level of the pension assets), would the employer be as likely to choose the lower yielding risk-free asset for the pension plan? (Hint: What is the relevant investment horizon for a pension plan if it is assumed to be an ongoing operation?)

2

Benefit Plan Objectives

It is reasonable to speculate that the first employee benefit plans were established to serve specific purposes—for example, to avoid "passing the hat" among employees when someone died. For many years, the design of these plans was influenced largely by the insurance industry's attitude toward underwriting, funding, and administration, since these were made available by insurers under the terms and conditions they chose to utilize.

Over the years, many factors have influenced the design of employee benefit plans, and a body of law has emerged that affects these plans in terms of minimum requirements and permissible provisions. The taxation of contributions and benefits has also influenced plan design, and the process of collective bargaining and the interests of organized labor have been a major influence, as has the availability of alternate funding mechanisms. These, and other factors, including a growing degree of sophistication and knowledge of the field, have created an environment in which an employer has a wide degree of choice and flexibility in benefit plan design.

The cost of employee benefits is significant. A well-rounded program (including paid time off) can easily generate a total cost in the vicinity of 30 percent or more of an employer's base payroll. If the cost of statutory benefits is also included, total cost can easily reach 40 percent of payroll or more. Indeed, some companies have total benefit costs that approach 50 percent of payroll. The amounts accumulated under these plans also are of major importance. For example, the assets accumulated by some companies in their pension plans alone exceed their net worth.

Given the substantial costs involved in employee benefits plans, the importance they have to millions of workers, and the complex legal, tax, and funding environment that exists, it is most important that such plans be designed with particular care, that they be fully supportive of the employer's philosophy, goals, and objectives, and that they at least partially satisfy the perceived needs of the employees. It should also be observed that this concept is of equal importance to small employers and to larger organizations.

The major focus of this text is on the various mechanisms that exist for the delivery of retirement benefits and the ways in which a specific retirement plan might be designed. However, matters that influence the design of a retirement plan also influence the design of other employee benefit plans. Thus, while the primary emphasis of this chapter is on retirement plans, the subject matter is broad enough to apply to all employee benefits.

In this chapter, some of the environmental considerations that can influence plan design are described first. Then employer philosophy and attitudes are discussed. The final portion of the chapter deals with specific employee benefit plan objectives.

ENVIRONMENTAL CONSIDERATIONS

Before passage of the Tax Equity and Fiscal Responsibility Act of 1982 (TEFRA), the employer's legal status often influenced plan design. Federal tax law was different as it applied to sole proprietorships, partnerships, Subchapter S corporations, nonprofit organizations, and regular corporations. For example, the defined *contribution* pension or profit sharing plan generally has been adopted by unincorporated organizations and by Subchapter S corporations because of the deduction limits previously imposed on these organizations. However, these deduction limits and the potential benefits of a defined *benefit* pension plan have often caused such organizations to incorporate either on a regular basis or as a professional corporation or association. Section 501(c)(3) organizations also have availed themselves of the defined contribution approach because of the availability of tax-deferred annuities under Section 403(b) of the Internal Revenue Code. The parity provisions of TEFRA eliminate most of the distinctions in tax law that formerly applied to partnerships and sole proprietorships. However, precedents established by prior practice and on account of prior law may still continue to influence plan design for some organizations.

The basic characteristics of the employer and its industry are part of the background for designing an employee benefit program. Is the firm a young, growing organization, or is it relatively mature? Is its history of profits stable and predictable, or have profits been, or are they likely to be, volatile? Does the firm anticipate moderate or significant growth, and what will its need for employees be in the foreseeable future? Is the industry highly competitive? Are profit margins narrow? Is the business cyclical? What are the firm's short- and long-term capital needs? The answers to these questions and others like them can be of great importance in structuring benefit plans that meet employee needs with funding patterns compatible with the employer's objectives and capabilities.

The characteristics of the individuals employed by the employer also play an important role in plan design. The distribution of employees by age, service, sex, and pay can have significant implications in terms of the type of benefit provided, cost levels generated, and similar matters. This distribution can be even more significant under certain funding methods and instruments.

An employer with diversified operations has special considerations when it comes to employee benefit plan design. For example, such an employer needs to consider whether the same benefit program is appropriate for all facets of the business. Factors such as cost, profit margins, competitive need, and geographic differences should be taken into account. Another factor related to this issue is the employer's attitude on the transfer of employees. A uniform program facilitates such transfers, while different plans at different locations may create impediments. Obviously, the employer's basic policy concerning employee transfers, whether encouraged or discouraged, bears on the matter. One approach used by some employers is to establish a basic or "core" program that applies in all areas of the business, with a flexible or varying program of supplemental benefits to accommodate different industry needs.

The communities in which the employer does business can also be an environmental factor in plan design. This is less the case in large, urban areas, but can become quite meaningful when the company is the dominant or a major employer in a discrete geographical area. In this case, the design and structure of an employee benefit plan could reflect the employer's degree of concern over the image it wishes to create in the communities in which it does business. If such a concern exists, it often indicates the need for liberal benefit provisions — not only by the employer's own industry standards, but by the standards established by different employers involved in the same communities.

The presence or absence of collective bargaining units can be a significant consideration. The demands of labor, both on a local and a national or "pattern" basis, can influence plan design, even for nonbargaining employees. Many employers follow the practice of extending bargained-for benefits to nonbargaining unit employees — or a practice of making the plans of the nonbargaining unit employees slightly better than those of the bargaining unit employees, to the extent that this does not violate labor laws. Others, however, treat the programs as totally separate, particularly in the context that benefit plans are part of total compensation and that basic salary and wage structures also are quite different between the two groups.

The foregoing is not intended to be an exhaustive discussion of environmental factors that influence plan design. Rather, it is intended to give some indication of items that should be considered. With these in mind, it is appropriate to turn to a discussion of employer philosophy and attitudes.

EMPLOYER PHILOSOPHY AND ATTITUDES

Specific objectives for employee benefit plans should be set in the context of the employer's philosophy and attitudes for the management of human resources. The following list of questions and observations, again not all-inclusive, is designed to suggest the nature of some of the items that need to be considered.

1. What is the employer's basic compensation philosophy? Many employers believe benefit plans are part of total compensation and that the cost and benefit structure of these plans should reflect the employer's basic attitude toward other compensation elements. Thus, the employer who has adopted a policy of paying high wages and salaries may very well adopt a liberal benefit program. On the other hand, an employer may choose to establish a benefit program that keeps total compensation costs at an acceptable level while presenting one element of compensation on a more favorable basis. For example, an employer may wish to establish highly competitive wages and salaries but, to keep total compensation costs in line, may provide only modest benefits. Such a compensation strategy, of course, can affect the type of employee attracted and also can influence matters such as turnover rates. It also is possible for an employer to adopt a reverse compensation strategy mix and have a liberal benefit program to go along with a cash compensation program that is not fully competitive. This type of compensation mix often is found in governmental units where cash compensation is fixed by law and where incentive compensation may not be payable. Here, it is common to find employees with a liberal benefit program.

2. Is the employer's basic attitude toward providing employee benefits one that emphasizes the protection and maintenance of income in the event of economic insecurity? Or is its attitude oriented more toward providing additional current, although tax deferred, compensation? Most employers do not have a clear-cut and total preference for one or the other of these positions; however, one position might be of greater significance than the other. The employer's leaning toward one or the other of these two concepts can find expression in a number of plan decisions. For example, a preference for the income-maintenance approach could suggest the choice of a defined benefit pension plan integrated to the maximum extent with social security benefits,[1] or of a death benefit that provides an income

---

[1]The basic concept of integration is that the benefits of the employer's plan must be dovetailed with social security benefits in such a manner that employees earning over the social security taxable wage base will not receive combined benefits under the two programs proportionately greater than the benefits for employees earning less than this amount. Therefore, although the benefit formula under the private plan may favor the higher paid employees, the combined social security and private plan benefits must produce a total retirement income that is a relatively equal percentage of compensation for all employees. This concept is presented in more detail in Chapter 6.

benefit but only to survivors of the employee's immediate family. A compensation-oriented approach, though, might suggest the use of a defined contribution plan as the basic program for providing retirement benefits.

3. Does the employer believe employees should share in the cost of meeting their own economic security needs? Many employers take the position that employees do have such a responsibility, and benefits in the event of medical expense needs, death, disability, and retirement should come from three sources—the government, the employer, and the employee's own savings. Where desired, employee involvement can be in the form of direct employee contributions, or it can be recognized in indirect ways as, for example, when income-replacement objectives in a noncontributory pension plan are consciously set below what might otherwise be desired levels, or through the use of deductibles, coinsurance, or inside plan limitations in a medical expense plan. Also, an employer can view this issue from the perspective of the total employee benefit program, making some specific plans contributory and some noncontributory, with the overall employee contributions achieving a total level the employer feels is satisfactory.

4. A long-term, advance-funded retirement program involves certain risks. Two of the most important relate to the impact of inflation and investment results. The employer's attitude on who should bear these risks—the employer or the employees—can play a significant role in the choice between a defined benefit and a defined contribution pension plan.[2] Under the former, these risks are assumed by the employer, although the risk of inflation can be tempered by the choice of a formula that is not pay-related, or by the choice of a career-pay formula, while the employee in effect assumes both of these risks under a defined contribution plan.

5. The selection of specific retirement plan provisions (normal retirement age, early retirement age and subsidies, the treatment of deferred retirement, and the benefit levels provided under all these events) and the amount of postretirement life and medical expense insurance provided can influence the pattern of retirements in any organization.[3] Many employers prefer to encourage employees to retire at or before normal retirement age, and for a variety of reasons, such as keeping promotional channels open. Others prefer to encourage deferred retirements and are reluctant to

---

[2]A defined benefit plan is a pension plan under which the employer provides a determinable benefit, usually related to an employee's service and/or pay. Under this approach, the employer's cost is whatever is necessary to provide the benefit specified. A defined contribution plan is a pension plan under which the employer's contribution is fixed and this contribution is accumulated to provide whatever amount of benefit it can purchase. Thus, an employee's benefit becomes the variable, depending upon factors such as age at entry, retirement age, and investment earnings (or losses). A defined contribution plan can involve a specific contribution or it can take the form of a profit sharing, thrift or savings, or employee stock ownership plan. These concepts are presented in more detail in Chapter 3.

[3]These provisions are discussed in Chapter 5.

see skilled workers leave while still capable of making important contributions to the firm's profitability. Still other employers take a neutral position and do not seek to exert any influence on the pattern of retirements in their organizations. In any event, this issue has taken on added significance in view of the 1986 amendments to the Age Discrimination in Employment Act (ADEA), which protect employment rights of all employees age 40 and over. This issue will also be influenced by the 1983 social security amendments, which will gradually extend the "normal" retirement age for social security benefits to 67, at the same time reducing the level of benefits available from ages 62 through 66.

6. A growing number of employers prefer to structure an employee benefit program on a basis that gives employees a wide choice of plans in which to participate and the extent to which they participate in these plans. This can be accomplished on the basis of before-tax credits in the form of flexible or "cafeteria" benefits, or it can be accomplished by developing various layers of after-tax contributory coverage. Such employers believe this type of flexibility makes the program more meaningful to employees and more efficient, since benefits are delivered only when needed or desired. Other employers prefer not to become involved in the administrative complexities and cost associated with such flexibility, nor do they wish to absorb any additional costs associated with the adverse selection permitted by such choices. Also, those employers who have a paternalistic attitude might feel many employees would not want to make choices or would not be able to make the right choices.

7. An employer's position concerning the cost levels it can assume can be a major determinant for a plan's benefit levels and the various ancillary benefits that might be included. The assumption of any given level of cost commitment also involves a balancing of employee interests with those of the organization's owners or shareholders. Another aspect relates to the employer's attitude about the need for maintaining controls over future cost levels. A high degree of concern in this area, for example, might lead to the selection of a career-pay or a defined contribution pension plan, to the use of pay-related deductibles in a medical plan, or to nonpay-related death benefits.

8. Whether the plan's benefits should be coordinated with social security benefits is a most important question. The employer's basic philosophy concerning this issue plays an important role in plan design. A great many employers believe that because of the very nature of social security benefits and their relatively larger value for lower paid employees, it would be impossible to achieve an equitable balancing of benefits and costs for employees at all pay levels without integrating pension and disability income plans in some fashion with the benefits provided by social security. Others believe the communications and administrative difficulties associated with integrated plans are such that integration is not desirable.

9. Should an employer provide a benefit program for executives that differs from that provided for its employees in general? Over the years, the majority of benefit programs have been applied across-the-board to all employees, and many employers still believe executives or highly paid employees should be treated the same as all employees. An increasing number of organizations, however, believe the unique needs of executives cannot be met by plans that must meet the nondiscrimination requirements of federal tax law. For example, it may be difficult for a firm to recruit a needed executive in midcareer because of the loss of pension benefits he or she will experience, since a large part of the executive's benefits will be frozen at the pay levels achieved with the prior employer. In such a case, a need may exist for the employer to have a retirement arrangement that restores the benefits such an executive might potentially lose. Similarly, an employer might find it desirable to provide executives with a supplemental pension that applies the basic pension plan formula to the executive's incentive pay, if the basic pension relates to base compensation only. Due to the nondiscrimination requirements described in Chapter 4, special benefits for executives such as those described cannot be provided through a qualified, nondiscriminatory pension or profit sharing plan. Instead, these benefits must be provided through some form of nonqualified supplemental pension arrangement (these nonqualified arrangements are described in Chapter 24). Many employers also provide executives with additional death benefits, both before and after retirement, as well as with additional disability income protection.[4]

10. An important question since the passage of the Employee Retirement Income Security Act of 1974 (ERISA) is whether the employer is willing to assume the plan termination obligations imposed upon the employer in the event of the termination of a defined benefit plan before all accrued and vested benefits have been funded. The impact this might have on net worth and on credit ratings and the ability to raise capital has caused a good deal of concern—particularly among small employers.[5] This potential liability can be avoided if a defined contribution pension plan is adopted and, indeed, over 80 percent of all new tax-qualified plans adopted since the passage of ERISA have been of the defined contribution variety.

---

[4] The tax laws now prohibit discrimination for virtually all forms of employee benefits (except disability income and employee-pay-all plans) and severely limit qualified retirement benefits for highly compensated employees. However, the cost of violating these discrimination requirements (employer-provided benefits become taxable to the employees) is less severe now that the maximum tax brackets have been lowered as a result of the Tax Reform Act of 1986. Many experts expect a proliferation of executive plans as a result.

[5] The employer's liability on termination of a single-employer plan is quite complex and a detailed discussion of this topic is deferred until Chapter 23. It should be noted that an employer can also be exposed to a liability in the case of a negotiated multiemployer plan.

EMPLOYER OBJECTIVES

With the preceding in mind, it is appropriate to consider specific employer objectives. The following discusses major employer objectives, as well as some of the factors relating to such objectives. Obviously, not all these objectives apply to each employer and, if they do have application, it is likely their relative importance may not be the same for each employer.

Attraction and Retention of Employees

Most employers recognize they must maintain some form of employee benefit program to attract and retain desirable employees. This is particularly so when the employer must compete with other employers for personnel.

Even so, many employers believe the presence of an adequate benefit program is not a positive influence in their efforts to attract and retain employees — at least to any significant extent. Rather, these employers reason the absence of such a program could have a negative effect on their recruiting and retention efforts. Put another way, these employers are of the opinion that an inadequate program can hinder their efforts to recruit and retain employees, while an overly generous program will not produce a corresponding increase in their ability to attract and hold desirable workers.

While this might be true as a general concept, it is worth noting that some benefit plans might have greater impact than others as far as employees are concerned. Thus, for example, the presence of a generous profit sharing plan might make employment with one employer more attractive than employment with another employer who maintains a more conventional benefit program. In the same vein, employees might find the choice and value of a flexible (or cafeteria) benefit plan of more interest than a plan that offers a standard fare of benefits.

Meeting Competitive Standards

The objective of having competitive employee benefit plans is closely related to the objective of being able to attract and retain good employees. It is, however, somewhat broader in concept and can reflect employers' attitudes concerning their standing in their own industry, as well as in the communities in which they operate. This objective also recognizes that, unlike other forms of compensation, employee benefit plans are highly visible and readily subject to external comparison.

An employer who wishes to have competitive employee benefit plans must establish standards for measuring these plans. Will competitiveness be measured against industry standards, geographic standards, or both? Many employers have a preference for measuring their plans against industry standards. However, it should be recognized that such standards are most appropriate for skilled or professional workers and for management personnel — those whose capabilities are more related to the employer's own industry. For workers whose capabilities are more readily transferred from one industry to another, a more realistic standard would be the plans maintained by the local companies with which the employer competes on a local basis for human resources. Thus, as a practical matter, most employers seek to compare their plans both on an industry and a geographic basis.

Having identified the standard against which the plans are to be measured, the employer also must decide the relative level of competitiveness to achieve. For example, the employer might decide the objective is to have an employee benefit program that meets the average of the companies that form its comparison base (or it can establish different positions for different plans). The employer also might decide it wishes to be a leader and have a program consistently among the best, or it might wish to rank somewhere between the 50th and 75th percentile. And, of course, the employer might elect to lag somewhat behind other companies because of cost or other considerations.

Even though the comparison base has been identified and the relative ranking within this base established, there remains the important matter of determining the technique to be used to establish the relative standing of the different plans. One method used quite frequently is to make comparisons of the benefits actually payable to representative employees under different circumstances. For example, the benefit payable under a retirement plan at normal retirement age might be projected for several employees with differing pay, service, and age characteristics. This method is relatively simple in concept, but should be used with caution. First, it shows benefits only and does not necessarily give any true indication of the relative cost of the plans involved. Also, by isolating a specific benefit, the importance and value of other benefits included in the same plan are not taken into account. For example, a company might be ranked as the highest in terms of benefits payable at normal retirement, but the other companies in the comparison may have much more valuable early retirement or survivor income benefits. Even if other benefits are illustrated and compared in the same way, the aggregate value of all benefits within the same plan may not be readily ascertainable. This method is also sensitive to the assumptions used in making the illustrations. If retirement benefits are being illustrated, for example, and if future pay increases are not taken into account, the benefit differences attributable to career-pay and final-pay[6] formulas will not be apparent (nor will there be any apparent difference between a final three-year average plan and a final five-year average plan).

---

[6]A final-pay provision bases benefits on the employee's earnings averaged, for example, over the last three or five years of employment, or over the three or five consecutive years in the 10-year period immediately prior to retirement during which the employee's earnings are the highest. In contrast, a career-pay provision bases benefits on the employee's earnings averaged over the entire career of employment. This concept is presented in detail in Chapter 6.

Another method used for comparative purposes is to compare actual costs to the employer for different benefit plans. The material used for this purpose usually is information acquired from both published and private surveys about actual employer cost patterns. A major difficulty with this approach is that there is often inconsistent reporting, by different employers, of the information requested. Also, actual contribution patterns do not necessarily reflect the real cost or value of the benefit involved. The cost reported, for example, might be the total annual cost of the plan including employee contributions and reflect the specific characteristics of the employee group involved. In the case of retirement plans, significant differences may exist in annual contributions because of the choice of a particular actuarial method and the combination of actuarial assumptions employed. For example, two employers with identical plans might report significantly different annual costs because of their different choices of assumptions for future investment earnings and growth in pay.

A third method is to measure plans on a basis that uses uniform actuarial methods and assumptions and focuses on the relative value of the different benefits provided. This technique establishes the value of specific plans, specific benefits within a plan, and the aggregate value of all plans. The method can also establish these relative values on the basis of employer cost only, or on the basis of combined employer and employee cost. By using uniform actuarial methods and assumptions, and by applying these to a database of employees held the same for all employer plans in the study, the actual differences in the value of different benefits are isolated and their relative values established. It should be noted that this technique does not establish actual costs or cost patterns, it simply establishes whether one particular benefit or plan is more valuable than another and the extent to which this is so.

Cost Considerations

Earlier in this chapter, reference was made to an employer's attitude on costs and how this can play a major role in plan design. Since a retirement plan often represents the largest part of an employer's total benefit program cost, it is particularly important that the employer have specific objectives in this area.

It is important to distinguish between ultimate real cost and estimated annual accruals. With this distinction in mind, an employer may establish specific objectives for actual liabilities assumed under a plan and specific objectives for annual accruals. The employer also may establish objectives in terms of the budgeting pattern to be assumed. For example, does the employer desire an accrual cost that remains level, as a percentage of payroll, or would it be preferable to have a pattern that starts with relatively low accruals, gradually building to higher levels in the future?

The employer's objectives for these cost levels influence the choice of retirement plan formula as well as the inclusion and level of ancillary benefits. These objectives also may influence the decision on whether the plan should be contributory and, if so, the level of employee contributions required.

There are other objectives an employer could have for matters concerning cost. The need for contribution flexibility might be one such objective and, if desired, could influence the choice of actuarial funding method and assumptions and could even lead the employer to adopt a profit sharing plan. Another objective could relate to the employer's willingness to assume the costs associated with future inflation. The extent to which the employer wishes to limit commitment might dictate the choice of a career-pay formula for a defined benefit plan or even the choice of a defined contribution plan of some type.

The need for a cost-efficient retirement program is an obvious objective. Thus, employers wish to avoid excessive or redundant benefits and to fund the plan in the most efficient manner possible. For this reason, many employers choose to coordinate benefits from all sources, and, for example, integrate their retirement plan benefits with those provided by social security.

It is also possible that an employer may view a retirement plan as a tax shelter for the benefit of key employees. When this is the case, the employer's objective might be to maximize benefits and contributions within the limits permitted by federal tax law.

Other employee benefit plans also involve cost considerations. If postretirement death and medical expense benefits are to be provided, should these liabilities be prefunded, and if so, how? Should inflation-sensitive benefits—medical expense and pay-related death benefits—be subjected to some degree of control through plan design? What type of funding mechanism should be utilized to gain greater control over cash flow? Clearly, cost considerations are becoming an increasingly important factor in plan design and in plan funding.

Compliance with Legal Requirements

Employee benefit plans have almost always been subject to some degree of regulation and other legal requirements. This has become much more the case in the last decade with the advent of ERISA, antidiscrimination laws, and the like. The recent enactment of the Tax Reform Act of 1986 will have a major impact on the design of plans. Thus, the design and maintenance of employee benefit plans must meet the requirements of federal tax law, antidiscrimination laws, securities laws, labor laws, and state insurance laws. In several areas, state as well as federal laws must be taken into account. Thus, an implicit, if not explicit, objective of any employee benefit plan is that it must comply with these legal requirements.

However, an employer often has a choice in the manner in which compliance is achieved and, in some cases, may avoid compliance requirements by the design of the plan. For this reason, it is desirable that the employer formulate specific objectives in this regard. The following examples should give at least some indication of areas where compliance choices are available.

1. The Age Discrimination in Employment Act (ADEA) prevents discrimination in employment for employees age 40 and over. However, this does not require all benefit plans to treat all employees alike, regardless of age. It is possible, for example, to reduce life insurance coverage for active employees by reason of age (but only within cost-justified limits). Although it is no longer possible to terminate pension accruals in a defined benefit plan or to discontinue allocations in a defined contribution plan after an active employee has attained age 65, a plan may limit the amount of benefit provided under the plan or the number of years of service or plan participation taken into account. An employer should establish basic objectives on how its over-65, active employees will be treated, and whether compliance with this law should be at or above the minimum level. The employer's decision is, of course, influenced by other objectives and attitudes, such as whether it is desirable to encourage earlier or deferred retirements, its public relations posture, and the like.

2. Federal tax law permits the exclusion from a defined benefit pension plan of employees who have less than one year of service or who are under age 21. Employers may include all employees in their plans or may seek to exclude the maximum number possible, depending upon their attitude on minimum compliance and other objectives.

3. An employer may wish to establish a defined benefit pension plan that includes incentive compensation for executives as part of the compensation base used to determine plan benefits, but may not want to include overtime pay and shift differential paid to other employees. It is unlikely the Internal Revenue Service would approve such a pay definition in a qualified pension plan. As discussed in Chapter 24, compliance with the nondiscrimination requirements of federal tax law could be satisfied by designing the qualified plan with a nondiscriminatory definition of compensation that relates to base pay only, and by instituting a nonqualified, supplemental executive retirement plan (SERP) that applies the base plan formula to incentive pay.

4. A savings plan can be designed so that some part of both employer and employee contributions can be invested in employer securities. Securities and Exchange Commission (SEC) requirements are such that the plan will have to be registered before employee contributions may be invested in this manner. These requirements can be avoided if employer securities can be purchased only by employer contributions.

Achieving Optimum Tax Benefits

Federal tax law is such that some advantages exist for distributions from employee benefit plans. This is particularly so in the case of tax-qualified retirement and profit sharing plans. For example: (1) investment income on plan assets is not taxed until it is distributed in the form of a benefit; and (2) certain lump-sum distributions may qualify for favorable tax treatment. Indeed, on the one hand these tax advantages very often are the motivating force behind the adoption of a plan—particularly in the case of a small employer. Larger employers, on the other hand, are not as apt to give a high priority to achieving optimum tax advantages for plan distributions. Since these plans cover large groups of employees, the employer's objectives more often are oriented toward benefit levels and costs.

If an employer wishes to achieve maximum tax advantages for a retirement program, this can find expression in many areas; for example, the choice of benefit formula, the degree to which the plan is integrated with social security benefits, the level of funding chosen, the funding instrument chosen, the adoption of both a defined benefit and a defined contribution plan, the use of a target benefit plan, and so on.[7]

The desire to maximize tax advantages may also affect other benefits and how they are funded. For example, a preretirement spouse benefit may be included as part of a retirement plan, or it may be funded by a separate group term life insurance program. If funded by life insurance, most of the benefit payments will escape income tax, however, the annual cost of insurance can represent taxable income to the employees under Section 79 of the Internal Revenue Code.[8] If the benefit is provided from retirement plan assets, the payments represent taxable income (except to the extent provided by employee contributions), but there will be no annual cost of insurance to be reported by the employee. The emphasis to be placed on these various tax considerations and the characteristics of the employee group involved influence the choice of how the benefit will be funded.

As mentioned earlier, lump sum distributions from a pension plan can qualify for favorable tax treatment. This could be very important for highly paid employees, and a desire to achieve maximum tax advantages could lead to the inclusion, in a retirement plan, of a provision that allows such lump-sum distributions. However, since the option also would have to be extended to all employees, consideration needs to be given to possible mis use of this feature by some employees and whether this could defeat overall plan objectives.

---

[7]A target benefit plan is one that combines the concepts of both defined contribution and defined benefit plans. The target benefit plan uses a defined benefit formula to determine an employee's projected pension at normal retirement date. A contribution to provide this benefit is determined. This contribution is not adjusted for future experience. Instead, contributions are accumulated for each employee in an individual account and, depending upon actual investment results, can accumulate to provide a greater or smaller benefit than that originally projected. This approach has the advantage of determining the initial amount to be allocated to each employee on a basis that reflects the employee's age as well as compensation, while at the same time preserving the accumulation aspects of a defined contribution plan. This concept is presented in more detail in Chapter 6.

[8]Life insurance proceeds generally are income tax free. However, if paid in installments, the portion representing interest payments will be taxable.

Efficiency of Design

The overall cost of employee benefits is quite substantial and, as noted earlier, can amount to one third or more of an employer's payroll costs. For this reason, it is important for an employer to structure its employee benefit program so benefits are provided in the most efficient manner possible and overlapping or redundant benefits are eliminated or, at least, minimized.

One of the most effective ways of doing this is to recognize that while any particular benefit plan has a primary focus (e.g., retirement, death, or disability), all benefit plans and some statutory plans must function in some fashion in the case of an event covered primarily by another plan. For example, the primary plan dealing with retirement is, of course, the employer's retirement plan. However, social security can be a major source of additional retirement income. Supplemental retirement income also can be provided by the employer's savings or profit sharing plan, if such a plan is in existence. The employer's group life insurance and medical expense plans may be the source of additional benefits for a retired employee. Viewing all these plans as a total retirement program can influence the choice of specific benefits and benefit levels. Thus, the existence of significant amounts of postretirement life insurance might suggest that, except for legally required joint and survivor protection, the normal form for payment of retirement benefits exclude any form of death benefit, such as a guarantee that benefits will be paid for a minimum period of time; otherwise, excessive or redundant postretirement death benefits might be provided.

The same approach can be applied to the events of preretirement death and disability. The primary plan in the event of preretirement death is the employer's group life insurance plan. However, additional death benefits may be provided by way of continuation of medical expense coverage for the employee's dependents and, in certain cases, the retirement plan must provide preretirement survivor benefits.[9] Social security can also be a source of substantial survivor benefits, as can a profit sharing or savings plan. In the case of disability, a need exists to coordinate the benefits available from the employer's plan (life insurance, short- and long-term disability income plans, savings and profit sharing plans, and medical expense plans) with those available from social security. Again, efficient plan design suggests the benefits from all these sources be coordinated to insure overall benefits in line with employer objectives.

Income-Replacement Ratios

Employer objectives as to income-replacement ratios are critical in the design of disability income and retirement plans.

---

[9] The preretirement survivor benefit requirements for a qualified plan are described in Chapter 6.

In the case of disability income plans, the issues are not as complex. The benefit usually is not service related (although some plans are), and it is generally designed to replace a percentage of current pay. There are no restrictions on the ability of a plan to integrate with social security benefits, and it is customary to offset 100 percent of the employee's primary social security disability benefit. In fact, most plans offset 100 percent of the total social security benefit payable, including family benefits. In general, the plan formula recognizes that some part or all of the social security and plan benefits may be income tax free, and that total after-tax income should provide adequate maintenance while at the same time creating an economic incentive for the employee to rehabilitate and return to active work. A typical formula might provide for a total gross before-tax benefit (including social security) of 60 percent of current pay.

Establishing income-replacement objectives for a retirement plan is more complex. Before selecting a specific benefit formula, it is important for an employer to identify the amount of an employee's gross income to be replaced by the retirement plan and under what circumstances.

From the employee's viewpoint, it would be desirable to have a situation where total retirement income permits the full maintenance of the standard of living the employee enjoyed just prior to retirement. For most employees, some part of this income consists of social security benefits. Indeed, for employees at lower income levels, a substantial portion of a preretirement gross income will be replaced by social security benefits. This is illustrated by Table 2–1, which shows estimated social security benefits at different final pay levels for both a single individual and a married couple, assuming the employee (and spouse) are both age 65 at the beginning of 1987. As can be seen, the replacement ratios, relative to gross pay, can be as high as 49 percent for an individual whose final pay is $10,000 (73 percent for the married couple). At a final pay level of $20,000,

TABLE 2–1: Social Security Replacement Ratios (1987 retirement)

Final Pay*	Social Security Benefit as a Percentage of Final Pay	
	Single	Married Couple
$10,000	49%	73%
15,000	42	63
20,000	38	58
25,000	35	52
30,000	30	45
35,000	26	39
40,000	23	35
45,000	21	31

*Assumes pay has grown at the rate of 6 percent a year.

social security can replace as much as 38 percent (58 percent for a married couple). Even at $45,000, the replacement ratio is 21 percent for a single individual (31 percent for a married couple). As is discussed later, the after-tax replacement ratios are even more significant.

An employee's personal savings, including equity in a home, can also be a source of retirement income. Also, many employers maintain supplemental profit sharing and savings plans that can be a source of additional income. In the absence of any such plan, however, it must be recognized that many individuals will not be able to save meaningful amounts of money to assist in meeting their retirement needs.

Another factor that should be considered in setting income-replacement ratios is that some reduction in gross income can take place without causing a significant reduction in a retiree's standard of living. Tax considerations are one reason why this is so. First, a retired employee is no longer paying a social security tax (unless he or she is in receipt of earned income). Moreover, social security benefits are income tax free for many individuals.[10] In addition, the standard deduction for federal taxes is increased for individuals 65 or over. The standard deduction for an unmarried taxpayer who is not a surviving spouse and is age 65 or over is increased by an additional standard deduction of $750. For a married taxpayer who is age 65 or over, the additional standard deduction is $600. Finally, retirement income is not subject to state or local taxes in many jurisdictions.

Another reason why some reduction in gross income can be tolerated is the removal of work-related expenses, such as commutation costs, the expense of maintaining a second car, lunch and clothing costs, and so on.[11] Also, many retired individuals no longer face the costs associated with child rearing (food, clothing, education, and the like) and many will have reduced housing costs because of the completion of mortgage payments and, in some localities, reduced real estate taxes.

With factors such as these in mind, most employers establish income-replacement objectives that generate something less than a 100 percent replacement of full preretirement gross income. Typically, these income-replacement objectives are set with several factors in mind:

1. They usually take the employee's (but not the spouse's) social security benefits into account.
2. The objectives usually are higher for lower paid employees than for higher paid employees.

---

[10]Under the social security amendments of 1983, up to one half of social security benefits will become taxable for single individuals whose income exceeds $25,000 and for married couples, filing a joint return, whose income exceeds $32,000.

[11]While it is difficult to estimate work-related expenses in any definitive way, it is interesting to note that the President's Commission on Pension Policy, in its Interim Report of May 1980, estimated these expenses to be 6 percent of after-tax preretirement income.

3. The objectives usually are set for the employee's pay level during the final year of employment or over a three- or five-year average just prior to retirement when the employee's earnings are highest.
4. Full income-replacement objectives are set only for individuals who have completed what the employer considers to be a "career" of employment; individuals who have less than this amount of service with the employer have objectives proportionately reduced.

A few comments are appropriate for each of these points. As indicated earlier, social security benefits can be of great importance to individuals at lower income levels, and they take on added significance since all or a portion of the benefits may be income tax free. Further, the employer has shared in the cost of providing these social security benefits. Thus, even though the particular pension formula for the employer's plan may not directly reflect social security benefits, the accrual rates chosen can be designed to produce a net plan benefit that, when added to the employee's primary social security benefit, produces the desired result.[12]

At one time, it was not uncommon for an employer to have a single income-replacement objective for employees at all pay levels. However, it was soon recognized that lower income employees need a higher level of income replacement simply because of minimum income needs. Moreover, it was reasoned that higher paid employees could accept lower income amounts without incurring a major reduction in living standards.

Most defined benefit plans utilize an employee's final average pay to determine benefit amounts. Typically, this is a five-year average, although there has been some trend toward the use of a three-year average. It is common for employers who have such a plan to state their income-replacement objectives in terms of the pay base used in the plan. Some employers, however, actually set objectives in terms of the employee's pay in the final year of employment, with the result that the plan benefit, when expressed as a percentage of the final average pay used in the plan, is somewhat higher than the employer's actual objective. It also should be noted that employers who adopt career-pay plans or who adopt defined contribution plans often do so with final pay income-replacement objectives in mind. Those who use career-pay plans frequently "update" accrued career-pay benefits to reflect current pay levels and to move benefits closer to objectives. Those with defined contribution plans find it more difficult to make such adjustments, but often set contribution levels so that, under reasonable expectations for salary growth and investment return, final-pay

---

[12]It is not customary to take the spouse's social security benefit into account in setting objectives. To do so would be difficult since a direct recognition of this benefit would not be permitted by the Internal Revenue Service, and to approximate its value on an across-the-board basis would result in inequities between employees who have a spouse and those who do not.

objectives might be achieved. Unfortunately, the inherent nature of defined contribution plans is such that, in most situations, these objectives will either be exceeded or not met at all.

Understandably, most employers do not feel an obligation to provide a full level of benefits to short-service employees. Thus, it is common practice to set objectives and design benefit formulas so that proportionately smaller benefits are provided for those individuals who work for an employer for less than what the employer considers to be a reasonable career. The number of years involved, of course, varies from employer to employer and reflects the nature of the employer's business and the degree of maturity it has achieved. However, reasonable career periods of from 25 to 35 years are common.

TABLE 2–2: Illustrative Income-Replacement Objectives (employee with 30 years of service)

Final Pay	Retirement Income as a Percentage of Final Pay*
Under $15,000	80–70%
$15,000 to $25,000	75–65
25,000 to 35,000	70–60
35,000 to 50,000	65–55
Over $50,000	60–50

*Including primary social security benefits.

With these factors in mind, Table 2–2 sets forth a typical set of income-replacement objectives. These objectives are merely examples. What is appropriate for one employer may be inappropriate for another and, in any event, what one employer might adopt as objectives necessarily must reflect that employer's own philosophy and environment.

Other Objectives

The foregoing has discussed some of the major employer objectives associated with employee benefit plans. Other employer objectives also play an important role in plan design. Some of these additional objectives are discussed below.

Social Obligations. Many employers feel a strong sense of social responsibility to their employees and to society in general. The adoption of adequate and meaningful employee benefit plans is a form of meeting this responsibility.

Employee Incentives. It would be a rare employer who is not interested in improving employee productivity. Profit sharing plans and plans that involve ownership of employer securities are plans that can create employee incentives and, as a result, improve productivity. Beyond this, employee morale is an important factor that can influence productivity. As noted earlier, the presence of employee benefit plans may not be a positive force in recruiting and retaining employees, and they may not be a positive factor in creating improved morale. However, their absence could be a negative influence and, for this reason, most employers believe a benefit program, along with other positive compensation and personnel practices, is an important factor in maintaining employee morale at a proper level.

Corporate Identification.   It may be desirable to have employees identify with overall employer business objectives. This might be accomplished by having employees acquire an ownership interest in the firm. Profit sharing plans, savings plans, and employee stock ownership plans (ESOPs) can achieve this objective. By having all or part of an employee's account invested in employer securities, the employee is made aware of progress of the company and the importance of achieving satisfactory profit results. The employee can also have the opportunity to vote the shares credited to his or her account; and the employer has the additional opportunity of being able to communicate with the employee as a shareholder by sending annual reports, proxy statements, and the like.

Administrative Convenience.   Generally, it is desirable that employee benefit plans be designed so that administrative involvement and cost are kept to a reasonable minimum. This objective has become especially important with increasing government regulations and requirements and as design and funding choices become greater and more complex. In this regard, employers should be aware of their own administrative capabilities, as well as those available from external sources. Also, while it is desirable to hold administrative costs to a minimum, these costs are not the most significant element of total plan costs. Thus, good plan design should not be sacrificed for the objective of holding down administrative costs.

QUESTIONS FOR REVIEW

1. Describe some of the environmental factors that should be considered in the pension plan design process.
2. Many employers believe employees should share in the cost of meeting their own economic security needs. This type of employee involvement in a private pension plan may take two alternative forms. Explain.
3. Describe the three techniques that may be used to establish the relative standing of various retirement plans.
4. What are some of the objectives an employer could have for matters concerning the cost of the pension plan?

5. An employer often has a choice in the manner in which compliance with legal requirements for pension plans is achieved. Give four examples of areas where compliance choices are available.

6. What are some of the plan design alternatives available to an employer who wishes to achieve maximum tax advantages for a retirement program?

7. An efficient pension plan design requires the identification of all sources of benefits for a retired employee. What plans should be considered as potential sources of benefits?

8. Why do some employers establish income-replacement objectives that generate something less than 100 percent of full preretirement gross income?

9. Identify the factors that are often considered by employers in setting income-replacement objectives.

10. Describe how retirement plans may be used to provide: (a) employee incentives and (b) corporate identification.

QUESTIONS FOR DISCUSSION

1. Assume that an employer wants to provide a reasonable combined replacement ratio (a ratio that combines both social security and private pension benefits in the numerator) for high-paid employees without providing an excessive replacement ratio for employees at lower income levels. Using the relationship between social security retirement benefits and final pay provided in Table 2–1, illustrate why it may be necessary for the employer to integrate the pension plan. (The mechanics of the integration procedure will be treated in Chapter 6.)

2. Provide a numerical example to explain why an executive might experience a loss of pension benefits under a final average defined benefit plan if he or she were to change jobs in midcareer.

3. The age at which unreduced social security retirement benefits may commence is scheduled to gradually increase from 65 to a maximum of 67 after the turn of the century. Assume that you are asked to give advice on how a firm's retirement benefits should be restructured as a result of this change. Discuss how your response will vary depending on the employer's objectives.

3

Defined Contribution versus Defined Benefit Plans

B efore discussing specific aspects of retirement plan design, it is important to recognize that an employer has two broad choices in selecting a plan to provide these benefits. One of these, of course, is the defined benefit plan under which the employer provides a determinable benefit, usually related to an employee's service and/or pay. Under this approach, the employer's cost is whatever is necessary to provide the benefit specified. The second approach is the defined contribution plan. Here, the employer's contribution is fixed and this contribution is accumulated to provide whatever amount of benefit it can purchase. Thus, an employee's benefit becomes the variable, depending upon factors such as level of contributions, age at entry, retirement age, and investment earnings (or losses). A defined contribution plan can involve a specific contribution (as in a money purchase pension plan), or it can take the form of a profit sharing, thrift or savings, or employee stock ownership plan (these topics are discussed in Chapters 15, 16, and 18, respectively).

Although only the two polar cases in selecting a pension plan are discussed in this chapter, it is important to note that in recent years some

SOURCE: This material was originally presented on May 20, 1982, at a policy forum sponsored by the Education and Research Fund of the Employee Benefit Research Institute. It was subsequently published by the Institute as a chapter in *Economic Survival in Retirement: Which Pension Is for You?* (Washington, D.C., 1982). It is reproduced here with the permission of the Institute.

employers have adopted plans that combine the best features of both approaches. These plans, generally referred to as target benefit plans, are best understood after the reader is fully cognizant of each of the specific features of a pension plan. Therefore, the discussion of these plans is deferred until Chapter 6.

The choice between a defined benefit or a defined contribution plan to provide or supplement retirement benefits is of great importance, both to employer and employees. Legislative developments in recent years have been a major factor influencing this decision. While a detailed discussion of all these plans is found in subsequent chapters of this text, it is important, at this stage, to provide an overview of the factors involved in making a choice between these two different approaches to providing retirement benefits. This chapter reviews the background and broad considerations involved, as well as the legislative activity that bears on this choice.

BACKGROUND

The vast majority of employees covered today by the private pension system in the United States participate in defined benefit plans. There are some notable exceptions. Educational and other nonprofit institutions, for example, have historically favored defined contribution pension arrangements because of the unique tax sanctions granted them under section 403(b) of the Internal Revenue Code. Also, a number of profit-making organizations have opted for deferred profit sharing arrangements to serve as retirement plans. Nevertheless, the defined benefit approach was favored by most employers both small and large—at least until the passage of the Employee Retirement Income Security Act of 1974 (ERISA).

This preference for defined benefit plans over defined contribution plans has been due to many factors:

1. Most employers have specific income-replacement objectives in mind when establishing a retirement plan. A defined benefit plan can be structured to achieve these objectives. The defined contribution approach, on the other hand, will produce plan benefits that fail to meet or that exceed such objectives as they affect individual employees. This depends on a number of factors such as length of participation, age at retirement, inflation, investment results, and the like.

2. By the same token, most employers wish to take social security benefits into account so that the combined level of benefits from both sources will produce desired results. Defined contribution plans can be integrated with social security benefits to some extent by adjusting contribution levels; however, integration cannot be accomplished as efficiently as is the case under defined benefit plans, where such coordination can be done on the basis of benefits provided.

3. The typical defined contribution plan provides that the employee's account balance is payable in the event of death and, frequently, in case of disability. This, of course, produces additional plan costs or, alternatively, lower retirement benefits if overall costs are held constant. An employer who is interested primarily in providing retirement benefits can use available funds more efficiently for this purpose under a defined benefit plan.

4. In the view of many, a more equitable allocation of employer contributions occurs under a defined benefit plan, since the employee's age, past service, and pay may all be taken into account. By contrast, the typical defined contribution plan allocates contributions only on the basis of pay. (Service is sometimes recognized in defined contribution plans; however, its impact in terms of allocations is rather minimal.) This characteristic of defined contribution plans is one of the reasons they do not lend themselves to achieving consistent income-replacement objectives.

5. A defined benefit plan can be (and often is) structured to provide a benefit that is related to an employee's final pay, thus protecting the employee against the effects of preretirement inflation. Equivalent protection cannot be provided under a defined contribution plan. Thus, in effect, the risk of inflation is assumed by employees, who must rely primarily on investment results to increase the value of their benefits during inflationary periods.

6. This last comment raises another issue in the comparison of defined benefit plans and defined contribution plans. Investment risk and reward are assumed by the employer under the former, by employees under the latter. Risk can be minimized by use of selected investment media. Absent such protection, however, many people feel that it is inappropriate for the average employee to assume such risk with respect to a major component of his or her retirement security.

The defined contribution approach is, of course, not without its advantages. Deferred profit sharing plans, for example, offer employers maximum flexibility in terms of cost commitment as well as opportunities to increase employee productivity. Through the use of employer securities as a plan investment, greater employee identification with the company and its goals also can be achieved. Additionally, if the employee group covered is relatively young, the defined contribution plan is apt to have greater employee relations value than a defined benefit plan.

LEGISLATIVE FACTORS

ERISA has had a significant impact on defined benefit plans. Despite the advantages noted, a defined benefit plan now exposes an employer to significant financial liability if the plan is terminated when there are unfunded liabilities for vested benefits. A minimum of 30 percent of an employer's net worth is subject to a lien in favor of the Pension Benefit Guaranty Corporation (PBGC) if necessary to meet any liabilities assumed by the PBGC in this event (the specifics of the employer's liability are discussed in Chapter 23). The lien, since it is in the nature of a tax lien, supersedes the liens of any other creditors. The problems of potential employer liabilities were exacerbated by the Multiemployer Pension Plan Amendments Act of 1980, which created substantial liabilities for an employer who wishes to or who must withdraw from a multiemployer plan that has unfunded vested liabilities. Here, the employer is liable for its share of unfunded vested liabilities (generally on the basis of the ratio of the employer's contributions to total contributions), and there is generally no limit on the percentage of the employer's net worth that can be used for this purpose.

The vast majority of employees who are not covered by a private retirement program work for smaller companies. According to the Employee Benefit Research Institute, 79 percent of such individuals work for firms that employ fewer than 100 employees. Clearly, these small employers, as well as newly formed companies, are apt to be reluctant to adopt a defined benefit plan and the potential liabilities that are imposed by ERISA. Many such employers will find the defined contribution alternative, with no such liabilities, to be a more palatable approach—despite the advantages offered by a defined benefit arrangement.

That this is so would seem to be borne out by Internal Revenue Service (IRS) statistics on the establishment of new plans. Since ERISA, approximately 80 percent of all new plans are defined contribution in nature. To be sure, many of these new plans (e.g., savings plans) supplement existing defined benefit plans. However, this is still a much higher percentage than was the case prior to the passage of ERISA.

Apart from the plan termination provisions of ERISA and their implicit but significant emphasis on defined contribution plans, it is important to note that the federal government—knowingly or unknowingly—has emphasized the defined contribution approach in many other ways. For example:

1. Long-standing provisions of the Internal Revenue Code (referred to earlier) permit and encourage the use of tax-deferred annuities (defined contribution plans) for employees of educational and other nonprofit organizations.

2. The basic structure of the Code, as it applied to H.R. 10 or Keogh plans for the self-employed, was strongly oriented toward defined contribution plans. Even though amended to specifically sanction defined benefit plans, the defined contribution approach proved to be the simplest and easiest way to take advantage of this law. Indeed, almost all such plans have utilized the defined contribution approach. This might change as a result of the parity provisions of the Tax Equity and Fiscal Responsibility Act of 1982 (TEFRA), which eliminated most of the distinctions in tax law that formerly applied to different organizations. However, precedents

established by prior practice and prior law may still continue to influence plan design for unincorporated organizations.

3. The Individual Retirement Arrangement (IRA) concept (described in Chapter 19) is totally a defined contribution approach.

4. Beginning in 1979, employers were permitted to adopt a simplified employee pension (SEP). A SEP utilizes the IRA concept but has higher contribution limits than an IRA and considerably less paperwork than a conventional retirement plan. Again, the defined contribution approach is mandatory.

5. Employee stock ownership plans (ESOPs), which are defined contribution plans, have also been the subject of special legislation. As will be described in Chapter 18, such plans, unlike defined benefit plans, can be involved with corporate debt financing. In addition, ESOPs have been the subject of special interest legislation—witness the Regional Rail Reorganization Act of 1973, the Foreign Trade Act of 1974, the Chrysler Corporation Loan Guarantee Act of 1979, the Small Business Employee Ownership Act of 1980, and the Tax Reform Act of 1986. It seems likely that special interest legislation of this type will recur in the future.

6. The Revenue Act of 1978 added section 125 to the Code. This section permits the adoption of *cafeteria* or *flexible* compensation plans and provides that an employee can choose between taxable and nontaxable compensation elements without problems of constructive receipt if certain conditions are met. One of these conditions is that deferred compensation plans cannot be one of the choices. However, this section was amended to allow the inclusion of profit sharing and stock bonus plans that meet the requirements of section 401(k) of the Code (described in Chapter 17). Thus, a flexible compensation plan can permit an employee to choose among welfare benefits (e.g., life insurance, disability income, medical expense), cash, deferred profit sharing or savings plan benefits. This legislation encouraged the defined contribution approach. This area is particularly significant since interest in flexible compensation plans is increasing and these plans are very likely to become a major factor in the employee benefit planning process of the future.

Some pressures exist to expand flexible compensation legislation so as to include defined benefit pension plans. Even if this does occur, it is still likely that the emphasis on defined contribution plans will remain. There are very real problems involved in trading defined benefits (particularly if they are pay related) for current cash or welfare contributions. It is possible to do this, but it will be necessary to resolve issues of equity and the relative value of choices. In many cases, it will be easier to limit employee elections as to how available dollars can be used—for example, to a choice of purchasing current benefits or of deferring these dollars under some type of defined contribution program. Indeed, it might be said that flexible compensation plans often apply the defined contribution concept to an employer's entire benefit program.

7. Closely related to flexible compensation plans are the section 401(k) cash/deferred profit sharing or savings plans. A key feature of these plans is that they permit the use of salary reduction arrangements—an approach that can be very tax effective and that has captured the interest of many employers. Much of the initial interest was in the conversion of existing plans. However, the approach presents attractive advantages and it seems likely that new programs will continue to be enacted. Employers who do not have pension plans may find the combination of tax savings for employees and the possible lesser financial obligations of the defined contribution approach to be an attractive way of establishing a retirement program. This could be particularly true when tied in with an overall flexible compensation program.

8. The plan termination and funding requirements imposed on defined benefit plans by the Omnibus Budget Reconciliation Act of 1987 may foster a much higher level of interest in the relatively unrestricted defined contribution approach.

OTHER FACTORS

As can be seen, there has been a significant amount of direct legislative activity that has enhanced the attractiveness of various defined contribution mechanisms. However, other legislation also may have an indirect effect that will encourage the growth of these plans. Some of the changes made by the 1983 social security amendments are a good example of how indirect legislation can affect the design of private retirement plans.

These amendments gradually change the normal retirement age for social security benefits from 65 to 67. While the earliest age for claiming social security retirement benefits was not increased from 62, the reduction for early benefit commencement will be gradually increased as the normal retirement age increases. Moreover, workers will have an additional incentive to remain in the work force beyond age 65, since delayed retirement credits will be increased[1] and the earnings test has been liberalized.[2]

These changes could affect the planning process associated with defined benefit plans. Most of these plans are designed to produce a specific amount of replacement income, together with primary social security benefits, when an employee reaches age 65. The actual income replacement objectives may vary, but they usually reflect the employee's pay level and length of service. While replacement ratios are generally expressed in

---

[1]In 1983, there was a credit of 3 percent a year for delaying retirement after the normal retirement age and before age 72. The new law gradually increases the credit for workers who reach age 62 in 1987 until it reaches 8 percent for workers reaching age 62 in 2005.

[2]In 1983, beneficiaries under age 70 who were still working were subject to a 50-cent reduction in benefits for every $1 of earnings when the earnings exceeded a base amount. The new law changed the earnings reduction, effective in 1990, to a $1 reduction for every $3 of earnings in excess of the base amount.

terms of before-tax income, they are often consciously set with reference to their after-tax value.

The fundamental concept of this planning process revolves around the coordination of two income sources—the private plan and social security—usually occurring around the time of the employee's 65th birthday. However, the idea that 65 is a typical retirement age has already begun to diffuse with recent trends toward early retirement. This diffusion will become even greater as the social security normal retirement age is changed, especially when accompanied by the elimination of permissible mandatory retirement in 1986. What may emerge is a concept that retirement age will become highly subjective for each employee. Actual retirement age may range over a span that begins when employees are in their late 50s and extends until employees reach their early 70s. If retirement becomes spread over such a wide range, it will become increasingly difficult to maintain a plan design structure that is predicated on the majority of employees retiring at age 65 and the coordination of two income sources at this point. Thus, one of the broad but important implications facing employers is the potential need to rethink their approach to plan design and the basic delivery of retirement benefits. Nonintegrated plans and greater use of defined contribution plans are examples of approaches that might be considered. These approaches allow an employer to opt for cost control in lieu of finely tuned benefit levels.

A mandatory private retirement system in the United States is still a long way off—if, indeed, it ever becomes a reality. Yet the possibility exists that such a system will become law. The President's Commission on Pension Policy, which filed its report in February 1981, recommended that a mandatory minimum pension system be established. More specifically, the Commission recommended that this program be in the form of a defined contribution plan with a minimum employer contribution of 3 percent of compensation. While the Commission did not divulge all of its reasoning in support of this defined contribution recommendation, it is likely that it was perceived as the simplest and most acceptable way of moving into a mandatory system. A mandatory defined benefit program would present a host of issues concerning pay-related benefits, the recognition of prior service, and the imposition of related liabilities.

The prospects of a mandatory private pension system are not clear at this time. Movement in this direction during the next few years is quite unlikely. But, on a long-term basis, there is the distinct possibility that some form of pension coverage will become mandatory. If this should happen, the defined contribution approach is most apt to be used. (Defined benefit equivalents would most likely be permitted—largely to accommodate existing defined benefit plans—but a defined contribution plan would be the probable choice for employers installing a plan for the first time.) A mandatory private pension system would have major implications for the expanded growth of defined contribution plans.

THE FUTURE

Despite all the foregoing, defined benefit plans are alive and well at this time. They are firmly entrenched in major companies and most of the employees now covered by private pensions participate in defined benefit arrangements. It is unlikely that many of these plans will be shifted—at least completely—to defined contribution plans. What might happen, however, is that employers with these plans will hold them at current levels, opting to make benefit improvements via some kind of supplemental defined contribution arrangement (e.g., a salary reduction, section 401(k) savings plan). For employers who do not yet have a pension plan, there has already been and is likely to be greater utilization of one form or another of the defined contribution approaches referred to in this chapter. IRAs, ESOPs, SEPs, flexible compensation and section 401(k) plans are all attractive and viable programs to consider. While defined benefit plans will remain a major component in the U.S. private pension system, the defined contribution plan has begun to take on a more significant role and this role is likely to become greater in the years ahead.

QUESTIONS FOR REVIEW

1. Describe the factors that will determine an employee's retirement benefit under the defined contribution approach.
2. Explain the primary advantages of a defined benefit plan.
3. Explain the primary advantages of a defined contribution plan.
4. Explain the ways in which the federal government emphasized the defined contribution approach.
5. Explain how the 1983 social security amendments might affect utilization of the defined benefit approach.

QUESTIONS FOR DISCUSSION

1. The text states that in the view of many, a more equitable allocation of employer contributions occurs under a defined benefit plan than under a defined contribution plan. Assume that a participant in a defined benefit pension plan, age 25, is currently paid $15,000 per year and will retire at age 65. At that time, he will receive a pension benefit equal to 1 percent of average salary in the last five years times years of service. Compute the present value of the pension benefit accrued from working an additional year, as a percentage of the participant's compensation, at ages 30, 35, 40, 45, 50, 55, 60, and 64. Perform the calculations under two sets of assumptions: (a) the participant has no wage growth and the discount rate is 3 percent, and (b) the participant's wage growth is 7 percent and the discount rate is 10 percent. Graph the change in the present value of

accrued benefits from an additional year's work (expressed as a percentage of compensation) against the participant's age under both scenarios. What conclusions can you draw about the allocation of employer contributions under defined benefit plans? (Notice that the discount rate exceeds the wage growth by 3 percent under both scenarios.)

2. Prepare a similar graph to the one in the preceding question for an employee participating in a defined contribution plan providing a contribution of 6 percent of compensation, and compare your results with the previous graphs. What conclusions can you draw about the allocation of employer contributions under a defined contribution plan vis-à-vis those of a defined benefit plan? What implications does this have for the retention of older employees?

3. Assume that you are an employee, age 25, and you are given your choice of participating in the defined benefit plan described in Question 1 or the defined contribution plan in Question 2. Which one would you prefer? Describe how you made the evaluation and any assumptions required.

4

Plan Qualification and Deductibility of Employer Contributions

While an employer may choose to use a nonqualified approach to providing retirement benefits for certain highly paid executives, the requirements of ERISA are such that a qualified plan is the only effective way to provide these benefits for a large group of employees. Morcover, the tax advantages provided under the Internal Revenue Code for qualified pension and profit sharing plans are most significant—both to an employer and to its employees. The principal tax advantages of such a plan are:

1. Contributions made by the employer, within the limitations prescribed, are deductible as a business expense.
2. Investment income on these contributions normally is not subject to federal income tax until paid in the form of benefits.
3. An employee is not considered to be in receipt of taxable income until benefits are distributed.
4. A lump-sum distribution to an employee after the employee attains age 59½ will be taxed on a favorable basis if it meets certain requirements.

To obtain these tax benefits, the plan must achieve a qualified status by meeting the requirements of the Internal Revenue Code and appropriate regulations and rulings issued by the commissioner of internal revenue. This chapter, while not intended as an exhaustive treatise on the tax aspects of qualified plans, should serve as a general guide to the major requirements of federal tax law that a plan must meet if this qualified status is to be obtained. This chapter also includes a summary of the procedures involved in submitting a plan to the Internal Revenue Service for the purpose of obtaining an advance determination letter, as well as a brief discussion of the provisions of federal tax law relating to trust investments for a qualified plan and the deductibility of employer contributions.

QUALIFICATION REQUIREMENTS

Coverage Requirements

The Tax Reform Act of 1986 has greatly altered the rules regarding coverage for qualified plans. Except for certain plans maintained under collective bargaining agreements, the changes are effective for plan years beginning after December 31, 1988.[1]

One of the most important requirements of a qualified plan is that it must be for the exclusive benefit of employees or their beneficiaries. Officers of a corporation and stockholders may participate in the plan if they are bona fide employees. However, a plan cannot be structured so that it discriminates in any fashion in favor of highly compensated employees. A highly compensated employee is defined as an employee who is:

1. A 5 percent owner.
2. A person earning over $75,000 a year in either the current or preceding year.
3. A person earning over $50,000 a year in either the current or preceding year and is or was in the top 20 percent of all active employees for such year.
4. An officer earning over 150 percent of the dollar limit for annual additions to a defined contribution plan ($45,000 in 1987) in either the current or preceding year.

In determining who is an officer, no more than 50 individuals (or 10 percent of the employee group, if smaller) need be taken into account.

If an employee is a family member (lineal ascendant or descendant and spouse) of a 5 percent owner or one of the top 10 highly paid employees, both will be treated as one person for purposes of the nondiscrimination tests. The $50,000 and $75,000 amounts will be indexed to reflect increases in the Consumer Price Index (CPI) beginning in 1988. If an employee (other than a 5 percent owner) earned less than the test amount in the year before the year he or she meets the definition of highly paid employee was

---

[1]The changes will not apply to plans maintained under one or more collective bargaining agreements that were ratified prior to March 1, 1986, before the earlier of the date the last collective bargaining agreement terminates, or January 1, 1991.

not an officer in that prior year, the employee will not be a member of the highly paid group for the entrance year unless he or she is among the top 100 employees for that year.

It is possible for an attorney or other professional person to be a bona fide employee and, as such, to participate in a qualified plan. The mere fact that a professional employee has income other than from the employer is immaterial. If such an individual is an employee for all purposes, including coverage for social security benefits, and income from the employer is subject to withholding for income tax purposes, he or she may be considered an employee under the plan.

Beginning in 1989, a plan will have to satisfy any one of the following three new tests:[2]

1. The *percentage test* is satisfied if the plan benefits at least 70 percent of the sponsoring employer's nonhighly compensated employees.
2. A plan may qualify under the *ratio test* if the percentage of nonhighly compensated employees who benefit under the plan is at least 70 percent of the percentage of highly compensated employees who benefit under the plan.
3. Two conditions must be met for a plan to satisfy the *average benefits test*. First, the plan must meet the fair cross section test applying to plan years beginning before January 1, 1989.[3] Second, the average employer-provided contributions (including forfeitures) or benefits for nonhighly compensated employees under all of the employer's qualified plans (including an amount deemed to represent the employer-provided portion of social security under rules to be issued) must be, as a percentage of compensation, at least 70 percent of the similar benefit for highly compensated employees.

These tests can be satisfied by combining comparable plans. Further, an exception to the general rule regarding the aggregation of all employees of a controlled group of corporations (see page 72) is permitted under certain circumstances. If an employer has separate lines of business or operating

---

[2]For plan years beginning before January 1, 1989, the Code requires that a plan, if it is to qualify, must meet *either* the mathematical test or the fair cross section test. The mathematical test states that the plan must cover 70 percent or more of all employees or, if the plan requires employee contributions and if 70 percent or more of all employees are eligible to participate in the plan, at least 80 percent of those eligible must elect to participate. Under this latter provision, if only 70 percent of the employees are eligible, only 56 percent of the total employees have to be covered (80% × 70%). In applying this requirement test, those employees who have not satisfied the minimum age and service requirements of the plan need not be taken into consideration. The fair cross-section test states that the plan must benefit such employees as qualify under a classification set up by the employer and found by the Internal Revenue Service not to be discriminatory in favor of officers, stockholders, or highly compensated employees. In applying these tests, employers may exclude certain employees from consideration, generally as allowed under the law in effect for plan years beginning after December 31, 1988.

[3]Technically, after 1988 the fair cross-section test will only prevent discrimination in favor of highly compensated employees.

units employing at least 50 employees that are established for bona fide business reasons, and if the plan meets the fair cross-section test applying to plan years beginning before January 1, 1989, any of the tests can also be satisfied separately for each such line of business or unit. The law provides a "safe harbor" test for determining whether a separate facility has been established for bona fide business reasons. To qualify for the safe harbor, the percentage of highly compensated employees at the separate facility may be not less than one half nor more than twice the average percentage of highly compensated employees companywide. Headquarter personnel are not considered a separate line of business.

If a plan fails to satisfy the coverage tests, nonhighly compensated employees will not be affected. Highly compensated employees, however, will be taxed on the present value of their employer-derived accrued benefits that are vested and income on any contributions to the extent such amounts have not been previously taxed.

In addition to meeting one of the basic coverage tests, plans (other than negotiated multiemployer plans) must meet a *minimum coverage test* beginning in 1989. Each plan must meet this test at all times; the test cannot be satisfied by combining comparable plans nor can the test be applied on a line of business or operating unit basis. Technical corrections to the Tax Reform Act of 1986 may permit this test to be applied on a "lines of business" basis. The minimum coverage test requires that a plan cover the lesser of: (*a*) 50 employees, or (*b*) 40 percent of all employees of the employer.

In applying these requirements, it will be permissible to exclude from consideration any employees covered by a collective bargaining agreement if there is evidence that retirement benefits were the subject of good faith bargaining. It is also possible to exclude nonresident aliens who receive no income from the employer from sources within the United States, certain airline pilots, and employees not meeting minimum age and service requirements.

Under the average benefit percentage test, it is possible, although difficult, to establish a plan solely for salaried employees or for those employees who work in certain designated departments or in other classifications, so long as the average benefit percentage for the nonhighly compensated employees is at least 70 percent of the average benefit percentage for the highly compensated employees and the plan does not discriminate in favor of the highly compensated employees. The Code itself states that a classification shall not be considered discriminatory merely because it is limited to salaried or clerical employees. This Code provision does not mean that a "salaried-only" plan will automatically be acceptable. Such a plan must still meet the overriding requirements of the average benefit percentage test.

The coverage requirements of federal tax law also limit the employer's choice of eligibility requirements (for example, minimum service and minimum ages).

The coverage requirements are also significant in the area of employee contributions. For example, while a plan may require employees to contribute, the employee contribution rate cannot be so high as to make the plan unattractive except to highly compensated employees. Traditionally, an employee contribution rate of 6 percent or less is not considered burdensome.

For purposes of several of the plan qualification requirements, including the coverage requirements, leased employees are treated as an employee of any person for whom a leased employee performs services, but contributions or benefits provided by the leasing organization which are attributable to service performed for the recipient are treated as provided by the recipient. The term *leased employee* refers to any person who is not an employee of the recipient and who provides service to the recipient if: such services are provided pursuant to an agreement between the recipient and a leasing organization, such person has performed such service for the recipient on a substantially full-time basis for at least one year, and such services are of a type historically performed in the business field of the recipient by employees. The plan qualification requirements do not apply to any leased employee if they do not constitute more than 20 percent of the recipient's nonhighly compensated work force and they are covered by a plan maintained by the leasing organization that meets the following requirements: the plan is a money purchase pension plan with a nonintegrated employer contribution rate of at least 10 percent of compensation, the plan provides for full and immediate vesting, and each employee of the leasing organization immediately participates in the plan.

The coverage requirements (except for the minimum coverage test) need be met on only one day in each quarter of the plan's taxable year.

Contribution and Benefit Requirements

Another major requirement of a qualified plan is that contributions or benefits provided cannot discriminate in favor of the highly compensated group of employees.

A plan will not be discriminatory merely because it uses a benefit formula that provides a larger percentage of benefit for earnings in excess of some amount such as the social security taxable wage base than it does for earnings under this amount.[4] However, if the benefit formula is in any way integrated with social security benefits, certain requirements are imposed to prevent discrimination in favor of the highly paid employees. The basic concept of these requirements is that the benefits from the employer's plan must be dovetailed with social security benefits in such a manner that employees earning over the taxable base will not receive combined benefits under the two programs that are proportionately greater than the

---

[4]For plan years beginning before January 1, 1989, a qualified plan is also able to exclude individuals who earn less than the maximum taxable wage for social security purposes.

bined benefits for employees earning under this amount. These integration requirements, as they apply to specific formulas and plan provisions, are discussed in Chapter 6.

Other Requirements

Must Be in Writing.   A qualified plan must be in writing and must set forth all the provisions necessary for qualification. This is normally accomplished by means of a trust agreement, a plan instrument, or both. In group pension programs, the plan provisions are sometimes contained in the group contract and, in this event, neither a trust agreement nor a separate plan instrument is necessary.

A trust agreement is generally required for trust fund plans and for plans using individual insurance or annuity contracts along with a conversion fund.[5] This allows the employer to make irrevocable contributions on a basis that permits the employee to defer including these contributions as taxable income until they are distributed. If a group pension contract is employed, an intervening trust usually is not necessary, since the same results can be achieved through the group contract itself; that is, the contract can be written so that employer contributions are irrevocably made without the employees being considered in receipt of these contributions until they are distributed.

Communication to Employees.   The plan must also be communicated to employees. An announcement letter or booklet is frequently used for this purpose. If employees are not given a copy of the actual plan, they should be told that a copy is available for inspection at convenient locations.

Nondiversion of Contributions.   The trust must specifically provide that it is impossible for the employer to divert or recapture contributions before the satisfaction of all plan liabilities — with certain exceptions, funds contributed must be used for the exclusive benefit of employees or their beneficiaries. One exception to this rule may occur at termination of a pension plan if any funds then remain because of "actuarial error" and all fixed and contingent obligations of the plan have been satisfied. In this event, such excess funds may be returned to the employer. A second exception makes it possible to establish or amend a plan on a conditional basis so that employer contributions are returnable within one year from the denial of qualification if the plan is not approved by the Internal Revenue Service. It is also possible for an employer to make a contribution on the basis that it

---

[5]A trust agreement is not necessary for plan assets held in insurance policies or nontransferable annuities, or for assets held by insurance companies, and for funds held in custodial accounts. However, a plan instrument of some type still would be required so that the plan provisions can be set forth in writing.

will be allowed as a deduction; if this is done, the contribution, to the extent it is disallowed, may be returned within one year from the disallowance. Further, contributions made on the basis of a mistake in fact can be returned to the employer within one year from the time they were made.

Definitely Determinable Benefits. A qualified pension plan must provide definitely determinable benefits. A defined contribution pension plan meets this requirement, since the employer's contribution formula is definite and, for this reason, benefits are considered actuarially determinable. Also, variable annuity plans or plans under which the benefit varies with a cost-of-living index will be acceptable.

Because of the definitely determinable benefit requirement, any amounts forfeited by terminating employees may not be used to increase benefits for the remaining participants under a *defined benefit* pension plan. Instead, these forfeitures must be used to reduce employer contributions next due. Moreover, a defined benefit plan will not be considered to provide definitely determinable benefits unless actuarial assumptions are specified in the plan whenever any benefit under the plan is to be determined using those assumptions. The assumptions must be specified in the plan in a way that precludes employer discretion. For defined contribution plans, forfeitures can be applied to increase benefits or to reduce contributions.

The definitely determinable benefit requirement does not apply to qualified profit sharing plans. Here, there is a requirement that the plan must provide for participation in the profits of the employer by the employees or their beneficiaries. While it is not required that there be a definite formula for determining the amount to be contributed to the profit sharing plan, it is required that there be a definite predetermined formula for allocating contributions among participants and for distributing funds after a fixed number of years, the attainment of a stated age, or upon the happening of some event such as layoff, illness, disability, retirement, death, or severance of employment.

Permanency. The plan must be a permanent one. While the employer may reserve the right to amend or terminate the plan at any time, it is expected that the plan will be established on a permanent basis. Thus, if a plan is terminated for any reason other than business necessity within a few years after it has been in force, this will be considered as evidence that the plan, from its inception, was not a bona fide one for the benefit of employees. This, of course, could result in adverse tax consequences.

In the profit sharing area, as previously noted, it is not necessary that the employer make contributions in accordance with a definite predetermined formula. However, merely making a single or an occasional contribution will not be sufficient to create a permanent and continuing plan.

The regulations require that "substantial and recurring" contributions must be made.

Vesting.   A plan will not qualify unless it provides for full vesting when an employee attains normal retirement age and unless it provides for fully vested rights in all participants upon termination of the plan or permanent discontinuance of plan contributions. Further, the plan must meet minimum vesting requirements. The permissible vesting schedules and the rules relating to the determination of an employee's accrued benefit are described in Chapter 6.

U.S. Trust.   If a trust is used, it must be one organized or created in the United States and maintained at all times as a domestic trust. The earnings of a trust created outside of the United States will be taxable, although if the trust would otherwise qualify, the employer will be allowed to take appropriate deductions for its contributions and the beneficiaries of the trust will be allowed the same tax treatment for distributions as if the trust had been qualified.[6]

Requirements Added by ERISA and Subsequent Legislation.   The Code was amended by ERISA, the Tax Equity and Fiscal Responsibility Act of 1982 (TEFRA), the Deficit Reduction Act of 1984 (DEFRA), the Retirement Equity Act of 1984 (REACT), and the Tax Reform Act of 1986 to require that qualified plans include a number of different provisions. Several of these provisions already have been noted in this chapter. The remaining requirements are discussed in greater detail in Chapters 5 and 6 and are only summarized below.

1. *Service*. The determination of service for purposes of eligibility to participate, vesting, and determining eligibility for benefit accruals must be made in accordance with detailed specifications.

2. *Survivor benefits*. All plans (other than certain exempt profit-sharing and stock bonus plans) must provide automatic survivor benefits in the form of qualified preretirement survivor and qualified joint and survivor annuities. Additional death benefits may be included in a qualified plan so long as such benefits considered together are "incidental." Each of these concepts will be discussed in detail in Chapter 6.

3. *Maximum benefits and contributions*. The benefit payable to a participant under a defined benefit plan and the annual addition made on behalf of a participant under a defined contribution plan must be limited; further, a combined limit is imposed in any situation where both a defined benefit and a defined contribution plan are in effect. These limits are often referred to as "Section 415" limits. (There is also a limit on the amount of compensation that may be used to determine contributions or benefits.)

---

[6]Special rules exist concerning the taxation of distributions to nonresident aliens.

4. *Plan termination*. The manner in which plan assets must be allocated in the event of plan termination is established by ERISA.

5. *Assignments*. The plan must prohibit assignments; however exceptions have been granted to: (*a*) the extent of 10 percent of benefit payments, (*b*) the extent of utilizing a vested interest as collateral for a loan made from the plan, and (*c*) qualified domestic relations orders (described in Chapter 6).

6. *Mergers and consolidations*. A provision must be included to protect an employee's benefits in the event of a merger or consolidation of plans, or in the event of a transfer of plan assets or liabilities.

7. *Payment of benefits*. Unless otherwise requested by the employee, benefit payments must commence within 60 days of the latest of the following three events: the plan year in which the employee terminates employment, the completion of 10 years of participation, or the attainment of age 65 or the normal retirement date specified in the plan.

8. *Increases in social security*. Any increase in social security benefits that takes place after retirement or after termination of employment cannot operate to reduce an employee's benefits.

9. *Required plan distributions*. Distributions to all participants must be completed or commence by the April 1 following the calendar year in which the participant reaches age 70½, even if the participant remains in employment. Alternatively, starting no later than the following April 1, distributions can be made over the life of the participant (or joint lives of the participant and beneficiary) or over a period no longer than the life expectancy of the participant (or joint life expectancies of the participant and beneficiary).[7]

Also, for general purposes of qualification, for the application of minimum participation and vesting standards, and for the application of the maximum limitation on benefits and contributions, all organizations under common control (that is, where there is 80 percent control) will be considered as a single employer.[8] (For purposes of applying the limitation on benefits and contributions, only 51 percent control is needed.)

OBTAINING AN ADVANCE DETERMINATION LETTER

The federal tax law does not require submission of a plan to the Internal Revenue Service for an advance determination that the plan meets the requirements of the Code and has achieved a qualified status. As a convenience to the taxpayer, however, the Internal Revenue Service will issue

---

[7]For plan years beginning before January 1, 1989, the required beginning date was the later of the employee's retirement date or the April 1 following the taxable year in which the participant reaches age 70½. However, 5 percent owners were already subject to the more stringent rules that apply to all participants after 1988.

[8]Note, however, that for the coverage requirements described on page 50, there is a separate line of business exclusion.

advance determination letters (often called "approval" letters) as to the qualified status of a plan. Most taxpayers take advantage of this and obtain such a ruling.

One reason for taking advantage of this procedure is the possibility that the Service will find some feature or features of the plan unacceptable. The Code permits a retroactive change in the plan (to its effective date) if the change is made within the time allowed by the Internal Revenue Service (usually by the time the employer's tax return for the year is due, including extensions). The period for making remedial amendments can be extended for 91 days after final notification by the Service if the plan was filed before the employer's tax return was due. If changes are necessary, the employer may make the appropriate amendments to the plan within this period and thus preserve the deductions to be claimed for the taxable year involved.

In contrast, if the employer does not file for an advance determination letter, the qualified status of the plan may be examined by the Service at the time the employer's tax return is audited. Any changes then required by the Service will, in all probability, be at a time beyond the period allowed for making a retroactive change. Thus, there would be the possibility of the employer losing at least one year's deduction.

The Internal Revenue Service has issued rulings that prescribe the information to be submitted in requesting an advance determination letter. The information required includes the following:

1. The name of the plan and the name and address of the employer.
2. Copies of any trust indenture involved.
3. Copies of any instrument constituting the plan.
4. Copies of any group annuity contract involved.
5. Copies of any amendments to any of the above items.
6. A detailed description of the plan (effective dates, eligibility requirements, employee contribution levels, retirement dates and provisions, vesting provisions, funding instrument, and so on).
7. A summary concerning the salaries, benefits, contributions, and other information relating to the 25 highest paid participants of each employer participating in the plan.[9]
8. A classification of all employees, with reasons indicated as to why certain employees are not eligible to participate.
9. Evidence that all interested parties (e.g., employees) have been properly notified of the application for the advance determination letter.

Any plan sponsor or plan administrator making a determination request for a plan of a single employer should file either Form 5300 (defined benefit plans) or Form 5301 (defined contribution plans) with one Form 5302

---

[9]While in most cases the employees affected are the same, this listing of the 25 highest paid participants should not be confused with the 25 highest paid employees on the effective date of the plan who are or who may become participants and whose benefits would be restricted in the event of early termination of the plan.

(employee census). A Schedule T (Form 5300), Supplemental Application Form for Approval of Employee Benefit Plans Under TEFRA, Tax Reform Act of 1984, Retirement Equity Act of 1984, and Tax Reform Act of 1986, should be attached to each application. A separate application must be filed for each defined benefit plan and for each defined contribution plan. Forms 5300 and 5301 may also be used to request a determination letter on amendment after initial qualification, to request a determination letter regarding the effect of a potential partial termination on the plan's qualification, and to give notice of merger, consolidation or transfer of plan assets or liabilities and request a determination on the remaining plan(s).

The application for an advance determination letter is filed with the "key" district director for the IRS district in which the employer's principal place of business is located (or where the parent company's principal place of business is located in the case of a plan covering a parent company and some or all of its subsidiaries). As indicated above, employees must be given written advance notice of the request. This notice must advise the employees that any employee (or class of employees) may comment to the district director on the application within 45 days. Moreover, the Pension Benefit Guaranty Corporation, or the secretary of labor (if requested by 10 percent of the employees or by 10 employees, whichever is less) also may comment upon the application. If the district director proposes to issue an adverse letter, this may be appealed to the Appeals Office of the appropriate region of the IRS and, if the proposed adverse determination is upheld, the national office of the IRS may be requested to consider the application.

It is customary to arrange for a conference at each appropriate level within the Internal Revenue Service before an adverse letter is proposed for issuance. Also, in addition to the appeal procedure described above, the district director may be requested to refer specific issues to the national office of the IRS for technical advice. If the national office issues such technical advice on any issue, it may not be the basis for a subsequent appeal.

If the employer has exhausted all remedies within the Internal Revenue Service (including all of the appeal procedures described previously), and if an adverse determination letter is issued, the employer may seek a declaratory judgment in the United States Tax Court as to the qualified status of the plan. Also, an employee who has filed comment with the district director and the Department of Labor also may seek a declaratory judgment concerning the qualified status of the plan after all administrative remedies have been exhausted.

TRUST INVESTMENTS

As previously noted, a qualified plan must be for the exclusive benefit of employees or their beneficiaries, and this primary purpose must be maintained with respect to the investment of trust funds as well as in other activities of the trust. Generally, the trustee may purchase any investments permitted by the trust agreement to the extent permitted by ERISA and by general law. The fiduciary provisions of ERISA also require that the fiduciaries[10] of the plan use the care, skill, prudence, and diligence in making investments that a prudent person who is familiar with such matters would use under the circumstances then prevailing — the so-called prudent expert rule. A fiduciary is also responsible for diversifying investments to minimize the risk of large losses unless it is clearly prudent not to diversify, and must invest only in assets subject to the jurisdiction of the U.S. courts.

Prohibited Transactions

The Internal Revenue Code prohibits certain transactions between the plan and parties in interest. A party in interest is broadly defined and includes, for example, any fiduciary, a person providing services to the plan, any employer or employee organization whose employees or members are covered by the plan, a direct or indirect owner of 50 percent or more of the business interest, a relative of any of the above, and an employee, officer, director, or a person having 10 percent or more of the ownership interest in any of the above.

The following are prohibited transactions between the plan and a party in interest:

1. The sale, exchange, or leasing of property.
2. Lending money or extending credit (including the funding of the plan by the contribution of debt securities).
3. Furnishing goods, services, or facilities.
4. Transfer to or the use of plan assets.
5. Acquisition of qualifying employer securities and real property in excess of allowable limits.

Additionally, a party in interest is prohibited from dealing with plan assets in his or her own interest or for his or her own account.

Prior to ERISA, it was possible for a party in interest to deal with the plan provided the transaction was at arm's length and the plan was protected adequately. Under ERISA, any transactions between a party in interest and the plan (with limited exceptions) are prohibited.

If a party in interest engages in a prohibited transaction, an excise tax of 5 percent of the amount involved in the transaction may be levied on the party in interest. If the situation is not corrected within the time allowed (90 days unless extended by the Internal Revenue Service), a further excise

---

[10]A fiduciary is defined as any person who exercises discretionary authority or control over a plan or its assets, actually provides investment advice for a fee with respect to plan assets, or has any discretion with regard to plan administration. Certain exceptions are available for investment advisers, however.

tax of 100 percent of the amount involved will be levied. Prior to ERISA, a plan lost its qualified status if it engaged in a prohibited transaction; this penalty no longer applies.

A significant aspect of the prohibited transaction rules concerns the investment of plan assets in qualifying employer securities and real property. Qualifying employer securities include stock. Marketable obligations are also considered to be qualifying employer securities if certain requirements are met. The first of these requirements relates to the purchase price of the obligation and is satisfied if any one of the following three tests is met:

1. The obligation is acquired on the market either at the price of the obligation prevailing on a national securities exchange that is registered with the Securities and Exchange Commission, or at a price not less favorable to the trust than the offering price as established by current bid and asked prices quoted by persons independent of the issuer.
2. The obligation is acquired from an underwriter at a price not in excess of the public offering price for the obligation as set forth in a prospectus or offering circular filed with the Securities and Exchange Commission if a substantial portion of the same issue is acquired by persons independent of the issuer at the same price.
3. The obligation is acquired directly from the issuer at a price not less favorable to the trust than the price paid currently for a substantial portion of the same issue by persons independent of the issuer.

The second requirement that must be satisfied is that immediately following the acquisition of the obligation, not more than 25 percent of the aggregate amount of obligations issued in such issue and outstanding at the time of acquisition is held by the trust and that at least 50 percent of such amount is held by persons independent of the issuer. A third requirement provides that immediately following such acquisition, not more than 25 percent of the assets of the trust is invested in obligations of the employer or related or controlled interests.

Qualifying employer real property is real property that is dispersed geographically, is suitable for more than one use, and has been leased to the employer.

Generally speaking, a pension plan may not acquire (by any means) employer securities and real property if the immediate effect of this would cause more than 10 percent of the fair market value of plan assets to be so held.

Deferred profit sharing and thrift and savings plans that specifically so provide may invest without limit in qualifying employer securities or real property. If such a plan does not specifically provide for the amount of employer securities or real property to be held, the 10 percent limit will apply. A defined contribution pension plan that so provided on September 2, 1974, may also invest without limit in qualifying employer securities or real property; otherwise, however, defined contribution pension plans are subject to the 10 percent limit.

Even though investment in qualifying employer securities and real property is permitted under the prohibited transaction rules (and under the requirements for diversity), investments of this type must still satisfy the overriding requirement that they be for the exclusive benefit of employees. Moreover, it is also necessary that any investment in employer securities and real property satisfy the requirements of prudence.

A number of exemptions to the prohibited transaction rules are specifically provided for in ERISA, and there also is a provision for applying for additional exemptions. Among the specific exemptions granted are the furnishing of office space and services for reasonable compensation, the providing of ancillary banking services where this is done without interference with the interests of the plan and the plan participants and, in the case of banks and insurance companies, the utilization of their own facilities to fund their own plans. Another exemption permits a wide variety of transactions by qualified plan asset manager's (QPAMs) such as banks and insurance companies.

UNRELATED BUSINESS INCOME

Generally, the income of a qualified trust is exempt under Section 501(a) of the Code. However, even though such a trust does not lose its qualified status, all or a part of its income may be subject to tax if such income is considered to be unrelated business income.

Unrelated business income is the gross income derived from any unrelated trade or business regularly carried on by the trust, less allowable deductions directly connected with the carrying on of such trade or business, together with any unrelated debt-financed income. An unrelated trade or business means any trade or business the conduct of which is not substantially related to the exempt purpose of the trust.

Only income resulting from the direct operation of the business is subject to tax. Thus, if the trust owns all the stock of a corporation and the corporation directly operates the business, the dividend income received by the trust will not be subject to tax.

The following income is not considered as unrelated business income: dividends, interest, annuities, royalties, rents from real property (including personal property leased with the real property where the rents for such property are incidental), and gains from the sale or exchange of capital assets.[11]

---

[11]Note, however, that income from the rental of personal property not leased with real property is considered unrelated business income. Also, the rent from real property that is leased with personal property will be taxed if 50 percent or more of the rent is attributable to the personal property. Both the rent from the real and the personal property will be taxable if rentals are based on a percentage of this net income from the property.

If the rent from a business lease is to be taxed to a trust, the unrelated business income is that part of the rent that bears the same relationship to the total rent as the indebtedness at the end of the taxable year bears to the adjusted basis of the property at that time. The same proportion of interest, depreciation, taxes, and so on, will be allowed as a deduction to the trust.

When a trust has unrelated business income in excess of $1,000, this must be reported by the trustee on Form 990-T. This return must be filed on or before the 15th day of the fourth month following the close of the trust's taxable year. Generally speaking, most qualified trusts will be taxed at the tax rates imposed on trusts and estates.

DEDUCTIBILITY OF EMPLOYER CONTRIBUTIONS

Apart from the specific provisions of the Internal Revenue Code dealing with the deductibility of employer contributions to a qualified plan, it is first required that if such a contribution is to be deductible, it must otherwise satisfy the conditions of an ordinary and necessary business expense under Code Sections 162 (relating to trade or business expenses) or 212 (relating to expenses for the production of income). Also, a deduction will not be allowed for any portion of the contribution for any employee that, together with other deductions allowed for compensation for such employee, exceeds a reasonable allowance for services the employee actually has rendered.

The employer's contributions to a qualified plan are generally deductible under Section 404(a) of the Internal Revenue Code. Expenses such as actuary's and trustee's fees that are not provided for by contributions under the plan are deductible under Sections 162 or 212 to the extent they are ordinary and necessary expenses.

Employer contributions are generally deductible only in the year in which paid. However, an employer will be deemed to have made a contribution during a taxable year if it is in fact paid by the time prescribed for filing the employer's return for such taxable year (including extensions) and if the employer claims the contribution as a deduction for such year. It is important, however, that the plan be in existence by the close of the employer's taxable year in the case of deductions claimed for the first plan year that begins in such taxable year.

Basically, two provisions determine the maximum amount an employer can contribute and take as a deduction to a qualified pension plan in any one taxable year. The first of these rules permits a deduction for a contribution that will provide, for all employees participating in the plan, the unfunded cost of their past and current service credits distributed as a level amount or as a level percentage of compensation over the remaining future service of each such employee. If this rule is followed, and if the remaining unfunded cost for any three individuals is more than 50 percent of the total unfunded cost, the unfunded cost attributable to such individuals must be distributed over a period of at least five taxable years. Contributions under individual policy pension plans are typically claimed under this rule.

The second rule, while occasionally used with individual policy plans, is used primarily in group pension and trust fund plans.[12] This rule permits the employer to deduct the normal cost of the plan plus the amount necessary to amortize any past service or other supplementary pension or annuity credits in equal annual installments over a 10-year period.

The maximum tax deductible limit will never be less than the amount necessary to satisfy the Code's minimum funding standards.[13] By the same token, the maximum tax-deductible limit cannot exceed the amount needed to bring the plan to its full funding limit (as described in Chapter 9).

If amounts contributed in any taxable year are in excess of the amounts allowed as a deduction for that year, the excess may be carried forward and deducted in succeeding taxable years, in order of time, to the extent that the amount carried forward to any such succeeding taxable year does not exceed the deductible limit for such succeeding taxable year. However, a 10 percent excise tax is imposed on nondeductible contributions by an employer to a qualified plan. For purposes of the excise tax, nondeductible contributions are defined as the sum of the amount of the employer's contribution that exceeds the amount deductible under Section 404 and any excess amount contributed in the preceding tax year that has not been returned to the employer or applied as a deductible contribution in the current year.

For profit sharing plans, the maximum deductible contribution is equal to 15 percent of the compensation paid or otherwise accrued during the employer's taxable year to all covered employees.[14] Carryover provisions apply in profit sharing plans when the contribution in one taxable year is greater than the deductible limit for such taxable year. This type of carryover is called a "contribution carryover." Thus, if a contribution is made in a given year in excess of the allowable deduction for such year, the employer will be allowed to take a deduction for such excess payment in a succeeding taxable year if it does not bring the deduction of the succeeding year to over 15 percent of the participating payroll for such succeeding year.

If both a defined benefit pension plan and a defined contribution plan exist, with overlapping payrolls, the total amount deductible in any taxable

---

[12]These funding instruments are discussed in Chapters 13 and 14, respectively.

[13]Section 412 of the Internal Revenue Code specifies the minimum annual contribution to be made by a sponsor of a qualified plan. See Chapter 9 for a detailed discussion.

[14]If the contribution to the profit sharing plan is less than this amount, the difference between the amount actually paid in and the 15 percent limit (called a "credit carryover") can be contributed and deducted in succeeding years, but only if the carryover was accumulated before 1987. However, the credit carryover contribution in any later year cannot exceed 15 percent of the compensation paid or otherwise accrued during such later year. Also, there is an overall annual limitation when a credit carryover is involved. This overall limit is 25 percent of current covered payroll.

year under both plans cannot exceed 25 percent of the compensation paid or accrued to covered employees for that year.[15] When excess payments are made in any taxable year, the excess may be carried forward to succeeding taxable years, subject to the limitation that the total amount deducted for such succeeding taxable year (including the deduction for the current contribution) cannot exceed 25 percent of the compensation paid or accrued for such subsequent year.

The 25 percent limitation does not eliminate the requirements that a currently deductible profit sharing contribution must not exceed 15 percent of the payroll of the participating employees and that a currently deductible pension contribution must not exceed the amount that would have been the limit had only a pension plan been in effect.

QUESTIONS FOR REVIEW

1. Why is it important to identify the highly compensated employees in reference to pension plan qualification?
2. Summarize the Internal Revenue Code's coverage requirements for qualified plans.
3. What employees may be excluded in applying the coverage requirements?
4. Summarize the general theory behind the nondiscrimination requirements for integrated pension plans.
5. Under what conditions is it possible for an employer to recapture contributions before the satisfaction of all plan liabilities?
6. Can amounts forfeited by terminated employees be used to increase benefits for the remaining participants under a pension plan? Explain.
7. Why must a pension plan be considered permanent for qualification purposes?
8. Why would an employer want to obtain an advance determination letter from the Internal Revenue Service?
9. The Internal Revenue Code prohibits certain transactions between the plan and parties in interest. What is a party in interest, and what types of transactions are prohibited?
10. Must all qualified retirement plans satisfy the same constraints with respect to the investment of plan assets in employer securities and real property?

QUESTIONS FOR DISCUSSION

1. Assume that, in 1989, an employer has 1,000 employees, 100 of them highly compensated, and three retirement plans. Plan A has 90 highly compensated employees, 90 nonhighly compensated employees, and an average benefit per-

---

[15]This 25 percent limit will be increased to the extent larger contributions are required by the Code's minimum funding standards for the defined benefit plan.

centage of 8 percent. Plan B has 10 highly compensated employees, 360 non-highly compensated employees, and an average benefit percentage of 7 percent. Plan C has no highly compensated employees, 405 nonhighly compensated employees, and an average benefit percentage of 6 percent. In addition, 45 employees are not eligible for coverage. Determine whether the employer satisfies the coverage tests.[16]

2. Assume that, in 1989, an employer has 1,000 employees all covered in either a salaried or hourly plan. The salaried plan has 50 highly compensated employees with an average benefit percentage of 30 percent, and 450 nonhighly compensated employees with an average benefit percentage of 36 percent. The hourly plan, which was not a result of collective bargaining, has 500 employees, all nonhighly compensated, with an average benefit percentage of 28 percent. Does the salaried plan satisfy the new coverage requirements?

---

[16]This question is based on material appearing in William M. Mercer-Meidinger, Inc., *Tax Reform: What It Will Mean to Benefits and Compensation* (New York: William M. Mercer-Meidinger, Inc., 1986), p. 20.

5

Basic Features of a Pension Plan

An employer adopting a qualified pension plan must make a number of decisions as to the basic features to be included in the plan. The employer must, for example, determine the class of employees to be covered; when and under what conditions these employees will be eligible for participation; what benefits they will receive upon retirement, death, disability, or severance of employment; how and when these benefits will be paid; and whether or not employees will contribute toward the cost of these benefits.

Legal requirements, of course, play a major role in plan design. The requirements of the Internal Revenue Code and appropriate regulations are of vital importance if the employer wishes to obtain the favorable tax benefits that flow from having a "qualified" plan. While the requirements for qualification were discussed at length in Chapter 4, it should be emphasized at this point that such a plan must not discriminate in any way (i.e., in benefits, contributions, or coverage) in favor of the highly compensated employees. Thus, the organization, if it is to have a qualified plan, cannot pick and choose the employees to be covered nor can it determine their benefits in a selective manner. Instead, the employer must adopt a plan that treats employees fairly and equitably and that does not produce discrimination in favor of the highly compensated employees.

As was pointed out in Chapter 2, the design of a pension plan for a particular employer should reflect a thorough evaluation of the objectives and circumstances of that employer. It often happens that an employer will adopt a "package" plan only to find, at a later date, that this plan is deficient in some respect. Unfortunately, the remedy to this type of problem frequently involves considerable expense and effort on the part of all concerned. This point deserves particular emphasis with the growing use of master and prototype plans. These plans, while they offer the distinct advantage of ease of installation, also create a situation where a plan may be designed without sufficient thought and analysis of the options available in structuring all of the plan provisions. These plans are discussed in Chapter 21.

This and the following chapter discuss the various factors that bear on an employer's decisions concerning the design of the more prominent features to be included in a pension plan. While much of this material applies equally well to profit sharing plans, it is oriented specifically toward *qualified pension* plans. The features discussed in this chapter include eligibility requirements, the determination of service, retirement ages, and employee contributions. Chapter 6 covers retirement, death, disability, and severance-of-employment benefits and the special requirements applicable to top-heavy plans. Chapter 6 also touches upon some of the other provisions essential to any pension plan (such as the employer's right to amend or terminate the program) but that are more or less straightforward in nature and do not require any major consideration by the employer.

ELIGIBILITY REQUIREMENTS

In the generally accepted sense, eligibility requirements are those conditions an employee must meet to become a participant in the plan. In noncontributory plans, an employee who meets the eligibility requirements automatically becomes a participant when first eligible. In contributory plans, the employee usually has the option of participating and must take some affirmative action before becoming a participant. Thus, the employee must usually sign an application for participation under which the employee agrees to make contributions and also designates a beneficiary.

Eligibility requirements fall into two broad categories — those that defer an employee's participation until some stipulated conditions are met, and those that exclude an employee from participation on a permanent basis (or, at least, until the employee has had some change in employment classification). An example of an eligibility requirement that defers participation would be a requirement that the employee must attain some minimum age before becoming eligible. On the other hand, a provision that excludes hourly employees is illustrative of a requirement that may exclude certain employees from ever participating in the plan.

Those eligibility requirements that defer participation often are included for administrative cost considerations. Inclusion of employees who are still in what might be termed the *high-turnover* stage of their employment will involve the creation and maintenance of records and, depending on the funding instrument involved, could create additional and unnecessary costs for the employer. For example, an employee who terminates employment shortly after becoming a participant under an individual policy plan creates a cost to the employer measured in terms of the difference between the premiums paid for the employee's coverage and the cash surrender value (including any dividends) that is available from the insurer under the employee's insurance or annuity contract (these funding instruments are described in Chapter 14). However, care must be exercised so that the eligibility requirements are not too stringent. The positive psychological effect of the plan may be lost if a number of employees find that they are not yet eligible to participate. The selection of appropriate eligibility requirements balances these factors so that within the employer's objectives as many employees as possible are eligible, while financial losses and administrative difficulties are kept to a minimum.

Those eligibility requirements that may permanently exclude employees from participation are generally dictated by the employer's objectives, by bargaining agreements, or by cost considerations. For example, if a bargaining unit is negotiating for a pension plan, coverage is generally confined to employees represented by the bargaining unit.

The most common eligibility requirements involve the use of a minimum age or a minimum period of service. In the broad sense, other eligibility requirements also may be considered, such as the use of employment classifications.

One further point is that eligibility requirements that defer participation also might affect the employee's benefit and the ultimate cost of the plan, since, for example, they could limit the time during which credited service may be accrued. Many plans, however, and particularly those negotiated by collective bargaining units, give credit for total service or give credit for all service up to some maximum such as 30 years.

In designing eligibility requirements, it often is helpful to prepare a chart that shows the distribution of employees by age and service. This type of chart often indicates the proper choice of eligibility requirements. Table 5–1 shows how such a chart might be prepared.

With the above discussion as general background, it is now appropriate to consider certain specific eligibility requirements in greater detail.

Years of Service and Minimum Age

In most situations, it is possible to demonstrate that an employer's highest rate of turnover occurs among employees who have been with the firm for a relatively short period of time. It is generally desirable that any minimum service and age requirements of the plan be set to provide that only those persons who have been employed beyond this period will be eligible.

TABLE 5–1: Analysis of Employees by Age and Service

Age	Under 1 Year	1	2	3	4	5–9	10–14	15–19	20 or More	Total
						Years of Service				
Under 20	1									1
20–24		1								1
25–29	1		1							2
30–34			1	1	1	2				5
35–39	1					1	3			5
40–44	2	2		1			1	1		7
45–49	1			5	1	3	1	2		13
50–54			1		1		1		1	4
55–59						1	2		1	4
60–64			1				1			2
65–69						1	1			2
70 and over							1			1
Total	6	3	4	7	3	8	11	3	2	47

Under federal tax law, however, eligibility cannot be delayed beyond the time an employee reaches age 21 and completes one year of service.[1] Thus, the maximum service requirement that may be used is one year, and the highest minimum age that may be used is age 21.[2] Further, the use of entry dates cannot delay the participation of an employee more than six months. Thus, if it is desired to use the most stringent minimum age and service requirements possible, the plan should permit entry at least every six months. The use of an annual entry date will be permissible only when the minimum age and/or service requirements are at least six months less than those permissible under the law (age 20½ or six months of service).

An exception to the one-year service requirement is available if the plan provides full and immediate vesting (an infrequent situation in a defined benefit pension plan). Here, a two-year service requirement, along with a minimum age requirement of 21, will be permissible (for plans that do not have a cash or deferred arrangement). For plan years beginning before January 1, 1989, a three-year service requirement is permitted for such plans.

Employment Classifications

At one time, it was quite common to establish plans with participation limited to salaried employees only. However, even prior to the new coverage requirements imposed by the Tax Reform Act of 1986, it had

[1]The definition of a year of service is extremely technical for some forms of employment. A detailed discussion of this topic is provided later in this chapter.

[2]The minimum age is increased from 21 to 26 in the case of a plan maintained exclusively for employees of an educational institution that provides that each participant having at least one year of service has full 100 percent vesting.

become increasingly more difficult to qualify plans with this limitation. As a general rule, if the salaried employees were all earning more than the hourly employees, the plan would not be acceptable to the IRS. The acceptability of such a plan increased, however, when the hourly employees earned substantially the same as some of the salaried employees.

It was also possible for a plan to be established for only those employees who worked in a specific plant or at a specific location, or who worked in a specific occupation. These classifications were not used too frequently and, when used, could not produce discrimination in favor of the prohibited group of employees.

Because many salaried-only plans relied on the old nondiscriminatory classification test, these plans will have to be reviewed for plan years beginning after December 31, 1988, to determine if they meet the new average-benefits test described in Chapter 4.

Salaried-only plans also may be acceptable where the employer is making contributions for the hourly employees as, for example, under a different plan. Thus, if the salaried-only plan does not qualify on its own, it may still qualify if the plan covering the hourly employees provides contributions or benefits that are comparable to those being provided for salaried employees.

Under federal tax law, a plan may exclude employees covered by a collective bargaining agreement if there is evidence of good faith bargaining on pensions. In many situations, this will effectively permit the establishment of a salaried-only plan, even in the absence of a plan providing comparable benefits or contributions for the noncovered employees. In addition, aliens employed abroad by a branch of a U.S. employer may be excluded from coverage even though U.S. citizens at the branch are included in the plan.

DETERMINATION OF SERVICE

An employee's length of service is an important factor in determining his or her rights and benefits under a pension plan. First, length of service may establish the employee's initial eligibility to participate in the plan, and may establish eligibility for death and disability benefits and the right to retire early. Length of service also establishes vesting rights in the event of termination of employment and, in most situations, service is a major factor in the plan's benefit formula, thus establishing the amount of the employee's benefit.

The law establishes specific requirements for the determination of service in three key areas: (1) initial eligibility to participate, (2) vesting, and (3) the right to a benefit accrual. The law does not mandate how service is to be determined for other purposes (e.g., the right to retire early) but for administrative convenience most plans determine service in the same manner for all purposes.

The basic concept of the law is that an employee must be given credit for a year of service for any computation period during which the employee works 1,000 hours. (A computation period is a 12-month period and may be established as a plan year, calendar year, or an employment year; however, in the case of service used for eligibility purposes, the initial 12-month period must begin with date of employment.) The employee also must be given a ratable benefit accrual, if participation has commenced, for any computation period in which he or she is credited with at least 1,000 hours of service.

If an employee completes fewer than 1,000 hours of service within a computation period, credit need not be given for a year of service and the employee need not be given any benefit accrual for the period in question. However, if the employee has completed at least 501 hours of service in the computation period, this will prevent the employee from incurring a "break in service."

Whether the employee has incurred a break in service is significant in terms of aggregating separate periods of employment. Prior to the passage of ERISA, it was relatively unusual for a plan to consolidate separate periods of employment. Such aggregation is now required under certain conditions. If an employee returns to work for at least one year after a break in service (which is defined to be a computation period during which the employee has been credited with 500 or fewer hours of service), the employee's prior service will have to be taken into account if: (1) the employee was vested (even though only partially) when the break in service occurred; or (2) the number of consecutive one-year breaks in service equals or exceeds the greater of five or the number of prebreak years of service. In recognition of the practical problems of reconstructing prior employment records, the break-in-service rules apply only for service incurred after the time a plan was required to comply with the terms of ERISA. Broken service before that time may continue to be determined by the terms of the plan as it existed then. In the case of either a defined contribution plan or a fully insured plan, it is not required that years of service after five consecutive one-year breaks in service be taken into account for the purpose of determining the employee's vested interest for employer contributions made prior to the five-year period.

Additional requirements of the law for the determination of service are as follows:

1. Service must include periods of employment with any corporation that is a member of a controlled group of corporations (i.e., where there is 80 percent control). Similar principles apply for service in an unincorporated business under common control.

2. Service with a predecessor employer must be taken into account for eligibility and vesting purposes if the employer maintains the plan of the

predecessor. If the employer maintains a plan that is not the plan of the predecessor, service with the predecessor will have to be considered to the extent prescribed in regulations.

3. In the case of service used to determine initial eligibility to participate in the plan, the initial computation period must begin with the employee's date of employment. The employer has the choice of converting the computation period to a plan or calendar-year basis after the first 12 months of employment, provided the beginning of such new computation period overlaps with the first employment year.

4. For vesting purposes, certain periods of service may be excluded. Specifically, the plan may exclude service prior to age 18.[3] Service need not include any period during which the employee did not elect to contribute under a plan requiring employee contributions. It may also exclude service prior to the adoption of the plan (or predecessor plan).

5. A new special rule for maternity or paternity absences has been added. This rule applies to an individual who is absent from work by reason of the pregnancy of the individual, the birth of a child of the individual, the placement of a child with an individual in connection with adoption, or for purposes of caring for such child for a period beginning immediately following birth or placement. The new law requires that, for purposes of determining whether a one-year break in service has occurred, the plan treat as hours of service the lesser of the hours that otherwise would have been credited to the individual or 501 hours. If a participant would be prevented from incurring a one-year break in service solely because the period of absence is treated as hours of service, the hours of service are credited only in the year in which the absence from work begins; otherwise hours are credited in the year immediately following.

The following describes specific ways in which service may be calculated under the law.

Hour of Service

The first issue involved in calculating service is determining what constitutes an hour of service. The regulation defines an hour of service as an hour for which an employee is paid, or entitled to payment, for the performance of duties for the employer; and an hour for which the employee is paid, or entitled to payment, by the employer on account of a period of time during which no duties are performed (irrespective of whether the employment relationship has terminated) due to vacation, holiday, illness, incapacity (including disability), layoff, jury duty, military duty, or leave of absence; and each hour for which back pay, irrespective of damages, is

---

[3]There is an exception to this rule for plan years beginning before January 1, 1989. If the plan's vesting provisions are based upon the rule of 45 (the details of this vesting alternative are described in Chapter 6), service prior to age 18 must be taken into account if it is rendered while the employee is a participant in the plan.

either awarded or agreed to by the employer. However, a plan need not credit an employee with more than 501 hours of service for any single, continuous period during which the employee performs no duties, or for any period of nonworking service for which payment is made under workers' compensation, unemployment compensation, or state disability laws.

Depending upon the compliance method selected, all or some of these hours of service will have to be taken into account. (Under the elapsed time method of compliance, the hours-of-service concept is not relevant, since total service is measured from date of employment to date of severance.)

Compliance Methods

An employer has three methods to choose from in crediting employees with hours of service. The same method may be used for all purposes or, under the decoupling provisions of the regulations, a different compliance method may be used within the same plan for eligibility, vesting, and benefit accrual purposes. Also, if discrimination does not result, a different method may be used for different classes of employees (a particularly helpful factor when distinguishing between part-time and full-time employees). Finally, the regulations permit the use of one compliance method for pre-ERISA service and another for post-ERISA service (again, an important factor in view of the lack, in many instances, of adequate pre-ERISA employment records).

The first method is the standard-hours-counting method under which all hours for which compensation is paid must be taken into account. While this method is, in one sense, the simplest to describe, many employers find it difficult to administer—particularly in the case of exempt employees who often do not keep a record of actual hours worked.

The second method involves the use of equivalencies. Under this method, four alternatives exist. The first uses hours worked where service is determined only on the basis of actual hours worked, including overtime and excluding all other nonworked hours for which compensation is received, such as vacations, holidays, and so forth. The second alternative involves only regular hours worked. Under this alternative, service is determined on the basis of actual hours worked, excluding overtime, and excluding all other nonworked hours for which compensation is received. The third alternative concerns a time period selected for the plan—day, by shift, weekly, semimonthly, or monthly—and an employee is credited with an imputed number of hours for the time period involved as long as he or she is credited with at least one hour of service during such time period. The fourth alternative involves the employee's earnings and here, hours of service are related to the earnings received by the employee during the period involved.

The third method is called the elapsed-time method. Under this method, service is measured from the employee's date of employment to date of severance.

An employer who wishes to use an equivalency in lieu of counting hours must pay a "premium." In the case of time-period equivalencies, this premium is measured in terms of the number of hours that must be credited for the time period selected. In essence, the hours credited will exceed a normal work schedule for the period involved to build in a credit for overtime or additional hours that might have been worked. The specific hours that must be credited under each of the time-period equivalencies are as follows:

One day — 10 hours.

One week — 45 hours.

Half-month — 95 hours.

One month — 190 hours.

Shift — actual hours included in the shift.

Under the daily time-period equivalency, for example, an employee must be credited with 10 hours for each day in which he or she is credited with one hour of service. Thus, after five such days, the employee will have been credited with 50 hours of service. This, of course, means that under the time-period equivalencies, an employee will be credited with 1,000 hours of service in a much shorter period of time (in the average situation) than would be the case under the actual hours-counting method.

The premium for using the other equivalencies is measured by reducing the 1,000-hour standard for a full year of service and the 501-hour standard for applying the break-in-service rules. The reductions for the different equivalencies are shown in Table 5–2. As indicated by this table, for example, under the hours-worked equivalency an employee will only have to be credited with 870 hours (instead of 1,000 hours) to be credited with one year of service, and need only be credited with 435 hours of service in a computation period (instead of 501 hours) to avoid having a break in service.

TABLE 5–2: Adjustments in Hours of Service
Required for Crediting a Year of Service and for
Break-in-Service Rules under Certain Equivalencies

Equivalency	Year of Service	Break in Service
Hours worked	870	435
Regular hours worked	750	375
Earnings		
Hourly-rated employees	870	435
Other employees	750	375

Under the elapsed-time method, service credit for eligibility and vesting must begin with the employee's date of hire (except for permissible statutory exclusions such as service prior to the effective date of the plan). For benefit-accrual purposes, service must be credited starting with the date the employee begins participation in the plan. Service must continue to be credited, for all purposes for which the elapsed-time method is used, until the employee's date of severance. In the case of quitting, discharge, retirement, or death, the employee's severance date will be immediate. In the case of absence from active employment for other reasons such as layoff, leave of absence, and disability, the employee's severance date will be 12 months after the beginning of the absence. After the employee's severance date, the plan need not credit service. However, there are two exceptions to this rule. The first exception is if the employee is reemployed within 12 months after quitting, discharge, or retirement, the plan must grant service credit for the period of the employee's severance (but only for eligibility and vesting purposes and not for benefit accruals). The second exception is if an employee quits, is discharged, or retires during a layoff, disability, or leave of absence, and is reemployed within 12 months after the absence began, the plan must grant service credit for the period of severance (again, for eligibility and vesting, but not for benefit accruals). Also, under the elapsed-time method, a one-year period of severance is treated the same as a one-year break in service.

EMPLOYEE CONTRIBUTIONS

A major question the employer must resolve is whether employees will be required to make contributions toward the cost of plan benefits. Sound arguments may be presented for both contributory and noncontributory plans, although the ability of the employer or employees to pay is often the controlling factor. In any event, the trend is clearly in the direction of noncontributory plans, at least in the case of defined benefit plans.

Arguments advanced in favor of contributory plans include the following:

1. From a philosophical viewpoint, employees are responsible for meeting part of their own economic security needs.
2. If employees contribute, it will mean a smaller employer contribution to provide the same overall plan benefits.
3. If employers do not want to use employee contributions to reduce their own contribution, then by making the plan contributory, the overall plan benefits will be larger.
4. Something for nothing is too often taken for granted, and the deductions from current earnings will continually remind employees that the employer is assuming a large share of providing the plan benefits. (It

would seem that this argument could be minimized by an effective method of repeatedly publicizing the plan and its value to employees.)

5. Employees are encouraged to save. The contributory plan also provides an employee with additional funds in the event of termination of employment.

The proponents of a noncontributory plan hold that the contributory plan has the following disadvantages:

1. Employer contributions represent dollars that have not been taxed. On the other hand, dollars received by the employee as earnings that are then contributed under the plan are dollars that have been taxed to the employee. Hence, dollar for dollar, employer contributions provide more than those of an employee.
2. Deductions from earnings are a source of constant irritation to employees.
3. The employer might be forced to increase salaries to compensate for the additional deductions.
4. The number of participants required for a qualified plan (or required by the insurer under certain funding instruments) might not enroll.
5. Some employees may refuse to participate, in which case the employer will still have a problem when these employees reach retirement age.
6. Additional records must be kept by the employer, thereby increasing administrative work and costs.

If the employer decides that employees should make contributions, the next decision will be the amount employees should contribute. While employee contributions may be related to the cost of benefits, generally it is much more satisfactory to relate these contributions to earnings. In this way, an employee's contributions are geared to the ability to make them. Furthermore, in most plans it is impossible to predict exactly what the cost of an employee's pension will be until actual retirement. Hence, any contributions made by the employee and related to cost necessarily are estimated and do not have an exact relationship.

Employee contribution rates of 2, 3, or even 4 percent of earnings are commonly used. If the plan is to qualify, however, the contribution rate generally should not exceed 6 percent. If the plan employs a formula integrated with social security benefits, the contribution rate should reflect the different levels of benefits relative to earnings. For example, if the benefit formula provides a 1 percent future service benefit for earnings under $800 a month and a 1.5 percent benefit on earnings in excess of this amount, the corresponding employee contributions could be 2 and 3 percent.

Contributory plans usually require that an employee, before becoming a participant, must sign a request for participation agreeing to make the required contributions and authorizing the employer to withhold contributions from earnings. If an employee fails to make such an election when first eligible, it is customary to impose some form of penalty. In plans using a unit credit formula,[4] for example, past service benefits as well as the future service benefits[5] that would otherwise have accrued might be forfeited until the employee joins the plan. If the plan employs a flat percentage of earnings formula,[6] the benefits might be reduced by multiplying the benefit the late entrant would otherwise have received by a fraction, the numerator being the years of actual contribution and the denominator the number of years the employee could have contributed. A few plans are even more severe and provide that if an employee does not join when first eligible, the right to participate will be forfeited for all time. Another approach used by some employers is to give employees the option of participating if they are employed when the plan becomes effective, but to require participation as a condition of employment for all future employees.

Another provision to be considered in contributory plans is the right of an employee to suspend or discontinue contributions. Many plans do not give an employee either of these privileges. Others permit a temporary suspension (for a year or so) without affecting benefits, and some permit a complete discontinuance at any time. Still others permit only a complete discontinuance. If discontinuance of contributions is permitted, further questions exist, such as whether the employee is permitted to rejoin the plan and, if so, what benefits the employee will then be entitled to receive.

Regardless of whether the plan requires employees to make contributions, it may permit an employee to make voluntary contributions (or additional contributions under a contributory plan) to supplement benefits. Prior to 1989, such a provision was acceptable to the Internal Revenue Service provided the voluntary additional contributions do not exceed 10 percent of aggregate compensation for all years of plan participation. Beginning in 1989, such contributions will have to meet the average contribution percentage (ACP) test described in Chapter 16. The advantage of such a provision is that the employee will not be required to include the investment income on accumulated contributions as income subject to tax until this income is distributed. Even then, favorable tax treatment accorded to distributions from a qualified plan could apply to the earnings on these additional contributions. When employees are permitted to make additional contributions, the plan should also contain provisions concerning

---

[4]A unit credit formula gives specific recognition for service as well as earnings. Under such a formula, an employee receives a benefit credit equal to a percentage of earnings for each year that he or she is a participant under the plan.

[5]Past and future benefits are defined relative to the date of plan inception. This concept is discussed in detail in Chapter 6.

[6]This type of formula does not take an employee's service into account, except in those plans that require that the employee must have completed a minimum period of service by normal retirement date and that provide for a proportionately reduced benefit if his or her service is less than the required number of years. Some percentage of earnings, usually ranging from 25 to 50 percent, is selected as the measure of the pension benefit.

the amounts that employees may contribute on this basis, how often (if at all) the rate of contribution may be changed by the employee, the conditions under which these contributions may be withdrawn, whether or not employees may suspend or discontinue these additional contributions, and if so, the effect of a suspension or discontinuance, and so on.

RETIREMENT AGES

Normal Retirement Age

The normal retirement age in most plans is 65. The choice of this age has been influenced not only by the fact that this is the age at which full social security benefits now commence but also that retiring employees before age 65 with full benefits often produces prohibitive costs. Federal law defines normal retirement age to be the age specified in the plan, but no later than age 65 or the completion of 10 years of participation (5 years in the case of a plan participant who commences participation in the plan within 5 years before attaining normal retirement age under the plan), whichever is last to occur. Occasionally, an earlier age such as 60 will be chosen as the normal retirement age although, to a great extent, this practice has been confined to public, quasi-public, and charitable institutions. Also, where an employee's occupation is such that his or her working career is shorter than in most other occupations, and when this does not result in prohibited age discrimination, a plan may provide for a normal retirement age lower than 65. It should be noted, however, that there has been a growing interest (both with management and employees) in retiring earlier than age 65—frequently by means of some form of subsidized early retirement benefit. On the other hand, the 1983 social security amendments gradually change the "normal" retirement age for collecting unreduced social security benefits from 65 to 67. It remains to be seen whether this will influence the choice of normal retirement age under private plans, assuming ERISA and the Code are amended to permit this action.

A staggered normal retirement schedule is used for older employees. A typical schedule would state that anyone over age 60 will retire at the end of 5 years of participation in the plan. Thus, an employee 61 years old at entry into the plan would retire at 66. The use of a staggered normal retirement schedule accomplishes several things. First, the cost of providing a given amount of pension will decrease as the employee's normal retirement age increases. Second, it enables the employer to accumulate the cost of an older employee's pension over a longer period of time. Third, if the plan bases benefits on service or uses a defined contribution (money purchase) formula, the employee will have an additional period of time in which to accrue benefits. Finally, both the employer and employee are given an adequate period of time in which to plan for the employee's retirement.

Early Retirement Age

Most plans provide that an employee may choose early retirement on a reduced pension, although a few plans limit this feature to cases of total and permanent disability. If an early retirement provision is included, it is customary to establish some requirements an employee must fulfill before being allowed to elect early retirement.

A typical requirement for early retirement would be that the employee must have attained at least age 55 and completed at least 10 years of service or participation in the plan. Requirements such as these limit the option to situations where the employee is actually retiring, as opposed to changing jobs. They also tend to create a situation in which the employee will receive a reasonable benefit.

Employer consent is generally not required for early retirement. If employer consent is necessary, the Internal Revenue Service requires that the value of the benefit payable at early retirement be not greater than the value of the benefit that the employee would have received under the plan's vesting schedule had employment been terminated on the date of retirement.

The benefit payable at early retirement typically is lower than the normal retirement benefit for two reasons. First, the full benefit will not have accrued by the employee's early retirement date. Second, the benefit, because it is starting several years earlier than anticipated, will be paid over a longer period of time. Thus, an actuarial reduction factor usually is applied to the value of the employee's accrued benefit to determine the amount of early retirement benefit.

Determining the value of the employee's accrued benefit is relatively simple under an allocated funding instrument.[7] In a pension plan funded entirely by individual insurance policies, for example, the value of the accrued benefit generally is the cash surrender value of the employee's insurance or annuity contract at the time of retirement. In this type of plan, the actuarial reduction is accomplished by the use of the settlement option rates contained in the contract. The employee's benefit is generally that amount that may be provided by applying the cash surrender value under the option at the employee's attained age on his or her retirement date.

In plans using an unallocated funding instrument, and where the benefit formula reflects the employee's service, the benefit is generally measured in terms of the employee's accrued benefit to the date of retirement. If the plan uses another type of formula, however, the determination of the value of the employee's accrued benefit is more difficult. One often-used

[7]Funding instruments are classified on the basis of whether contributions are allocated to provide benefits to specific employees or whether contributions are accumulated in an unallocated fund to provide benefits for employees.

approach is to multiply the value of the employee's projected benefit at normal retirement date by a fraction, the numerator being the years of participation or service the employee has completed at early retirement date and the denominator the years of participation or service the employee would have completed at normal retirement date.

In any event, an employee's accrued benefit at early retirement must meet the accrued benefit requirements of federal tax law that apply to vested benefits (discussed in Chapter 6).

The reduction factor applied to the value of the employee's accrued benefit might be something as simple as a reduction of one half of 1 percent for each month by which early retirement precedes normal retirement; or, as often is the case, an actuarial reduction factor is determined from a table included in the plan or group contract. Table 5–3 shows a typical set of actuarial reduction factors that apply where the normal form for the payment of benefits is a pure life annuity.

As noted earlier, there has been a growing interest in recent years in the possibility of retiring earlier than age 65. While some plans actually establish a normal retirement age earlier than age 65, a greater number encourage early retirement by not applying a full actuarial reduction if certain conditions are met. One approach, for example, is to provide for no actuarial reduction at all if the employee retires after attaining some age (such as 60) and after completing some period of service (such as 30 years). A similar approach would be to apply no reduction factor (or a minimum factor) if early retirement occurs when the employee's age and service total to some number such as 90—for example, an employee who is age 62 and who has completed 28 years of service would satisfy this requirement. Still another

TABLE 5–3: Early Retirement Factors*

Years Prior to Normal Retirement Date†	Percentage
1	89.9
2	81.0
3	73.2
4	66.4
5	60.3
6	54.9
7	50.1
8	45.8
9	42.0
10	38.5

*Based on a normal retirement age of 65.
†Years prior to normal retirement date means years and complete months from early retirement date to normal retirement date. Allowance for such months is made by interpolating in the table.

approach would be to apply some simple factor, such as one fourth of 1 percent for each month by which early retirement precedes normal retirement, that is considerably less than the reduction that would otherwise be called for by full actuarial reduction factors. Approaches such as these will, of course, increase the cost of the pension plan; however, employees generally find such a provision to be attractive, and quite frequently the employer finds its overall interests are best served by a provision that encourages early retirement.

Late Retirement Age

Plans must also include a provision allowing an employee to defer retirement. This feature could also be important to the employer, since it permits a greater degree of flexibility in scheduling the actual retirement of a key employee when there is a problem in obtaining or training a replacement.

The Federal Age Discrimination Law and some state laws protect employment rights without an upper age limit. The right to elect late retirement is subject to these legal requirements and the employer's consent to late retirement cannot be required for deferrals.[8]

QUESTIONS FOR REVIEW

1. The law establishes specific regulations for the determination of service in what key areas?
2. When will an employee incur a break in service? Why is this significant?
3. Explain (a) how hours of service are generally related to the calculation of service for plan participants, (b) the break-in-service rules for maternity or paternity absences, and (c) the compliance methods available for counting hours of service.
4. What is the purpose of eligibility requirements that defer participation?
5. Describe the advantages of a contributory plan.
6. Describe the advantages of a noncontributory plan.
7. Why would an employee elect to make voluntary nondeductible contributions to a pension plan?
8. What are the advantages of a staggered normal retirement schedule?
9. Why is the benefit payable at early retirement lower than the normal retirement benefit?
10. What options are available to an employer who would like to encourage early retirement through provisions in a qualified plan?

---

[8]Individuals who are bona fide executives or who are in high policymaking positions and whose annual employer-provided retirement income from all sources is at least $44,000 may be required to retire at age 65.

QUESTIONS FOR DISCUSSION

1. Corporation A is divided into two divisions. In order to work in division 2 an employee must first have been employed in division 1 for five years. If employees in division 1 are covered by a pension plan that contains a plan provision that requires division 2 employment for participation, will the plan satisfy the minimum age and service requirements?[9]

2. (a) A calendar year plan provides that an employee may enter the plan only on the first semiannual entry date, January 1 or July 1, after he or she has satisfied the applicable minimum age and service requirements. Does the plan satisfy the requirements for plan participation? (b) A plan provides that an employee is not eligible to participate until the first day of the first plan year beginning after he or she has satisfied the minimum age and service requirements. Does the plan satisfy the requirements for plan participation? (c) A calendar year plan provides that an employee may enter the plan only on the first semiannual entry date, January 1 or July 1, after he or she has satisfied the applicable minimum age and service requirements. After 10 years of service employee A separated from service in 1976 with a vested benefit. On February 1, 1990, A returns to employment covered by the plan. Assuming A completes a year of service after his return, when will his participation in the plan resume?[10]

3. Prior to 1989, a qualified plan requires as a condition of participation that an employee complete a minimum of three years of service. Assuming that the plan computes service by the actual counting of hours and provides full and immediate vesting, how soon would an employee become eligible to participate if (a) she worked 1,000 hours in each of the first six years, (b) she worked 1,000 hours in each of the first six years, except for year 3 (700 hours), (c) she worked 1,000 hours in each of the first six years, except for year 2 (500 hours) and year 4 (700 hours).[11]

---

[9]Regulation Section 1.410(a)-3(e)(2).
[10]Regulation Section 1.410(a)-4(b)(2).
[11]Regulation Section 1.410(a)-5(c)(2)(ii).

6

Basic Features of a
Pension Plan
(continued)

Chapter 5 discussed those elements of plan design dealing with eligibility requirements, determination of service, employee contributions, and retirement ages. In this chapter, attention is focused on the benefits payable under a pension plan at retirement, death, disability, or upon severance of employment. The requirements applicable to top-heavy plans are also discussed. The chapter concludes with a brief discussion of general provisions included in most plans—the right to amend or terminate the program, administrative provisions, and the like.

RETIREMENT BENEFITS

The formula selected for determining an employee's retirement benefit is a vital provision in a pension plan. The employer's financial capacity and general philosophy concerning the desired level of retirement benefits, as well as the employer's specific objectives as to the distribution of benefits among employees, all play an important role in selecting such a formula.

Many employers believe that a plan should be designed to provide a higher paid career employee with an income after retirement that, together with primary social security benefits, will be about 50 to 55 percent of earnings just before retirement. For lower paid employees, the percentage generally is set at a higher level—perhaps as much as 80 to 85 percent.

For employees considered to be less than career employees (usually those employees with fewer than 25 or 30 years of service with the employer), these percentages would be proportionately smaller. From the employer's viewpoint, the benefit formula selected should in no event result in a plan that produces unacceptable costs so as to endanger the continuation of the plan if corporate earnings are decreased or if current tax advantages are reduced.

Basically, there are two types of benefit formulas for the employer to consider. The first is called a *defined contribution* or a *money purchase* formula. Under this type of formula, contribution rates are fixed, and an employee's benefit varies depending upon such factors as the amount of the contributions made, investment earnings on plan assets, and the employee's entry age and retirement age.[1]

The second type is called a *defined benefit* or an *annuity purchase* formula. Here, a definite benefit is established for each employee, and contributions are determined to be whatever is necessary to produce the desired benefit results. Defined benefit formulas may be subdivided into several different classifications.[2]

Determination of Compensation

Since the amount of benefit under most formulas is based on an employee's compensation, it is important, before discussing specific formulas, to have a clear idea of the various considerations involved in selecting the compensation base to which the benefit formula will be applied.

The Tax Reform Act of 1986 provided a uniform definition of compensation for purposes of the nondiscriminatory requirements. Generally, compensation is compensation for service performed for an employer that is currently includable in income. An employer may elect to include salary reduction contributions to cash or deferred arrangements (described in Chapter 17), tax sheltered annuities (described in Chapter 20), or simplified employee pensions (described in Chapter 19) as compensation, provided that these contributions are treated as compensation on a consistent basis. The secretary of the treasury is directed to prescribe regulations providing for alternate definitions of compensation. However, such alternate definitions will only be available to employees if they do not discriminate in favor of highly compensated employees.

Another aspect of the problem of determining earnings used for the benefit formula is the question of whether plan benefits should be based on the

---

[1]This chapter is concerned only with defined contribution pension plans. Other defined contribution plans, such as profit sharing and thrift and savings plans, are discussed in later chapters.

[2]It has been said that a third type of benefit formula is emerging, one in which the employee's benefit will vary depending upon the performance of the common stock market or upon changes in a cost-of-living index. Actually, this is not so, since variable benefit plans involve either a defined contribution or a defined benefit formula.

average of the earnings paid over the entire period of the employee's participation in the plan or on an average of the employee's earnings during some shorter period of time that is near the employee's normal retirement age. The latter type of provision, often called a *final-pay provision*, would base benefits on the employee's earnings averaged, for example, over the last three or five years of employment, or over the three or five consecutive years in the 10-year period immediately prior to retirement during which the employee's earnings are the highest.

The advantage of a final-pay plan is that it relates benefits to the employee's earnings and standard of living during a period just preceding retirement. As a result, the employee's initial benefit keeps pace with any preretirement inflationary trends. Moreover, a final-pay plan is more likely to meet employer objectives as to benefit levels than is a career-pay plan. This type of plan, however, is usually more expensive than one that bases benefits on career average earnings. Many employers believe it is best to use a career average earnings plan and to make periodic adjustments in the benefit formula when economic trends justify such an action.

While a final-pay plan has the disadvantage of committing an employer to increased costs during an extended inflationary period, it should be remembered that in many situations the employer's capacity to absorb these increases also may be increased. Moreover, a final-pay plan generally produces more favorable results for key employees than the career average approach.

A final point to be noted concerns the requirement of federal tax law that an employee's *normal* retirement benefit can never be less than the highest early retirement benefit that he or she could have received. Thus, any salary reductions that occur after an employee first becomes eligible to retire early cannot have the effect of reducing the employee's *normal* retirement benefit.

Defined Contribution Formulas

As previously noted, a defined contribution formula does not provide a fixed benefit for employees. Instead, the rate of contribution of the employer is fixed, usually as a percentage of the employee's earnings, and this contribution is applied (together with the employee's contribution under a contributory plan) to provide whatever pension benefits can be purchased. Since the cost of a given amount of benefit varies by entry age and retirement age, the benefits for any employee depend on these factors, as well as on contribution levels and investment income. Beginning in 1989, the combined total of employer and employee contributions under a defined contribution plan must satisfy the average contribution percentage (ACP) test described in Chapter 16.

In the past, the employee's sex was also a factor in determining the amount of retirement benefit that could be provided under a defined contribution pension plan. If a male and female employee were the same age and had exactly the same amount accumulated under such a plan, the male employee would receive a higher lifetime pension than the female employee. This was because the female employee was expected to live longer and, in anticipation of this, the same initial amount was expected to be paid over a longer period of time. Because of this difference in life expectancies, the actuarial value of the pension, in both cases, was considered to be the same. In 1983, however, the Supreme Court ruled (in *Arizona Governing Committee* v. *Norris*) that life annuities under an employer-sponsored defined contribution plan must be provided on a unisex basis for contributions made on or after August 1, 1983.[3]

Defined contribution plans are often contributory. In this case, the employer's contribution either matches or is a multiple of the employee's contribution. For example, the plan could call for the employer and employee each to contribute 5 percent of the employee's compensation; or the employee's contribution could be set at 3 percent of compensation with the employer contributing 6 percent.

It should be recognized that the defined contribution formula has several inherent limitations. First, an employee who joins the plan at an older age will have only a short period of time to accumulate funds, with the result that the employee's benefit often will be inadequate. Since the owners of a business are often advanced in years when a plan is being established, and since a defined benefit formula generally produces more favorable results for them, it is not hard to see why they frequently find little appeal in a defined contribution formula. It is possible, of course, to include a past service benefit at the time the plan is established; on balance, however, most firms still find a defined benefit formula to be more desirable from this point of view. Table 6–1 indicates the results that could flow under a defined contribution formula and the disparity in benefits often produced in such a plan. This table assumes that the compensation

TABLE 6–1: Illustration of Defined Contribution Formula without Earnings Projection

Age at Entry	Normal Retire- ment Age	Compen- sation	Contribu- tion	Fund at Retirement	Monthly Benefit	Benefit as a Percent of Compen- sation
30	65	$12,000	$1,200	$141,745	$1,274	127.4
40	65	14,000	1,400	81,419	732	62.7
45	65	9,500	950	37,043	333	42.1
53	65	30,000	3,000	53,646	482	19.3
55	65	12,000	1,200	16,766	151	15.1

---

[3]It should be noted that employees can buy annuities from insurance companies on the open market (i.e., apart from the qualified retirement plan). At this time insurers are not required to offer such annuities on a unisex basis, although legislation requiring this has been proposed.

shown for each employee will continue until normal retirement; that the contribution made by the employer each year is 10 percent of the employee's compensation; that this contribution will accumulate at 6 percent compound interest until retirement; and that the fund accumulated at retirement will be applied under representative annuity purchase rates to provide a monthly retirement benefit.

As Table 6–1 shows, younger employees have a much longer time to accumulate funds and receive a proportionately larger benefit. Moreover, the defined contribution plan has an additional weakness since, because of the effect of compound interest, greater weight is given to the employee's lower compensation at the younger ages than will be given to the higher compensation the employee is likely to receive when he or she is older.

An additional comment about the potential disadvantages of the defined contribution formula has to do with its ability to respond to growth in an employee's earnings — particularly during periods of inflation. Table 6–1 projected benefits for employees on the assumption that earnings would remain constant. This is not a realistic assumption since, in all probability, most employees will receive a number of pay increases over their working careers. Thus, it is important to illustrate and compare the results depicted in Table 6–1 with what would be the case if all assumptions remain the same except for future earnings growth. This comparison for the same group of employees is set forth in Table 6–2, which assumes earnings will grow at the rate of 4 percent a year. As can be seen, the potential benefit, as a percent of final compensation, is considerably lower when future earnings growth is taken into account. In effect, a defined contribution plan is a career-pay plan; however, unlike the practice for career-pay defined benefit plans, it is relatively uncommon for an employer to "update" accrued benefits under a defined contribution plan.

Another observation about the deficiencies of a defined contribution formula is that the employee's benefit under this formula can only be estimated. This lack of certainty as to benefits could prove to be an unsatisfactory employee relations feature of such a plan. Finally, the variations in benefit levels for different employees make it difficult, if not

TABLE 6–2: Illustration of Defined Contribution Formulas with and without Earnings Projection

| | Compensation | | Fund at Retirement | | Monthly Benefit | | Benefit as a Percentage of | |
Age at Entry	At Entry	Final	Flat Earnings	With Projected Earnings	Flat Earnings	With Projected Earnings	Earnings at Entry	Final Earnings
30	$12,000	$45,532	$141,745	$237,864	$1,274	$2,139	127.4	56.4
40	14,000	35,886	81,419	120,652	732	1,085	62.7	36.3
45	9,500	20,015	37,043	51,156	333	460	42.1	27.6
53	30,000	46,184	53,646	65,375	482	588	19.3	15.3
55	12,000	17,080	16,766	19,754	151	178	15.1	12.5

impossible, to design a formula that produces benefit levels uniformly responsive to employer objectives.

Target Benefit Plans.   These aspects of the defined contribution pension plan have caused growing interest in the so-called target benefit plan — one that combines the concepts of both defined contribution and defined benefit plans. The target benefit plan uses one of the defined benefit formulas defined later in this chapter to determine an employee's projected pension at normal retirement date. Depending upon the actuarial cost method and assumptions employed, a contribution to provide this benefit is determined. The actuarial cost method is usually the projected benefit without supplemental liability method (described in Chapter 9), and the interest assumption, to avoid potential problems of discrimination, is usually set as at least 5 but not more than 6 percent. This contribution is not adjusted for future mortality or investment experience. Instead, contributions are accumulated for each employee in an individual account and, depending upon actual investment results, can accumulate to provide a greater or smaller benefit than that originally projected. This approach has the advantage of determining the initial amount to be allocated to each employee on a basis that reflects the employee's age as well as compensation, while at the same time preserving the accumulation aspects of a defined contribution plan.

Under ERISA and Internal Revenue Service requirements, a target benefit plan is treated as a defined benefit plan for some purposes and a defined contribution plan for others. For example:

The maximum amount that may be contributed for any one individual is determined on the basis applicable to defined contribution plans.

Forfeitures must be used to reduce employer contributions, as is the case with defined benefit plans.

The plan termination insurance provisions of ERISA are not applicable to target benefit plans, as is the case with defined contribution plans.

Special integration rules apply to target benefit plans.[4]

Union-Negotiated Plans.   Union-negotiated plans, particularly multiemployer plans, possess characteristics of both defined contribution and defined benefit plans. In many of these situations, an employer's contribution to the plan is fixed, most frequently as a contribution of so many cents for each hour worked by each covered employee or as a percentage of compensation. An actuarial cost method,[5] with appropriate actuarial assumptions, is then employed to make an estimate of the benefit levels the

---

[4]See pages 115–22 for a detailed discussion of these rules.

[5]An actuarial cost method is a particular technique for establishing the amounts and incidence of the normal costs and supplemental costs pertaining to the benefits of a pension plan.

aggregate employer contributions will provide. The plan is then established with a defined benefit formula, even though funds are received on a defined contribution basis. Only rarely will it turn out that the contribution level precisely supports the benefit level so determined, with the result that future contributions, or benefits, or both, are adjusted periodically to conform with the actual experience of the plan.

Defined Benefit Formulas

Broadly speaking, there are four basic defined benefit formulas. These include: (1) a flat amount formula, which provides a flat benefit unrelated to an employee's earnings or service; (2) a flat percentage of earnings formula, which provides a benefit related to the employee's earnings but which does not reflect service; (3) a flat amount per year of service formula, which reflects an employee's service but not earnings; and (4) a percentage of earnings per year of service formula, which reflects both an employee's earnings and service. Deined benefit formulas also may be integrated with social security benefits; however, since the requirements for integrated formulas are detailed and specific, they are discussed separately later in this chapter.

Flat Amount Formula.   As indicated above, this type of formula provides for a flat benefit that treats all employees alike, regardless of their service, age, or earnings. For example, the benefit might be $100 or $150 a month. The flat amount formula, since it is considered to produce inequitable results, seldom is used by itself. On occasion, this formula is used in conjunction with some other type of formula; for example, a plan may provide a flat benefit of $150 a month for a covered employee, plus a percentage of his or her earnings in excess of the current social security taxable wage base.

While the employee's length of service is not reflected directly in this type of formula, service is in effect recognized since most plans require that an employee, upon attaining the normal retirement age specified by the plan, must have been employed for some period of time, such as 25 years. Plans that include such a requirement provide for a proportionately reduced benefit if the employee has accumulated fewer than the required number of years, thus creating, in effect, a formula weighted for service.

Flat Percentage of Earnings Formula.   This type of formula is used frequently today, particularly in plans that cover salaried or clerical employees. Some percentage of earnings, usually ranging from 25 to 50 percent, is selected as the measure of the pension benefit. It may be used with either career average or final average earnings, although it is used most frequently in final-pay plans.

This type of formula does not take an employee's service into account, except in those plans that require that the employee must have completed a minimum period of service by normal retirement date and that provide for a proportionately reduced benefit if his or her service is less than the required number of years.

An administrative device used with many formulas, sometimes including the flat percentage of earnings formula, is the "earnings bracket" schedule. Instead of using actual earnings under the benefit formula, the benefit is determined by an earnings bracket approach and is expressed as a dollar amount per bracket of earnings. Table 6–3 shows a typical earnings bracket schedule. Actually, a 30 percent of earnings formula has been applied to the midpoint of each earnings bracket.

TABLE 6–3: Illustrative
Earnings Bracket Schedule

Monthly Earnings	Monthly Pension
$650–683	$200
684–716	210
717–749	220
750–783	230
784–816	240

Flat Amount per Year of Service Formula.   This type of formula is often found in negotiated plans. It provides a flat dollar amount for each year of service accumulated by the employee. The dollar amount varies from plan to plan, but a benefit of $14, or $16, or even as much as $18 or $20 a month for each year of service is common. Thus, in a plan that provides for a benefit of $10 a month for each year of service, an employee with 27 years of employment would receive a monthly pension of $270.

This type of formula frequently requires that an employee must have worked for a minimum number of hours during a plan year to receive a full benefit credit for such year. Minimums often used for this purpose are 1,600 and 1,800 hours. An employee who works fewer than the required number of hours in a given year usually receives some proportionate credit for the actual hours worked. Federal tax law requires that a proportionate credit be given if the employee is credited with at least 1,000 hours of service in the 12-month computation period used by the plan.

Some plans limit benefits to service performed after the plan was made effective, although in most cases credit is given for service prior to the inception of the plan. When this is done, credit may or may not be given for service needed to meet any eligibility requirements of the plan. Also, it is not uncommon to include a provision that limits the total service that may be credited for benefit purposes to a period such as 30 years.

Percentage of Earnings per Year of Service Formula.   A formula that gives specific recognition for service as well as earnings is considered by many pension practitioners to produce the most equitable results in terms of a benefit formula that provides benefits for employees in relation to their value or contributions to the firm. A formula producing this result is often called a *unit credit* or *past and future service* formula. Under such a formula, an employee receives a benefit credit equal to a percentage of earnings for each year that he or she is a participant under the plan. This benefit credit is called the employee's future service or current service benefit. The percentage of earnings credited varies from plan to plan, but a typical percentage would be 1 percent or 1.25 percent. It may be used with either career average or final earnings, and works particularly well with career average plans.

Many plans also include a "past service" benefit for employees who enter the plan on its effective date. In a plan that bases future service benefits on career average earnings, the past service benefit is usually expressed as a fixed percentage of the employee's earnings on the effective date of the plan multiplied by the employee's years of past service. In determining past service benefits, however, it is customary to exclude service that would have been required to join the plan had it always been in effect. It is also possible to limit the total years of past service credited. For example, past service could be limited to a given number of years (such as 10), to service completed after a certain calendar year (such as the year in which the firm was acquired by the current ownership interests), to service completed after attaining a certain age (such as 21), or to a combination of these factors. The percentage applied to earnings to determine past service benefits is usually a lower rate than is applied for future service benefits. The reason for this is that the earnings of an employee on the effective date of the plan generally are higher than the average of the employee's earnings over the period of his or her past service. Rather than determine the employee's actual average earnings during his or her past service, which is often difficult or even impossible because of the lack of records, a rough approximation is made by reducing the percentage applicable to the employee's higher earnings at the time the plan is established.

If the plan bases benefits on final earnings, a distinction is usually not made between past and future service benefits. Here, the employee's total service (subject to any limitations such as a maximum service credit provision or excluding service needed to meet eligibility requirements) is applied to the percentage of final earnings to determine the total retirement benefit.

To illustrate the operation of a past and future service formula in a career average earnings plan, assume the benefit formula of a plan provides a monthly pension of one half of 1 percent of a participant's earnings on the effective date of the plan multiplied by the employee's years of past service, and a future service benefit of 1 percent of earnings during each year that the employee is a participant. The plan has an eligibility requirement of one year of service, and service needed to meet this requirement is excluded when determining the employee's total past service. Normal

TABLE 6–4: Past and Future Service Formula

(1)	(2)	(3)	(4)	(5)	(6)	(7)
Years of Total Past Service	Years of Credited Past Service	Monthly Earnings	Past Service Benefit (2) × (3) × ½%	Years of Future Service	Future Service Benefit (3) × (5) × 1%	Total Benefit (4) + (6)
20	19	$1,000	$95	25	$250	$345

retirement under the plan will occur at 65. Table 6–4 shows how the monthly pension benefit would be calculated for a 40-year-old employee who had 20 years of service when he joined the plan at its inception date. This table assumes, for illustrative purposes, that the employee's monthly earnings are $1,000 and remain constant at this level during the period of future service.

Variable Benefit Formulas.   Variable benefit plans are designed to protect against the effects of inflation on a retired employee's pension benefit. They take either of two general forms: (*a*) the benefit varies to reflect changes in the value of a specific portfolio of common stocks and similar investments, or (*b*) the benefit varies to reflect changes in a recognized cost-of-living index such as that published by the Bureau of Labor Statistics. In either case, the plan attempts to adjust benefits to keep an employee's purchasing power on a relatively level basis. These plans are discussed in greater detail in Chapter 7.

Integrated Formulas

The Tax Reform Act of 1986 drastically altered the rules for integrating qualified plans with social security, effective generally for plan years beginning after December 31, 1988. A detailed explanation of integrated formulas for plan years beginning before January 1, 1989, can be found in the appendix to this chapter.

For most individuals, retirement income will be derived from both social security benefits and private pension plans. Since the employer bears part of the cost of social security benefits, it is only logical for the employer to recognize these benefits in the benefit formula of the plan. Thus, it is common for an employer to establish a retirement plan on a basis that provides a higher level of benefits for earnings above the social security taxable wage base than is provided for earnings below this amount. While at first glance such a plan would appear to discriminate in favor of highly compensated employees, federal tax law expressly permits this type of plan provided the benefit formula *integrates* with social security benefits. The basic concept of integration is that the benefits of the employer's plan must be dovetailed with social security benefits in such a manner that employees earning over the taxable wage base will not receive combined benefits under the two programs proportionately greater than the benefits for employees earning less than this amount. Therefore, although the benefit formula under the private plan may favor the higher paid employees, the combined social security and private plan benefits must produce a total retirement income that is a relatively equal percentage of compensation for all employees. Thus, the integration requirements are designed to prevent discrimination in favor of the highly compensated employees.

These integration rules allow a "permitted disparity in plan contributions or benefits." Excess plans (whether defined benefit or defined contribution) will be permitted to use an integration level of any amount up to the social security taxable wage base in effect at the beginning of the plan year; however, the permitted disparity will be reduced for excess defined benefit plans if the plan's integration level is higher than the social security covered compensation level. The disparity will also be reduced for defined benefit plans that provide for unreduced benefits commencing before the social security retirement age but will not be reduced for other ancillary benefits.

For defined benefit excess plans, the accrual rate for pay above the plans's integration level cannot be more than two times the accrual rate for pay below this amount. In addition, this spread between the upper and lower percentage cannot exceed 0.75 percent of pay for each year of participation up to a maximum of 35 years — or a maximum total spread of 26.25 percent. This limit applies both to unit benefit and flat benefit plans. All other plan benefits and features must apply equally to accruals below and above the integration level. There is no longer a distinction between career and final average pay plans in terms of integration capability; if a plan uses final average pay, it must be averaged over at least three years. However, that statute itself requires use of three-year final average pay; technical corrections to resolve the inconsistency are expected.

For defined contribution plans, the contribution rate for pay above the integration level is also limited to two times the rate of pay below the integration level. There is a further limit, however. The spread between the two contribution rates cannot exceed the greater of 5.7 percent or the social security tax for old-age benefits.

These changes mean that pure excess plans — where no benefit or contribution is provided for pay up to the plan integration level — will no longer be permitted.

Offset plans will still be permitted, but the benefit otherwise accrued by such plans may not be reduced by more than 50 percent. The dollar amount or formula used for the offset must be specified in the plan. The offset may not exceed 0.75 percent of final average pay multiplied by years of service up to a maximum of 35 years. For this purpose, final average pay is determined by ignoring pay in excess of the social security taxable wage base. The 0.75 percent factor will be reduced, in regulations to be issued, for individuals whose final average pay exceeds covered compensation.

Final-pay offset plans must also use a three-year final average pay definition; as noted, technical corrections are expected.

An additional change permits employers to establish a plan maximum that limits an employee's pension to 100 percent of final pay less the employer-provided portion of his or her primary social security benefit attributable to service with the employer. For this purpose, an employee's primary social security benefit is assumed to accrue ratably over 35 years. Final pay under this provision is the highest single year's pay in the five years preceding the employee's termination of employment. This change recognizes but restricts the practice of some plans that now apply this type of maximum by subtracting as much as the full amount of the employee's social security benefit.

Minimum Benefits

Closely related to the choice of an adequate benefit formula is the question of whether provision for a minimum pension should be included in the plan.

A minimum pension provision is generally a desirable feature of any pension plan. It is often possible for a benefit formula to produce a very small pension benefit as applied to certain employees. The use of a minimum pension can result in the payment of at least a minimum amount to these employees, while at the same time avoiding the embarrassment and ill will that might otherwise be generated in these situations. Apart from these considerations, if the plan is insured, the insurer may insist on the inclusion of a minimum pension provision as a part of its general underwriting requirements — particularly in the case of a plan funded with individual policies. The minimum sometimes used is $20 a month.

Limits on Benefits and Contributions

ERISA imposed limits on the benefits and contributions that can be provided under qualified plans. For a defined benefit plan, the annual employer-provided benefit for an employee cannot exceed a stipulated dollar amount or, if lesser, 100 percent of the first $200,000 of the employee's average annual pay for the three consecutive years of highest pay.[6]

The dollar limit was initially established at $75,000 to be adjusted annually to reflect increases in the Consumer Price Index. By 1982, this limit had reached $136,425. Under changes made by TEFRA, however, this limit was rolled back to $90,000, beginning in 1983. It will be increased for future increases in the Consumer Price Index, but not until 1988 and then only for post-1986 increases. These limits do not apply to employee-provided benefits and need not be adjusted for preretirement ancillary

---

[6]If an employee has never been covered by a defined contribution plan, an annual pension of up to $10,000 can be paid even if it exceeds 100 percent of pay.

benefits such as death or disability benefits. The maximum permissible benefit will be reduced if payments begin before the social security retirement age and will be increased if they begin after that age.[7] The reduction will be 5⁄9 of one percent for the first 36 months of early retirement plus 5⁄12 of one percent for each additional month of early retirement after age 62. The reduction for ages before age 62 will be based on actuarial factors using the plan's interest rate (but not less than 5 percent) for early retirement. The *dollar* limit is reduced proportionately if the employee completes fewer than 10 years of *participation* before retirement; the *percentage* limit is reduced proportionately if the employee completes fewer than 10 years of *service* before retirement. The limits also must be reduced for the value of any pension-related, postretirement death benefits; however, a reduction will not be required if payments are made on a qualified joint and survivor basis (even if the percentage continued is 100 percent) and the joint annuitant is the employee's spouse.

In the case of a defined contribution plan, the limitation is expressed in terms of the maximum annual addition that may be made to the employee's account. This maximum annual addition is limited to the lesser of 25 percent of the first $200,000 of annual pay or a stipulated dollar amount. This dollar amount was originally set at $25,000 also to be adjusted annually to reflect increases in the Consumer Price Index. This limit had reached $45,475 in 1982, but was rolled back by TEFRA to $30,000, beginning in 1983. The Tax Reform Act of 1986 redefined the defined contribution dollar limit as the greater of $30,000 or 25 percent of the dollar limit for defined benefit plans. Thus, there will be no further increase in the defined contribution dollar limit until the defined benefit dollar limit reaches $120,000. The annual addition is defined to include employer contributions, the employee's own contributions, and forfeitures.[8]

If a participant is covered by both a defined benefit plan and a defined contribution plan maintained by the same employer, then a special expanded annual limit applies. The defined benefit plan projected annual benefit and the defined contribution plan annual addition are converted into fractions, added, and then tested against a 1.0 limit. The defined benefit fraction is the participant's projected annual benefit (as of the close of the limitation year) divided by the lesser of 125 percent of the defined benefit dollar limit or 140 percent of the average high compensation. The defined contribution fraction is the sum of the annual additions of a participant's account (as of the close of the limitation year) divided by the lesser of

---

[7]Effective for distributions made after December 31, 1986, certain transitional rules exist to protect a participant whose previously accrued benefit under a defined benefit plan would otherwise be reduced by the actuarial reduction for benefits beginning before the social security retirement age.

[8]For years beginning before January 1, 1987, the term *annual addition* meant the sum of employer contributions, nondeductible employee contributions in excess of 6 percent of the participant's compensation (or 50 percent of employee contributions, if less), and forfeitures. This distinction is important for purposes of the combined limits (described later) because of its cumulative nature.

125 percent of the defined contribution dollar limit for all years of service or 140 percent of compensation eligible under the defined contribution percentage limit for all years of service.

The application of this combined limit might best be illustrated by the following example, which, for the sake of simplicity, ignores the cumulative aspects of the limit. Under the employer's profit sharing plan, a highly compensated employee will receive a contribution of 12.5 percent of annual pay in 1986. Because this contribution equals 50 percent of the limit otherwise allowable for a defined contribution plan (12.5% ÷ 25%) the allowable limit for the defined benefit plan for this employee will be 90 percent or less of the otherwise allowable limit (140% − 50%). For example, if the employee's compensation was $80,000, the defined contribution fraction would be:

$$.125 \times 80,000 \div \min[1.25 \times 30,000; 1.4 \times .25 \times 80,000] = .3571$$

Therefore, the maximum defined benefit fraction would be:

$$1 - .3571 = .6428$$

Computing the maximum numerator for the defined benefit fraction:

$$.6428 \times \min[1.25 \times 90,000; 1.4 \times 1.0 \times 80,000] = 72,000$$

or 90 percent (72,000 ÷ 80,000) of the otherwise allowable limit.

If, instead, the employee earned $150,000, the defined contribution fraction is:

$$.125 \times 150,000 \div \min[1.25 \times 30,000; 1.4 \times .25 \times 150,000] = .5$$

Therefore, the maximum defined benefit fraction must be .5 (which is again obtained by subtracting the defined contribution fraction from 1.0) and the numerator in the defined benefit fraction is:

$$.5 \times \min[1.25 \times 90,000; 1.4 \times 1.0 \times 150,000] = 56,250$$

or 62.5 percent (56,250 ÷ 90,000) of the otherwise allowable limit.

Where the limits are applicable, the employer may establish an excess benefit plan to restore the benefits or contributions lost by reason of the application of the limit. Such a plan is not subject to the provisions of ERISA.

If an employee is participating in the plans of another incorporated or unincorporated business under common control (only a 51 percent interest is necessary for this purpose), the plans of all such businesses must be aggregated for purposes of applying the limitations on benefits and contributions.

These limits must be applied on the basis of a limitation year that is the calendar year, unless a different 12-month period is elected by the employer. This could be of significance where a noncalendar year plan does not have a limitation year that parallels the plan year. For example, assume the plan year for an employer's profit sharing plan ends on January 31, and that on that date an employee was credited with $1,000 or 10 percent of compensation during the plan year. If the employee terminates employment at the end of February and the employee's compensation for the two months of the current calendar year was $2,000, and if the limitation year is the calendar year, the addition to the employee's account for such calendar year would be 50 percent of compensation (the $1,000 allocation divided by the $2,000 of compensation received). This would exceed the allowable contribution limit and could cause disqualification of the plan.

DEATH BENEFITS

Mandatory Death Benefits

The two death benefits required by the law are: (1) in the case of a vested participant who retires under the plan, the accrued benefit must be provided in the form of a qualified joint and survivor (QJS) annuity, and (2) in the case of a vested participant who dies before the annuity starting date and who has a surviving spouse, a qualified preretirement survivor (QPS) annuity must be provided to the surviving spouse. However, the plan may provide that the annuity payment will be reduced to reflect the additional cost of the survivorship provision. The only plans that may be exempted from these new requirements are defined contribution plans that are not subject to the minimum funding standards and certain employee stock ownership plan (ESOP) benefits. For a defined contribution plan to be exempt, it must meet the following requirements: (a) the plan must provide that the participant's nonforfeitable accrued benefit is payable in full to the surviving spouse on the death of the participant, and (b) the participant does not elect a payment or benefit in the form of a life annuity. The ESOP exemption is described in Chapter 18.

The law defines a QJS annuity as an annuity for the life of the participant with a survivor annuity for the life of the spouse that is not less than 50 percent of (and is not greater than 100 percent of) the amount of the annuity that is payable during the joint lives of the participant and the spouse. The QJS must also be the actuarial equivalent of a single annuity for the life of the participant.

In general, the QPS annuity provides a survivor annuity for the life of the spouse in an amount not less than the amount that would be payable as a survivor annuity under the QJS annuity (or the actuarial equivalent thereof). In the case of a participant who dies after the date on which the participant attained the earliest retirement age, it is assumed that he or she had retired with an immediate QJS annuity on the day before the date of death. In the case of a participant who dies on or before the day on which the earliest retirement age would have been attained, it is assumed that he or she had separated from service on the date of death, survived to the earliest retirement age, retired with an immediate QJS annuity at the earliest retirement age, and died the next day. A plan may not delay the commencement of QPS annuity payments beyond the month in which the participant would have attained the earliest retirement age under the plan. In the case of a defined contribution plan, the term *QPS annuity* means an annuity for the life of the surviving spouse, the actuarial equivalent of which is not less than 50 percent of the account balance of the participant as of the date of death.

The law also provides detailed notification requirements for QJS and QPS annuities. The rules for QJS annuities require that each plan provide to each participant a written explanation of:

1. The terms and conditions of the QJS annuity.
2. The participant's right to make, and the effect of, an election to waive the joint and survivor annuity form of benefit.
3. The rights of the participant's spouse.
4. The right to make, and the effect of, a revocation of an election.

This explanation must be provided within a reasonable period of time before the annuity starting date.

The rules for QPS annuities require a qualified plan to provide to each participant a written explanation with respect to the QPS annuity comparable to that required for the QJS annuities. This explanation must be provided within the applicable period defined as the later of:

1. The period beginning with the first day of the plan year in which the participant attains age 32 and ending with the close of the plan year preceding the plan year in which the participant attains age 35.
2. A reasonable period after the individual becomes a participant.
3. A reasonable period after the plan ceases to fully subsidize the costs of the annuity.
4. A reasonable period after the survivor benefit requirements become applicable with respect to a participant.
5. A reasonable period after separation from service in case of a participant who separates before attaining age 35.

The law requires that each participant may elect at any time during the applicable election period[9] to waive the QJS annuity form of benefit or the QPS annuity form of benefit (or both), and may revoke any such election at any time during the applicable election period. Moreover, the spouse must consent to the election. This requirement is satisfied if the spouse of the participant consents in writing to such election, and the spouse's consent acknowledges the effect of such election and is witnessed by a plan

---

[9]The applicable election period is defined as the 90-day period ending on the annuity starting date in the case of an election to waive the QJS annuity form of benefit, or the period that begins on the first day of the plan year in which the participant attains age 35 and ends on the date of the participant's death in the case of an election to waive the QPS annuity.

representative or a notary public, or it is established to the satisfaction of a plan representative that this consent cannot be obtained because there is no spouse, or because the spouse cannot be located. It should be noted, however, that these rules do not apply where the plan fully subsidizes the costs of the benefits.[10] The law defines this as a situation under which the failure to waive the benefit by a participant would not result in a decrease in any plan benefit with respect to the participant and would not result in increased contributions for the participant.

The law permits that survivor annuities need not be provided if the participant and spouse were married less than 1 year. In general, the QJS and QPS annuities will not be required to be provided unless the participant and spouse had been married through the one-year period ending on the earliest of the participant's annuity starting date, or the date of the participant's death. However, if a participant marries within one year before the annuity starting date, and the participant and the participant's spouse have been married for at least a one-year period ending on or before the date of the participant's death, the participant and spouse must be treated as having been married throughout the one-year period ending on the participant's annuity starting date.

Optional Employer-Provided Death Benefits

An employer-provided death benefit is an optional benefit under a pension plan; however, a great many plans include such a benefit. Broadly speaking, such a death benefit may take one of two forms — the first consists of life insurance provided under some form of individual policy or group life insurance contract issued by an insurer, and the second consists of cash distributions from plan assets. Death benefits also may be classified as being payable in the event of death either before or after retirement.

Death benefits provided under individual policy plans and death benefits provided from plan assets are considered a part of the plan and, as such, are subject to the requirement of the Internal Revenue Service that the death benefit must be "incidental." In a defined benefit plan using life insurance, the incidental test is satisfied if the benefit does not exceed 100 times the expected monthly pension benefit or, if greater, the reserve for the pension benefit. For pension plans using a defined contribution (money purchase) formula, the incidental test for the use of life insurance is satisfied if: (1) the aggregate of the premiums paid for a participant's life insurance is less than one half of the contributions allocated to the participant at any particular time; and (2) the plan requires the trustee to convert the entire value of the life insurance contract at or before retirement into

---

[10]A plan may take into account, in any equitable manner, the increased costs of providing a QJS or QPS annuity. The cost may be placed on the participant or beneficiary by reducing the benefit otherwise provided. A plan may, however, fully subsidize the cost of the QJS annuity, QPS annuity, or both.

cash, or to provide periodic income so that no portion of such value may be used to continue life insurance protection beyond retirement or to distribute the contract to the participant. The incidental test is not violated if the death benefit does not exceed the sum of the reserve of the life insurance policy and the amount held for the employee in the conversion fund. Also, as long as less than 50 percent of the employer's contributions for an employee have been used to purchase life insurance, the face amount of the life insurance plus the employee's share of the conversion fund may be paid as the death benefit under a defined benefit plan without violating the incidental death benefit rules.

A plan may provide both a lump-sum preretirement death benefit and a QPS annuity, as long as the incidental death benefits rule (described in Chapter 4) is not violated. A plan under which the only preretirement death benefit is a QPS annuity satisfies the incidental death benefits rule. However, a QPS annuity is considered an integral part of a preretirement death benefit. Thus, for defined benefit plans, the QPS annuity must be considered with other preretirement benefits to determine whether the benefits provided are incidental. A plan that provides a lump-sum preretirement death benefit equal to 100 times the monthly annuity amount and a QPS annuity violates the incidental death benefits rule.

According to Revenue Ruling 85-15, however, there are several amendments that would enable a plan with a lump-sum preretirement death benefit to satisfy the incidental death benefits requirement. For example, the plans could offset the (otherwise) incidental preretirement death benefit by the value of the QPS. In this regard, if life insurance contracts are purchased by the plan to provide the lump-sum preretirement death benefit, the proceeds could be paid to the plan's trust with the trust providing the QPS to the surviving spouse and the excess, if any, of the lump-sum preretirement death benefit over the value of the QPS annuity to the participant's beneficiary (who could also be the surviving spouse).

DISABILITY BENEFITS

While most employers recognize the possibility of short-term disabilities and usually provide a reasonable level of benefits for this contingency through their wage continuation plans, such is not generally the case in the area of total and permanent disabilities. With the increased availability of insured long-term disability programs, however, more employers are seeking to provide benefits in the event of total and permanent disability via this device, and on a basis that is completely apart from any benefits available under the employer's pension plan.

In the pension area, disability benefits, even in insured plans, generally have been provided on a self-insured basis; that is, the benefits are paid in some form directly from plan assets, and the employer's experience in this regard is reflected in the cost level of the plan.

A number of pension plans, particularly those funded with individual policies, provide for full vesting if an employee becomes totally and permanently disabled. Other plans treat such a disability as an early retirement if the employee has completed some minimum period of service or participation in the plan and has attained some minimum age. Unfortunately, the disability benefits provided under such provisions are either nonexistent or inadequate for disabilities occurring at younger ages.

Some group pension and trust fund plans, however — particularly those that have been union negotiated — provide for a separate and distinct benefit in the event of total and permanent disability. The benefit provided under such plans sometimes is a specified dollar amount, a specified percentage of earnings, or an amount equal to the employee's accrued or projected pension credits (with or without actuarial reduction). Often, the disability benefit under the plan is integrated with benefits available under government plans such as worker's compensation or social security benefits. Frequently, the plan provides that the disability benefit will terminate when the employee reaches normal retirement age, at which time the accrued normal pension benefit will be payable.[11]

Most plans will continue to accumulate pension credits during disability and while long-term disability benefits are being paid. If the pension benefit is based on the participant's salary, additional credits are often frozen at the level of the pre-disability salary.

SEVERANCE OF EMPLOYMENT BENEFITS

The right of an employee to the benefits attributable to employer contributions under a pension plan in the event of termination of employment prior to retirement has been the subject of considerable discussion for many years. A major accomplishment of ERISA was to require that an employee achieve such rights, or a vested interest, after some reasonable period of service.

The Internal Revenue Code requires that the employee's rights to that portion of his or her accrued benefit attributable to his or her own contributions be fully vested at all times. This does not require a minimum benefit equal to the amount the employee has contributed. In a defined

---

[11]It would seem such a provision is consistent with the Age Discrimination in Employment Act, as amended in 1986. However, the Department of Labor and the Equal Employment Opportunity Commission have indicated, in their opinion, such a provision might be in violation of the law concerning disabilities occurring after age 60 — where the continuation of some disability income benefit might have to be provided for some period after age 65.

contribution plan, for example, there may have been investment losses that result in the value of the employee's contribution being less than the amount actually contributed by the employee. In such a situation, the plan would not have to return to the employee an amount greater than the value of the employee's contributions after taking investment losses into account.

In any event, accrued benefits attributable to employer contributions must vest when the employee reaches normal retirement age. Beginning in 1989, only two vesting standards will be available, and both will require more rapid vesting than was previously the case.[12] The first standard requires that all accrued benefits must be 100 percent vested after five years of service.[13] The second standard permits graded vesting, with 20 percent of accrued benefits vesting after three years of service and that percentage increasing in 20 percent multiples each year until 100 percent vesting is achieved after seven years. Of course, more liberal vesting schedules than required will be acceptable.

Determination of Accrued Benefit.   The Code also stipulates minimum standards to be followed in determining an employee's accrued benefit for purposes of applying a vesting schedule. A plan will be acceptable if it meets any one of three rules:

1. *The 3 percent rule.* The employee's accrued benefit must be at least equal to 3 percent of the projected normal retirement benefit for each year of *participation*, to a maximum of 100 percent after 33⅓ years of participation.

2. *The 133⅓ percent rule.* The accrued benefit may be the employee's actual benefit earned to date under the plan, provided any future rate of benefit accrual is not more than 133⅓ percent of the current benefit accrual rate.

---

[12]For plan years beginning before January 1, 1989, accrued benefits attributable to employer contributions must be vested upon termination of employment in accordance with one of the three following rules:

1. *The 10-year rule.* The employee must be 100 percent vested after 10 years of service.
2. *The 5 to 15 rule.* Graduated vesting is provided, beginning with 25 percent after 5 years of service, increasing 5 percent a year for the next 5 years, and 10 percent for the next 5 years, thus producing a 50 percent vested interest after 10 years of service, and a 100 percent vested interest after 15 years of service.
3. *The rule of 45.* The employee achieves a 50 percent interest after the earlier of 10 years of service or when the combination of service (minimum of five years) and the employee's age totals 45; thereafter, the employee's vested interest increases 10 percent per year for the next five years.

The Internal Revenue Service was given the authority to impose more stringent vesting requirements if such action is necessary, in the opinion of the Service, to prevent discrimination. The Congressional Committee Report, however, directed the Internal Revenue Service not to require a vesting schedule more stringent than 40 percent vesting after four years of service, with 5 percent additional vesting for each of the next two years, and 10 percent vesting for each of the following five years.

[13]Multiemployer plans that are collectively bargained may continue to use 10-year cliff vesting.

3. *The fractional rule*. The employee's accrued benefit is not less than the projected normal retirement benefit prorated for years of plan participation.

Most plans are expected to be able to satisfy either or both the 133⅓ percent rule and the fractional rule. However, any plan that permits the accrual of benefits for more than 33⅓ years will not be able to satisfy the 3 percent method.

If a defined benefit plan requires employee contributions, the accrued benefit attributable to employer contributions is determined by subtracting the life annuity value of the employee's contributions. In making this calculation, the employee's contributions are accumulated with interest compounded annually at the applicable rate, and are multiplied by a factor of 10 percent—for example, if the employee's contributions with interest amount to $5,000, the annual annuity attributable to the employee's contributions will be $500.[14] The applicable interest rate for pre-ERISA years is the plan rate; it is 5 percent for subsequent years through 1987 and, beginning in 1988, it will be 120 percent of the midterm applicable federal rate as in effect for the first of the plan year. This amount will be subtracted from the total accrued benefit to determine the accrued benefit attributable to employer contributions. The Internal Revenue Service has the authority to revise the factor from time to time.

An employee's accrued benefit is established on a pure life annuity basis only, and does not have to include any ancillary benefits such as death or disability benefits.

Other Vesting Requirements.   The Internal Revenue Code also establishes a number of other requirements concerning the vesting and payment of an employee's benefits.

1. If an employee is less than 50 percent vested and withdraws his or her contributions, any benefits attributable to employer contributions may be canceled, but any such employee must be permitted to "buy back" the forfeited benefits upon repayment of the withdrawn contributions plus, if a defined benefit plan, compound interest. If the employee's vested interest is 50 percent or more, withdrawal of employee contributions cannot result in a cancellation of benefits attributable to employer contributions.

2. Except as provided above, an employee's vested interest cannot be forfeited under any circumstances (other than death), even if termination of employment is due to dishonesty.[15]

---

[14]The 10 percent factor applies if normal retirement age is 65 and normal retirement benefits are provided as straight life annuities. Other circumstances are controlled by Revenue Ruling 76-47.

[15]Plans can provide that nonforfeitable accrued benefits derived from employer contributions will not be paid if the participant dies—except to the extent that a QPS or QJS annuity is payable. See pages 99–101 for a description of these annuities.

3. An automatic cash-out of an employee's entire interest is permitted upon termination of employment where the value of this benefit does not exceed $3,500. Under such circumstances and for purposes of determining the employee's accrued benefit, the plan may disregard service for which the employee has received such a payment. If the amount exceeds $3,500 the same will hold true but only if the employee agreed in writing to the cash payment.[16] In any event, if the plan wishes to disregard such service, a terminating employee who has received a cash-out and is later reemployed must be permitted to "buy back" the accrued benefit by repaying the cash payment with compound interest (currently 5 percent per year). (In the case of a defined contribution plan, such a buy-back is required only before the employee has incurred five consecutive one-year breaks in service, and interest need not be paid.)

4. Any employee who terminates employment must be given written notification of his or her rights, the amount of his or her accrued benefits, the portion (if any) that is vested, and the applicable payment provisions.

5. A terminated employee's vested benefit cannot be decreased by reason of increases in social security benefits that take place after the date of termination of employment.

6. If the plan allows an active employee to elect early retirement after attaining a stated age and completing a specified period of service, a terminated employee who has completed the service requirement must have the right to receive vested benefits after reaching the early retirement age specified. However, the benefit for the terminated employee can be reduced actuarially even though the active employee might have the advantage of subsidized early retirement benefits.

7. Any plan amendment cannot decrease the vested percentage of an employee's accrued benefit. Also, if the vesting schedule is changed, any participant with at least three years of service (at least five years of service are ·required for plan years beginning before January 1, 1989) must be given the election to remain under the preamendment vesting schedule (for both pre- and postamendment benefit accruals).

8. The accrued benefit of a participant may not be decreased by an amendment of the plan.[17] This includes plan amendments that have the effect of eliminating or reducing an early retirement benefit or a retirement-type subsidy or eliminating or reducing the value of an optional form of benefit with respect to benefits attributable to service before the amendment. In the case of a retirement-type subsidy, this applies only with

---

[16]To be considered made on account of termination of participation in the plan, the distribution (whether voluntary or involuntary) must be made no later than the close of the second plan year following the year in which the termination occurs.

[17]Technically, there are two very limited exceptions to this rule. Amendments described in IRC section 412(c)(8) and ERISA section 4281 are permissible.

respect to a participant who satisfies the preamendment condition for the subsidy, either before or after the amendment.

TOP–HEAVY PLANS

One of the most dramatic changes made by TEFRA was the introduction of the concept of top-heavy plans and the imposition of complex rules upon such plans beginning in 1984. These rules are applicable to qualified plans and:

1. Require the plan to meet one of two accelerated vesting schedules.
2. Call for minimum contribution and/or benefit levels for nonkey employees.
3. Reduce maximum contribution/benefit limits for key employees if an employer maintains both a top-heavy defined benefit plan and a top-heavy defined contribution plan.

This portion of the chapter first discusses the definition of a top-heavy plan. It next discusses the definition of a key employee. The remaining material considers the qualification rules that apply to top-heavy plans and the implications of these rules.

Top-Heavy Plans Defined

A defined contribution plan is top-heavy in a plan year if, as of the determination date (generally, the last day of the preceding plan year), either: (1) the sum of the account balances of all key employees participating in the plan is more than 60 percent of the sum of the account balances of all covered employees; or (2) the plan is part of a top-heavy group, as explained below.

A defined benefit plan is top-heavy in a plan year if, as of the determination date, either: (1) the present value of the accumulated accrued benefits of all key employees participating in the plan is more than 60 percent of the present value of the accumulated accrued benefits of all covered employees; or (2) the plan is part of a top-heavy group.

A top-heavy group is the combination of two or more plans and, under the law, it may be either required or permissible to aggregate two or more plans to determine top-heaviness. It is required to aggregate into a group (1) all plans covering a key employee and (2) any plan upon which a key-employee plan depends for qualification under the coverage and discrimination requirements of the Code. It is permissible for an employer to expand the group by aggregating other plans as long as the resulting group continues to satisfy the coverage and discrimination rules.

The 60 percent test applies to the top-heavy group. If the group is top-heavy, then each plan is also deemed to be top-heavy. However, a plan included solely at the employer's election is not necessarily considered top-heavy. In applying the top-heavy group rules, all plans of all employers who are part of the same controlled group are treated as a single plan.

In determining the present value of accrued benefits and account balances, the employer may count both employer and employee contributions. Accumulated deductible employee contributions, however, must be disregarded.[18] Also, the employer must count any amount distributed to or for a participant under the plan within the five-year period ending on the current determination date.

Rollover contributions and similar transfers to a plan made after 1983 will not be part of the top-heavy plan computation, unless they are made to a plan maintained by the same, or an affiliated, employer. Presumably, rollovers made before 1983 will have to be considered.

Key Employees Defined

Key employees are defined as: (1) all officers[19] (up to a maximum of 50) with an annual compensation greater than 150 percent of the maximum dollar limit for annual additions to defined contribution plans (in 1987 this would be equal to $1.5 \times \$30,000 = \$45,000$); (2) the 10 employees who own the largest interest in the employer with an annual compensation greater than 100 percent of the maximum dollar limits for the annual addition to defined contribution plans; (3) an employee who owns more than a 5 percent interest in the employer; and (4) an employee who owns more than a 1 percent interest in the employer and whose annual compensation is more than $150,000. An employee who falls into more than one category, of course, is counted only once.

An employee is considered to be a key employee if the employee falls into one of the above classifications at any time during the current plan year or the four preceding plan years. Thus, the group of key employees may be larger than the actual operating group of key employees for any period of time.

If an employer has more officers than are required to be counted, the officers to be considered are those with the highest compensation.

In determining stock ownership, an employee is treated as owning stock even if it is owned by other members of his or her family or certain partnerships, estates, trusts, or corporations in which the employee has an interest. The rules for determining ownership in noncorporate entities are similar to those for determining corporate ownership.

---

[18]A federal income tax deduction was available for qualified voluntary employee contributions prior to 1987.

[19]If the employer has between 30 and 500 employees, the number of officers included will never have to be greater than 10 percent of all employees. Also, Regulation §1.416-1, T-13 states that the determination of whether a person is an officer will be based on all the facts and circumstances. Thus, not all individuals with the title of officer will be deemed officers for this purpose.

Qualification Rules

A top-heavy plan must meet certain additional requirements if it is to be qualified under the Code. Moreover, the IRS currently requires all plans (except governmental plans and certain plans covering only employees who are members of a collective bargaining unit), even if they are not top-heavy, to include provisions that will automatically take effect if that event should occur. These additional requirements are as follows.

Vesting.   A top-heavy plan must meet one of two alternative "fast" vesting schedules for all accrued benefits. The two vesting schedules are: (1) 100 percent vesting after three years of service; and (2) graded vesting of at least 20 percent after two years of service, 40 percent after three, 60 percent after four, 80 percent after five, and 100 percent after six years

Minimum Benefits for Nonkey Employees.   A top-heavy plan must provide a minimum benefit or contribution for all nonkey employee participants. Social security benefits or contributions may not be applied toward these minimums. For each year (maximum of 10) in which a defined benefit plan is top-heavy, each nonkey employee participant must accrue an employer-provided benefit of at least 2 percent of compensation (generally defined as the average of the five consecutive highest years of pay). For each year in which a defined contribution plan is top-heavy, an employer must contribute at least 3 percent of compensation for each nonkey employee participant; however, in no case does an employer have to contribute more than the percentage contributed for key employees. Reallocated forfeitures and any amounts contributed on account of salary reduction arrangements (see Chapter 17) are counted as employer contributions under defined contribution plans. When a nonkey employee participates in both a defined benefit and a defined contribution plan, the employer does not have to provide minimum benefits under both plans.

Limitations on Contributions and Benefits.   In the case of any top-heavy plan, the aggregate Section 415 dollar limit described on page 98 is reduced to 100 percent. The dollar limit can be increased back to 125 percent, however, if the plans meet the "concentration test" and provide an extra minimum benefit for nonkey employees. The concentration test is satisfied if the present value of the key employees' accrued benefits (or account balances) is not more than 90 percent of the total value for all covered employees. The extra minimum benefits to be provided for each nonkey employee are: (1) for defined benefit plans, a benefit accrual of one percent of compensation for each year of service during which the plan is top-heavy, up to a maximum of 10 years; and (2) for defined contribution plans, a contribution of 1 percent of compensation for each year of service during which the plan is top-heavy.

GENERAL PLAN PROVISIONS

Chapter 5 and the preceding portion of this chapter have dealt with the major plan provisions an employer must consider when establishing a pension plan. There are, of course, a number of other provisions that are a part of any plan and that relate generally to the rights and duties of the interested parties and to the administrative aspects of the program. The following discusses, very briefly, the most significant of these general provisions.

Employer's Right to Amend or Terminate the Plan

While a pension plan is established on an indefinite and presumably permanent basis, an essential plan provision is one that gives the employer the unilateral right to amend or terminate the program at any time. As will be seen, however, the rights reserved to the employer under such a clause are limited to some extent by federal law.

The right-to-amend clause is usually straightforward and reserves the right of the employer to make plan amendments without the consent of employees or their beneficiaries. However, as discussed in Chapter 4, if a plan is to maintain its qualified status, an amendment may not reduce benefits related to contributions made prior to the amendment, deprive any employee of the employee's then accrued vested interest, nor permit the employer to recover any funds previously contributed to the plan. Thus, the amendment clause normally restricts the employer's rights to this extent unless the amendment itself is required to make the plan conform to federal or state laws. Also, as previously noted, if an amendment changes the plan's vesting schedule, any participant with at least three years of service must be given the election to remain under the preamendment vesting schedule.

The typical right-to-terminate clause gives the employer the unilateral right to terminate the plan (or to discontinue contributions) for any reason and at any time. However, as discussed in Chapter 4, for a plan to achieve a qualified status under federal tax law, it must be permanent and, while the Internal Revenue Service will approve a plan with such a termination provision, restrictions are imposed on the employer's right to terminate the program. Thus, if an employer terminates the plan for reasons other than "business necessity" within a few years of its inception, the plan may lose its qualified status for all prior open tax years, since this action will be considered by the Service as evidence that the plan, from its inception, was not a bona fide program for the exclusive benefit of employees in general. If business necessity exists, the employer may terminate the plan without adverse tax consequences. Valid reasons for a plan termination include financial incapacity, bankruptcy, insolvency, change of ownership, and so on.

The termination-of-plan clause must make provision for the distribution of plan assets if the plan is terminated or contributions are discontinued.

Since federal tax law prohibits the return of any funds to the employer on plan termination (other than excess amounts remaining because of "actuarial error" after satisfaction of all plan liabilities), the plan assets must be applied for the benefit of the employees or their beneficiaries in a specified order of priorities.[20]

The Internal Revenue Service requires the inclusion of a provision that limits the benefits payable to certain highly paid employees in the event of plan termination. The provision limits benefits payable to the 25 highest paid employees of the employer at the inception of the plan whose anticipated individual annual retirement benefit from employer contributions will exceed $1,500. An employee could be within this group even though not a participant when the plan was established. This limitation on benefits applies if the plan is terminated within 10 years after its effective date. (It also will apply to any benefits that become payable with respect to this group during the first 10 plan years even though the plan has not been terminated if, when the distribution is made, the "full current costs" of the plan have not been met.) Under Regulation §1.401-4(c)(7), the limitation is the greater of:

1. A dollar amount equal to the present value of the maximum termination benefit guaranteed by the PBGC (described in Chapter 23).[21]
2. The greater of $20,000 or 20 percent of the first $50,000 of annual compensation times the number of years between plan establishment and termination.

Exculpatory Provisions

To the extent permitted by ERISA (if at all), the trustee, if a trust is involved, and the insurer, in an insured plan, will want to have provisions that protect them in their relationships with the employer, the employees and their beneficiaries, and with each other. These provisions set forth the rights of the insurer and trustee as well as the limits of their responsibilities and liabilities.

Miscellaneous Provisions

The plan must also contain a number of provisions relating to the broad administration of the program, many of these provisions being dictated by the funding instrument employed to provide benefits. The following list, while by no means all-inclusive, indicates some of the provisions that must be considered.

---

[20]This topic is described in detail in Chapter 19.

[21]For purposes of the 25 highest paid employees, the amount of the PBGC guarantee depends on whether the employee is a substantial owner. A substantial owner is an individual who owns the entire interest in an unincorporated trade or business, is a more-than-10 percent partner, or owns (directly or indirectly) more than 10 percent in value of either the voting stock of a corporation or all classes of stock.

Beneficiary Provisions.   If the plan contains a death benefit, there must be a provision for the employee's right to name and change beneficiaries. The provision also should cover such matters as the form that any such designation or change should take; when and under what conditions it will become effective; the rights and duties of the interested parties if payment has been made (or has commenced) before a change has been properly recorded; and the distribution of the proceeds in the event the employee dies without having made a beneficiary designation.

Facility of Payment.   A related provision is one that permits the trustee or insurer to distribute proceeds to certain individuals if the employee or beneficiary is in any way incompetent to receive the proceeds.

Trustee Provisions.   If a trust is involved, several points concerning the trustee should be covered; for example, there should be a provision covering the details of the resignation or removal of the trustee and the manner in which a successor trustee will be appointed. There also should be a provision authorizing payment of the trustee's expenses and, if applicable, payment of the trustee's fee. The powers and duties of the trustee for the plan should be covered, with special emphasis on investment authority. If more than one trustee is involved, there should be a provision indicating whether the trustees are required to act unanimously or whether majority action will suffice. If the trustees are to have the right to allocate or delegate authority, a provision to this effect should be included.

Mergers and Consolidations.   A plan must provide that the value of an employee's accrued benefit cannot be diminished in any way by any merger or consolidation with, or transfer of assets or liabilities to or from, any other plan.

Payment of Benefits.   Benefit payments must commence, unless otherwise elected by the employee, no later than the 60th day after the *latest* of the close of the plan year in which the participant attains age 65 (or the normal retirement age specified in the plan), completes 10 years of participation, or terminates employment. In any event, for distributions before January 1, 1989, all qualified plans must provide that, except in the case of death, a participant's entire interest will be distributed by the April 1 following the year the participant reaches age 70½, or retires, whichever is later. Also, any interest remaining in a plan at an employee's death must be distributed to a beneficiary within five years unless distribution has already begun and is payable over a period not greater than the joint life expectancy of the employee and his or her spouse. Five percent owners are subject to special distribution rules. Their lifetime distribution must be completed or commence by the April 1 following the year they reach age 70½ even if retirement is later. For distributions commencing after December 31, 1988, the rule applicable to 5 percent owners applies to all plan participants. That is, distribution to any participant must be completed or commence by the April 1 following the calendar year in which the participant reaches age 70½, even if the participant remains in employment.

Small Benefits.   Many plans include a provision that permits payment of the employee's retirement benefit in a lump sum if its value is less than $3,500. However, an involuntary cash-out may not be made after a participant's annuity starting date unless the participant and spouse consent in writing to the distribution. If the participant dies, the surviving spouse must consent to a cash-out after the annuity starting date. Obviously, the payment of small amounts on a periodic basis is of little value to the retired employee, and the administrative problems involved in maintaining the necessary records and making the small payments could be significant. Thus, payment of the benefit in a lump sum is generally desirable for all concerned.

Leaves of Absence.   A well-designed plan should have a provision dealing with the possibility of an employee going on leave of absence (other than the maternity or paternity leaves discussed on page 73) and the effect this might have on plan benefits. A typical provision would protect an employee's rights while on military leave (normally for the period of time employment rights are protected by law) or while on any other authorized leave for a period not exceeding one or two years. The plan should indicate whether time spent on such a leave will be considered as credited service for retirement benefits. If such time is considered as credited service, however, and if the employee fails to return to work within the time allowed, he or she usually is considered as having terminated employment when the leave began, subject, of course, to the law's requirements concerning the determination of service for vesting purposes. Also, if such credit is given and if the plan is contributory, there is need for a further provision for any employee contributions that might otherwise have been due during the leave of absence. If, under the funding instrument involved, the employer advances the employee's contribution during the leave, there is usually a feature that allows the employer to recover this amount if the employee fails to return to work within the time allowed.

Governing Law.   Most plans include a provision stating that the plan and its provisions will be construed in accordance with the laws of a specific state to the extent not preempted by ERISA.

Spendthrift Provision.   The Code requires that the plan prohibit the assignment or alienation of benefits, with three exceptions: an employee may be permitted to assign up to 10 percent of any benefit payment, an employee may use his or her vested interest as collateral for a loan from the plan (if such loan is not a prohibited transaction), and a payment may be made to an alternate payee pursuant to a qualified domestic relations order (QDRO).

A QDRO is a domestic relations order that satisfies all the following requirements:

1. It must create or recognize the existence of an alternate payee's right to, or assign to an alternate payee the right to, receive all or a portion of the benefit payable with respect to a participant under a plan. An alternate payee is a spouse, former spouse, child, or other dependent of a participant who is recognized by a domestic relations order as having a right to receive all, or a part of, the benefits payable under a plan.

2. It must clearly specify certain facts about the participant's benefits. The order must clearly specify the name and the last known mailing address of the participant and the name and mailing address of each alternate payee covered by the order; the amount or percentage of the participant's benefit to be paid by the plan to each such alternate payee, or the manner in which such amount or percentage is to be determined; the number of payments or period to which such order applies; and each plan to which such order applies.

3. It must not alter the amount or form of the benefits. The QDRO may not require a plan to provide: any type or form of benefit, or any option, not otherwise provided under the plan; (actuarially) increased benefits; or the payment of benefits to an alternate payee that are required to be paid to another alternate payee under another order previously determined to be a QDRO. In the case of any payment before a participant has separated from service, a QDRO may require that payment be made to an alternate payee on or after the date on which the participant attains the early retirement age[22] as if the participant had retired on the date on which payment is to begin under the order. In this case, the amount of the payment is determined by taking into account the present value of the benefits actually accrued and not the present value of an employer subsidy for early retirement. The QDRO must be limited to a form that may be paid under the plan to the participant.

Limitation of Employee's Rights.   A desirable provision in any plan is one that stipulates that the existence of the plan and the employee's participation do not give the employee any right to be retained in the employ of the employer, nor any legal or equitable rights against the employer, except as provided by law.

ERISA-Required Provisions.   In addition to some of the provisions already mentioned, ERISA requires that several other items be covered in

---

[22]This has been defined as the earlier of (1) the earliest date benefits are payable under the plan or (2) the later of the date the participant attains age 50 or the date on which the participant could obtain a distribution from the plan if the participant separated from service.

the plan. For example, the plan must provide for named fiduciaries as well as a procedure for establishing and carrying out the plan's funding policy. The plan also should describe clearly any procedure for the allocation of fiduciary and administrative duties and responsibilities, and should stipulate the basis on which payments will be made to and from the plan.

APPENDIX—INTEGRATED FORMULAS FOR PLAN YEARS BEGINNING BEFORE JANUARY 1, 1989

The concepts and rules described in the following material were developed and promulgated by the Internal Revenue Service in 1971. They have not been changed although the social security law has since been amended several times. In particular, these concepts and rules do not reflect the 1977 or 1983 amendments to the social security law. These amendments made major changes in the level of social security benefits provided and also changed the way in which wages are determined for calculating social security benefits from an average monthly wage to average indexed monthly earnings. Thus, what follows, although a correct statement of current integration requirements, does not relate to current social security benefits and provisions.

The integration requirements in effect prior to 1989 take the form of establishing the maximum benefits that may be provided for employees under various circumstances. In arriving at these maximums, a value was placed on the employee's total social security benefits. Essentially, these benefits were valued at 162 percent of the employee's maximum primary benefit. This amount, in turn, was 70 percent of the average monthly wage on which the employee's social security benefit was computed. However, the integration rules also recognize that employees pay a social security tax. Since the tax rate is divided equally between employers and employees, the 70 percent figure was reduced by 50 percent, to a resulting figure of 35 percent. In recognition of possible future increases in social security benefits, the 35 percent figure was raised to 37.5 percent. Thus, for integration purposes, social security benefits currently are considered to be worth 37.5 percent of the wages on which social security benefits are computed. This percentage, however, applies only to a pure life annuity plan without integrated death or disability benefits. If the plan includes such benefits, this percentage is reduced.

It is important to note that an employee's *average monthly wage* for integration purposes is not the same as his or her current social security *taxable wage base*. This, of course, is because of the fact that in computing an employee's wages for social security, only earnings subject to social security tax are taken into account. Since the taxable wage bases in prior years were lower than the current taxable wage base, it is impossible, under current social security laws, to develop such an average monthly wage equal to the current taxable wage base until the 21st century. For this reason, the provisions of federal tax law relating to integration set forth a schedule showing the maximum average wage for each year of retirement. Thus, the year in which an employee reaches age 65 determines the earnings level for testing integration. This schedule refers to the maximum average wage as *covered compensation* and sets forth covered compensation levels ranging from $13,800 for the year 1985 up to $39,600 for the year 2020. A schedule of covered compensation levels, as of 1985, is set forth in Table 6A–1.

TABLE 6A–1: Schedule of Integration Periods and Applicable Covered Compensation Levels

Period Employee Reaches Age 65	Covered Compensation
1985	$13,800
1986	15,000
1987	15,600
1988	16,200
1989	17,400
1990	18,000
1991	18,600
1992	19,200
1993	19,800
1994	20,400
1995	21,600
1996	22,200
1997	23,400
1998	24,600
1999	25,200
2000	26,400
2001	27,600
2002	28,200
2003	29,400
2004	30,000
2005	31,200
2006	31,800
2007	33,000
2008	33,600
2009	34,800
2010	35,400
2011	36,000
2012	36,600
2013	37,200
2014	37,800
2015	38,400
2016	39,000
2017	39,000
2018	39,600
2019	39,600
2020 and later	39,600

The following is by no means an exhaustive discussion of the integration requirements of federal tax law. It does, however, describe the major requirements for typical integrated formulas. It also assumes normal retirement under the plan will not occur before age 65 and that employees will not make contributions.[23]

Flat Percentage-Excess.   In plans of this type, benefits are provided only for final average pay in excess of the appropriate covered compensation level or some stated dollar amount uniformly applied to all employees. In a plan that provides no integrated death or disability benefits, the maximum percentage that can be provided for final average pay in excess of the appropriate covered compensation level is 37.5 percent. (The appropriate covered compensation level for a particular plan is determined by the first year in which it is possible for an employee or future employee to retire at age 65 under the plan provisions.) If the plan provides benefits for final average pay in excess of some amount higher than the appropriate covered compensation level, the maximum percentage must be reduced. This is done by multiplying 37.5 percent by a fraction, the numerator of which is the appropriate covered compensation level for the plan and the denominator of which is the level actually set in the plan. Thus, for example, if the appropriate covered compensation level for a plan is $12,000 and the plan provides benefits only for final average pay in excess of $15,000, the maximum percentage for the plan would be 80 percent of 37.5 percent, or 30 percent.

Several important requirements must be observed if a flat percentage-excess plan is to completely meet the integration requirements of federal tax law:

1. The plan benefit must be based on *average* pay that is determined over a period of at least five *consecutive* years.[24]

2. This employee must have completed at least 15 years of service with the employer (not necessarily as a participant in the plan) in order to qualify for the maximum percentage. For an employee with fewer than 15 years of service, a proportionate reduction in benefits must be made.

3. Benefits payable in the event of early retirement or termination of employment cannot exceed the actuarial equivalent of the maximum normal retirement benefit multiplied by a fraction, the numerator of which is the actual number of years of service completed by the employee at early retirement or termination, and the denominator of which is the total number of years of service the employee would have completed at normal retirement.

---

[23]A decrease in the allowable benefit is required when normal retirement may occur before 65 or when retirement at ages below 65 is permitted on a basis that provides benefits that are higher than the actuarial equivalent of an employee's accrued benefit. An increase in the allowable benefit is permitted when employees contribute.

[24]It is permissible to use four or three consecutive years in the averaging period; however, the maximum percentage will be reduced by 5 or 10 percent, respectively, if this is done.

Flat Percentage-Stepped Up.   Under a plan of this type, all earnings are taken into account in applying the plan formula; however, the formula contains two percentages — a lower percentage for earnings up to some stipulated level and a higher percentage for earnings in excess of this amount. For integration purposes, the lower percentage is considered a base plan, applicable to all earnings, and only the excess portion must meet the requirements previously discussed. To illustrate, if a plan provides for a monthly benefit of 10 percent of the first $1,000 of final average pay plus 40 percent of such pay in excess of $1,000, the plan, for the purpose of meeting integration requirements, would be considered as a flat percentage-excess plan of 30 percent of final average pay in excess of $1,000. This portion, then, would have to meet the requirements set forth above.

Unit Credit-Excess.   A unit credit-excess plan provides a pension benefit of some percentage of average pay in excess of a stipulated amount for each year of credited service. An important factor in determining the maximum percentage applicable to such a plan is whether the plan bases benefits on career average or final average pay. For a career pay plan, the maximum percentage applicable to each year of future service is 1.4 percent of the employee's earnings in excess of the current social security taxable wage base. There is no limit as to the number of years of service that may receive benefit credit. This maximum percentage is applicable only in a plan without integrated death or disability benefits.

For a final average pay plan with no integrated death or disability benefits, the maximum percentage to be applied to excess earnings is 1 percent, with no limit on the number of years of service that may be credited for benefit purposes. However, unlike the unit credit career pay plan, this percentage can apply only to compensation in excess of the appropriate covered compensation level; and, if a higher level is used, the percentage must be reduced in the same manner applicable to a flat percentage-excess plan; that is, the 1 percent is multiplied by a fraction, the numerator of which is the appropriate covered compensation level, and the denominator of which is the actual level being used by the plan.

It should be noted that a unit credit final average pay excess plan may still be acceptable, even though it does not meet the foregoing rules, if it satisfies the requirements for a flat percentage-excess plan. This could be the case where there is a limit on the number of years of service that will be credited for benefit purposes. In this event, the appropriate maximum percentage for the flat percentage-excess plan is divided by the maximum number of years of credited service under the plan. To illustrate, a unit credit final pay excess plan with an applicable covered compensation level of $12,000 that provides a monthly benefit of 1 percent of monthly final average pay in excess of $1,250 for each year of service up to 30 years would meet the integration requirements (assuming that no integrated death or disability benefits are included in the plan). Such a formula would not meet the normal test applicable to such a plan — that is, the maximum allowable percentage would be only 80 percent of 1 percent (the ratio of the covered compensation of $12,000 to the actual compensation breakpoint of $15,000). However, it does satisfy the requirements of a flat percentage-excess plan, since 80 percent of 37.5 percent is 30 percent, and 30 percent divided by 30 (the maximum years of credited service) results in an allowable maximum percentage of 1 percent — a percentage equal to that set forth in the plan formula. When a unit credit-excess plan is integrated under the requirements relating to a flat percentage-excess plan, it is necessary that the benefits payable in the event of early retirement or termination of employment be limited to the actuarial equivalent of the maximum projected normal retirement benefits multiplied by a fraction, the numerator of which is the actual number of years of service completed by the employee at early retirement or termination, and the denominator of which is the total number of years of service the employee would have completed at normal retirement. This restriction does not apply to other unit credit-excess plans, where the benefit payable in the event of early retirement or termination of employment may be based upon the benefit accrued by the employee under the plan formula up to the time of retirement or termination of employment.

Just as with a flat percentage-excess plan, a unit credit final average pay excess plan must base benefits on an average pay that is determined over a period of at least five consecutive years.[25]

Unit Credit-Stepped Up.   As is the case with a flat percentage-stepped up formula, a unit credit-stepped up plan bases benefits on all earnings, but applies two percentages — a lower percentage with respect to earnings up to some stipulated amount and a higher percentage for earnings in excess of this level. Again, for integration purposes, the lower percentage is considered a base plan applicable to all earnings, and only the excess portion must meet the requirements previously described for a unit credit-excess plan.

Social Security Offset.   Many plans provide a retirement benefit inclusive of benefits payable under social security. This type of formula deducts a percentage of the employee's primary social security benefit from the pension benefit otherwise payable under the plan. In other words, any of the earlier described formulas can be used, with social security benefits being deducted from the amount of benefit the formula would otherwise provide. Only the employee's primary insurance amount (i.e., exclusive of dependent's benefits) is taken into account for this purpose. The integration limit in these plans applies not to the percentage of compensation

---

[25]If the otherwise allowable limit is reduced by 5 or 10 percent, respectively, an averaging period of four or three consecutive years may be used.

being credited, but to the percentage of the permissible social security off-set. For a plan without integrated death or disability benefits, the maximum offset is 83⅓ percent of the employee's primary insurance amount if the offset is based on the benefits payable under the social security laws in effect when the employee retires. If the offset is based on the benefits payable under the 1967 social security amendments, the maximum offset is 105 percent of the employee's primary insurance amount; if based on the 1969 social security amendments, the maximum offset is 92 percent of the primary insurance amount.

It should be noted that the integration rules as such do not require an offset plan to base benefits on a final average pay determined over any specific period of time. Also, the 15 years of service requirement for full benefits does not apply to this type of formula.

Defined Contribution Formulas. It also is possible to integrate defined contribution formulas with social security benefits. If no contribution is being made for earnings up to the current social security taxable wage base, the maximum percentage that may be contributed for earnings in excess of this amount is the amount of social security tax assessed for old-age, survivors, and disability income benefits; that is, the social security tax excluding that portion attributable to medicare. For 1984 through 1987, this tax rate will be 5.7 percent; for 1988. If a contribution is being made for earnings below the social security taxable wage base, the percentage applicable to earnings above this amount may be increased by the amount of this base contribution.

Death Benefits. If a pension plan provides for the payment of employer-provided integrated death benefits (other than a return of employee contributions with interest) either before or after retirement, the maximum percentages otherwise determined must be reduced, depending upon the level and type of death benefit provided. This reduction is accomplished by multiplying the otherwise allowable percentage by an appropriate factor. No reduction is required in the case of a preretirement spouse benefit as required by the Internal Revenue Code. However, in the case of other preretirement survivor benefits in the form of a life income equal to a percentage of the employee's accrued pension, a formula is employed to determine the factor. This formula is $7 \div (7 + 2k)$, where k is the percentage of accrued pension payable to the survivor. Thus, in the case of a 50 percent continuation, the factor is 87.5 percent ($7 \div [7 + 2 \times 1/2] = 7 \div 8 = 87.5$ percent). Factors for other forms of death benefits are set forth in Table 6A–2. It should be noted that if a plan provides for both a pre- and postretirement death benefit, both reduction factors must be employed.

TABLE 6A–2: Reduction Factors for the Inclusion of Death Benefits in Integrated Plans

Type of Death Benefit	Reduction Factor
Preretirement:	
Amount not exceeding reserve	89%
Amount equal to 100 multiplied by expected monthly pension	80
Amount equal to greater of reserve or 100 multiplied by expected monthly pension	78
Postretirement:	
Life annuity with 5 years certain	97
Life annuity with 10 years certain	90
Life annuity with 15 years certain	80
Life annuity with 20 years certain	70
Life annuity with installment refund	90
Life annuity with cash refund	85
Life annuity with 50 percent continued to surviving spouse	80

If any part of the death benefit consists of pure life insurance, the cost of which was includable in the employee's taxable income, no reduction is required for this portion of the death benefit. Also, it is not necessary to apply reduction factors if the only form of postretirement death benefit is that which might be created under an optional form of payment on an actuarially equivalent basis. Finally, it is not necessary to adjust the maximum permissible contribution under an integrated defined contribution formula if any form of death benefit is included. The reason, essentially, is that since the contribution is fixed, these features automatically affect the amount of the employee's retirement benefit.

Disability Benefits.   If a pension plan contains an integrated benefit payable before age 65 in the event of disability, the maximum percentage otherwise applicable for normal retirement benefits must be reduced by 10 percent — that is, the maximum percentage is multiplied by 90 percent. The integrated disability benefit itself also must satisfy integration requirements. The preretirement disability benefit under an excess plan cannot be greater than the employee's accrued benefit (without actuarial reduction) or a percentage of the employee's projected pension. This percentage is the greater of 70 percent or the percentage derived by dividing the employee's actual service by his or her projected service. If the preretirement disability benefit offsets social security benefits, the maximum offset permitted before age 65 is 64 percent of the employee's primary social security benefit; a 75 percent offset is permitted after age 65.

It should be noted that these rules apply only when plan disability benefits are payable for a disability that also qualifies the employee for social security disability benefits. If disability benefits may be payable to employees who do not satisfy the eligibility requirements for social security disability benefits, then for integration purposes they are treated as early retirement benefits.

Variable Benefit Plans.   If the base investment rate under a variable annuity plan is at least 5.5 percent, the maximum integration percentages are the same as for a regular defined benefit plan.[26]

At lower base investment rates, the maximum integration percentages must be reduced by $\frac{1}{15}$ for each one half of 1 percent that the base investment rate is less than 5.5 percent.

QUESTIONS FOR REVIEW

1. Describe the advantages and disadvantages of a final-pay pension plan.
2. For what purpose is a target benefit plan treated as a defined benefit pension plan? For what purposes is it treated as a defined contribution pension plan?
3. Explain the four basic defined benefit formulas.
4. Describe how (a) defined benefit pension plans and (b) defined contribution pension plans may be integrated with social security.
5. Describe the dollar limits for defined benefit and defined contribution pension plans. Under what conditions must these limits be reduced?
6. Describe a qualified joint and survivor annuity (QJS).
7. Describe the payments that must be provided under a qualified preretirement survivor annuity (QPS) if (a) a participant dies after reaching the earliest retirement age, and (b) a participant dies on or before the date of attaining the earliest retirement age.
8. Describe the vesting requirements for accrued benefits attributable to (a) the employee's contributions and (b) the employer's contributions.
9. Does an employer have complete flexibility in determining the minimum benefit amount that must be credited to a participant who terminates from the plan in a vested status? Explain.
10. How is top-heaviness determined for a qualified pension plan? What are the consequences of such a status?

QUESTIONS FOR DISCUSSION

1. Assume that an employer sponsors an integrated defined contribution pension plan. What is the maximum allowable contribution for compensation in excess of the social security taxable wage base in 1989 if the contribution for compensation less than the social security taxable wage base is: (a) 5 percent; (b) 6 percent?

---

[26]The base investment rate for a variable annuity is the assumed rate with which actual investment yields are compared to determine future changes in benefits.

2. An employer maintains two plans. Plan A covers key employees, while Plan B covers nonkey employees. Both plans independently satisfy the coverage and nondiscriminatory requirements of the IRS Code. (*a*) Must the employer aggregate the two plans to determine top-heaviness? (*b*) May the employer aggregate the two plans to determine top-heaviness? (*c*) Why would an employer want to aggregate the two plans if this option is available?

3. Assume that a calendar year defined contribution plan has a one-year minimum service requirement. An employee is hired on January 1, 1984, at $90,000 with increases of $10,000 each January 1. By 1987, the annual additions for the employee amount to $72,500. If the same employer establishes a defined benefit pension plan that covers this employee, what is the maximum annual benefit that can be provided to this employee from the second plan?

7

The Impact of Inflation on Pensioner Income

Everyone, in one way or another, bears the burden of inflation. For many individuals, this burden can be lightened or even eliminated by improvements in pay, investment opportunities, changes in lifestyle, and the like. One segment of the population, however — pensioners who are living on a fixed income — has limited opportunity to counteract the effects of inflation and, as a result, can suffer to a greater extent than those who are still actively employed or those who have accumulated independent wealth.

During the 1970s, the financial plight of pensioners did not go unnoticed. Erosion of their purchasing power and fear of future inflation:

1. Prompted Congress to adjust social security benefits automatically to reflect changes in the Consumer Price Index and to liberalize the conditions under which pensioners can work and still collect social security benefits.
2. Generated union and employee pressure for "inflation-proof" pension benefits.
3. Caused employees eligible for early retirement to defer actual retirement for as long as possible.

SOURCE: The material in this chapter is reprinted with the permission of Towers, Perrin, Forster, and Crosby. All rights reserved.

4. Motivated many employers to provide ad hoc benefit increases to their pensioners.
5. Stimulated interest in pension planning techniques that automatically provide for some degree of protection against inflation.

These steps have treated only the symptoms of inflation. In the long run, the only adequate and equitable solution to the problems caused by inflation is to bring inflation itself under control. Thus, the ultimate solution rests with the federal government and the adoption of appropriate fiscal and monetary policies.

The rate of inflation slowed down to a considerable extent during the early 1980s. Even so, the general expectations that inflation will continue, at least to some extent, and that the number of years employees will spend in retirement will increase (as a result of recent trends in early retirement and increases in life expectancy), make it important to consider the needs of the retired population. It is also significant that the size of this population is increasing not only in numbers, but also as a percentage of the total population; according to some projections, by the turn of the century there will be one person over age 65 for every two workers under that age.

This chapter reviews the general background of the problems that inflation has created for pensioners, identifies the conventional ways in which some employers have addressed these problems in the past, and discusses current problems and issues as well as additional plan design techniques that might be used to alleviate these problems.

BACKGROUND

Before considering specific methods of treating the financial problems inflation has created for pensioners, it is important to review the way in which the impact of inflation is measured, the role played by social security in alleviating these problems, and the nature of employer commitments under private pension plans.

Measuring Inflation

The most commonly accepted measure of inflation is the Consumer Price Index (CPI). In February 1978, the Bureau of Labor Statistics began issuing two indexes—the All-Urban Households Index and the Wage-Earner and Clerical Workers Index. The new indexes were designed to provide a more accurate picture of the market basket of some 400 goods and services that form the basis of measuring price movement. The Wage-Earner Index is an updated version of the old index. The All-Urban Index represents 80 percent of the national population (as against 40 percent for the Wage-Earner Index) and is based on the market basket of goods and services supposedly bought by city dwellers and not just workers.

Many authorities question whether the CPI is an appropriate measure of inflation and, indeed, whether it exaggerates or even escalates inflation rates. Among the concerns expressed is the fact that the CPI fails to distinguish, in adequate fashion, price increases due to quality improvements. Moreover, it is based on infrequent surveys of consumer expenditures. Its appropriateness as the measure of lost purchasing power for pensioners is even more questionable. For example:

1. The CPI does not reflect federal, state, and local income taxes. This is particularly important when considering the needs of pensioners since:

    a. Social security benefits (which can form a significant portion of a pensioner's total income) are income tax free for middle to lower income pensioners.[1]

    b. Social security taxes are no longer payable (unless the pensioner continues in some form of covered employment).

    c. Higher standard deductions are provided under federal tax law for individuals age 65 or over.

    d. A number of states and local governments do not tax retirement income.

2. Although the utilization of medical services increases with age, significant coverage is provided to pensioners and their dependents, beginning at age 65, under the medicare provisions of social security. Moreover, many employers provide postretirement medical expense coverage, often on a basis that requires no contributions from the pensioner.

3. A relatively high weighting is given to housing costs; many pensioners have completed the financing of home ownership by the time they retire and many localities provide for some form of property tax relief for individuals beyond a stated age.

4. Many localities also provide free or reduced-cost transportation for the elderly; similarly, discounts for food and entertainment are often made available.

5. A number of work-related expenses (e.g., additional clothing and upkeep, commutation costs, the need for a second car) may no longer apply to pensioners.

6. Costs associated with children (food, clothing, education, and the like) have been eliminated for most pensioners.

7. The absence of regular working relationships along with lesser family responsibilities sometimes gives pensioners a mobility permitting movement to parts of the country that offer more favorable tax treatment and lower living costs.

---

[1]A portion of social security benefits will be included in the gross income of any individual whose modified adjusted gross income (AGI plus interest earned or accrued on tax-exempt investments) plus one half of benefits that exceed the base amount. The base amount is $32,000 for a married couple filing jointly; zero for married taxpayers who live together during the taxable year but file separately; and $25,000 for all other individuals.

On the other hand, it must be recognized that most pensioners have less total income than individuals who are actively employed. As a result, a greater percentage of a pensioner's total income is spent for necessities such as food, shelter, energy, and medical care. Thus, as inflation increases the cost of these items, pensioners find it necessary to allocate a greater portion of their total income to purchasing necessities. In contrast, actively employed individuals also share in productivity gains, with the result that the portion of their total income devoted to necessities does not increase as rapidly as that of pensioners.

It also should be recognized that social pressures discourage any drastic change in standards of living upon retirement and that an increasing tendency exists for retired persons to remain active, particularly in civic, social, travel, and recreational activities. However, it is likely that these and other activities, along with their related costs, will diminish as the pensioner grows older.

Role of Social Security

Since 1975, social security benefits have been increased automatically to reflect changes in the CPI. This has been a major factor in softening the impact of inflation on pensioners. Prior to 1975, social security benefits were increased by frequent legislative action to accomplish the same result and, in fact, were increased by amounts greater than those required by increases in the CPI.

The role of social security in countering the effects of postretirement inflation, particularly since it is income tax free for individuals in the lower to middle income ranges (defined as modified AGI plus one half of social security benefits less than $25,000 or $32,000, depending upon filing status for tax purposes), is quite important. This significance is illustrated by Tables 7–1, 7–2, and 7–3. (Table 7–1 deals with a single pensioner; Table 7–2 focuses on a married pensioner; and Table 7–3 summarizes the information included in Tables 7–1 and 7–2.) These tables depict the total income payable to a single pensioner and to a pensioner with a spouse, from social security and a conventional private plan at two final gross pay levels — $15,000 and $25,000. The total pension income is shown on an after-tax basis for 1983 — the assumed year of retirement — and again at the end of 1998, after 15 years of inflation at an assumed rate of 4 percent a year.[2]

The 1983 total pension may be compared with preretirement after-tax income, and the 1998 total pension may be compared with preretirement after-tax income adjusted at the 4 percent annual inflation rate for the same

---

[2]This rate of inflation was used for illustrative purposes and in view of the long-term nature of the projections. The relative impact of different inflation rates can be observed.

TABLE 7–1: Illustration of Significance of Social Security in Countering Effect of Postretirement Inflation (single pensioner)

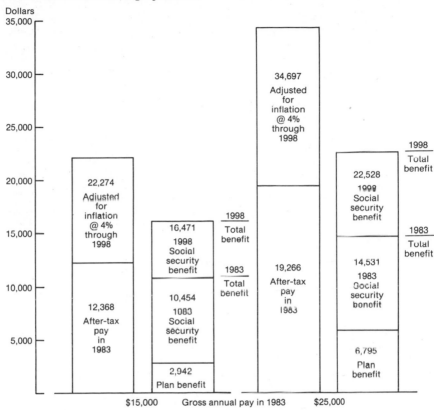

Dollars

35,000

30,000 — 34,697 Adjusted for inflation @ 4% through 1998

25,000 —

1998 Total benefit

22,528 1998 Social security benefit

1983 Total benefit

20,000 — 22,274 Adjusted for inflation @ 4% through 1998

15,000 — 16,471 1998 Social security benefit · 1998 Total benefit

14,531 1983 Social security benefit

10,454 · 1983 Total benefit · 19,266 After-tax pay in 1983 · 1083 Social security benefit

10,000 — 12,368 After-tax pay in 1983

5,000 — 2,942 Plan benefit · 6,795 Plan benefit

$15,000   Gross annual pay in 1983 $25,000

15-year period. In addition to the items already mentioned, these charts are based on the following factors:

1. The private plan formula is a final-pay offset formula that produces a pension at age 65 of 50 percent of final average pay, less 50 percent of the pensioner's primary social security benefit.
2. The calculations reflect social security taxes and assume average federal, state, and local income taxes for the pay levels shown.
3. Pensioners and their spouses are assumed to be age 65 on January 1, 1983.
4. The social security benefits shown for the married pensioners include the 50 percent spouse benefit.
5. To be consistent with the inclusion of the social security spouse benefit, the amount of private plan benefit shown for the married pensioners has been reduced from the amount the plan formula would otherwise produce, to provide a 50 percent joint and survivor benefit for the pensioner and spouse.

TABLE 7–2: Illustration of Significance of Social Security in Countering Effect of Postretirement Inflation (married pensioner)

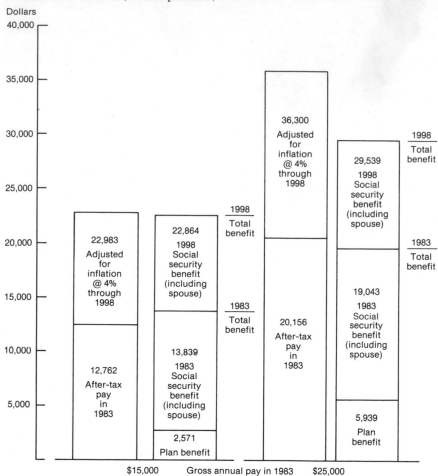

6. To isolate the effect of social security, the private plan benefit was assumed to remain constant during the entire 15-year period illustrated.

A number of observations may be made concerning the results depicted on these charts. First, quite apart from the issue of meeting the problems created by inflation, social security benefits play a major role in meeting the income replacement needs of individuals at low- to middle-income levels. Also, when viewed and related on an after-tax basis, social security benefits are much more powerful than suggested when these benefits are compared to gross pay prior to retirement. For example, the total social security benefit payable to the married pensioner whose 1983 gross pay level was $15,000 amounts to 75 percent of this gross pay—but it actually replaces

TABLE 7–3: Illustration of Significance of Social Security in Countering Effect of Postretirement Inflation

	Single Employee Final Pay		Married Employee Final Pay	
	$15,000	$25,000	$15,000	$25,000
Preretirement:				
1. Final pay	$15,000	$25,000	$15,000	$25,000
2. Taxes	2,632	5,734	2,238	4,844
3. Spendable income	12,368	19,266	12,762	20,156
Upon retirement:				
4. Pension income:				
Private plan	2,942	6,795	2,571	5,939
Social security	7,512	8,736	11,268	13,104
Total	10,454	15,531	13,839	19,043
5. Taxes	—	—	—	—
6. Spendable income	10,454	15,531	13,839	19,043
Fifteen years after retirement (with inflation of 4 percent per year):				
7. Pension income:				
Private plan	2,942	6,795	2,571	5,939
Social security	13,529	15,733	20,293	23,600
Total	16,471	22,528	22,864	29,539
8. Taxes	—	—	—	—
9. Spendable income	16,471	22,528	22,864	29,539
10. Preretirement spendable income, adjusted for inflation	22,274	34,697	22,983	36,300
Comparison:				
11. Spendable income upon retirement as a percentage of preretirement Spendable income: (6) ÷ (3)	85	81	108	94
12. Spendable income 15 years after retirement as a percentage of inflation-adjusted preretirement Spendable income: (9) ÷ (10)	74	65	99	81
13. Loss in purchasing power: (11) − (12) ÷ (11)	13	20	8	14

88 percent of the pensioner's preretirement after-tax income. Social security replaces 52 percent of gross income for the married pensioner who retired at the $25,000 level, but 65 percent of preretirement after-tax pay. Although smaller, both in dollars and as a percentage of preretirement take-home pay, social security benefits are also of significant value to the single pensioner.

For the single pensioner who retired at the $15,000 pay level, the combined income from the private plan and social security replaces 85 percent of preretirement take-home pay. For the married pensioner who retired at the same pay level, the combined income from the private plan and social security actually exceeds the amount of that individual's preretirement take-home pay. Even after 15 years of inflation at the rate of 4 percent a year, the married pensioner whose final pay was $15,000 is still receiving a total benefit, solely because of social security increases, that replaces 99 percent of the purchasing power he or she enjoyed prior to retiring; in the case of the single pensioner, 74 percent is replaced.

The effect of social security on the pensioner who retired at the $25,000 level is not as dramatic but, nevertheless, is substantial. The total income (private plan and social security) payable to the married pensioner at retirement replaces 94 percent of preretirement after-tax income; the effect of social security increases during 15 years of annual 4 percent inflation is that this pensioner is able to retain 81 percent of preretirement purchasing power. For the single pensioner, the corresponding figures are 81 percent and 65 percent, respectively.

As final-pay levels go up, the relative value of social security decreases and, as a result, the effect of the automatic increase provisions of social security is less significant. Using the same assumptions as those underlying Tables 7–1, 7–2, and 7–3, this is illustrated by Table 7–4, which compares the percentage of preretirement after-tax income replaced at the time of retirement (January 1, 1983) with the percentage replaced after 15 years, with adjustment for inflation at the rate of 4 percent a year.

Table 7–4 suggests that because of social security, and assuming the existence of a modest private pension plan, the loss in purchasing power caused by inflation will be greater for pensioners at middle to upper income levels than for pensioners at lower income levels. In fact, under the assumptions employed, the loss of purchasing power over the 15-year period of retirement would be as shown in Table 7–5.

Changing the underlying assumptions in a comparison of this type, made in Tables 7–4 and 7–5, will, of course, change the results. As would be expected, a higher assumed rate of inflation will erode purchasing power at a more rapid rate; however, because this same higher rate of

TABLE 7–4: Effect of Inflation on Total Income (including social security) at Various Income Levels; Inflation at Annual Rate of 4 Percent

	Percentage of After-Tax Income Replaced			
	Single Pensioner		Married Pensioner	
Final Gross Pay	At Retirement	Inflation Adjusted for 15 Years	At Retirement	Inflation Adjusted for 15 Years
$ 15,000	85%	74%	108%	99%
25,000	81	65	94	81
40,000	74	54	80	64
100,000	61	40	61	42

TABLE 7–5: Loss in Purchasing Power at Various Income Levels; Inflation at Annual Rate of 4 Percent

Final Gross Pay	15-Year Loss in Purchasing Power	
	Single Pensioner	Married Pensioner
$ 15,000	13%	8%
25,000	20	14
40,000	27	20
100,000	34	31

inflation will be reflected in social security benefits, the effect will be that higher paid pensioners will lose purchasing power more rapidly than will lower paid pensioners.

It also might be observed that at the lower income levels very little loss in purchasing power can be sustained because of the subsistence needs of these individuals. However, this seems to be primarily a matter of the basic salary or wage structure that exists at the time an individual retires, rather than a problem associated with postretirement inflation. If the combination of a modest private plan and social security can replace all or a substantial part of an individual's preretirement take-home pay, and if this level of purchasing power can be largely sustained over an extended period of inflation, the problem of income adequacy is not so much caused by inflation as by the level of income that existed at retirement.

In any event, it seems clear that for a high percentage of pensioners, social security benefits have been and will continue to be of major importance in meeting the problems associated with inflation.

Nature of Commitment

To the extent there is a need, real or perceived, to provide pensioners with some form of financial relief, a question arises as to who should bear the cost of providing this relief. The logical sources are: (1) the government, (2) employers, and (3) employees and/or pensioners. Although the incidence and short-term distribution of this cost are affected by who assumes the primary burden, the ultimate cost will be borne by the general public in the form of increased taxes, higher consumer prices, lower wages, and/or lower returns on savings.

It has been suggested that pension plans be required to make some provision for cost-of-living increases for retired participants. Presumably, the cost of any such required benefit would be assumed by the employer in the case of a noncontributory plan, or by the employer and employees in the case of a contributory plan.

Proponents of requiring private plans to provide for automatic cost-of-living increases point out that this type of benefit is now provided under social security and under the federal civil service and military retirement systems, as well as under many state and local government plans. However, this argument fails to recognize that governments are in a unique position to make these promises and raise needed revenues by increasing the tax liabilities of future generations of taxpayers. Private industry has no such ability and, in fact, would be required to prefund any such obligation. Indeed, questions of equity are raised by the government's practice of promising inflation-proof benefits to its employees, who are just a segment of the population, and then taxing the future population at large to provide those benefits that result from the government's failure to control inflation. Also, it would appear that these generous benefits are not currently taken into account by the government in determining equitable pay levels for its employees.

Mandating automatic cost-of-living adjustments raises a host of questions and could have a very serious, negative effect on the development of the private pension system. A major problem is that legislating such a requirement fails to recognize the nature of the commitment made by employers for private plans. Many employers, for example, have assumed no obligation at all to provide pension benefits for their employees. Many of the employers who have adopted plans have chosen to make their commitment not in the form of providing a fixed amount of retirement income but, rather, in the form of a fixed or variable annual contribution during the worker's active employment. Examples of employers who have followed this course of action are those who have adopted deferred profit sharing plans as their primary retirement programs and those who have adopted money purchase pension plans (such as colleges and universities and many self-employed individuals). Although these employers are still in the minority, in terms of people covered, it should be observed that since the passage of ERISA, more than 80 percent of all new pension plans are defined contribution in nature.

Even among those employers who have adopted defined benefit plans, a wide range of difference exists in the level and type of benefit provided. The initial level of pension benefit, for example, will vary from employer to employer because of differences in the percentage rates used to accrue benefits or the pay base used to calculate benefits. Many plans, of course, are the result of collective bargaining and provide only the dollar level of benefits agreed to by management and the union.

Given the variable nature of employer commitments, if any, to provide pension benefits, it is impossible to arrive at any mandatory system of employer-provided financial relief for pensioners that is equitable and fair to all.

The financial burden of inflation is presently borne primarily by employers, pensioners, or both. Those employers who have done nothing to alleviate the problem have, in effect, made their pensioners assume the burden of lost purchasing power. Other employers, including many of the large U.S. corporations, periodically have arranged for supplemental benefits for their pensioners. Active employees have rarely been called upon to assume any direct share of this burden; however, there appears to be a growing interest in alternative methods of involving employees in this regard. Some of these approaches are discussed later in this chapter.

Many employers who in effect have asked their pensioners to assume the loss in purchasing power caused by inflation have not done so in a thoughtless manner. Public opinion to the contrary, corporations do not have unlimited financial capacities. Typically, any organization has limited resources that must be allocated carefully to achieve a number of different purposes. This, in turn, requires that priorities be established and met. Thus, for example, an employer might find that even though increasing pensioner benefits would be highly desirable, available funds are more immediately needed to increase pay levels for active employees, who are also affected by inflation, to maintain a competitive pay structure to attract and retain needed personnel. Similarly, the collective bargaining process and the interests of active members of the bargaining unit could take precedence over the interest of pensioners. In short, the balancing of shareholder, management, and active employee interests often have prevented employers from assuming all or even part of the cost associated with increasing benefits for pensioners.

To date, the government has not shared the burden of protecting pensioners under private plans from the eroding effects of inflation. The government could, in fact, assume some of this burden and spread its cost over a broader base by selling indexed bonds to pension funds, at least in amounts sufficient to cover plan liabilities for pensioners, selling indexed annuities, and/or granting tax credits to employers who provide for increasing benefits to pensioners.

TRADITIONAL APPROACHES TO ADDRESSING PROBLEMS OF INFLATION

Inflation affects pensioners not only in the period following retirement, but also during the period of active employment while their pensions are being accrued. The following discusses, first, the plan design approaches used to counteract the effect of preretirement inflation and, second, approaches used to offset postretirement inflation. Although the primary focus relates to retirement income levels, the material concludes with a brief discussion of postretirement death and medical expense benefits often provided by employers for their pensioners.

Preretirement Inflation

As noted earlier, employer commitments to provide private plan retirement benefits vary from none at all to a replacement of a substantial part of an employee's pay determined at or shortly before retirement.

If an employer's plan provides a specific amount of retirement benefit, the amount of this benefit is expressed either as a dollar amount or in relation to the employee's pay. If pay-related, the benefit may be determined as a percentage of pay averaged over the employee's career or over a relatively short period such as three or five years—often the high three- or five-year average during the last 10 years of employment.

Dollar amount plans (e.g., plans that provide a benefit such as $15 per month per year of service) do not directly reflect inflation because they are not pay related. However, these plans are typically union negotiated and, in practice, the dollar amount is increased periodically via the collective bargaining process. Thus, in fact, these plans tend to provide initial retirement benefits that allow for preretirement inflationary trends. Of course, the extent to which this is so for any specific pensioner will depend upon the time of actual retirement and the dollar level then in effect for benefits under the plan.

Those plans that base benefits on final pay provide a retiring employee with an initial benefit that reflects inflation that has taken place prior to retirement. In fact, the majority of the nonnegotiated defined benefit plans in effect today use some form of final-pay base to determine benefits and thus recognize most of the inflation that takes place prior to retirement. The use of a five-year average for this purpose has been quite common. More recently, however, partially in response to inflation, there has been growing use of three-year averaging periods. Because most of these plans are noncontributory, the cost of accommodating preretirement inflation is being borne primarily by employers. This cost becomes dramatically evident in inflationary periods as total pension plan costs rise, relative to payroll costs, because of pay movement in excess of that anticipated.

Some employers have chosen to develop benefit and cost commitments on the basis of career-pay plans. These plans, of course, reflect some part of the inflation that takes place prior to retirement. However, unless the rates of accrual are set unusually high, or the employer has updated the benefits that have accrued for employees, or the plan also has a minimum benefit formula based on final pay, the initial level of benefit provided for a pensioner will not fully reflect the inflation that has taken place during a working career. In many situations, employers periodically update career-pay plans by recalculating accrued benefits on the basis of then current pay. Although the career-pay approach, with periodic updates, provides less assurance to employees than the final-pay approach concerning the adequacy of their benefits, there are definite advantages to the employer. First, the employer retains control over the timing and extent to which the cost of inflation is assumed. Second, the employer also receives credit for making periodic benefit improvements.

Those employers who utilize a defined contribution approach to providing pension benefits usually determine or allocate each year's contributions on a basis that reflects then current pay levels. Thus, from year to year, there is some reflection of inflation. However, the philosophical basis for many of these plans does not involve any commitment by the employer to the income adequacy of funds at retirement; in such situations, the ultimate benefit may or may not be adequate depending upon a number of factors such as the length of the employee's plan participation, actual contribution rates, investment return, and the like. Some plans, however, in recognition of the possible inadequacy of retirement benefits (not only because of inflation, but also because of other inherent features of this type of plan), provide for a minimum benefit related to the pensioner's final pay. This can be accomplished by a separately stated final-pay minimum benefit, or by a "floor" plan under which the pensioner is assured that if the defined contribution plan does not produce a minimum benefit, the difference will be provided by the floor plan itself.

It also should be observed that in the typical defined contribution plan, all or part of an employee's account may be placed in equity-type investments, with the employee being credited with the actual investment results realized. Over a long period, it might be argued that the effects of inflation will be offset by gains in such equity holdings. Historically, a long-range relationship between the cost of living and the investment performance of diversified portfolios of common stocks has existed. However, short-term patterns reveal dissimilar and even opposite movements. Although protection against inflation is not assured by such equity investments, they do offer some possible degree of protection.

Postretirement Inflation

The techniques utilized to adjust benefits for employees who have already retired may be automatic or nonautomatic. The automatic adjustments provide for increases, at stated intervals, that are related to some form of index such as the CPI or to rates of return on an investment fund. The nonautomatic increases are provided on an irregular basis, at the employer's discretion, with the amount of increase determined in a variety of ways. The following discusses and evaluates these different techniques.

Automatic Adjustments.   Four basic forms of automatic adjustment techniques have been used for making postretirement benefit changes:

1. Equity pensions.
2. Cost-of-living formulas.
3. Wage-related formulas.
4. Specified percentage formulas.

Equity Pensions.   An equity pension, often called a variable annuity, provides retirement income that varies in dollar amounts to reflect the investment results of an underlying fund of common stocks. The equity feature (usually affecting only a portion of the retirement income amount) may operate during the years of active employment as well as during the postre-tirement payout period. In either case, the assumption is that stock price movement will vary with the movement of all other prices and, hence, reflect the general level of inflation. Proponents of the equity pension approach argue that active employees and pensioners have some assurance their retirement income will fluctuate with the general level of economic activity. Until the late 1960s and early 1970s, calculations of stock market performance indicated that only in a few periods would the pensioner have been better off with fixed-dollar retirement income. Also, from the employer's standpoint, the cost of equity pensions can be predicted before-hand. This is because the risk of potential investment gains and losses has been shifted to plan participants. Another potential advantage to the employer is that equity pensions may eliminate or reduce the need for other pension benefit liberalizations. Finally, an equity pension plan, at least during a rising market (such as the one experienced from late 1982 until mid-1987), could prove to be popular with employees, particularly where preretirement accruals are geared to stock performance.

Despite these points, equity pensions have some disadvantages:

1. Employees and/or pensioners are required to assume the risk of investment loss as well as the reward of investment gain. It is questionable whether individuals at lower income levels should be asked to assume this risk/reward situation for an item that constitutes an important part of their economic security.

2. The downward fluctuations in pension payments, which invariably occur from time to time, may cause hardship for pensioners. Recognizing this problem, employers may limit the amount of annual downward (or upward) adjustment through use of a securities fluctuation reserve.

3. Equity pensions are more complicated than fixed-dollar pensions and are often more difficult to explain than other methods of adjusting pen-sions. This could be particularly important in a situation where the employer's fund fails to perform as well as recognized equity indexes.

4. If the objective is to have an employee's retirement income vary directly with cost- or standard-of-living changes, equity pensions may not be appropriate in the timing and magnitude of the pension fluctuations. At best, equity pensions are only an indirect means of relating retirement income to economic trends. At worst, and particularly over the short term, equity pensions may result in decreasing pension amounts during periods of rampant inflation.

5. From the employer's viewpoint, the equity pension approach may, in fact, produce additional or unnecessary costs. If the value of equities increases faster than the cost of living, benefits will be greater than may be needed to maintain the original income-replacement ratios of pensioners. At the same time, the excess investment return that causes this result will not be available to reduce employer costs. On the other hand, if the cost of living outpaces the performance of the equity market, the employer may

very well feel the need to assume the additional cost of providing some form of supplemental benefit for pensioners. Thus, the employer reaps none of the gain of superior investment performance and might become involved in the cost of underwriting this performance when it falls short of cost-of-living changes.

The difficulties encountered in the late 1970s, when relatively high rates of inflation occurred during periods of depressed stock values, have caused many companies to move from the equity pension concept to some other form of pension adjustment technique. At this time, equity pensions are used primarily by private colleges and universities.

Cost-of-Living Formulas. A direct approach to automatic pension adjustments involves linking retirement income amounts by formula to upward (and in some cases, downward) changes in a cost-of-living or price index such as the CPI. Under these plans, pension amounts increase periodically, subject to limits, if the increase in the price index equals or exceeds a predetermined level. The major advantages of this approach are that employees have advance assurance their retirement income will be adjusted periodically to help preserve their purchasing power and that the CPI, used almost exclusively in such plans, is well known and at least partially understood by most employees. Consequently, the employer has a good chance of avoiding criticism that the pension adjustment technique is faulty.

The following are possible disadvantages:

1. The employer assumes a largely undeterminable future liability tied to a government index over which it has no control. (However, the adjustment formula may be designed to provide ceilings on the amount of the increase in benefits and thus the maximum additional costs that are assumed.)
2. No allowance is made for any rising standard of living that may be experienced by active employees.
3. The CPI may, in fact, overstate rates of inflation and the presumed needs of pensioners, thus resulting in additional and unnecessary costs.
4. The tax law requires that any automatic increases be given to vested terminations — individuals for whom the employer may feel little or no continuing obligation.
5. If the pension plan provides for subsidized early retirement benefits, the cost of this subsidization very possibly will increase because the assurance of protection against inflation will most likely cause an increase in the incidence of early retirement.
6. Providing automatic cost-of-living adjustments for pensioners could create pressure to follow the same approach (i.e., automatic cost-of-living adjustments for wages) for active employees.

The cost implications of providing automatic cost-of-living increases for pensioners can be quite significant. The actual cost increases associated with such a benefit will, of course, vary from plan to plan and can range from about 8 to 20 percent for each 1 percent annual increase in benefits. Paradoxically, the greater the degree of funding achieved by a plan, the greater the percentage increase in plan costs when pensioner benefits are increased (as would be true whenever any of the benefits of such a plan are increased). Also, the greater the proportion of females covered by the plan, the greater the cost of pensioner increases. Assuming that a plan is approximately 50 percent funded and that the majority of pensioners are male, one rule of thumb is that pension costs will increase by about 10 percent for each 1 percent annual increase in pensioner benefits. Increases in accrued benefit liabilities would generally follow the same increase pattern. The extent of the increase in accrued benefit liabilities would be different for each plan and would be most significant where existing pensioner liabilities are small compared to total plan liabilities and where females form a substantial portion of all plan participants.

Cost-of-living formulas are frequently found in the public sector (e.g., the federal civil service and military retirement systems, and various state and municipal plans), but are still relatively rare in the private sector. Although there is growing interest in this approach, many employers are wary of its cost implications, particularly if the feature is not needed to provide retirement benefits that are competitive either on the basis of industry or geography.

Wage-Related Formulas. This method involves the automatic fluctuation of retirement income payments in response to changes in some designated wage index. This permits pensioners to benefit from standard-of-living improvements enjoyed by active employees. The index could be one of a general nature, such as the Bureau of Labor Statistics index of the average wage for industrial workers, or a more specialized one, such as the average wage paid by the individual employer. The former alternative normally would seem most appropriate as a measure of general standard-of-living variations, but it might have limited application to a specific employee group. The latter could have a significant impact on pension plan costs if an employer maintains a liberal salary or wage increase policy. Some governmental units sponsor plans with wage-related formulas for pension adjustments; however, this type of plan is relatively uncommon, particularly in the private sector.

Specified Percentage Formulas. Under this approach, a predetermined percentage formula governs the amount of annual increase in retirement income. Unlike cost-of-living or wage-related plans, the company, in a sense, estimates future economic trends and commits itself to a specific increase on this estimation. For example, the pension may be increased automatically by 1.5 percent a year on the assumption that this increase will offset, at least partially, upward trends in prices. When compared with cost-of-living and wage-related formulas, a specified percentage formula permits a more reliable prediction of plan costs. The primary disadvantage is that no assurance exists that the retirement income increases will actually reflect shifts in the cost of living, particularly over the short run. It is only by coincidence that such a plan would respond precisely to inflation and fulfill employee needs. This approach is not commonly employed except in some state and municipal pension plans.

Nonautomatic Adjustments.   The most popular method of coping with postretirement inflation, and the one that has been adopted by a majority of large, well-known organizations, has been the nonautomatic or discretionary form of adjustment made at irregular intervals and with varying ways of determining the amount of increase provided. Reasons for adopting a discretionary rather than an automatic approach to pension increases include the following:

1. Because the rate of inflation is uncertain, an organization should not commit itself to a predetermined or formula method.
2. Discretionary adjustments have a predictable cost because they remain under the employer's control, both as to timing and amount.
3. Both the scope and level of social security benefits may eliminate or reduce substantially the need for future retirement income improvements.
4. The employer receives credit for making a plan improvement each time benefits are increased.

One obvious disadvantage of the discretionary approach is the lack of assurance for pensioners that retirement income levels will continue to meet their needs. Another possible disadvantage is that this technique offers no possibility of prefunding the cost of the increases or having employees share in this cost during their active employment.

The discretionary adjustment techniques most frequently used are either fixed percentage, or flat-dollar formulas, or a combination of the two.

A flat percentage increase may be applied uniformly to the retirement income of all pensioners. Alternatively, graded percentages may be used with variations based on a pensioner's age group, years of service prior to retirement, or the number of years since retirement date or the last pensioner increase. In a few instances, the pension increase may be limited to a defined "subsistence" income group — that is, a percentage increase is applied only if a pensioner's total income from the company's plan and social security falls below certain dollar amounts. The percentage increase may be at least indirectly contingent on changes in the CPI. Frequently, the increase is subject to a stated dollar minimum and/or maximum; for example, the minimum monthly increase might be $10, with the maximum established at $75 or $100. The usual rationale for having a maximum is that the need for additional income is not as acute for pensioners who are receiving substantial pension payments. However, the higher the level of total pension income, the greater will be the loss of purchasing power because of inflation. This, of course, is because of the effect of automatic social security increases and the significance they have for pensioners at lower income levels.

A flat-dollar increase may be applied uniformly or on a variable basis. The latter approach is often used for nonunion, salaried pensioners to provide them with the same level of benefit increases provided for union pensioners.

The choice of formula and the level of percentage or dollar amount chosen depend upon a number of factors including the cost and funding implications involved, the original level of pension provided, actual CPI movement, changes in social security benefits, the timing and form of the last pensioner increase (if any), competitive practices, and the cost and level of other benefits (death and medical expense) being provided.

It also should be noted that nonautomatic adjustments have been negotiated for retired members of a collective bargaining unit. Although these increases are not a mandatory subject of collective bargaining, there is nothing to prevent voluntary negotiations on this issue. Contracts negotiated in recent years between the United Auto Workers and the major automobile manufacturers are examples of this type of negotiation.

These discretionary adjustments are sometimes made part of the underlying formal plan. At other times, particularly when the formula will not meet Internal Revenue Service requirements for a qualified pension plan, discretionary adjustments are provided as a separate, nonqualified benefit. Even so, such nonqualified benefits are still subject to the labor provisions of ERISA unless they qualify for the exemptions provided.

Although the nonqualified approach has the advantage of permitting flexibility in the design of the formula, it has potential funding disadvantages; for example, the liability for the increase must be funded on a current disbursement basis over the remaining lifetimes of the pensioners, and there is no ability to vary this funding level from year to year without affecting the benefits payable to pensioners. (However, the possibility of some overall funding flexibility is available if the funded position of the underlying formal plan is such that its funding level can be reduced to reflect payments being made under the nonqualified supplement.) Although the same rate of funding probably is desirable if the benefit is funded as part of the formal plan, the flexibility does exist for amortizing this additional liability over as much as a 30-year period.

Supplemental Benefits

Many employers provide some form of death and/or medical expense benefit for their pensioners. Often the benefits are provided at no cost to the pensioner or on the basis of only a modest contribution. Although these benefits do not provide a form of direct income, they do assist pensioners in meeting their economic security needs and, in so doing, reduce the amounts pensioners would otherwise have to spend to obtain this protection. Employer practices in this regard vary to a considerable extent. The following very briefly discusses the benefits most frequently provided.

Death Benefits.   Group life insurance is almost always provided for active employees. Often, some basic amount of coverage is provided at no cost to the employee, with optional amounts available on a contributory basis. In other situations, the entire amount of group life insurance is available only on a basis that requires employee contributions.

Very few major employers completely discontinue noncontributory group life insurance at retirement; on the other hand, very few continue the full amount of such coverage throughout retirement. Typically, the coverage is reduced either all at once or in equal installments over a 5- or 10-year period. The ultimate amount of insurance provided is often a flat amount such as $5,000, or an amount equal to 25 or 50 percent of the pensioner's final pay before retirement. In the case of early retirement, it is common to continue the full coverage until the pensioner reaches age 65, at which time the scheduled reductions begin.

In situations where the full amount of group life insurance requires employee contributions, the pattern of postretirement reductions and coverage is similar to that described above. However, when the coverage is provided by a combination of noncontributory and contributory coverage, the contributory coverage is almost always terminated at retirement (although, in the case of early retirement, full coverage might be made available to the pensioner until age 65 if he or she continues to make any required contributions).

Survivor benefits are another form of postretirement death benefit for pensioners. Typically, the benefit is in the form of continuing all or part of the pensioner's income to a designated survivor. Survivor benefits may be provided at no cost to the pensioner, at full cost to the pensioner, or on a basis where the cost is shared by both the employer and the pensioner.

Most employers do not assume the full cost of providing postretirement survivor benefits. Those that do often provide the benefit only for the pensioner's spouse. In this event, the benefit is usually in the form of continuing 25 or 50 percent of the pensioner's income to the spouse for his or her lifetime.

If the pensioner is paying all or part of the cost of the postretirement survivor benefit, the typical method of making the benefit available is through the use of the optional payment provisions of the pension plan. Thus, the form of payment could guarantee that the benefit would be paid for a minimum number of years or, as is more often the case, the benefit could be payable on a joint-and-survivor basis with all or part of the pensioner's benefit being continued to the spouse. (The Code requires that the automatic payment form for a married pensioner, subject to a right of revocation, be a life annuity with at least 50 percent of the pensioner's benefit continued after death to the pensioner's spouse. However, the full cost of this benefit can be passed on to the pensioner.) The cost of providing such postretirement benefits is met by reducing the amount of benefit otherwise payable to the pensioner. If the pensioner is paying all of the cost, the reduction will be the full amount necessary to create a benefit that is the actuarial equivalent of the amount payable to the pensioner as a life annuity; those employers who assume part of the cost do so by subsidizing the amount by which the pensioner's benefit is reduced—that is, the amount of the reduction is not a full actuarial equivalent.

Medical Expense Benefits.   Many of the employers who provide retirement benefits also provide some form of postretirement coverage for medical expenses.

In the case of early retirement, it is common to provide a pensioner and spouse with the full level of coverage provided for active employees. When the pensioner or spouse reaches age 65, adjustments are made. Some employers terminate the coverage; others continue coverage, sometimes with lesser benefits, and in some fashion recognize that the pensioner or spouse has become eligible for medicare. The two most common approaches are to: (1) "carve out" medical payments from the employer's plan; or (2) supplement medicare benefits by paying all or part of the deductibles and coinsurance features of medicare or, possibly, by paying for certain items not covered by medicare such as prescription drugs and private duty nursing. Some employers also pay the pensioner's premium cost for Part B coverage under medicare.

Medical coverage provided for pensioners after age 65 is frequently but not always noncontributory. If contributions are required from active employees and if full coverage is continued from early retirement to age 65, it is customary to continue collecting contributions from the pensioner, at least for coverage prior to age 65.

THE FUTURE

Inflation and, in particular, its effect on pensioners continues to be a matter of concern for most employers. Employers who have a genuine concern over the financial plight of their pensioners must consider a number of issues—with many conflicting viewpoints—in arriving at a decision on what, if anything, they might do to alleviate this burden. The following questions are by no means all-inclusive, but they do suggest many of the issues that must be addressed.

1. Given the range of commitment assumed by private employers in terms of pension promises, should the treatment of inflation, as it affects pensioners, be left to the federal government?

2. Further, if private industry provides for protection against inflation, will this be undesirable in the long run because it removes a major source of pressure on the government to control its fiscal and monetary policies?

3. On the other hand, if private industry fails to respond to the problem, will this hasten some form of legislation, such as mandatory, automatic cost-of-living protection or fully provided government pensions?

4. Even if pensioner needs are acknowledged, is it appropriate to expend corporate funds for a group of individuals no longer making a productive contribution to the employer's success?

5. In allocating available corporate resources, how should priorities be established among active employees, shareholders, and pensioners?

6. Assuming the availability of some funds to apply to the benefit of pensioners, would it be more effective to provide or increase death and medical expense benefits than to increase income levels?

7. Will the assumption of additional pension costs have a positive or negative effect on the company's public or competitive position (e.g., public image, product cost, competitive employment practices, or attitude of active employees)?

8. How can the real loss of purchasing power of a specific group of pensioners be fairly assessed, taking into account factors such as their unique needs and the role of social security?

9. In measuring pensioner needs, should improvements in the standard of living be taken into account as well as increases in the cost of living?

10. If increases are to be provided, should they be limited to pensioners or should they be extended to other groups such as surviving contingent annuitants and beneficiaries under optional forms of payment; surviving spouses or beneficiaries under preretirement death benefit features; employees who previously terminated employment and who are now drawing a pension; or disabled employees who are receiving benefits either under the pension plan or under a long-term disability plan?

11. If an automatic increase formula is adopted for pensioners, what will be the implications of this for salary and wage administration policies for active employees?

12. Has the effect of inflation on a company's pensioners been dampened or exaggerated by reason of the original level of benefit provided to employees at the time they retired—that is, did original benefit levels provide generous or minimal income-replacement ratios?

13. If an ad hoc increase is to be provided, should it be made part of the underlying tax-qualified plan or should it be a nonqualified supplement, taking into account for each alternative the requirements imposed by law?

14. What is the company's overall strategy for encouraging retirement (particularly in light of age discrimination laws) and how will the company's treatment of pensioners affect this strategy (e.g., will providing

automatic protection against inflation for pensioners encourage earlier retirement)?

15. If a company has provided ad hoc increases on several different occasions, would it be appropriate to formalize the practice and gain some of the funding and employee relations advantages associated with an automatic increase formula?

16. Should employees be asked to assume part of the cost of protection against inflation, either directly or indirectly?

17. What alternative techniques might be employed to protect pensioners, at least to some degree, from the effects of inflation while at the same time retaining desirable controls over the cost implications of providing such protection?

These questions, and others like them, may be difficult to answer, and it is quite likely they will be answered in different ways by different employers. Nevertheless, they must be addressed in arriving at a thoughtful and orderly conclusion about ways in which an employer might respond to the problem of inflation's impact on the purchasing power of its pensioners.

Possible Approaches

Undoubtedly, the majority of employers who wish to provide some form of financial protection for their pensioners will opt to use one or more of the traditional approaches described earlier in this chapter. Thus, it can be expected that there will be continued use of final-pay plans (or periodic updates for career-pay plans), coupled with discretionary or ad hoc adjustments for pensioners from time to time. If high levels of inflation return, however, it is reasonable to expect that more and more employers will explore the possibility of providing some limited form of automatic postretirement benefit adjustments. The following lists some of the techniques employers might use, alone or in combination, to provide such adjustments while retaining control of costs.

1. Provide for increasing benefits in each year of retirement by movement in the CPI but with a maximum for each year's increase (e.g., 3 percent, or with a specific dollar limitation).

2. Provide for increasing benefits in each year of retirement by a fraction of the movement in the CPI (e.g., 50 percent).

3. Provide for increasing benefits in each year of retirement by a graded percentage of movement in the CPI (e.g., 100 percent of the first 2 percent increase in the CPI, 75 percent of the next 2 percent, 50 percent of the next 2 percent, and 25 percent of the balance).

4. Provide for increasing benefits in each year of retirement at a stipulated percentage, regardless of CPI movement (e.g., 3 percent).

5. Provide for increasing benefits by all or a part of the CPI movement, but only for increases that occur after a specific period of retirement or

after a certain age (e.g., no increases will be provided with respect to increases in the CPI during the first five years of retirement or prior to age 70).

6. Provide for increasing benefits by all or part of the CPI movement, but only for the first years of retirement (e.g., increases during the first five years of retirement or prior to age 70 would be the only increases taken into account).

7. Provide for increasing benefits in each year of retirement by all or part of the CPI movement, but only for part of the individual's pension (e.g., the increase would be applied only to the first 25 or 50 percent or the first $1,000 of monthly pension payable).

8. Provide for increasing benefits in each year of retirement by all or part of the CPI movement, but only for pensioners whose annual pension is less than a stipulated amount (e.g., the maximum primary social security benefit).

9. Provide for increasing benefits in each year of retirement by all or part of the CPI movement, but only to the extent that the percentage increase, when applied to an individual's pension, would cause an increase in excess of a stipulated dollar amount (e.g., if the stipulated dollar amount is set at $500 and if the percentage increase in the CPI for a year, when applied to the individual's total company pension, would result in a gross increase of $700, the amount of the actual increase that year would be $200 [$700 − $500 = $200]).

To ease the cost impact of providing for automatic adjustments, it would also be possible to adopt the ultimate provision desired by making gradual improvements. For example, the first step might be to provide for automatic increases but only for CPI movement that occurs after a pensioner reaches age 70 and with a maximum increase each year of 3 percent. At a later time or times, the age could be reduced to 68 or 65 and the maximum could be increased to 4 or 5 percent or even eliminated.

Providing for some form of automatic adjustment in pension benefits has the clear advantage of assuring employees that they will have some degree of protection against postretirement inflation. In turn, this should encourage employees to retire at or before age 65 — a factor that might be particularly significant in light of recent legislation concerning mandatory retirement. Another possible advantage of the automatic benefit provision is that it permits prefunding of the cost of the benefit over the working lives of employees rather than over the relatively short period of their retirement years or over a period that extends beyond their lifetimes. The most obvious disadvantage of an automatic increase provision is the additional cost involved — even with the inclusion of cost controls. Other disadvantages include the inability to reflect social security changes and the loss of ability to take credit for improving the plan from time to time.

Other approaches include having employees share directly in the cost of providing postretirement inflation protection. One such approach would be to develop an optional form of payment under which retiring employees could accept a reduction in initial pension in return for automatic annual increases in benefit for their remaining lifetimes. For example, the reduction in pension required to provide a 3 percent annual increase in benefit for an employee age 65 would be approximately 19 percent. The employer could, of course, subsidize this type of benefit by requiring a lesser reduction than might otherwise be required. In the above illustration, for example, the reduction in benefit might be limited to 10 percent with the additional cost being absorbed by the employer. Under the optional form of payment approach, the increase in benefit would be a fixed percentage (or choice of percentages) regardless of the CPI movement. It would also be possible to relate the increase in benefit to actual movement in the CPI. However, this would introduce a greater degree of uncertainty into the establishment of reduction factors and would be less attractive to the employee who would probably want more definite assurance of benefit increases before agreeing to a reduction in pension.

Another possible approach that involves having employees share directly in the cost of their own protection is to introduce a contributory pension supplement. Under this type of arrangement, an active employee might be given the option of making a supplementary contribution (determined by his or her age at the time contributions begin) to "purchase" a benefit whereby the employee's pension would increase automatically by a predetermined percentage or percentages. Establishing an appropriate contribution schedule would, of course, be difficult because of the likelihood of future benefit increases because of future pay increases. However, the extent to which the employer is willing to subsidize the cost of this benefit could minimize or eliminate this problem. One disadvantage of this approach is that it is a long-term solution involving a transition period (e.g., the needs of current pensioners would continue to be a problem and contributions for older active employees might be too high at the outset), thus requiring the use of other techniques until the transition period is over. Another potential disadvantage is that pressures might ultimately develop to have the supplement provided on a noncontributory basis. Also, there will always be the problem of how to treat the pensioner who, for a variety of reasons, chose not to participate; however, the availability of an optional form of payment, as described above, could be, at least, a partial solution for this pensioner.

A more realistic variation of this concept is the utilization of a savings plan to accumulate a capital sum for supplemental retirement benefits. Savings plans are growing in popularity and are found in a large number of major U.S. industrial corporations.[3] Although these plans typically accumulate funds for a variety of purposes, they can, by design and by communications emphasis, be used to provide an additional source of retirement

---

[3]These plans are discussed in Chapters 16 and 17.

benefits. If used in tandem with a pension plan, the savings plan has the potential of delivering annual postretirement benefit increases at a predeterminable compound rate. The economics of this concept appear in Table 7–6, which shows the approximate annual contribution needed, as a percentage of payroll, of a savings plan that supplies postretirement increases of 3 percent a year in the pension benefit of an employee retiring at age 65. (The table assumes that rates of investment return and pay increases are equal.)

As would be expected, the percentage that must be contributed for the employee depends upon the age of entry into the plan and the number of savings plan contributions made on the employee's behalf. Thus, for example, if the basic pension plan generates a pension of approximately 40 percent of final pay, a contribution each year of 2.8 percent of pay would be required for an employee age 35 on entry into the plan; 4.3 percent if entry is at age 45.

A typical savings plan permits employee contributions of up to 6 percent of pay with a 50 percent matching employer contribution. Thus, under such a plan, the maximum contribution would be 9 percent. The solid line drawn across Table 7–6 indicates that such a contribution level could produce a 3 percent automatic pension increase for all combinations of entry ages and pension benefit levels, except for an employee entering a 50 percent plan at or after age 55. The broken line indicates the results for a savings plan with a maximum employee contribution of 4.5 percent, matched 50 percent by the employer, for a total maximum contribution of 6.75 percent.

Again, the use of a savings plan in this manner represents a long-term solution and provides no assistance for current pensioners, active employees who are close to retirement when the plan is adopted, or those employees who do not elect to participate. Nevertheless, it is a mechanism with significant potential for meeting the problem of inflation.

TABLE 7–6: Percentage of Pay that Must Be Contributed to Achieve 3 Percent Annual Increase in Pension (annual savings plan contribution as a percentage of payroll)

Entry Age	Annual Pension as a Percentage of Final Pay			
	20 Percent	30 Percent	40 Percent	50 Percent
35	1.4	2.1	2.8	3.5
40	1.7	2.6	3.4	4.3
45	2.1	3.2	4.3	5.3
				(6.75% plan)
50	2.8	4.3	5.7	7.1
				(9% plan)
55	4.3	6.4	8.5	10.6

SUMMARY

The extent to which pensioners have suffered a real loss in purchasing power because of inflation is less than clear because of the nature of the CPI and its questionable relevancy to the different circumstances and needs of the retired population. For low- and middle-income wage earners, substantial relief has been provided through legislated and automatic increases in income tax free social security benefits. Nevertheless, it is apparent that some loss of purchasing power has occurred and that the "cost" of this has been borne by the pensioners in those situations where private plan benefits do not exist or where they have not been improved. In many other situations, employers have voluntarily assumed at least part of this cost and have increased benefits to pensioners, usually on an ad hoc basis. The nature of the private plan commitment is such that legislating mandatory protection against inflation for pensioners seems neither appropriate nor equitable. The government could assume a role in addressing this problem by making indexed bonds or annuities available or by providing tax credits and by taking the value of indexed benefits into account when setting pay levels for government employees.

The majority of defined benefit plans provide for a benefit based on the pensioner's pay close to the time of retirement, thus reflecting both increases in the CPI and improvements in the standard of living that have taken place prior to retirement. Collectively bargained plans of the dollar-per-month variety are frequently updated by means of the collective bargaining process. Benefits received under career-pay plans, which are fewer in number, are updated frequently to achieve the same general result but under conditions that give the employer control over the timing and extent of the additional costs associated with such improvements. Defined contribution plans reflect some degree of inflationary pressure in that contributions (currently and prospectively but not retroactively) either are made or allocated on a basis related to pay. However, because these plans often permit equity investments and because investment results inure to the benefit (or loss) of employees, some possible long-term protection against inflation exists if the equity market moves in the same general direction as prices. Also, some defined contribution plans provide a degree of protection against preretirement inflation by means of final-pay minimum benefit formulas or through the use of floor plans.

With the exception of governmental plans and those adopted by private colleges and universities, the use of automatic adjustment techniques for handling postretirement inflation is relatively uncommon. By far, the discretionary or ad hoc adjustment technique is the most prevalent method used by private industry. The major reason for this has been the unwillingness to assume the unknown liability involved in an open-ended commitment to increase benefits for postretirement inflation. In addition to retaining control over cost considerations, the discretionary approach also permits the employer to retain control over the design of the increase.

Additional protection against postretirement inflation also is provided by many employers under programs that continue some form of life insurance and/or medical expense coverage for pensioners.

The employer who is considering ways of alleviating the impact of inflation on the pension benefits of employees must resolve a number of complicated questions, while at the same time reconciling the viewpoints of groups with conflicting interests. In the near future, it is likely that most employers, if they do anything at all, will utilize traditional approaches with particular emphasis on discretionary or ad hoc adjustments. However, there is growing interest in the use of limited forms of automatic postretirement adjustment techniques, coupled with a growing interest in methods that involve employees in some form of direct cost sharing.

QUESTIONS FOR REVIEW

1. How does the effect of the automatic increase provision of social security change as final-pay levels go up?
2. Will higher paid pensioners lose purchasing power more or less rapidly than lower paid pensioners if the rate of inflation increases? Explain.
3. What argument is put forth by those in favor of requiring private pension plans to provide for automatic cost-of-living adjustments? What are the fallacies with this argument?
4. Describe how preretirement inflation would be treated in (a) dollar amount plans and (b) career-pay plans.
5. From the employer's viewpoint, what advantages are offered by a career-pay approach with periodic updates?
6. Describe two methods for treating the impact of preretirement inflation that may be adopted by employers who utilize the defined contribution approach.
7. Describe the potential advantages and disadvantages of an equity pension.
8. Describe how wage-related formulas may be used to treat the impact of postretirement inflation on pensioner income.
9. Describe the advantages and disadvantages associated with the use of a specified percentage formula.
10. Why might an employer adopt a discretionary rather than an automatic approach to pension increases?

QUESTIONS FOR DISCUSSION

1. Assume that you have been asked to prepare a report on the relative advantages and limitations of preparing a separate Consumer Price Index based solely on the buying habits of retirees that would be used to determine the cost-of-living adjustments paid to retirees. What are the major points that need to be covered in such a report?

2. Assume that you have been asked to prepare a report to determine if the current system of benefit adjustments for private pension plans could be replaced by automatic benefit increases tied to specific price indicators. What are the major points that need to be covered in such a report?

3. An employer asks you to comment on a new concept of providing pension adjustments for retirees. Under this concept, employees are provided with an option to receive benefits in the form of an increasing annuity. Describe the plan design considerations of such an approach and its relative advantages and limitations.

8

Cost and Funding Considerations

A pension plan, in its simplest form, is a promise by the employer to pay a periodic benefit (usually for life) to employees who meet the requirements set forth in the plan. For a given pension benefit, the amount of annual benefit payments under the plan depends upon the number of retired workers. The number of retired workers, in turn, depends upon the rate at which already retired workers die and the rate at which new employees are added to the retirement rolls. Since the average life expectancy for a 65-year-old is about 15 years, it is quite likely that for some time after the plan is established, more new members are added to the retired employee group than are removed from the group as a result of death. Therefore, under a typical plan, the aggregate annual benefit payout should increase for a substantial number of years after the inception of the plan. The annual benefit payout continues to increase until a point is reached at which the size of the retired employee group tends to stabilize; that is, the point at which the number of retired workers dying is about equal to the number of new additions to the retired group.

However, when the employer funds the plan, the pattern of the annual contributions under the plan will differ from the benefit payout pattern because, as indicated earlier, the benefit payout pattern for a given level of pension benefit is dependent upon the number of retired workers eligible for benefits during each year and will be the same regardless of the manner in which contributions are made.

The objective of this chapter is to consider some of the important implications of funding and to acquaint the reader with the factors affecting the *ultimate cost* of a pension plan, apart from specific plan provisions and benefits. Particular reference is made to the various actuarial assumptions and cost methods that can be used in determining the incidence and amount of pension costs. The discussion later in this chapter assumes a fixed set of plan specifications and also assumes, for the purpose of simplicity, that the plan is noncontributory.

ESTIMATED COST VERSUS ULTIMATE COST

The only way to determine the true cost of a pension plan would be to wait until the last retired employee has died, add up all the benefit payments and administrative expenses that have been paid since the inception of the plan, and subtract the investment earnings. The ultimate cost of the plan could then be stated as the benefits paid plus administrative expenses less investment earnings over the total life of the plan.

However, no business firm would ever establish a pension plan if the cost of the plan were completely uncertain until the plan is terminated at some date in the distant future. The obvious solution is that although the specific ultimate cost is unknown, actuaries are able to estimate the ultimate cost of the plan with reasonable accuracy and thus arrive at a level of estimated plan contributions. To do this, assumptions must be made regarding the factors that affect the plan's ultimate cost. In subsequent years, adjustments in the estimated amounts of contributions required may have to be made, based on comparisons between the actual experience under the plan and the assumed experience. Experience more favorable than expected permits a reduction in future contributions. Conversely, adverse experience under the plan requires an increase in future contributions.

The point that pension cost projections are *estimates* and not *actual cost* figures cannot be overstressed. A moment's reflection regarding the nature of a pension plan should make this point quite clear. Assume, for example, that a pension plan provides employees with a retirement benefit only after attainment of age 65 and completion of a minimum of 5 years of service with the employer. It is obvious that not all current employees of the firm will be entitled to a retirement benefit under the plan. Some employees may die and others may quit, be laid off, or become disabled prior to age 65. Other employees may defer their retirement beyond age 65; and, also, the number of years that retired workers will live cannot be predicted with certainty. Furthermore, in the case of funded plans, the rate of investment income to be earned in the future on accumulated assets in the pension fund can only be estimated.

But, how does the pension actuary make an estimate of the ultimate cost of a pension plan? The first step is to make estimates of the various components of the ultimate cost; that is, estimates of the benefits paid, the expenses, and the investment return expected. The estimate of benefits paid depends on three things: the benefit provisions of the pension plan; the characteristics of the participants in the plan (age, sex, salary, and length of service); and the actuarial assumptions used to predict the amount of future benefit payments. The benefit provisions and characteristics of plan participants are unique to the plan being valued, while the actuarial assumptions are determined by the pension actuary valuing the plan. Selection of the appropriate actuarial assumptions for predicting future benefit payments along with actuarial assumptions as to expenses and investment return are discussed in the next section of this chapter.

Once an estimate of the ultimate cost of the plan is determined, the next step is to determine the contributions required to pay for the estimated cost in an orderly manner. One of several actuarial cost methods will be used to allocate the costs to the various years and will be discussed in the next chapter.

CHOICE OF ASSUMPTIONS

Two important points should be made regarding the choice of assumptions for the calculation of estimated pension costs.

First, the flexibility available in choosing a particular set of actuarial assumptions depends in large part upon the funding instrument involved.[1] The greatest flexibility is available under trust fund plans and under unallocated group pension contracts such as a group deposit administration contract. If the employer has competent advice, the assumptions used will be reasonable for the type of plan and the characteristics of the employee group covered. Fully insured individual policy plans and group permanent and group deferred annuity instruments offer the employer the least choice in cost assumptions, since the insurance company effectively establishes the assumptions to be used by its premium rates.

Second, the choice of a particular set of assumptions does not normally alter the ultimate cost of the plan. The choice of assumptions will affect the cost allocated to a given year, but the ultimate cost is primarily dependent on actual experience over the life of the pension plan. Obviously, the ages at which employees retire or the rate at which they die or leave their jobs is not conditioned by the assumptions in these areas made by the pension actuary. The relative magnitude of actuarial gains and losses under the plan will vary, given different original assumptions, but the end result will be an approximately similar ultimate cost picture except to the extent that investment earnings are affected by the incidence of contributions produced by the funding assumptions chosen. This conclusion does not apply fully in the case of plans funded with individual policies. In the case of individual

---

[1]Funding instruments are described in Chapter 14.

contracts, there is a certain degree of pooling of experience among the whole class of business. For example, the mortality or expense experience under a particular plan is not directly reflected in the insurance company's dividends paid to that group, since the dividend scale for individual policies is determined by the experience for that class of business as a whole. There is also an element of pooling in some group plans.

COST ASSUMPTIONS

As discussed above, one approach in considering the factors affecting the cost of a pension plan is to relate these factors to the formula for determining the ultimate cost of the plan; that is, benefits paid plus administrative expenses less investment earnings.

Benefits Paid

Number of Employees Retiring.   The amount of benefits paid under a plan depends upon several factors. The first factor is the number of workers who will ultimately be entitled to receive benefits under the plan. The number of employees who will be eligible for benefits will depend on four factors: (1) mortality rates among active employees, (2) rates and duration of disabilities among active employees under a plan that offers a disability benefit, (3) layoffs and voluntary terminations of employment, and (4) rates of retirement at different ages. Let us now turn to a consideration of each of these cost factors.

Mortality.   The higher the rate of mortality among active employees, the lower will be the cost of retirement benefits under the plan. However, if a participant is entitled to a preretirement death benefit, this will increase the cost of the plan, as additional benefits are being provided.

Mortality among active employees can be an important cost-reducing factor in those plans providing little or no death benefit. This is particularly true for small plans, where a few deaths can have a significant impact on the cost of the plan.

Actuaries generally use the same mortality table in projecting mortality among both active and retired employees.[2]

---

[2]One exception is individual policy combination plans. Here, an annuity table is used for mortality after retirement and, often, a Commissioners Standard Ordinary (CSO) mortality table for mortality prior to retirement. CSO tables are based on the mortality experience of purchasers of life insurance and generally indicate higher rates of mortality at all ages than the rates indicated in annuity tables. Conservatism in the construction of mortality tables suggests the use of higher-than-expected mortality rates for insurance tables and lower-than-expected mortality for annuity tables.

Several mortality tables are available for pension cost calculations. Projections have also been developed to reflect the probable continuing improvements in mortality. Thus, as improvements in mortality occur, or are expected to occur, the actuary often uses a group annuity mortality table with the projection that he or she believes to be appropriate for the given case. Mortality gains or losses will develop from year to year, and the actuary can keep abreast of the experience through subsequent modifications of the mortality assumption. Table 8–1 shows the probability of surviving to 65 under the 1937 Standard Annuity Table, the 1951 Group Annuity Table, and the 1971 Group Annuity Mortality Table. Obviously, the results are considerably different, which indicates the impact on estimated costs caused by the mortality assumption chosen by the actuary.

The question is often raised whether a mortality assumption should be used in calculating the amount of contributions to be paid into a conversion fund under combination plans — particularly those plans covering a small group of employees.[3] Pension practitioners seem to be divided in their opinions on this point. Some planners prefer to use a mortality assumption in these cases, while others believe that the size of the covered group generally involved in plans of this type is too small to permit the expectations to be realized. If the expected mortality among a small group of employees does not materialize, the employer will be faced with the need for additional contributions in future years. Those favoring the use of a mortality assumption in these situations argue that its use results in a lower initial contribution requirement, which might be best suited to the current financial needs of some employers, and that any actuarial losses due to the use

TABLE 8–1: Probability of Surviving
to Age 65 for Males

Age	1937 Standard Annuity	1951 GAT	1971 GAT
20	.698	.776	.809
25	.703	.779	.812
30	.709	.782	.814
35	.718	.787	.818
40	.730	.793	.824
45	.749	.803	.832
50	.778	.822	.848
55	.821	.856	.876
60	.890	.910	.922

[3]A combination plan is an arrangement under which two funding instruments are used, with a portion of the contributions placed in a trust fund (or a conversion fund held by an insurer) and the balance paid to an insurance company as contributions under a group annuity contract or as premiums on individual life insurance or annuity contracts. The entire pension for each participant is generally paid by the insurance company, with transfers from the trust fund or conversion fund being made as required.

of such an assumption may be offset by actuarial gains due to severance of employment. Furthermore, it is argued that if the expected mortality is realized, the use of a mortality assumption produces a more realistic projection of future costs. Although there is merit in the latter position, the pension planner should clearly point out to the employer the full implications of using a mortality assumption with relatively small groups.

Rate and Duration of Disability. If a pension plan offers a disability benefit, cost projections for that plan should include a disability assumption. The plan actuary must establish two sets of probabilities in evaluating the cost of providing a disability benefit. First, a rate of occurrence (frequency) of disabilities of the nature entitling the disabled employee to a benefit under the plan must be estimated. The rates of disability will vary with the plan's definition of disability, the age and sex composition of the covered employee group, the nature of the employment, and the general level of economic activity. At the inception of a plan, the disability experience projected for a particular plan may be based on insurance company data, or on the actual experience of the employer, or on the experience of a large company in the same or a comparable industry. Ultimately, the plan's own experience may be used as a yardstick.

Having determined the probable incidence of disability, the actuary must then project the duration of the disability. The duration of the disability will be affected by reemployment opportunities, which in turn are related to the nature of the employment and general economic conditions. The duration of the benefit period also will be affected by the mortality rates among disabled workers.

It can be seen, then, that the ability to project future disability rates is a difficult task. The actuary must keep a careful check on the actual disability experience evolving under the plan.

Turnover. Employees who voluntarily quit or who are laid off represent a cost-reducing factor to a pension fund, assuming the absence of full vesting. Also, as indicated above, in plans that do not provide death or disability benefits, terminations of employment due to these causes also represent cost-reducing factors. In the latter case, separate assumptions may be made regarding mortality, disability, and turnover; or, as is quite common, the plan actuary may use one set of termination rates covering all causes of termination of employment among nonretired workers.

TABLE 8–2: Present Value of $1 of Monthly Benefit Beginning at Age 65

Male Age	(1) No Turnover	(2) Scale A	(3) Scale B	Ratio (2) ÷ (1)	Ratio (3) ÷ (1)
25	$ 8.78	$ 4.86	$ 2.64	55%	30%
35	15.85	13.03	10.67	82	67
45	28.87	28.22	27.59	98	96

Source: Based on 1971 GAM, 6 percent interest.

Table 8–2 shows the effect on costs using three different turnover assumptions. The yearly withdrawal rates under Scale A and Scale B are as follows:

Male Age	Scale A	Scale B
25	5.00%	10.00%
35	2.50	5.00
45	0.75	1.50
50	0	0

As indicated in these examples, most turnover tables assume a greater withdrawal rate at the younger ages than at the older ages, which normally would be the case.

The problems of developing accurate turnover rates for a specific plan are obvious. Future withdrawal rates vary among employers and industries and with changing economic conditions. The age composition of the covered group has a significant impact on turnover rates. It is generally recognized that turnover rates for younger workers are very high. Turnover rates also vary depending on the length of service of employees. Furthermore, working conditions and the personnel policies and benefit programs of a particular employer may affect turnover rates in that firm. Lastly, economic recessions or periods of prosperity may significantly alter turnover rates. During periods of recession, employees will be less likely to quit, while the rate of layoffs will probably increase. The opposite situation generally prevails during periods of economic prosperity.

The concept of turnover is broader for multiemployer plans than it is for single-employer pension funds. In the former, the employee's coverage is terminated only if he or she fails to be reemployed by a participating employer within a specified time period, usually one or two years. In the skilled trades, withdrawal from the industry is less likely than separation from an individual employer. One of the basic assumptions justifying the existence of a multiemployer pension arrangement is the high degree of job mobility of the covered employees. But it is also assumed that there is a tendency for employees to be reemployed within the scope of coverage of the plan.

It is not surprising, therefore, that two actuaries may recommend considerably different withdrawal rates for the same plan. The choice of turnover assumption must rest, in the final analysis, on the sound judgment of the actuary. This judgment is based on the characteristics of the employee group, the factors discussed above, and the actuary's overall experience in pension cost projections. Some turnover tables have been developed to guide pension consultants.[4]

---

[4]See, for example, T. F. Crocker, H. M. Sarason, and B. W. Straight, *Actuaries Pension Handbook* (Los Angeles: Pension Publications, 1957).

These tables are of assistance for initial cost calculations, and adjustments in assumed turnover rates can be made as the actual experience under the plan evolves.

The question arises whether a turnover assumption should be used in calculating the level of annual contributions to be made under a plan using an unallocated funding instrument (including the conversion fund under a combination plan) when the plan covers a relatively small number of employees. The arguments for and against the use of a turnover assumption in these cases are somewhat similar to the arguments set forth earlier regarding the advisability of a mortality assumption under these plans. There is one more argument against use of a turnover assumption, and that is the fact that turnover is even less predictable than mortality for relatively small groups of employees. However, those pension planners who take the opposite stand say that there will obviously be some turnover in a plan (where there may be no mortality) and to ignore it is not to be realistic.

Rate of Retirement. In estimating the cost of pension benefits, one must make an assumption regarding the ages at which individuals will retire under the plan.

For those plans that allow retirement at ages other than the normal retirement age, it would be appropriate to make an assumption about the percentage of people retiring at each age (just as the turnover assumption varies by age). However, for practical reasons, most actuaries assume that all employees retire at one age.

The higher the retirement age, the lower will be the cost of a given amount of retirement benefit. For example, if an employee decides to work to age 65 rather than retiring at age 62, there is an additional three-year period during which the employee may die, with the resulting possibility that the employee will never receive retirement benefits. More importantly, the requirement of retiring at 65 will reduce the length of the benefit period. In most plans, offsetting these two factors is the fact that the individual will continue to accrue benefits and hence will be entitled to a larger basic pension.

An actuary generally will use a retirement age assumption lower than the normal retirement age specified in the plan when the plan provides some form of subsidized early retirement benefit (i.e., an early retirement benefit that is greater than the actuarial equivalent of the normal retirement benefit) and when it is expected that many employees will, in fact, retire early.

It is not unusual to find that some employees defer retirement beyond the normal retirement age. Thus, it may be logical to assume in cost estimates that the actual average retirement age is higher than the normal retirement age. This will tend to lower the estimated costs for the plan. Although not typical, some plans provide actuarially equivalent (larger) benefits to persons deferring retirement beyond normal retirement age. In these plans, no discount should be reflected in the cost calculations for postponed retirements.

Length of Benefit Period.   In addition to the number of employees retiring, the amount of benefit paid under the plan is affected by the length of time that retired workers receive their pension benefits (or the length of time payments will be continued under the normal form to a beneficiary of the retired worker after his or her death). The length of the benefit period depends upon the longevity of retired workers and the normal annuity form. Therefore, an assumption must be made regarding mortality among retired lives. As indicated earlier, the mortality table used for retired lives is generally identical to the table used for active lives, except in the case of individual policy plans.

Benefit Formula.   The last factor affecting the total amount paid under the plan is the amount of pension paid to each retired worker. It goes with out saying that the higher the benefit level, the greater will be the cost of the plan.

However, projecting benefit levels is more difficult under some benefit formulas than under others. The least difficult formula is one that provides a flat benefit for all retired workers, for example, a $100-a-month benefit. On the other hand, if the benefit formula calls for a pension benefit related to compensation, cost projections may include an assumption regarding expected future increases in the salaries of covered employees. For example, if a plan provides a pension benefit of 1 percent of salary per year of covered service, future increases in salary will increase benefit levels and, therefore, the cost of the plan.

The decision on the size of the salary progression assumption is an extremely important one, because of its dramatic impact on the level of projected costs. Other things being equal, the use of a salary progression assumption substantially increases cost estimates, but the absence of such an assumption may significantly understate future plan costs. The substantial impact on a cost estimate that results from use of a salary progression can be illustrated as follows: if a salary progression in the future is at the rate of 5 percent a year, the employee hired at age 20 for $10,000 a year would be receiving about $90,000 a year at age 65.

Prior to 1975, social security benefits and the maximum taxable wage base only changed by action of Congress, but commencing in 1975, social security benefits were automatically adjusted for changes in the cost of living while the maximum taxable wage base was adjusted to reflect changes in average wages in the country. Therefore, in the case of plans that are integrated with social security benefits, it is appropriate to project future levels of social security benefits or maximum taxable wage bases.

Also, in the case of negotiated plans providing a flat benefit per year of service, there is generally no advance provision for future increases in the unit benefit amount, and, in fact, current IRS regulations do not allow an assumption of future increases. It is generally recognized that benefit levels will be increased periodically due to inflationary pressures, but recognition is not given to this fact in cost projections until increases are actually negotiated.

Expenses

The expenses of administering the pension plan must be added to the benefits paid in arriving at the ultimate cost of the plan. The expense assumption used depends on the type of administration and the funding instrument involved. Under individual policy plans and some group pension contracts, the insurance company includes a loading for expenses in the gross premiums charged for purchased benefits. The expense loading is largest under individual policy plans and decreases considerably under group pension contracts. Additionally, some administrative fees necessitated by ERISA may be charged separately from the gross insurance premium.

In the case of trust fund plans, the employer may pay the actuarial, legal, administrative, and investment expenses associated with the plan separately from the contribution payments to the plan. Nevertheless, these expenses must be added to the amount of benefit payment in arriving at the ultimate cost of the plan, even though they are not included in the actual cost estimates.

Possible differences in the handling of expenses, then, must be recognized in comparisons of cost projections involving different funding instruments.

Investment Return

The investment income earned on the accumulated assets of a funded pension plan reduces the ultimate cost of the plan. Thus, the higher the investment return assumption, other things being equal, the lower will be the projected cost of the plan. For example, under one mortality table and assuming a 5 percent loading factor, the single-premium sum required for a 45-year-old to purchase a pure life annuity of $1 a month beginning at age 65 is $30.27 using a 6 percent investment return assumption, as compared with a single premium of $23.48 using a 7 percent investment return assumption. Thus, in this example, an increase of 1 percent in the investment return rate assumption results in a reduction of about 22 percent in the estimated cost of the plan. For a given plan, the impact of a change in the investment return assumption on the estimated cost of the plan depends on the age distribution of participants and their relative benefit credits.

The investment return assumption used should recognize the total anticipated rate of return including investment income, dividends, and realized and unrealized capital appreciation (or depreciation). Therefore, selection of an appropriate investment return assumption should take into account the size of the fund, the anticipated investment policy of the plan trustees, current and projected long-term rates of return, and any other factors that might affect the future pattern of investment earnings of the fund. The choice of an appropriate rate of investment return is particularly difficult if a sizable portion of the assets is invested in common stocks, since these investments are subject to significant fluctuations in value. In addition to having an impact on the selection of an investment return assumption, investments in equities raises the rather difficult issue of when to recognize unrealized capital gains or losses.

For a number of reasons, current market values of securities have seldom been used in actuarial valuations. Two of the most important reasons are: (1) market values will generally be relatively high in periods of high corporate earnings, thereby reducing the apparent need for contributions (and also the tax deductible limits) at times when the employer may be best able to make large contributions toward the pension fund (in periods of low corporate earnings the reverse will often be true, with required contributions and tax deductible limits increased at a time when the employer's capacity to contribute is at a minimum); and (2) because of market value fluctuations, to measure a plan's unfunded liabilities on any given date by the current market values of the fund's equities could produce a very irregular funding pattern— the antithesis of the orderly procedure, which is an essential characteristic of a satisfactory pension funding program.[5]

In spite of the above objections, current market values are used in some situations. In fact, the Internal Revenue Code requires that the value of a defined benefit plan's assets shall be determined by any reasonable actuarial valuation method that takes into account fair market value. Money purchase plans must base assets solely on the basis of fair market value. Generally, the IRS has taken the position that this condition is satisfied if the asset valuation method generates an asset value that is within 80 percent of fair market value.[6] Obviously, fair market value alone would be an acceptable method. Market values also often are used in valuing the conversion fund under a combination plan.

A number of approaches have been developed to overcome the drawbacks noted above to the use of current market value. For example, to

---

[5]William F. Marples, *Actuarial Aspects of Pension Security* (Homewood, Ill.: Richard D. Irwin, 1965), p. 107.

[6]The valuation of assets rules do not apply to bonds (or other evidences of indebtedness) if a plan administrator makes a special election to value these instruments on an amortized basis.

minimize the effects of short-term market fluctuations, a moving average (e.g., a five-year average) of market values may be used. Another method used to minimize such fluctuations is to recognize appreciation annually, based on an expected long-range growth rate (e.g., 3 percent) applied to the cost (adjusted for appreciation previously so recognized) of common stocks. When this method is used, the total cost and recognized appreciation (or depreciation) usually are required to be within a specified percentage (e.g., 80 percent) of the market value.

SUMMARY

Historically, pension actuaries have used actuarial assumptions considered reasonable "in the aggregate" while each assumption might not be "individually realistic." For example, when making cost estimates where the benefit is related to final five-year average earnings, a zero percent salary increase assumption might be used, but the corresponding understatement in costs is offset by a conservative (low) investment return assumption.

Beginning in 1988, however, actuaries will be required to use actuarial assumptions that are individually realistic. As can be seen from the above discussion, the choice of actuarial assumptions has a significant impact on the *estimated* costs of a pension plan. It must be repeated, however, that the choice of a particular set of assumptions generally has little effect on the *ultimate* cost of the plan. As with the choice of an actuarial cost method discussed in the next chapter, the choice of assumptions can have an impact on the incidence of plan costs. As gains or losses arise in the future the annual contribution account will be affected, even though the ultimate cost of the plan is unchanged. Table 8–3 illustrates the impact of varying sets of assumptions on the cost estimates for an actual plan. The plan provides a benefit of 1 percent of compensation per year of service, with a normal retirement age of 65. The individual level cost method with a supplemental liability was used to project the cost of the plan. It is assumed that the supplemental liability will be funded over a 30-year period. The nature of the various actuarial cost methods is discussed in detail in the next chapter.

Unfortunately, an employer is sometimes unduly influenced by these cost estimates in the choice of a funding instrument. In the case illustrated in Table 8–3, proposal 6 may be misinterpreted as the lowest cost arrangement available to the employer. It may well turn out that one of the other cost projections is in fact closer to the cost that is eventually experienced under the plan. The important factors that an employer should consider in the choice of a funding instrument are examined at length in Chapter 14.

TABLE 8–3: Effect of Varying Sets of Actuarial Assumptions on Estimated Cost of a Pension Plan

Assumptions	Estimated Annual Cost	
1. *a*. 5 percent investment return	1. Normal cost	$43,331
b. 5 percent salary	Initial Supplemental Liability	
c. Light turnover	($506,805)	31,398
d. 1971 Group Annuity Mortality		
Table with projection	Total cost	$74,729
e. Average retirement age 65		
2. *a*. 5 percent investment return	2. Normal cost	37,558
b. 4 percent salary	Initial Supplemental Liability	
c. Light turnover	($479,144)	29,685
d. 1971 GAM with projection	Total cost	$67,243
e. Average retirement age 65		
3. *a*. 6 percent investment return	3. Normal cost	29,302
b. 4 percent salary	Initial Supplemental Liability	
c. Light turnover	($408,317)	27,985
d. 1971 GAM with projection	Total cost	$57,287
e. Average retirement age 65		
4. *a*. 6 percent investment return	4. Normal cost	26,130
b. 4 percent salary	Initial Supplemental Liability	
c. Heavy turnover	($412,198)	28,251
d. 1971 GAM with projection	Total cost	$54,381
e. Average retirement age 65		
5. *a*. 6 percent investment return	5. Normal cost	23,407
b. 4 percent salary	Initial Supplemental Liability	
c. Heavy turnover	($369,737)	25,341
d. 1971 GAM with projection	Total cost	$48,748
e. Average retirement age 67		
6. *a*. 6 percent investment return	6. Normal cost	21,894
b. 4 percent salary	Initial Supplemental Liability	
c. Heavy turnover	($346,779)	23,767
d. 1951 Group Annuity Table	Total cost	$45,661
e. Average retirement age 67		

QUESTIONS FOR REVIEW

1. Can cost uncertainties be eliminated by using a fully insured individual policy approach? Explain.
2. What factors enter into the determination of the number of employees who will be eligible for benefits under a pension plan?
3. Describe how the type of benefit formula used may present difficulties in projecting the costs of a pension plan.
4. How does administrative expense relate to ultimate pension plan costs? What are some of the major administrative costs?

5. Does the federal law require the use of current market value in the valuation of securities used to fund pension plans? Explain.
6. Describe the approaches used to overcome the drawbacks of using current market value in the valuation of pension plan assets held in the form of securities.
8. Does the choice of an actuarial cost method affect the ultimate cost of a pension plan? Explain.
9. Explain how the investment rate assumption affects the ultimate cost of a pension plan.

QUESTIONS FOR DISCUSSION

1. Assume that you are asked to set assumptions for a new defined benefit pension plan. Describe the procedure you would follow.
2. How often should the assumptions established in Question 1 be updated?
3. Comment on how you would expect each of the following to influence retirement age: (a) changes in social security, (b) government regulation, such as the Age Discrimination in Employment Act, (c) early retirement incentives, and (d) cost-of-living adjustments to retirees.

9

Cost and Funding Considerations (continued)

BUDGETING PENSION COSTS

The discussion in Chapter 8 set forth the various factors that affect the ultimate cost of a pension plan and how the choice of actuarial assumptions can significantly affect the estimated costs. What is still needed, however, is some actuarial technique to determine how the estimated costs of the plan are to be spread over future years. These techniques are referred to as *actuarial cost methods*. More specifically, an actuarial cost method is a particular technique for establishing the amounts and incidence of the normal costs and supplemental costs pertaining to the benefits (or benefits and expenses) of a pension plan.[1]

Two approaches have been used to finance pension plans in the past. Before describing the different actuarial cost methods, it might be helpful to review the current disbursement approach and the terminal funding approach. Though basically no longer permitted by the Internal Revenue Code for qualified plans, knowledge of these two approaches should provide a better basis for understanding advance funding required by law, a discussion of which follows later.

---

[1]The terminology pertaining to the actuarial aspects of pension planning reflects, wherever possible, the thinking of the Committee on Pension and Profit Sharing Terminology, sponsored jointly by the American Risk and Insurance Association and the Pension Research Council, University of Pennsylvania.

Current Disbursement Approach

Under the current disbursement approach, the employer pays each retired worker's monthly pension as each payment becomes due. There is no accumulation of pension funds in an irrevocable trust or through a contract with an insurance company.

An illustration of the current disbursement approach would be a supplemental executive retirement plan (described in Chapter 24) under which the employer promises all employees with at least 10 years of service a lifetime pension of $100 a month beginning at age 65. If no employees are eligible for benefits during the first two years after the plan is established, the employer would not make any pension plan payments during that period. The employer's pension outlay of $100 a month begins with the retirement of the first eligible employee; the outlay increases by that amount as each new retired worker is added to the pension rolls and decreases by $100 a month as each retired worker dies. These monthly pension outlays are provided out of current operating income and, in effect, are treated as a part of wage costs.

Terminal Funding

Under the terminal funding approach, the employer sets aside for each employee, on the date the latter retires, a lump-sum amount sufficient to provide the monthly pension benefit promised under the plan. The lump-sum amount needed to provide the promised benefit is a function of the amount of benefit assumptions as to the expected benefit period, and the rate of investment return expected to be earned on the investment of this principal sum. For example, assuming mortality rates will occur in accordance with the 1971 Group Annuity Mortality Table (for males) and assuming the rate of investment return will be 6 percent, the sum needed to provide $100 a month for life to a male, age 65, is $11,122.[2]

If the mortality and investment return assumptions prove to be accurate, the principal plus investment earnings will be sufficient, on the average, to provide the $100-a-month benefit.

The employer, therefore, sets aside the appropriate single-premium sum as each employee retires. Like the current disbursement approach, terminal funding does not require the employer to make any contributions on behalf of employees who are still actively at work.

The benefits can be funded through the purchase of single-premium

---

[2]An expense assumption is ignored in the above calculation, since the authors are interested solely in illustrating the concept of terminal funding. In practice, the expenses of administering the benefit would be taken into account in the single-premium rate charged by an insurance company or in determining the amount to be set aside in a trust fund under noninsured plans, if expenses associated with the plan are paid from the trust fund. Normally, the expenses under trust fund plans are paid directly by the employer and, therefore, no expense allowance is required.

annuities from insurance companies, or the employer can transfer the estimated single-premium sums to a trust fund.

The reader should not confuse the concept of terminal funding with the
practice of split funding that is prevalent in the pension field. The term
split funding, as it is commonly used in pension planning, refers to the use
of two different funding agencies in administering the assets of a pension
plan. For example, a plan may provide that contributions on behalf of
active employees are to be administered by a corporate trustee. When an
employee retires, the trust agreement may require the corporate trustee to
withdraw from the trust fund and transfer to an insurance company the single-premium sum needed to purchase a life annuity equal to the monthly
pension earned by the employee under the terms of the pension plan. This
type of plan is considered to be an advance funded plan unless the
employer is paying to the corporate trustee an annual sum exactly equal to
the amount of single premiums needed to provide the benefits for workers
retiring each year—a highly unlikely situation.

Advance Funding

Under advance funding, the employer (and the employee, under contributory plans) sets aside funds on some systematic basis prior to the
employee's retirement date. Thus, periodic contributions are made on
behalf of the group of active employees during their working years. This
does not mean that each dollar of contributions is necessarily earmarked for
specific employees. As will be noted in subsequent chapters, contributions
are not allocated to specific employees under certain funding instruments;
for example, trust fund and group deposit administration plans. Thus, it is
true that in some plans using unallocated funding instruments, contributions in the early years may only be sufficient to provide lifetime benefits to
the first group of employees retiring under the plan. However, if contributions are continued on an advance funding basis, the accumulated assets in
the pension fund will soon exceed the aggregate single-premium sums
needed to provide benefits to those workers who are already retired. This
excess of pension assets, then, represents the advance funding of benefits
that have been accrued or credited to the active (nonretired) employees.

Pension plans operating on an advance funded basis are invariably qualified with the Internal Revenue Service. An employer is generally not willing to make advance contributions to an irrevocable trust fund unless it
receives the tax advantages of a qualified plan.

The three approaches to financing a pension plan can be illustrated
graphically as follows. Suppose it is desired to fund benefits of $100 a year
for a male employee, now age 40. For simplicity it is assumed benefits will
be paid from age 65 to age 80, with no benefits paid after age 80. In
Table 9–1, section A represents the benefit payments that will be made to
the individual from age 65 to age 80. The three approaches to financing his
benefit may now be examined.

TABLE 9–1: Illustration of Methods to Finance a Pension Plan for One Employee

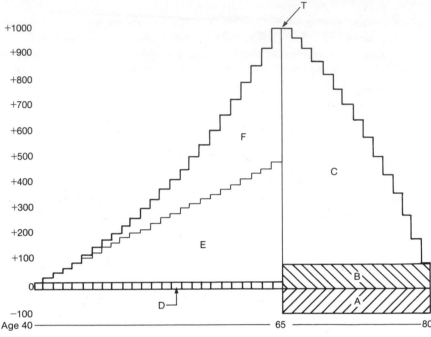

Legend: A = Benefit disbursements
B = Employer contributions under current disbursement approach
C = Assets remaining after disbursements
D = Annual contribution under advance funding approach
E = Accumulation of annual contribution under advance funding approach
F = Investment earnings under advance funding approach
T = Amount required at age 65 to fully fund benefit payable

1. Under the current disbursement approach, section B represents the contribution required by the employer—exactly equal to the benefit disbursements in section A.

2. Under terminal funding, the employer makes a contribution at age 65 equal to the amount indicated by the T. This amount is sufficient either to buy the benefit from an insurance company or to be deposited in a trust fund that, together with investment earnings, will be sufficient to pay the benefits. Section C represents the assets remaining in the trust fund at each year from age 65 to age 80.

3. Under advance funding, section D represents the annual contribution made by the employer at each age from 40 to 65, while section E represents the accumulation of these contributions over time. Section F represents investment earnings on the contributions. As can be seen, at age 65 the combination of accumulated employer contributions and investment earnings is equal to the amount required to fully fund the benefit at age 65 (the amount shown by T).

The relatively even distribution of annual pension outlays under advance funding produces a more equitable reduction of the firm's cash flow over the years. The pension is being provided to employees for the year of service rendered to the firm. Thus, it would seem that the funds available to the owners of the firm (e.g., stockholder dividends) should be reduced by pension contributions in an amount approximately equal to the present value of benefits accruing under the plan. It is true that credit for past service, offered at the inception of the plan, creates a problem. Since the plan was not in existence during those past service years, it is highly improbable that previous generations of owners would be willing to retroactively refund a portion of the funds they received from the firm. The next best solution seems to be to amortize past service cost in the first 20 or 25 years after the inception of the plan. ERISA requires that for new plans, past service costs must be amortized over no more than 30 years.

The accumulation of assets in a pension fund resulting from the advance funding of benefits serves as a buffer during periods of financial stress. During a period of low earnings or operating losses, an employer may find it advisable to reduce or eliminate pension contributions for a year or even a longer period. This can be done in those cases where the pension fund is of sufficient size that a temporary reduction of contributions does not violate the minimum funding requirements imposed by ERISA. It should be noted that this financing flexibility does not necessitate any reduction or termination of pension benefits.

Under advance funding, then, the plan actuary uses a set of assumptions and an actuarial cost method in estimating the annual cost of a plan. Annual contribution payments usually are based on these estimated annual costs. However, it should be noted that actual annual contribution payments need not be identical to the estimated annual costs generated by a given actuarial cost method. As will be noted in later chapters, the employer has some flexibility in the timing of contribution payments under unallocated funding instruments.

There are several different actuarial cost methods, each producing different patterns of annual costs under the plan. Having different actuarial cost methods to calculate annual pension costs is analogous to having different methods for determining the annual amount of depreciation of plant and equipment to charge against operations. The depreciation methods that can be used may produce different annual charges, but the total value of the building and equipment to be depreciated is constant regardless of the depreciation formula used. Similarly, the various actuarial cost methods will produce different levels of annual cost, but the choice of a particular actuarial cost method will not affect the ultimate cost of the plan. One important exception to the latter conclusion is the fact that if an actuarial cost method is chosen that produces higher initial contributions than other methods, then the asset accumulation will be greater (assuming a positive rate of return) in the early years of the plan, thereby producing greater investment income. An increase in investment income will decrease the ultimate cost of the plan.[3]

If the choice of actuarial cost method usually has little effect on the ultimate cost of a pension plan (after taking into consideration interest, and so on), what factors determine which method will be used in calculating the amount and incidence of pension contributions? The answer to this question will become more apparent after the following discussion of the specific cost methods. However, the reader may find it helpful to keep in mind that the choice of a specific actuarial cost method is influenced to a great degree by the degree of flexibility in annual contribution payments desired by the employer and available under the particular funding instrument used.

ACTUARIAL COST METHODS

Actuarial cost methods can be broadly classified into (1) accrued benefit, and (2) projected benefit cost methods.[4]

As further explained below, the class into which a particular cost method falls depends upon whether, for cost determination purposes, an employee's benefits under the pension plan are deemed to "accrue" in direct relation to years of service or are viewed as a single "projected" total.

Most actuarial cost methods break down the total actuarial cost into the normal cost and the supplemental cost of the plan. The normal cost of the plan is the amount of annual cost, determined in accordance with a particular actuarial cost method, attributable to the given year of the plan's operation.

Most plans provide credit for service rendered prior to the inception date of the plan. If the normal cost under the particular cost method is calculated on the assumption that annual costs have been paid or accrued from the earliest date of credited service (when in fact they have not), the plan starts out with a supplemental liability. At the inception of the plan, the supplemental liability, often called the actuarial or past service liability, arises from the fact that credit for past service is granted, or part of the total benefit is imputed, to years prior to the inception of this plan. The annual contribution normally will be equal to the normal cost of the plan plus at least enough of a contribution to amortize the supplemental liability over a 30-year period. If it is desired to fund this supplemental liability in a more rapid manner (10 years is generally the minimum period over

---

[3]More precisely, the timing of contribution payments has additional cost implications if federal income tax rates change; or if alternative uses of capital vary over time; or if investment return rates vary over the life of the plan.

[4]Parts of the material in this section were drawn from Joseph J. Melone, "Actuarial Cost Methods—New Pension Terminology," *Journal of Insurance* 30, no. 3 (September 1963), pp. 456–64.

which it can be funded on a deductible basis), larger annual contributions will be required. The portion of the annual cost applied toward the reduction of the supplemental liability is referred to as the plan's supplemental cost. As the plan continues in operation, the size of the supplemental liability normally will change. In addition to normal changes in the supplemental liability that may occur as a result of the actuarial method being used, these changes in the size of the supplemental liability may result from variations in benefit formulas, deviations of actual from expected experience, and changes in the actuarial assumptions or in the actuarial cost method used in subsequent normal cost calculations. Offsetting any increase in the supplemental liability will be any unanticipated increase in the size of pension fund assets. The unfunded supplemental liability, then, is the difference between the supplemental liability and any assets that may have accumulated under the plan as a result of prior contributions.

Accrued Benefit Cost Method

An accrued benefit cost method is one under which the actuarial costs are based directly upon benefits accrued to the date of cost determination, such benefits being determined either by the terms of the plan or by some assumed allocation of total prospective benefits to years of service. To determine the actuarial cost of the plan for a given year, the method assumes that a precisely determinable unit of benefit is associated with that year of a participant's credited service.

This method of calculating the actuarial costs of pension plans is sometimes referred to as the single-premium, unit credit, unit cost, or step-rate method.

The accrued benefit method is limited to those plans that provide a unit benefit type of formula based on career average compensation (for example, a percentage of each year's compensation), or a specified dollar amount for each year of credited service.[5] Under these benefit formulas, a precisely determinable unit of benefit is associated with each year of a participant's credited service.

Although best adapted to those plans that use a unit benefit type of formula, the accrued benefit cost method also can be used when the plan provides a composite benefit based on the participant's total period of credited service. For example, the plan may provide a $100 monthly pension benefit at age 65 after 25 years of service, or the plan may use a benefit formula based on final average compensation. In these instances, the accrued benefit method requires that a portion of the prospective benefit be imputed to each year of credited service. This requires some arbitrary basis of allocating total prospective benefits to particular years of service. When used for

---

[5]Because of sharply increasing costs, regulations do not permit use of the accrued benefit cost method for minimum funding requirements for final average plans.

plans of this type, it is usually referred to as the projected unit credit method.

The first step in the calculation of the normal cost under the accrued benefit cost method is to determine the present value of each participant's benefit credited during the year for which costs are being calculated. The cost per dollar of benefit is a function of the participant's age and sex and of the mortality, interest, and other assumptions used. Thus, the normal cost per dollar of benefit under the accrued benefit cost method increases with the age of the participant, assuming that all other assumptions are held constant. For example, using the 1971 Group Annuity Mortality Table, a 6 percent interest assumption and a 5 percent loading, the normal cost per $1 of monthly benefit beginning at age 65 for a male employee at various ages would be as follows:

Age	Normal Cost
25	$ 9.24
30	12.41
35	16.69
40	22.48
45	30.39
50	41.45
55	57.31
60	80.70

If the benefit formula is related to salary, increases in compensation would also increase the normal cost for a given participant.

The normal cost of the plan as a whole is simply the sum of the separate normal costs for the benefits credited for each participant during that particular year. Although the normal cost for a given participant increases over time under the accrued benefit cost method, the normal cost for the plan as a whole generally does not increase as rapidly, or may even remain fairly constant or decrease. The reason for this is that some older employees will die or terminate, and they will probably be replaced by much younger workers. If the distribution of current service benefit credits by age and sex remains constant, the total normal cost of the plan will remain constant.

At the inception of the plan, the supplemental liability under the accrued benefit cost method arises from the fact that either past service credits have been granted or a part of the benefits of the plan is imputed to past service. The supplemental liability at the inception of the plan under the accrued benefit cost method is simply the present value of the accrued past service benefits credited as of that date. Using the single-premium rates indicated above, the supplemental liability for a male employee, age 40, at the inception date of the plan, would be $22.48 per $1 a month of past-service benefit payable beginning at age 65. If the benefit formula provides a $10-a-month benefit per year of service and the employee has 10 years of credited past service, the supplemental liability for that individual would be $2,248.00 ($22.48 × $100 past-service benefit). The supplemental liability for the plan as a whole at the inception would be the sum of the supplemental liabilities for each of the covered employees.

It should now be clear why the accrued benefit method is readily adaptable to unit benefit formula plans. Also, this method generally is used under group deferred annuity plans, since a unit of benefit usually is purchased for each year of credited future service under these contracts. The employer has some flexibility in funding the supplemental liability.

Projected Benefit Cost Methods

Rather than costing the benefits credited during a specific period, one can project the total benefits that will be credited by retirement date and spread the costs for these benefits evenly over some future period. These costing techniques are referred to as projected benefit cost methods. More specifically, a *projected benefit cost method* is one under which the actuarial costs are based upon total prospective benefits, whether or not they are attributed to any specific periods of service. The actuarial cost determination assumes regular future accruals of normal cost, generally a level amount or percentage of earnings, whose actuarial present value is equal to the present value of prospective benefits less the value of plan assets and unfunded supplemental liabilities. From the preceding definition one can see that projected benefit cost methods differ from accrued benefit cost methods in two important respects. First, the normal cost accrual under a projected benefit cost method is related to the total prospective benefit, rather than the benefit for a particular year. The projected benefit methods generally are used when the plan provides a composite benefit based upon the participant's total period of credited service, such as $100 per month or 30 percent of average earnings for the last five years of service. These latter formulas do not allocate benefits to any particular year. However, it may be necessary, in the case of early retirement or termination of service with vested rights, to allocate the total potential benefit to actual years of service or to define the accrued benefit in terms of the amount purchasable by the accrued level annual cost. A projected benefit cost method can be, and is, used with benefit formulas that do allocate units of benefit to particular years of service. When so used, the normal cost accruals are still calculated on the basis of total projected benefits rather than annual units of benefit. For example, if a plan provides a retirement benefit of $10 a month per year of service, the normal cost computation is based on a projected monthly retirement benefit of $10 times the expected number of years of credited service as of normal retirement age. If the employee is age 35 upon entry into the plan and the normal retirement age is 65, then the total projected benefit is $300 a month.

A second distinguishing characteristic of projected benefit cost methods is that these techniques are generally applied with the objective of generating a normal cost that is a level amount or percentage of earnings for either the individual participants or the participants as a group. Therefore, these methods can be characterized as level cost methods. A cost method is characterized as level if it is based on an actuarial formula designed to produce a constant year-to-year accrual of normal cost (either in amount or as a percentage of payroll or other index) if (*a*) the experience conforms with the actuarial assumptions, (*b*) there are no changes in the plan, and (*c*) certain characteristics of the employee group remain unchanged.

However, the actual experience of the plan seldom conforms precisely with the actuarial assumptions used, and it is likely that there will be changes in the composition of the group for which cost accruals are assumed. Nevertheless, these methods are characterized as level cost methods, since the theoretical objective of most of these methods is to produce a level normal cost. By contrast, the accrued benefit cost method theoretically should produce increasing annual costs until the plan matures. However, as noted earlier, changes in the composition of the group may, in practice, result in fairly level normal costs under the accrued benefit cost method.

Projected benefit cost methods may be subdivided into (1) individual level cost methods and (2) aggregate level cost methods.

Individual Level Cost Methods. The individual subcategory of projected benefit cost methods is characterized by the assumed allocation of the actuarial cost for each individual employee, generally as a level amount or percentage of earnings, over all or a part of the employee's period of service or period of coverage under the plan, or some other appropriate period uniformly applied. Under individual cost methods, the total actuarial cost is generally separable as to the various participants; that is, costs are calculated individually for each employee or are calculated by group methods in such a way as to produce essentially the same total result as though individually calculated.[6]

The individual level cost methods may be further subdivided as to whether or not a supplemental liability is created.

Without Supplemental Liability. As indicated above, projected benefit cost methods have as their objective the spreading of the costs of total projected benefits evenly over some future period. One logical period over

---

[6]It should be noted, however, that this does not mean that it is possible, at any given time, to identify a participant's "share" in the plan assets. For example, a turnover assumption reduces the normal cost attributable to each participant. However, this normal cost figure is too low for the participant who does not terminate and eventually retires under the plan. Likewise, this normal cost figure is excessive for those participants who subsequently terminate with no vested benefits. For the plan as a whole, however, this normal cost figure may be entirely appropriate. This point should be kept clearly in mind, particularly in those sections of the chapter illustrating the calculations of normal costs under the various actuarial cost methods in terms of an individual participant. The authors recognize the weakness of this approach, but feel that the basic nature of each method is illustrated more clearly through use of individual participant examples.

which costs can be spread is the period from the attained age of the employee at the time he or she entered the plan to normal retirement age under the plan.

The normal cost accruals are determined by distributing the present value of an individual's total projected benefits as a level amount or percentage of earnings over his or her assumed future period of coverage under the plan. Total projected benefits include past-service benefits, if any, as well as future-service benefits to be credited by retirement age. Thus, no unfunded supplemental liability is created under this cost method at the inception of the plan, since the present value of future benefits is exactly equal to the present value of future normal cost accruals. Thereafter, there is still no supplemental liability if contribution payments have been made equal to the normal costs that have accrued in prior years. It must be reemphasized that a supplemental liability may be created for other reasons. The point to be made here is that this actuarial cost method, other things being equal, does not of itself generate a supplemental liability.

This actuarial cost method requires, then, a projection of total benefits distributed by age at inception of coverage, and calculation of the normal cost based on a set of level premium deferred annuity rates.[7]

The latter may be determined by dividing the present value of an annuity at normal retirement age by the present value of a temporary annuity running to normal retirement age. For example, assume that the total projected benefit for a participant age 35 at the inception date of the plan is $200 a month beginning at age 65. The normal cost for this participant's benefit would be equal to the present value at age 35 of an annuity of $200 a month beginning at age 65, divided by the present value of a temporary annuity due of $1 for 30 years.

If there is no change in the projected benefits of any employee and the covered group remains constant, the normal cost under the plan will remain constant (subject to adjustment to the extent that actual experience deviates from the assumptions employed). Obviously, this will not prove to be the case in most plans. For example, if the benefit formula is related to compensation, employees will be entitled to larger projected benefits as they receive salary increases. Where salary scales have not been used in the original cost calculations, the increase in projected benefits due to salary increases is spread evenly over the period from the year in which compensation is increased to the year in which the employee reaches

---

[7]Regardless of which actuarial cost method is used, there is the question of whether to include in the cost calculations employees who have not yet met the plan participation requirements. One view is that a certain percentage of the currently noneligible employees will eventually qualify for participation in the plan and, therefore, the cost calculations should recognize this fact. Some actuaries, however, project costs only for those employees who are actually eligible for participation in the plan. The latter approach generally produces lower cost estimates. Either approach can be justified, but the reader should recognize that differences in cost projections may be due, at least in part, to the approach used.

normal retirement age. This, of course, results in an increase in annual contributions for the plan as a whole. Also, new employees will become eligible for participation in the plan, and some currently covered workers will terminate their participation under the plan. Since the age and sex distribution and the benefit levels of new employees are not likely to be identical to those of terminated participants, there are bound to be variations in the annual contributions for the plan as a whole.

The reader will recognize that the individual level cost method without supplemental liability is, in effect, the actuarial cost method used under fully insured individual policy and group permanent plans. Indeed, this cost method is analogous to the level premium concept used in Individual life insurance premium calculations. For this reason, this actuarial cost method is sometimes referred to as the individual level premium method or the attained age level contribution method.

With Supplemental Liability. This cost method is similar to the previous method except that the assumption is made, for the initial group of participants, that the period over which costs are spread begins with the first year they could have joined the plan had it always been in effect. For an employee who enters after the inception date of the plan, the normal cost under this method is the same as would be generated by the previous method.[8]

This follows since that employee's entry year coincides with the year in which participation began. In the case of the initial group of participants, a supplemental liability is automatically created because of the assumption that normal cost payments have been made prior to the inception date of the plan.

Using the example cited above, assume that an employee is entitled to a total projected benefit at age 65 of $200 a month. The employee is age 35 at the inception of the plan, but would have been eligible at age 30 had the plan been in effect. Under the individual level cost method with supplemental liability, the normal cost for this participant's benefit would be equal to the present value at age 30 (rather than age 35, as is the case under the previous cost method) of an annuity of $200 a month beginning at age 65, divided by the present value of a temporary annuity due of $1 for 35 years (rather than 30 years). In the above example, the numerator is smaller and the denominator larger than the corresponding values calculated under the individual cost method without a supplemental liability. The result, of course, is that the normal costs are lower under the individual cost method with a supplemental liability. However, since the normal costs have not been paid for the prior years, there is a supplemental liability on behalf of this employee. Unlike the accrued benefit cost method, the initial supplemental liability under the individual cost method does not bear a precise relationship to past service benefits.

---

[8]This statement assumes that the normal cost is calculated in a consistent manner for both the original group and subsequent entrants.

The difference between the two individual level cost methods can be made clear by reference to a situation in the individual life insurance field. Let us assume that an individual, age 25, purchased a 10-year convertible term life insurance contract. At age 30, the insured decides to convert the policy to an ordinary life insurance policy. If the conversion is made as of issue age (25), the ordinary life premium for age 25 can be viewed conceptually as the annual normal cost under the individual level cost method with supplemental liability. The sum of the annual premiums from issue date (age 25) to conversion date (age 30), improved at the assumed rate of interest and adjusted to reflect the insurance cost, would be analogous to the supplemental liability under this method. If the conversion were made as of attained age, the annual premium for age 30, adjusted to reflect the insurance cost, would be analogous to the annual cost required under the individual cost method without supplemental liability.

In valuations after the first year of the plan, the normal cost and supplemental liability would be calculated in the same manner as at the plan's inception. However, the annual contribution would be a payment of the normal cost and some payment toward the unfunded supplemental liability (the supplemental liability less any assets that have accumulated). The normal cost calculation would be affected by any changes in assumptions or plan provisions, while the calculation of the unfunded supplemental liability would be affected not only by changes in assumptions or plan provisions, but also by any actuarial gains or losses since the plan actually started.

The individual level cost method with a supplemental liability also is referred to as the entry age normal method. This appears to be the primary cost method among large defined benefit plans. In a national survey of pension plans covering 1,000 or more participants, 49 percent of the final average plans and 34 percent of the career average plans chose this method.[9]

Aggregate Level Cost Methods.   The distinguishing characteristic of aggregate level cost methods is that the normal cost accruals are calculated for the plan as a whole without identifying any part of such cost accruals with the projected benefits of specific individuals. The cost accruals are expressed as a percentage of compensation or as a specified dollar amount.

The normal cost accrual rate under an aggregate method can be determined by dividing the present value of future benefits for all participants by the present value of the estimated future compensation for the group of participants. This accrual rate is then multiplied by the total annual earnings to determine the initial normal cost of the plan. If the normal cost accrual rate is to be expressed in terms of a dollar amount, then the present value of $1 per employee for each year of future service must be computed. Since there is no assumption that any normal costs have been accrued prior

---

[9]The Wyatt Company, *1984 Survey of Actuarial Assumptions and Funding* (Washington, D.C.: The Wyatt Company, 1985), p. 4.

to the inception date of the plan, the above method does not create a supplemental liability.

In the determination of cost accruals after the inception of the plan under the above method, recognition must be given to the plan assets that presumably have been accumulated to offset prior normal cost accruals. Thus, for those years subsequent to the establishment of the plan, the accrual rate is determined by dividing the present value of aggregate future benefits, less any plan assets, by the present value of future compensation.

The normal cost accrual can be calculated under an aggregate method to produce a supplemental liability. This can be done in many ways, but the most clearly understood approach to creating a supplemental liability under the aggregate method is to exclude past service benefits in the projection of aggregate future benefits. This decreases the numerator of the fraction, thereby producing a smaller normal cost accrual rate. Or the actuary may simply use a supplemental liability generated by one of the individual cost methods. However the supplemental liability is calculated, the unfunded supplemental liability must be subtracted (along with plan assets) from the present value of aggregate future benefits in the calculation of subsequent accrual rates.

The aggregate level cost method without supplemental liability is also referred to as the percentage of payroll, the aggregate, or the remaining cost method. When there is a supplemental liability in connection with this method, it is sometimes referred to as the attained age normal or entry age normal method with initial supplemental liability.

Amortization of Supplemental Liability. The actuarial cost methods that create a supplemental liability offer the employer greater flexibility in annual contribution payments than is available under the cost methods without supplemental liability. Under the former cost methods, the employer has the alternative of funding the initial supplemental liability at a pace consistent with its financial objectives and, of course, applicable law in addition to the annual normal costs under the plan. In most cases, the employer makes some contribution toward the amortization of the supplemental liability. The length of the period over which the supplemental liability should be funded varies with the circumstances surrounding each plan. However, amortization periods of 20, 25, or 30 years often are used. The initial supplemental liability must be amortized by sufficient contributions over no more than 30 plan years (the initial supplemental liability may be amortized over 40 years for plans in existence on January 1, 1974). Under federal tax law, the minimum period over which the supplemental liability can be funded (and tax deductions allowed) is 10 years; beginning in 1988, however, a contribution to bring a plan to a funding level of 100 percent of current plan liabilities will be tax deductible even though it exceeds the otherwise applicable limit.

DEFINED CONTRIBUTION PLANS

The discussion thus far in this chapter has been concerned primarily with the role of actuarial assumptions and actuarial cost methods in calculating the annual cost of a plan. The question arises as to the degree to which this discussion is pertinent in the case of defined contribution (money purchase) plans. In these plans, the employer's contribution commitment is fixed and is usually expressed as a specified percentage of the compensation of covered employees. Thus, it would seem that there is little need for actuarial assumptions and cost methods to determine annual costs under these plans. To allow the employer to estimate future costs or benefits under the plan, projections are required based on appropriate actuarial assumptions and a specific actuarial cost method. In estimating ultimate costs under a defined contribution plan, the actuary could use either the accrued benefit method or a projected benefit cost method, depending on how benefits are defined. Also, under traditional defined contribution plans, the annual contribution on behalf of each employee is viewed as a single-premium payment for a unit of deferred annuity to begin upon attainment of normal retirement age. Indeed, many of the defined contribution plans are funded through group deferred annuity contracts. Thus, the age of the employee and mortality and interest assumptions determine the amount of benefit being credited each year. The amount of benefit credited each year for a given employee will vary with the size of the contribution payment and the number of years to retirement age.

A variation of the traditional defined contribution plan is found in some negotiated plans that have both a fixed contribution and a fixed benefit. Negotiated multiemployer plans are established on this basis. The union negotiates a fixed pension contribution rate with all participating employers, and the rate is usually expressed in terms of cents per hour worked or unit of production, or as a percentage of the compensation of covered employees. The contributions are paid into a single trust fund, and a uniform benefit schedule applicable to all covered employees is established. Actuarial assumptions and an actuarial cost method are needed to determine the level of benefits that can be supported by the fixed contribution commitment. In these plans, an additional assumption must be made in actuarial computations that was not mentioned earlier in the chapter; that is, the expected level of future contributions. Since the contribution commitment is usually related to compensation or hours worked, changes in levels of economic activity affect the contribution income of the plan. The actuary, therefore, must project the future flow of contribution income to determine an appropriate benefit formula for the plan.

The cost method normally used in actuarial computations for fixed contribution-fixed benefit plans is the projected benefit cost method with a supplemental liability. One reason is that this method tends to produce annual normal costs that may be expected to remain fairly stable as a percentage of payroll or in terms of cents per hour, if the actuarial assumptions are in fact realized; and this is consistent with the contribution commitment under these plans, which is normally expressed as a percentage of payroll or in cents per hour of work. Another reason is the existence of a supplemental liability, which permits some flexibility in annual contribution income. As indicated above, changes in levels of employment will result in fluctuations in the annual aggregate contribution income of the plan, which may not match fluctuations in the amount of benefits credited. During periods of prosperity, the excess of actual over expected contribution income can be applied toward amortizing the supplemental liability at a rate faster than anticipated; likewise, periods of recession result in extensions of the period over which the supplemental liability is to be amortized. Of course, in both cases, the amortization periods must be in line with the minimums and maximums permitted under federal law.

MINIMUM FUNDING STANDARDS

The basic minimum funding standard required by the Code is that a pension plan having supplemental liabilities must amortize such liabilities over a specified period of time in addition to the funding of normal cost.

The requirement for amortizing supplemental liability applies only to defined benefit plans, since a defined contribution plan cannot technically have a supplemental liability. For defined contribution plans, the minimum contribution is the amount indicated by the plan formula. The requirements also apply to negotiated plans that have both a fixed contribution rate and a fixed benefit. Such plans may use the "shortfall" method described later in this chapter.

In meeting the minimum funding standards, the liabilities of a pension plan must be calculated on the basis of actuarial assumptions and actuarial cost methods that are reasonable and that offer the actuary's best estimate of anticipated experience under the plan; beginning in 1988, each individual assumption must be reasonable.

For plans in existence on January 1, 1974, the maximum amortization period is 40 years; for single-employer plans established after January 1, 1974, the maximum amortization period is 30 years. Moreover, experience gains and losses for single-employer plans must be amortized over a shorter period of time:[10] prior to 1988, this was a 15-year period; beginning in 1988, it will be a 5-year period. The shorter amortization period for gains and losses was designed to stimulate the use of realistic actuarial assump-

---

[10]It should be noted that one type of actuarial technique (the spread gain–type funding method) spreads experience gains and losses over future periods as part of the plan's normal cost.

tions. Beginning in 1988, changes in supplemental liabilities associated with changes in actuarial assumptions must be amortized over a period not longer than 10 years; previously, the period was 30 years.

Under ERISA, the secretary of labor may extend, for a period of up to 10 years, the amortization period for supplemental liabilities and experience losses for both single-employer and multiemployer plans. Such potential extensions are advantageous for those cases where a substantial risk exists that unless such an extension were granted, a pension plan would be terminated, or greatly reduced employee benefit levels or reduced employee compensation would result.

The Treasury Department can also allow some flexibility in employers meeting the minimum funding standards of the Code. In those circumstances where an employer would incur temporary substantial business hardships and if strict enforcement of the minimum funding standards would adversely affect plan participants, the secretary of the treasury may waive for a particular year payment of all or a part of a plan's normal cost and the additional liabilities to be funded during that year. Beginning in 1988, the law provides that no more than three waivers may be granted a plan within a consecutive 15-year period; the amount waived, plus interest, must be amortized not less rapidly than ratably over 5 years. Transition provisions are included with a fresh start allowing pre-1988 plan years to be excluded from the 15-year look-back period for waivers requested after December 17, 1987.

The Omnibus Budget Reconciliation Act of 1987 established additional minimum funding requirements for plans covering more than 100 participants and that are not at least 100 percent funded for current liabilities. This change becomes effective in 1989. The additional contribution is based on an 18-year amortization of the 1988 unfunded current liability, additional payments for any benefit improvements, and a payment toward current benefits for "unpredictable contingent events" (such as a plant shutdown) that have taken place. For this purpose, the current liability is the present value of all plan liabilities; i.e., the value of accrued benefits projected to the end of the current plan year, but excluding the value of unpredictable contingent events that have not occurred. The present value of this liability is calculated using the plan's valuation interest rate, provided that it is between 90 percent and 110 percent of the weighted average of rates of interest on 30-year Treasury securities during the four-year period ending on the last day of the prior plan year. Furthermore, the interest rate should be consistent with current insurance company annuity rates. The IRS may, by regulation, extend this range downward if 90 percent of the weighted average is unreasonably high, but to no lower than 80 percent of the weighted average. Also, the unfunded liability is calculated by subtracting the actuarial value of assets; any credit balance in the funding standard account must first be subtracted from the actuarial value of assets.

Along with these changes, the maximum deductible contribution will be increased to whatever contribution is required to bring the plan to a funded position of 100 percent of the current liability.

There are certain exemptions from the mandated minimum funding standards. Generally, the minimum funding standards apply to pension plans (as opposed to profit sharing and stock bonus plans) of private employers in interstate commerce, plans of employee organizations with members in interstate commerce, and plans that seek a qualified status under the tax laws. Exempt plans include government plans and church plans, unless they elect to comply with the requirements of the Code. Fully insured pension plans (funded exclusively through individual or group permanent insurance contracts) are exempt from the minimum funding rules as long as all premiums are paid when due and no policy loans are allowed. Additionally, plans that are also exempt are arrangements designed to provide deferred compensation to highly compensated employees, plans that provide supplemental benefits on an unfunded, nonqualified basis, and those plans to which the employer does not contribute.

Funding Standard Account

All pension plans subject to the minimum funding requirements must establish a "funding standard account" that provides a comparison between actual contributions and those required under the minimum funding requirements. A determination of experience gains and losses and a valuation of a plan's liability must be made at least once every three years.[11] The basic purpose of the funding standard account is to provide some flexibility in funding through allowing contributions greater than the required minimum, accumulated with interest, to reduce the minimum contributions required in future years.

Operation of the Account.   For each plan year, the funding standard account is charged with the normal cost for the year and with the minimum amortization payment required for initial supplemental liabilities, increases in plan liabilities, experience losses, the net loss resulting from changes in actuarial assumptions, waived contributions for each year, and adjustments for interest in the preceding items to the end of the plan year.[12] The

---

[11]Under certain circumstances, the IRS may require an actuarial valuation more frequently than once every three years. Valuations will generally be required for plan amendments that increase the plan's costs; plan years in which the number of participants changes by more than 20 percent; changes in funding methods or actuarial assumptions; adoption of the alternative funding standard account or attaining the full funding limitation (both concepts are explained later in this chapter); and spinoffs and mergers. See Proposed Regulation Section 1.412(c)(9)-1(d).

[12]Plan sponsors are able to change their funding methods with the (sometime automatic) approval of the IRS. See Revenue Proceeding 85-29.

account is credited in each plan year for employer contributions made for that year, with amortized portions of decreases in plan liabilities, experience gains, the net gain resulting from changes in actuarial assumptions, amounts of any waived contributions, and adjustments for interest in the preceding items to the end of the plan year. If the contributions to the plan, adjusted as indicated above, meet the minimum funding standards, the funding standard account will show a zero balance. If the funding standard account has a positive balance at the end of the year, such balance will be credited with interest in future years (at the rate used to determine plan costs). Therefore, the need for future contributions to meet the minimum funding standards will be reduced to the extent of the positive balance plus the interest credited. If, however, the funding standard account shows a deficit balance, called the *accumulated funding deficiency* (minimum contributions in essence have not been made), the account will be charged with interest at the rate used to determine plan costs. Moreover, beginning in 1989, the plan will be subject to an excise tax of 10 percent of the accumulated funding deficiency (100 percent if not corrected or paid off within 90 days after notice of a deficiency by the secretary of the treasury); previously, the initial excise tax was 5 percent. All members of the employer's controlled group are liable for payment of the minimum contribution and excise tax, with a lien on the employer's assets imposed for a deficiency in excess of $1 million. In addition to the excise tax, the employer may be subject to civil action in the courts for failure to meet the minimum funding standards. Also, beginning in 1989, minimum funding contributions must be made on a quarterly basis with the final payment due 8½ months after the close of the plan year. Interest on unpaid quarterly installments is charged in the funding standard account at a rate equal to the larger of the plan annuity rate or 175 percent of the Federal mid-term rate.

Shortfall Method.   A negotiated plan that has both a defined contribution rate and a defined benefit may elect to determine entries to the funding standard account under the shortfall method. Under the shortfall method, the net charge to the funding standard account for a year is based on the fixed contribution rate for the year times the actual number of units of service or production during the year; that is, hours worked or tons of coal mined. The difference between the net charge so computed and the amount that would otherwise have been computed under the funding standard account is the shortfall gain or loss that must be amortized over future years. In general, the shortfall gain or loss is amortized over the 15 years following the year in which it arose. For plans maintained by more than one employer, the start of the amortization period may be deferred up to five years after the shortfall gain or loss arose, but the amortization period still ends 15 years after the gain or loss arose. If the shortfall method is adopted after 1980 (or if it is decided to abandon use of the shortfall method after it is once used) it requires prior approval from the secretary of the treasury.

Alternative Minimum Funding Standard

A pension plan using a funding method that requires contributions in all years not less than those required under the "entry age normal funding method" can elect compliance under the alternative minimum funding standard. Under this standard, the minimum annual contribution to the pension plan would be the lesser of the normal cost determined for the plan or the normal cost determined under the accrued benefit cost method plus the excess, if any, of the actuarial value of the accrued benefits over the fair market value of the assets. All assets, under this standard, are valued at their actual market value on the date of valuation without benefit of averaging or amortization, while the actuarial value of accrued benefits is calculated based on assumptions appropriate for a terminating plan; for example, rates published by the Pension Benefit Guaranty Corporation (PBGC). Adherence to this standard would assure that the pension plan would have assets, valued at market, at least equal to the actuarial value of all accrued benefits, whether vested or not. The rationale for this alternative approach is that a pension plan should not be required to hold assets in excess of those needed to meet accrued benefits.

A pension plan using this approach must set up an alternative minimum funding standard account. Such an account is charged each year with the lesser of the normal cost of the plan or the normal cost determined under the accrued benefit cost method plus the excess of the actuarial value of accrued benefits over plan assets (not less than zero) and will be credited with contributions. All entries are adjusted for interest to the end of a plan year. There is no carryover of contributions over the required minimum from one year to the next, since any excess contributions simply become a part of the plan assets for the following year's comparison of assets and liabilities. Conversely, as with the regular funding standard account, any deficiency of contributions is carried over from year to year, with interest, and the excise tax described earlier is payable on the cumulative funding deficiency.

A pension plan electing the alternative funding standard must maintain both an alternate funding standard account and the basic funding standard account. The basic funding standard account is charged and credited under the normal rules, but an excise tax will not be levied on any deficiency in that account if there is no deficiency in the alternate account. A pension plan making this choice is required to maintain both accounts, since the minimum required contribution in a particular plan year is the lesser of the contributions called for by the basic and alternate standards. If a plan switches from the alternate standard back to the basic standard, the excess of the deficiency in the standard account over the deficiency in the alternate standard account must be amortized over five years.

Full Funding Limitation

Beginning in 1989, the full funding limit and, hence, an overriding limit on tax-deductible contributions, will be the lesser of 100 percent of the plan's actuarial accrued liability (including normal cost) or 150 percent of the plan's current liability (as previously defined), reduced by the lesser of the market value of plan assets or their actuarial value. Contributions in excess of the deductible limit will result in the imposition of a 10 percent excise tax on the amount of the excess.

Overstatement of Pension Liabilities

An excise tax will be imposed on an underpayment of taxes that results from an overstatement of pension liabilities. If the tax benefit is at least $1,000, the excise tax will be 10 percent of the overstatement for overstatements between 150 percent and 200 percent, 20 percent for overstatements of 200 percent to 250 percent, and 30 percent for overstatements exceeding 250 percent.

QUESTIONS FOR REVIEW

1. Define the following terms: (a) normal cost, (b) supplemental cost, and (c) past service liability.
2. Explain the steps in the calculation of (a) the normal cost and (b) the supplemental liability at plan inception under the accrued benefit cost method.
3. How does a projected benefit cost method differ from an accrued benefit cost method?
4. Distinguish between the individual level and aggregate level cost methods.
5. How does an employer amortize a supplemental liability? Over what time period can this be done, according to ERISA?
6. What are the amortization periods for unfunded supplemental liabilities for single-employer plans? In what situations will variance from the standards be permitted?
7. What are the exemptions from the mandated minimum funding standards?
8. What are the annual charges and credits in the funding standard account?
9. What is the impact of (a) a positive balance and (b) a negative balance for the funding standard account at the end of the year?
10. What alternate minimum funding standard exists for plans that use the entry age normal method?

QUESTIONS FOR DISCUSSION

1. Discuss why an employer might prefer to use an accrued benefit cost method instead of a projected benefit cost method, and vice versa.

2. Discuss why an employer might prefer to use an aggregate level cost method instead of an individual level cost method.

3. Discuss the factors that might influence an employer's choice of an amortization period for the supplemental liability.

10

Employers' Accounting for Pensions

Accounting procedures for pension plans consist of three components, each of which is controlled by a separate Financial Accounting Standards Board (FASB) Statement. FASB Statement No. 35, *Accounting and Reporting by Defined Benefit Pension Plans* (FASB 35), establishes standards for financial accounting and reporting for the annual financial statement of a defined benefit pension plan. FASB Statement No. 87, *Employers' Accounting for Pensions* (FASB 87), establishes standards for financial reporting and accounting for an employer that offers pension benefits to its employees.[1] Because of the unusually high number of inquiries received, the FASB staff determined that a special report, *A Guide to Implementation of Statement 87 on Employers' Accounting for Pensions*, should be issued as an aid in understanding FASB 87. Closely related to FASB 87, FASB Statement No. 88, *Employers' Accounting for Settlements and Curtailment of Defined Benefit Pension Plans and for Termination Benefits* (FASB 88), establishes standards for an employer's accounting for settlement of defined benefit pension obligations, for curtailment of a defined benefit pension plan, and for termination benefits.

SOURCE: Part of this chapter is based on material from Steven B. Johnson and Jack L. VanDerhei, "An Economic Perspective on the Pension Accounting Controversy," *Benefits Quarterly* (First quarter, 1985), pp. 36–45.

[1]In FASB parlance, pension benefits are defined as periodic (usually monthly) payments made pursuant to the terms of the pension plan to a person who has retired from employment or to that person's beneficiary.

189

This chapter focuses primarily on the consequences of sponsoring a single-employer pension plan on the employer's financial statements. Therefore, the major emphasis is on FASB 87[2] and 88. A brief discussion of the evolution of pension accounting standards is presented first, and then the FASB statements are described in detail and their impact on pension plan sponsors is analyzed.

THE EVOLUTION OF PENSION ACCOUNTING STANDARDS

Although various accounting conventions were applied to pension plans prior to 1966,[3] this was an era in which the accounting profession exercised little control over pension *accounting* while the government exercised considerable control over pension *funding*. As a result, pension accounting during this time has been characterized as essentially a discretionary system that typically resulted in the amount of pension expense recorded for a year being equal to the employer's pension contribution.

Since 1966, employer pension accounting has been governed by Accounting Principles Board *Opinion No. 8, Accounting for the Cost of Pension Plans* (APB 8). This pronouncement eliminated the previous discretionary method of accounting for pension costs and replaced it with a methodology that established a range of minimum and maximum annual costs based on a number of approved actuarial cost methods. For a variety of reasons, however, the appropriateness of this standard has been questioned since the passage of ERISA in 1974. In that year, the FASB added two pension projects to its agenda: one to cover accounting principles for the pension plan itself and another to cover accounting by employers for pensions.

As a result of these projects, FASB 35 and FASB Statement No. 36, *Disclosure of Pension Information* (FASB 36), were issued in 1980. FASB 35 established rules governing the measurement and reporting of plan assets and plan obligations by the plan itself. Under this pronouncement, plan assets must typically be measured at market value, while plan liabilities (both vested and nonvested) must be measured on a basis that ignores future salary progression. FASB 36, which established rules governing how the employing firm must disclose plan assets and liabilities on its financial statements, required a measurement procedure compatible with FASB 35. Although FASB 36 was heralded by some financial analysts as a significant

---

[2]Although they are beyond the scope of this chapter, FASB 87 also contains provisions treating multiemployer plans, non-U.S. pension plans, and business combinations.

[3]For an interesting historical analysis of the evolving relationship between the employer contributions and the charge for pension expense, see E. L. Hicks and C. L. Trowbridge, *Employer Accounting for Pensions: An Analysis of the Financial Accounting Standards Board's Preliminary Views and Exposure Draft* (Homewood, Ill.: Richard D. Irwin for the Pension Research Council, 1985), pp. 16–18.

improvement in disclosure, it was intended to serve only as a stopgap measure until the more contentious issues raised in response to the perceived limitations for APB 8 could be resolved.

FASB 87

Even with the modifications imposed by FASB 36, the APB 8 approach to pension accounting was criticized for the following reasons:

1. Pension costs were not comparable from one company to another.
2. Pension costs were not consistent from period to period for the same company.
3. Significant pension obligations and assets were not recognized in the body of the financial statements (although FASB 36 did require footnote disclosure in the balance sheet).

The Board had four basic objectives in the preparation of FASB 87. The first objective was to provide a measure of pension cost that better reflects the terms of the plan and recognizes the cost of the employee's pension over his or her service with the employer. As shown in Chapter 9, many of the actuarial cost methods chosen for funding purposes allocate pension contributions as a percentage of payroll. Of the actuarial cost methods acceptable for minimum funding purposes, only the accrued benefit cost method determines an amount that is based directly upon benefits accrued to the valuation date. Second, the Board wanted to provide a more comparable measure of pension cost. Not only were pension plan sponsors able to choose from a number of acceptable actuarial cost methods, but they were also given a degree of flexibility in choosing the amortization period for supplemental liabilities (in essence, anywhere from 10 to 30 years for liabilities created after 1974). Third, they desired to have disclosures that would allow users to understand the effect of the employer's undertaking. Previous pension accounting standards allowed the sponsor to record one net amount for the pension expense. It was believed that disclosure of the individual components of this amount would significantly assist users in understanding the economic events that have occurred. In theory, those disclosures also would make it easier to understand why the reported amount changed from period to period, especially when a large cost is offset by a large revenue to produce a relatively small net reported amount. Finally, as mentioned above, there was a desire to improve reporting of financial position. This relates primarily to the inclusion of underfunded pension liabilities on the balance sheet of the sponsor.

The new accounting requirements mandated by FASB 87 are phased in with a two-step process. The income statement (expense) provisions must be applied for years beginning after December 15, 1986, while the balance sheet (liability) provisions must be applied for years beginning after December 15, 1988.

Scope

Although FASB 87 applies primarily to qualified pension plans, there is reason to believe it may apply to any practice of paying postretirement benefits. Some accounting firms believe this will also apply to the supplemental executive retirement plans described in Chapter 24. However, FASB 87 definitely excludes postretirement health care and life insurance benefits. Although these benefits were originally part of the Board's project on accounting for pension benefits, it has since been spun off into a separate endeavor and is currently controlled by FASB Statement No. 81, *Disclosure of Postretirement Health Care and Life Insurance Benefits*.

Use of Reasonable Approximations

FASB 87 is intended to specify accounting objectives and results, rather than specific computational means of obtaining those results. Pension plan sponsors are allowed to use shortcuts if they will not result in material differences from the results of a detailed application.

Single-Employer Defined Benefit Pension Plans

The most significant elements of FASB 87 involve an employer's accounting for a single-employer defined benefit pension plan. After describing the basic elements of pension accounting, this section first explains the recognition procedures for the net periodic pension cost and then for the pension liabilities and assets. Certain details concerning measurement procedures are demonstrated and the new disclosure requirements are presented. Finally, certain miscellaneous provisions are presented.

Basic Elements of Pension Accounting.   It is important to note that FASB 87 does not apply to the government constraints on minimum or maximum (deductible) funding. Although the accrued benefit cost method (or projected unit credit method in FASB parlance) mandated for use in computing the net periodic pension cost is one of the acceptable actuarial cost methods under the Internal Revenue Code, Section 412, it is highly likely that the FASB 87 net periodic pension cost will differ substantially from the ERISA minimum funding amount. Furthermore, it is important to understand that FASB 87 incorporates two different definitions of the sponsor's pension liability. The projected benefit obligation is the amount used to measure pension cost and is defined as the actuarial present value of all benefits attributed by the plan's benefit formula to employee service rendered prior to that date, assuming future salary levels if the formula is based on future compensation.[4] In contrast, the accumulated benefit obligation is used for balance sheet recognition. It is determined in the same manner as the projected benefit obligation but without salary assumptions. Therefore, for those plans with nonpay-related pension benefit formulas, the projected benefit obligation and the accumulated benefit obligation are the same.

Recognition of Net Periodic Pension Cost.   Under FASB 87, the net periodic pension cost is made up of six components:

1. Service cost.
2. Interest cost.
3. Actual return on plan assets, if any.
4. Amortization of unrecognized prior service cost, if any.
5. Gain or loss to the extent recognized.
6. Amortization of the unrecognized net asset or obligation existing at the date of the initial application of FASB 87.

Service cost is the actuarial present value of benefits attributed by the pension benefit formula to employee service during that period.[5] Interest cost is the increase in the projected benefit obligation due to the passage of time. This can be thought of simply as the accrual of interest on a present value or discounted amount. The actual return on plan assets is based on the fair value of plan assets at the beginning and the end of the period, adjusted for contributions and benefit payments.[6]

The prior service cost component for accounting purposes is conceptually similar to the amortization of supplemental liability described in Chapter 9; however the allocation procedure does not result in a level dollar amount assigned to each year in the amortization period. Under FASB 87, the cost of retroactive benefits is the increase in the projected benefit obligation at the date of the amendment. This cost is then amortized by assigning an equal amount to each future period of service of each employee active at the date of the amendment who is expected to receive benefits under the plan. Once determined, the amortization period does not change for that amendment.

The basic notion represented by this new amortization procedure can be illustrated by the following simple example. Assume that a defined benefit pension plan is amended on January 1, 1988, generating an unrecognized prior service cost of $100,000. At that time, the employer has three

---

[4]Turnover and mortality also are assumed.

[5]There are obvious similarities between this component of net periodic pension cost under FASB 87 and the normal cost under the accrued benefit cost method described in Chapter 9.

[6]While the return is titled actual for disclosure purposes, FASB 87 states that the difference between the actual and expected return on plan assets must be accounted for as a part of the gain or loss component of pension expense. The net result of this treatment is that the expected return on plan assets is used to calculate pension cost for the period.

employees who are expected to receive benefits under the plan. Employee A is expected to leave after one year, employee B after two years, and employee C after three years. The expected years of service in 1988 from this employee population would be equal to three (one year from all three employees), in 1989 there would only be two expected years of service (since employee A would already have left), and in 1990 there would only be one expected year of service. Summing these figures gives an aggregate expected years of future service of six (three from 1988, plus two from 1989, plus one from 1990).

The amortization rate for each year is determined by taking the ratio of expected years of service for that year and dividing it by six (the aggregate expected years of service). The amortization rate for the year is then multiplied by the increase in the projected benefit obligation resulting from the plan amendment to determine the amortization for the year. In this example, the 1988 amortization amount would be $100,000 \times (3 \div 6) = $50,000. The amount in 1989 would be $100,000 \times (2 \div 6) = $33,333; in 1990 the amount would be $100,000 \times (1 \div 6) = $16,667.

In certain cases, the amortization of prior service cost must be accelerated. A history of regular plan amendments may indicate that the period during which the employer expects to realize benefits (through employee goodwill, etc.) for an amendment is shorter than the remaining service period. This is likely to transpire in collective bargaining agreements with flat dollar plans in which the dollar amount is renegotiated upward every several years.[7]

The fifth component of net periodic pension cost (gain or loss) results from changes in either the projected benefit obligation or plan assets. These changes result either from experience different from that assumed or from changes in assumptions. Gains and losses include both realized and unrealized gains and losses. Asset gains and losses are equal to the difference between the actual return on assets during a period and the expected return on assets for that period. The expected return on plan assets is determined from the expected long-term rate of return on plan assets and the market-related value of plan assets.[8] Amortization of unrecognized net gain or loss is included as a component of net pension cost if, at the beginning of the year, the unrecognized net gain or loss (excluding asset gains and losses not yet reflected in market-related value) exceeds a so-called corridor amount. This corridor was designed to minimize the volatility in pension expense that would otherwise result from application of the new accounting convention and is defined as 10 percent of the greater of the projected benefit obligation or the market-related value of plan assets. The amortization for the year will be equal to the amount of unrecognized gain

---

[7]It is also possible for a plan amendment to decrease the projected benefit obligation. In that case, the reduction must be used to reduce any existing unrecognized prior service cost, and the excess, if any, must be amortized on the same basis as the cost of benefit increases.

[8]The market-related value of assets must be either fair value or a calculated value that recognizes change in fair value in a systematic and rational manner over not more than five years.

or loss in excess of the corridor divided by the average remaining service period of active employees expected to receive benefits under the plan.

In addition to the amortization of the unrecognized net gain or loss from *previous* periods, the overall gain or loss component of net periodic pension cost also consists of the difference between the actual return on plan assets and the expected return on plan assets.[9]

The final component of net periodic pension cost is the amortization of the unrecognized net asset or obligation existing at the date of initial application of FASB 87. At the time the plan sponsor first applies FASB 87, the projected benefit obligation and the fair market value of plan assets must be determined.[10] The difference between these two amounts is then amortized on a straight line basis over the average remaining service period of employees expected to receive benefits under the plan. There are two exceptions to this general rule, though. First, if the average remaining service period is less than 15 years, the employer may elect to use a 15-year period. Second, if all, or almost all, of a plan's participants are inactive, the employer must use the inactive participant's average remaining life expectancy period instead.

Recognition of Liabilities and Assets.   Under FASB 87, a balance sheet entry will be made if there is a discrepancy between net periodic pension cost and employer contributions. Specifically, a liability (unfunded accrued pension cost) is recognized if net periodic pension cost exceeds employer contributions, and an asset (prepaid pension cost) is recognized if net periodic pension cost is less than employer contributions. Moreover, a balance sheet entry will be made if the firm sponsors an "underfunded" plan. If the accumulated benefit obligation is greater than plan assets, employers must recognize a liability (including unfunded accrued pension cost) equal to the unfunded accumulated benefit obligation. It should be noted, however, that the treatment is not symmetrical: FASB 87 does not permit recognition of a net asset if plan assets are greater than the accumulated benefit obligation.

If an additional liability is recognized, an equal amount is recognized on the balance sheet as an intangible asset, provided that the asset recognized does not exceed the amount of unrecognized prior service cost. In the case where the additional liability is greater than the unrecognized prior service cost, then the excess is reported as a reduction of equity, net of any tax benefits.

Measurement of Cost and Obligations.   FASB 87 provides much more guidance than its predecessors with respect to the interest rate assumptions chosen by the plan sponsor. In essence, the interest rate assumption used

---

[9]See footnote 6.

[10]Technically, this amount will be increased by any previously recognized unfunded accrued pension cost and reduced by any previously recognized prepaid pension cost. These terms are defined in the next paragraph.

for funding calculations actually has two separate elements in the pension accounting context. The first is the assumed discount rate, which must reflect the rates at which the pension benefit could be effectively settled. FASB 87 states that it is appropriate to consider rates used to price annuity contracts that could be used to settle the pension obligation (including the rates used by the PBGC to value the liabilities of terminating pension plans). Rates of return on high-quality, fixed income investments currently available and expected to be available during the period to maturity of the pension benefits also may be considered.

The second assumption deals with the expected long-term rate of return on plan assets and is not necessarily equal to the discount rate assumption. FASB 87 states that this assumption must reflect the average rate of earnings expected on the funds invested or to be invested to provide for the benefits included in the projected benefit obligation. This will necessitate an assumption as to the rate of return available for reinvestment as well as for the current assets.

Disclosures.   An employer sponsoring a defined benefit pension plan must disclose the following:[11]

1. A description of the plan including employee groups covered, type of benefit formula, funding policy, type of assets held, significant nonbenefit liabilities, if any, and the nature and effect of significant matters affecting comparability of information for all periods presented.
2. The amount of net periodic pension cost for the period, showing separately the service cost component, the interest cost component, the actual return on assets for the period, and the net total of other components.
3. A schedule reconciling the unfunded status of the plan with amounts reported in the employer's statement of financial position, showing separately:
    a. The fair value of plan assets.
    b. The projected benefit obligation, identifying the accumulated benefit obligation and the vested benefit obligation.
    c. The amount of unrecognized prior service cost.
    d. The amount of unrecognized net gain or loss (including asset gains and losses not yet reflected in market-related value).
    e. The amount of any remaining unrecognized net obligation or net asset existing at the date of initial application of FASB 87.
    f. The amount of any additional liability recognized as a result of underfunded accumulated benefit obligation.
    g. The amount of net pension asset or liability recognized in the statement of financial position (the net result of combining (a) through (f).

---

[11]FASB 87, ¶54.

4. The weighted-average assumed discount rate and rate of compensation increase (if applicable) used to measure the projected benefit obligation and the weighted-average expected long-term rate of return on plan assets.
5. If applicable, the amounts and types of securities of the employer and related parties included in plan assets, and the approximate amount of annual benefits of employees and retirees covered by annuity contracts issued by the employer and related parties. Also, if applicable, the alternative amortization methods used to amortize prior service cost and gains or losses and the existence and nature of commitment beyond the written terms of the plan.

Employers with Two or More Plans.   If an employer sponsors more than one defined benefit pension plan, all provisions of FASB 87 apply to each plan separately. Moreover, unless an employer has a right to use the assets of one plan to pay benefits of another, the excess assets of an overfunded plan cannot offset the additional liability for unfunded accumulated benefit obligations of another plan sponsored by the same company.

Contracts with Insurance Companies.   Benefits covered by annuity contracts are excluded from the projected benefit obligation and accumulated benefit obligation. If the benefits are covered by nonparticipating annuity contracts, the cost of the contract determines the service cost component of net periodic pension cost for that period. If participating annuity contracts are used, the excess premium (over that available from a nonparticipating annuity contract) must be recognized as an asset and amortized systematically over the expected dividend period under the contract.

Defined Contribution Plans

Under FASB 87, the net periodic pension cost for the typical defined contribution plan will be the contribution called for in that period. However, if a plan calls for contributions for periods after an individual retires or terminates, the estimated costs must be accrued during the employee's service period. An employer that sponsors one or more defined contribution plans must disclose the following separately from its defined benefit plan disclosures:

1. A description of the plan(s), including employee groups covered, the basis for determining contributions, and the nature and effect of significant matters affecting comparability of information for all periods presented.
2. The amount of cost recognized during the period.

FASB 88

FASB 88 defines one event (a settlement) that requires immediate recognition of previously unrecognized gains and losses and another event (a curtailment) that requires immediate recognition of previously unrecognized prior service cost. It also changes the method of computing gains or losses recognized on asset reversions and specifies special transition rules for companies that have undergone previous asset reversions. Companies are required to adopt FASB 87 and 88 simultaneously.

Definitions

Before discussing the mechanics behind these new accounting procedures, it is important to note the Board's interpretation of the following terms.

Settlement. A settlement is defined as a transaction that is an irrevocable action, relieves the employer of primary responsibility for a projected benefit obligation, and eliminates significant risks related to the obligation and the assets used to effect the settlement. Examples of settlements include making lump-sum cash payments to plan participants in exchange for their rights to receive specified pension benefits, and purchasing nonparticipating annuity contracts to cover vested benefits. For an example of a transaction that would not qualify as a settlement, assume that a sponsor invests in a portfolio of high-quality, fixed income securities with principal and interest payment dates similar to the estimated payment dates of benefits. Note that in this case, the decision can be reversed, and such a strategy does not relieve the employer of primary responsibility for an obligation, nor does it eliminate significant risks related to the obligation.

Annuity Contract. If the substance of a participating annuity contract is such that the employer remains subject to most of the risks and rewards associated with the obligation covered or the assets transferred to the insurance company, the purchase of the contract does not constitute a settlement.

Curtailment. A curtailment is an event that significantly reduces the expected years of future service of present employees or eliminates for a significant number of employees the accrual of defined benefits for some or all of their future services. Examples of a curtailment include the termination of employees' services earlier than expected (e.g., closing a facility) and termination or suspension of a plan so that employees do not earn additional defined benefits for future services.

Accounting for Settlement of the Pension Obligation

The maximum gain or loss in this case is the unrecognized net gain or loss plus any remaining unrecognized net asset existing at the date of initial application of FASB 87.[12] The entire maximum amount is recognized in earnings only if the entire projected benefit obligation is settled. However, if only part of the projected benefit obligation is settled, the employer will recognize in earnings a pro rata portion of the maximum amount equal to the percentage reduction in the projected benefit obligation.

If a participating annuity contract is purchased, the maximum gain is reduced by the cost of the participation right. Also, a provision is included to allow flexibility for employers who annually purchase annuities as a funding vehicle. If the cost of all settlements in a year is less than or equal to the sum of the service cost and interest cost components of net periodic pension cost for the plan for the year, gain or loss recognition is permitted but not required for those settlements. However, the accounting policy adopted must be applied consistently from year to year.

Accounting for a Plan Curtailment

Under FASB 88, the unrecognized prior service cost associated with years of service no longer expected to be rendered as the result of a curtailment is treated as a loss. This includes the cost of retroactive plan amendments and any remaining unrecognized net obligation existing at the date of initial application of FASB 87.

It should be noted that the projected benefit obligation may be decreased or increased by a curtailment. To the extent that such a gain exceeds any unrecognized net loss (or the entire gain, if an unrecognized net gain exists), it is a curtailment gain. To the extent that such a loss exceeds any unrecognized net gain (or the entire loss, if any unrecognized net loss exists), it is a curtailment loss. Any remaining unrecognized net asset existing at the date of initial application of FASB 87 is treated as an unrecognized net gain and is combined with the unrecognized net gain or loss arising subsequent to transition to FASB 87.

Special Transition Rules for a Reversion

Employers that entered into a reversion before the effective date of FASB 88 must recognize a gain as the cumulative effect of a change in accounting principle at the time of initial application of FASB 87. The amount of gain recognized is the lesser of:

---

[12]This will include any net gain or loss first measured at the time of settlement. This may happen if the insurance company uses an interest rate assumption for determining the annuity purchase price that differs from the discount rate assumed by the employer.

1. The unamortized amount related to the asset reversion.
2. Any unrecognized net asset for the plan (or the successor plan) existing at the time of transition.

QUESTIONS FOR REVIEW

1. Describe the accounting conventions used for pension plans prior to FASB 87.
2. What were the limitations of the pre–FASB 87 accounting conventions for pension plans?
3. Explain the scope of FASB 87.
4. Explain the difference between accumulated benefit obligation and projected benefit obligation.
5. Identify the six components of pension expense under FASB 87.
6. Under what circumstances must a pension plan sponsor recognize a pension liability on its balance sheet?
7. What types of interest rate assumptions are required under FASB 87?
8. Describe how contracts with insurance companies are handled under FASB 87.
9. Describe the FASB 88 accounting treatment for settlement of pension obligations.
10. Describe the FASB 88 accounting treatment for plan curtailments.

QUESTIONS FOR DISCUSSION

1. Discuss the likely impact of FASB 87 on funding levels for defined benefit pension plans.
2. Discuss the likely impact of FASB 87 on asset allocation decisions for defined benefit pension plans.
3. Assume an employer has an overfunded defined benefit pension plan and is currently considering the merits of terminating the plan and replacing it with a defined contribution pension plan. Discuss how FASB 88 might influence the employer's decision.

11

Investment of Pension Plan Assets

The next four chapters focus exclusively on the investment of plan assets for defined benefit pension plans. Chapters 11 and 12 describe the management of pension plan assets while Chapters 13 and 14 explain the basic types of funding instruments used by pension plans. Although investment of pension plan assets is also important in individual account plans (i.e., money purchase, profit sharing, thrift and savings, and cash or deferred arrangements—CODAs), a fundamental difference exists in that the investment risk is borne directly by the employees covered by these plans. As a result of this difference, sponsors of individual account plans typically provide participants with a choice of investment vehicles. Alternative funds provided under individual account plans generally include company stock, diversified funds, equity funds, fixed income funds, guaranteed investment contracts (GICs), and a money market fund.

In contrast, the investment risk under a defined benefit pension plan is borne almost entirely by the plan sponsor. It should be noted that active and retired employees may have at least an indirect interest in the performance of the plan assets, however. As discussed in Chapter 7, many defined benefit pension plans grant ad hoc increases every few years to counter the effects of inflation. To the extent that these increases depend upon a particular "cushion" of plan assets, the sponsor's investment performance may indeed have an impact on the participants. The participants may also have a stake in the adequacy of plan assets if a plan is terminated with unfunded liabilities.

INVESTMENT POLICY

An investment policy prescribes an acceptable course of action to the fund's investment managers. It communicates a risk policy in that it states the degree of investment risk that the sponsor is willing to assume.

Determining Investment Objectives

In contrast to an investment policy, an investment objective is a desired result of the investment process. Before such objectives can be established, the various risk-return characteristics of the alternative investments must be recognized.

Types of Risk.   Modern portfolio theory (described later in this chapter) defines risk in terms of the volatility of an investment (or portfolio of investments) in relation to the market. However, it is useful to consider the individual components of this aggregate concept:[1]

1. Purchasing power risk.
2. Business risk.
3. Interest rate risk.
4. Market risk.
5. Specific risk.

Purchasing power risk reflects the relationship between the nominal rate of return on an investment and the increase in the rate of inflation. Business risk involves the prospect that the corporation issuing the security may suffer a decline in earnings power that would adversely affect its ability to pay interest, principal, or dividends. Interest rate risk comprises the well-known inverse relationship between interest rates and (long-term) bond prices; that is, when interest rates increase, the value of long-term bonds will fall. This relationship often holds for equities as well.

The final two types of risk are usually used exclusively to explain stock price behavior. Market risk can be thought of as an individual stock's reaction to a change in the "market." In general, most stock prices will increase if the stock market increases appreciably and decrease if the market decreases appreciably; however, the price of one stock may change half as fast as the market, on average, while another may change twice as fast. This relationship is quantified later in the chapter by a measure known as "beta."

Obviously, market risk cannot account for the entire fluctuation of a stock's price. For example, if a biotechnology firm suddenly patents an unexpected cure for cancer, there would most likely be a rapid increase in

---

[1] Jerome B. Cohen, Edward D. Zinbarg, and Arthur Zeikel, *Investment Analysis and Portfolio Management*, 5th ed. (Homewood, Ill.: Richard D. Irwin, 1987), pp. 6-11.

its stock price in expectation of the future profit stream. In contrast, if the product developed by this firm later resulted in a massive product liability award for which the firm was not adequately insured, the stock price would most likely fall. These factors, intrinsic to the firm, are known as specific risks.

Characteristics of Investments.   There are four primary characteristics of pension plan investments that need to be considered:

1. Tax advantages.
2. Liquidity.
3. Stability in value.
4. Ability to preserve purchasing power.

The tax aspect of the investment is important due to the tax-exempt status of the pension fund, mentioned in Chapter 4. Because investment income of qualified pension plans is tax-exempt, certain types of investments may not be as attractive to pension funds as they would be for other types of funds. For example, the price of municipal bonds is likely to be bid up by individual investors in the highest marginal tax rates until they reach a point where their before-tax rates of return are below those that can be realized on corporate bonds or U.S. government bonds of a similar maturity.

Liquidity refers to the ability to convert an investment to cash within a short time period with little, if any, loss in principal. This may be an important attribute for at least a portion of the pension plan assets in case the plan has to weather a short period of time when the plan sponsor is unable to make contributions (or contributions are less than the amount of the benefit payments for the year) and at the same time the securities markets are depressed. If the plan did not possess an adequate degree of liquidity, the sponsor would have to sell securities at an inopportune time, perhaps resulting in the realization of capital losses.

Stability in value is closely akin to liquidity in that it emphasizes investments with minimal fluctuations in value. Achieving maximum stability in value is not particularly difficult   one need only limit investments to U.S. Treasury bills and money market instruments. However, the opportunity cost of forgone higher investment returns in riskier assets may be prohibitive. Instead, the objective of the sponsor should be to construct a portfolio that will maximize investment income for the desired level of risk.

The ability to preserve purchasing power is important because many defined benefit pension plans attempt to provide at least a partial offset against inflation for their retirees.

Historical Returns Achieved by the Various Classes.   Although there have been several empirical studies of the historical risk-return trade-off exhibited by the major classes of investments, the seminal work is that of

Ibbotson and Sinquefield.[2] They statistically analyzed a 53-year time series of the four major classes of investments and found, as expected, that the riskiest investments also generated the highest yields. Common stocks provided the highest annual return with a mean of 8.9 percent.[3] However, investors purchasing common stocks paid a price in terms of the volatility of their investment—the standard deviation for common stocks was 22.2 percent.[4] Long-term corporate bonds yielded a mean return of 4 percent over this period with a standard deviation of 5.6 percent, while long-term bonds issued by the government had a slightly higher risk (5.7 percent) but a somewhat lower return (3.2 percent). U.S. Treasury bills were obviously the safest investment and had a standard deviation of only 2.2 percent; however, they only generated a mean return of 2.5 percent.

These figures cannot be viewed in isolation, and it is important to consider how they fared after the effects of inflation had been removed. During this 53-year period, the geometric mean for inflation was 2.5 percent, an amount that should be subtracted from the nominal rate of return to find the real rate of return produced by an investment. For example, the real rate of return of common stocks during this period was 6.4 percent, while U.S. Treasury bills generated a real rate of return of 0 percent.

Guidelines for Investment Managers

After the investment objectives have been developed, they need to be expressed in a manner that is useful to the investment manager. Often, this expression takes the form of a guideline statement. The guideline statement should cover such questions as:[5]

1. How much risk is the plan sponsor prepared to take to achieve a specific benchmark rate of return?
2. What is the time period for measurement of performance relative to objectives?
3. What is the sponsor's preference in terms of asset mix, especially as it relates to stocks?

[2]Roger G. Ibbotson and Rex A. Sinquefield, *Stocks, Bonds, Bills and Inflation: Historical Returns 1926–1978* (Charlottesville, Va.: The Financial Analysts Research Foundation, 1979).

[3]Technically, the returns reported in this chapter are geometric average returns (sometimes referred to as compound annual returns). The figure can be obtained by multiplying (1 + rate of return) for each of the n years in the time series and then taking the nth root of the product. It should be noted that this is not the same as computing an arithmetic average, which is obtained by simply adding the rates of return for each of the n years in the time series and then dividing by n. Unless the rate of return is constant over the n-year time series, the geometric average will be less than the arithmetic average.

[4]The standard deviation is simply a statistical measure of the variability of a distribution of observations around its mean value. In general, the greater the standard deviation for a distribution, the greater the variability of the observations.

[5]Martin D. Sass, "How (Not) to Manage Your Pension Fund Manager," *FE Manual*, August 1985, pp. 38–39.

4. What is the liability outlook for the plan and what should the fund's investment strategy be in light of this outlook?
5. What are the sponsor's cash flow or liquidity requirements?
6. How much discretion is the manager permitted regarding foreign investment, private placements, options, financial futures, and so on?

Another matter that needs to be discussed at an early stage is exactly what constitutes an acceptable level of turnover. In a study released by the Department of Labor in 1986, it was revealed that ERISA plans had tripled their equity turnover between 1975 and 1983.[6] Moreover, analysis of the sample period (1968–1983) failed to demonstrate conclusively the significance of turnover as a factor in explaining total plan performance or the performance of equity and fixed income portfolios.[7] If the sponsor has decided that extensive turnover activity does not add value to the portfolio performance, guidelines to limit this activity should be established. If the sponsor has come to the conclusion that turnover expenses should be virtually eliminated, a tactic known as passive investment should be considered.[8]

Performance Measurement

The primary purpose of performance measurement is to "obtain information on which to base decisions in regard to investment objectives, portfolio strategy, and manager selection. In addition, performance measurement should improve communications with managers by creating a standard format for discussion."[9]

Effective performance measurement requires four steps:[10]

1. *Definition*. Establishment of investment objectives and, to the extent practical, clearly formulated portfolio strategy.
2. *Input*. Availability of reliable and timely data. Incorrect and tardy data will render the most sophisticated system ineffective.
3. *Processing*. Use of appropriate statistical methods to produce relevant measurements. The complex interaction of objectives, strategies, and

---

[6]Berkowitz, Logue & Associates, *Study of The Investment Performance of ERISA Plans*, study prepared for the Office of Pension and Welfare Benefits, Department of Labor, July 21, 1986.

[7]A subsequent study conducted by researchers at the U.S. Department of Labor has demonstrated that over the period 1977–1983, when measured net of investment fees and expense, pension plans underperform broad market indexes on the order of 100 basis points per annum. However, the hypothesis that this finding is attributable to excessive fees and turnover is uniformly rejected by the data. (Richard A. Ippolito and John A. Tuner, "Turnover, Fees and Pension Plan Performance," Mimeograph, September 1986.)

[8]See Chapter 12 for a detailed discussion of this topic.

[9]Sidney Cottle, "Pension Asset Management — Measuring Performance," *Financial Executive*, September 1981, p. 24.

[10]Ibid, p. 25.

managers' tactics cannot be understood if inappropriate statistical methods are used. A meaningful summary will make possible analysis of the investment process at the necessary depth.

4. *Output*. Analysis of the process and results presented in a useful format. Presentation should relate realized performance to objectives and preestablished standards. Enough material should be available to understand and analyze the process. Exhibits should be designed to highlight weaknesses in the investment process and to suggest possible improvements.

Four important caveats must be kept in mind in choosing a performance measurement system:[11]

1. There is a danger that a hastily chosen system, poorly related to real needs, can rapidly degenerate into a mechanistic, pointless exercise.
2. The system should fit the investment objectives and not the reverse.
3. Measuring the process may alter it.
4. To save time and cost, it is important that overmeasurement be avoided.

Performance Measurement Methodology.   Before any performance is measured, it is necessary to agree upon the correct definition for the return that is measured. Two alternative definitions, internal rate of return and time-weighted rate of return, have been used in the investment community for over 20 years. It is quite likely that the two rates of return will vary considerably. Therefore, it is critical that the sponsor understand the differences.

The internal rate of return (or dollar-weighted rate of return) is the rate that accumulates all of the cash flows (C) of a portfolio, including all outlays, to exactly the market value of the ending balance (MVEB). Assuming that the portfolio experienced j separate cash inflows and k separate cash outflows during the year,[12] the internal rate of return is the value of r that satisfies the following equation:

$$\text{MVEB} = C_1 \times (1 + r)^{t_1} + C_2 \times (1 + r)^{t_2} + \ldots + C_j \times (1 + r)^{t_j}$$
$$- C_{j+1} \times (1 + r)^{t_j + 1} - C_{j+2} \times (1 + r)^{t_j + 2} - \ldots$$
$$- C_{j+k} \times (1 + r)^{t_j + k}$$

The term t_1 denotes the time elapsed from the first investment until the end of the year, t_2 denotes the time elapsed from the second investment until the end of the year, and t_j denotes the time elapsed from the last investment until the end of the year. The term t_{j+1} denotes the time elapsed from the first cash withdrawal from the portfolio until the end of

---

[11]Cottle, "Pension Asset Management," p. 25.
[12]Any time period can be used for this measurement. The end of the year was selected as the measurement date in this example merely to simplify the discussion.

the year, the term t_{j+2} denotes the time elapsed from the second cash withdrawal from the portfolio until the end of the year, and the term t_{j+k} denotes the time elapsed from the last cash withdrawal from the portfolio until the end of the year.

The following example illustrates the calculation of an internal rate of return. Assume that a fund allocates $100 million to a new manager on January 1, and withdraws $50 million on July 1. If the market value of the assets increased by 5 percent during the first six months, the value on July 1 would be $100,000,000 × (1.05) − $50,000,000, or $55,000,000. If the market value of the assets increased by 10 percent during the next six months, the value on December 31 would be $55,000,000 × (1.1), or $60,500,000.

The internal rate of return (X) for this portfolio can by determined by choosing a value for r and solving the following equation (all dollar amounts are expressed in millions):

$$X = 100 \times (1 + r)^1 - 50 \times (1 + r)^{1/2}$$

If the value of X obtained for a particular value of r is larger (smaller) than the market value of the ending balance, then the chosen value of r is most likely too high (low).[13] For example, assume that the first estimate of r in the above equation is 15 percent. Substituting .15 for r gives a value of 61.00 for X. Since this value is larger than the market value of the ending balance (60.5), a smaller estimate of r is chosen. Assume a value of 10 percent is used in the second iteration. The new value of X is 57.56, which is lower than the market value of the ending balance. At this point, it is known that a solution will exist in the range of 10 to 15 percent. Subsequent iterations eventually produce an answer of 13.9 percent.

The internal rate of return is valuable in that it allows the sponsor to determine whether the investment is achieving the rate of return assumed for actuarial calculations; however, it is largely ineffective as a means of evaluating investment managers because it is contaminated by the effects of the timing of investments and withdrawals—a factor over which the investment manager presumably has no control. In response to this limitation of the internal rate of return approach, the Bank Administration Institute published a study in 1968 that suggested a different performance measurement technique known as the time-weighted rate of return. This value is computed by:[14]

> dividing the interval under study into subintervals whose boundaries are the dates of cash flows into and out of the fund and by computing the internal rate of return for each subinterval. The time-weighted rate of return is the [geometric]

---

[13]A major limitation of the internal rate of return approach is that it may produce multiple solutions for some cash flow patterns.

[14]*Measuring the Investment Performance of Pension Funds for the Purpose of Inter-Fund Comparison* (Park Ridge, Ill.: Bank Administration Institute, 1968).

average for the rates for these subintervals, with each rate having a weight proportional to the length of time in its corresponding subinterval.

This method can be illustrated by continuing the above example. Dividing the interval under study (one year) into subintervals of one-half year each and computing the internal rate of return for each, it is determined that the internal rate of return for the first six months was 10.3 percent and 20.9 percent for the second six months. The time-weighted rate of return can be determined by solving the following equation:

$$(1 + r_1) \times (1 + r_2) = (1 + r)^2.$$

The values of r_1 and r_2 represent the internal rate of return for the first and second halves of the year, respectively. Solving for r, the time-weighted rate of return, gives a value of 15.5 percent.

The reason that the time-weighted rate of return was larger than the internal rate of return in this example is due to the fact that the investment manager achieved a higher return during the period that less assets were available for investment.

Assessing Risk.   Having correctly measured the time-weighted returns, it is necessary to evaluate the risk-adjusted performance of investment managers. Although some investment managers still report their performance by comparing their equity portfolio return with a common stock index (such as the Standard & Poor's 500 Stock Average [S&P 500] index) and their bond portfolio results with a bond index (such as the Shearson Lehman Brothers government and corporate bond index) without any adjustment for their portfolio's risk, there is a growing realization that return cannot be meaningfully evaluated without simultaneously considering the risk of the investment. Portfolio risks are commonly measured in one or more of three ways:[15]

1. Total variability in absolute terms.
2. Total variability in relative terms.
3. Market-related variability.

Absolute risk can be measured in one of two ways. The most common is to compute the standard deviation of the periodic returns. Another method is to rank in order the returns over a particular period and to divide the distribution into percentiles. The range from the 25th to the 75th percentile, referred to as the semi-interquartile range in several measurement systems, is then used as a measure of the portfolio's absolute risk.

Relative risk measurements start with one of the two absolute risk measurements for the portfolio in question and then divide it by a similar measure for the market during the same time period. For example, if the

---

[15]Cottle, "Pension Asset Management," p. 28.

absolute risk measure for an equity portfolio was its standard deviation based on quarterly returns for the last five years, the denominator for the relative risk measure might be the standard deviation of the S&P 500 based on quarterly returns for the last five years.

Although relative risk measurement is an improvement over absolute risk measurement in that it factors in the activity of the market over the measurement period, at present the state of the art for adjusting returns for risk is to use the capital asset pricing model (CAPM).[16] The CAPM uses standard statistical techniques (simple linear regression) to analyze the relationship between the periodic returns of the portfolio and those of the market (e.g., the S&P 500). Although several modifications of the basic regression analysis exist, most applications will begin by subtracting out a risk-free rate of return (e.g., the Treasury bill rate) from both the portfolio and market returns.

For those not familiar with regression analysis, this technique can be thought of as simply plotting the periodic returns of the portfolio (on the vertical axis) against the periodic returns of the market (on the horizontal axis). A minimum number of data points are required for the statistical procedure to operate with a desired degree of confidence. The number of observations plotted depends upon the type of returns measured—five years of data are typically used in the case of quarterly returns, while three years of data are typically considered to be sufficient if monthly information is used. The straight line that provides the "best fit" for the observations is drawn on the graph and two features of this line are noted. The first is the point at which the line crosses the vertical axis and zero on the horizontal axis. This is referred to as the portfolio's "alpha" value, and can be thought of as the amount of return produced by the portfolio, on average, independent of the return on the market. The second feature is the slope of the line measured as the change in vertical movement per unit of change in the horizontal movement. This is referred to as the portfolio's "beta" value, and represents the average return on the portfolio per 1 percent return on the market. For example, if the portfolio's beta is 1.25, then a 2 percent increase (decrease) in the market would be expected to be associated with a 2.5 percent (1.25 × 2) increase (decrease) in the portfolio, on average.

Assessing Performance.   Once the portfolio's beta has been computed, it is possible to use the CAPM to provide a risk-adjusted measure of the

---

[16]It should be noted that this theory is based on a number of very restrictive assumptions: investors are risk-averse individuals who maximize the expected utility of their end-of-period wealth; investors make their investment decisions based on a single-period horizon; transaction costs are low enough to ignore; taxes do not affect the choice of buying one asset versus another; all individuals can borrow and lend unlimited amounts of money at a single-period riskless rate of interest; and all individuals agree on the nature of the return and risk associated with each investment. However, extensions of the CAPM have solved many of these problems. See Thomas E. Copeland and J. Fred Weston, *Financial Theory and Corporate Policy* (Reading, Mass.: Addison-Wesley Publishing, 1983), pp. 197–204.

portfolio's performance. The CAPM asserts that the predicted risk-adjusted rate of return for the portfolio (R_p) will be equal to the risk-free rate (R_f) plus a risk premium that is equal to the amount of risk, beta (β), times a market risk premium that is equal to the difference between the market rate of return (R_m) and the risk-free rate:

$$R_p = R_f + (R_m - R_f) \times \beta.$$

To illustrate this concept, assume that an investment manager's portfolio has a beta of 1.25, the risk-free rate of return is 6 percent, and the market rate of return is 10 percent. If the portfolio yielded a rate of return of 11.5 percent, what is the risk-adjusted rate of return? The answer is found by first finding the predicted risk-adjusted rate of return for the portfolio. This is accomplished by simply substituting the values in the equation above:

$$R_p = .06 + (.1 - .06) \times 1.25 = .11.$$

This predicted value is then subtracted from the portfolio's actual value to produce a risk-adjusted rate of return of a positive 0.5 percent $(11.5 - 11)$. The risk-adjusted rate of return can be used to measure risk-adjusted performance and to compare portfolios with different risk levels developed by actual portfolio decisions.

ALLOCATION OF FUND ASSETS

The asset allocation decision is a process that determines the best portfolio composition among the various major types of assets (stocks, bonds, etc.). This decision takes into account the sponsor's investment objective and, as a result, reflects the level of risk desired by the sponsor.

Major Factors to Be Considered

In addition to the type of plan (i.e., defined benefit versus individual account), there are three considerations that must be assessed in setting investment objectives:

1. Characteristics of the sponsor and its industry.
2. Demographics of the work force and maturity of the plan.
3. Possibility of plan termination.

Characteristics of the sponsor and its industry must be considered in determining policy. For example, a sponsor with thin profit margins, high labor costs, and in a highly cyclical industry has less tolerance for variability in pension costs than does a company with relatively large profit margins, low labor costs, and a less cyclical earnings pattern. Whether the industry as a whole is growing, stagnant, or declining also will affect the degree of conservatism built into the investment strategy.

Demographics is also important because a rapidly growing company with a young work force has less concern for cash flow and investment liquidity than does a company with a more mature work force and many pensioners. A sponsor in the first category would be more likely to have the ability to withstand several years of capital losses on the pension plan portfolio without impeding benefit payments.[17]

The possibility of plan termination is important for companies with some risk of plan shutdown, merger, acquisition, or other corporate reorganization because the investment policy must take into account the possibility that the Pension Benefit Guaranty Corporation (PBGC) will take over the plan and value the plan assets at the time of termination at the current market value. If a plan termination occurs during a business recession and the PBGC steps in, the claim against the sponsoring company will be larger.

QUESTIONS FOR REVIEW

1. Describe the major types of investment risk.
2. Describe why an investment's relative liquidity may be important to a pension plan's investment manager.
3. What have historical studies demonstrated with respect to the risk-return characteristics of the major classes of investments?
4. What types of questions should the investment manager's guideline statement cover?
5. Describe the steps involved in effective performance measurement.
6. Explain how the internal rate of return and the time-weighted rate of return are calculated.
7. Which of the two rates of return mentioned in the previous question should be used for performance measurement? Explain.
8. Explain the importance of the alpha and beta values produced by the capital asset pricing model (CAPM).
9. Explain the importance of the risk-adjusted rate of return.
10. Explain the factors that should be considered in the allocation of pension fund assets.

---

[17]This statement only considers the cash flow aspects of the plan. As described in Chapter 9, many of the actuarial cost methods used to determine the minimum funding standard for a defined benefit pension plan will amortize investment gains and losses over a maximum of 15 years. Therefore, if the sponsor desires to control volatility of the contribution stream from year to year, it is important that pension plan investments do not experience a large decline in value. Moreover, with the advent of FASB 87, there are now several accounting consequences of pension plan asset allocation that must take into consideration the goals of the plan.

QUESTIONS FOR DISCUSSION

1. If common stocks are assumed to produce a higher long-term rate of return than bonds, discuss why many defined benefit pension plan portfolios contain a significant percentage of bonds.

2. Discuss how the beta value produced by the capital asset pricing model could be used to construct an investment portfolio suited to the employer's objectives.

3. Discuss why performance measurement based exclusively on rate of return may lead to nonoptimal investment strategies.

12

Investment Objectives: Tactics

Chapter 11 described the essential elements of an investment policy and provided a brief introduction to the major factors to be considered in the asset allocation decision. This chapter concludes the discussion of investment objectives by considering the various tactics available to achieve these objectives. The most popular classes of assets used for pension plan investments are described, the process of selecting an investment manager is explained, and the relative advantages and limitation of passive management of pension assets are explored. The trust fund mechanism for holding and accumulating assets is discussed in Chapter 13, and special insurance and annuity products are discussed in Chapter 14.

CLASSES OF ASSETS

Retirement plan assets are estimated to be more than $1 trillion for the 1,000 largest U.S. plans. The largest 200 funds held the following assets in their portfolios in 1985:

Stocks: 41.6 percent.
Bonds: 33.3 percent.
Money market instruments: 8.5 percent.
Real estate: 4.2 percent.
GICs: 3.7 percent.
Mortgage-backed securities: 3.1 percent.

Mortgages: 2.2 percent.
Annuities: 0.8 percent.
Other: 2.6 percent.

Annuities are discussed in Chapter 14. The other major classes, as well as mutual funds and financial futures, are discussed below.

Money Market Instruments

As discussed in Chapter 11, pension plans will typically have a need to retain at least a portion of their assets in vehicles that will be readily convertible to cash. The exact portion will depend upon the specifics of the plan design (e.g., loan features and employee's ability to select lump-sum distributions) and the demographics of the plan participants. This portion of the portfolio should be invested in assets that have a low default risk, a short maturity, and are readily marketable. There are five major categories of this type of investment alternative: U.S. Treasury bills and notes, federal agency issues, certificates of deposit, commercial paper, and money market mutual funds.

U.S. Treasury Bills and Notes.   Treasury bills have maturities at issue ranging from 91 to 360 days, while Treasury notes have initial maturities ranging from 1 to 5 years. There is no default risk on these investments. In other words, the probability that either interest or principal payments will be skipped is zero.

Federal Agency Issues.   The Treasury is not the only federal agency to issue marketable obligations. Other agencies issue short-term obligations that range in maturity from one month to over 10 years. These instruments will typically yield slightly more than Treasury obligations with a similar maturity.

Certificates of Deposit.   These certificates are issued by commercial banks and have a fixed maturity, generally in the range of 90 days to one year. The ability to sell a certificate of deposit prior to maturity usually depends upon its denomination. If it is over $100,000, it can usually be sold in a secondary market; if it is under that amount, banks will usually assess a penalty if they buy it back early. The default risk for these certificates depends upon the issuing bank, but it is usually quite small. Therefore, their yield is generally only slightly higher than similar maturities in the previous two categories.

Commercial Paper.   This is typically an unsecured short-term note of a large corporation. This investment offers maturities that range up to 270 days, but the marketability is somewhat limited if an early sale is required.

The default risk depends upon the credit standing of the issuer, but commensurately higher yield is available.

Money Market Mutual Funds.   These funds invest in the money market instruments described above. As a result, investors achieve a yield almost as high as that paid by the direct investments themselves and at the same time benefit from the diversification of any default risk over a much larger population of investments. In addition, these funds allow the pension plan to maintain complete liquidity with respect to this portion of their portfolio.

Bonds

The use of bonds in pension plan portfolios can typically be attributed to one of two reasons. First, if the sponsor realizes that (to a large extent) the pension plan's obligations are fixed dollar obligations that will be paid out several years in the future, there may be a desire to purchase assets that will generate a cash flow similar to the benefit payments. This technique is referred to as dedication or immunization and is described in detail later in this chapter. Second, the investment manager may be willing to purchase assets with a longer maturity than the money market instruments described above. This assumption of interest rate risk is presumably compensated by a higher yield than that available from shorter maturities.

Bonds are simply long-term debt claims entitling the holder to periodic interest and full repayment of principal by the issuer. For purposes of this discussion, the universe of bonds will be dichotomized into corporate bonds and government bonds.

Corporate Bonds.   There are several characteristics of corporate bonds that are important to pension plan investment managers. For example, there are different degrees by which the promises of future cash flow are secured. Under a mortgage bond, a corporation pledges certain real assets as security for the bond. In contrast, a debenture is a long-term bond that is not secured by a pledge of any specific property. However, it is secured by any property not otherwise pledged.

The ability of the issuing corporation to call in the bond for redemption prior to the stated maturity date is known as a call provision. Although the issuer must typically pay some type of penalty (known as a call premium) for exercising this right, the holder of a bond with a call provision must be cognizant of the fact that the amount received (call premium plus principal) may be less than the value of the bond if the call had not been exercised. This will typically be the case in times of declining interest rates.

The marketability of corporate bonds is usually not an issue. However, if the investment manager sells them prior to the maturity date, the price received will be subject to both the business risk and interest rate risk described in Chapter 11. Investment managers must also be concerned with business risk, even if there is an intention to hold the bonds until maturity.

Government Bonds.   As mentioned in Chapter 11, pension plans will limit their investments in government bonds to those that generate taxable investment income. Hence, municipal bonds are not candidates for inclusion in a pension plan portfolio. Federal government bonds are possible candidates and they are evaluated in a manner similar to the corporate bonds. The major exception is that the default risk is nonexistent and, as a result, the yield would be expected to be lower than that available on corporate bonds of similar maturities.

The field of government bonds has expanded to include mortgage-related securities. Government National Mortgage Association (GNMA) pass-through certificates have an interest in a pool of single-family residential mortgages that are insured by the Federal Housing Authority or the Veteran's Administration. The timely payment of principal and interest on these securities is guaranteed by the U.S. government. The Federal Home Loan Mortgage Corporation (FHLMC) issues another mortgage-backed security, known as Freddie Mac. Although this instrument is not guaranteed by the U.S. government, it is unconditionally guaranteed by the FHLMC.

Common Stocks

Although there is no definitive manner of categorizing common stocks, it is customary to speak of them in the following terms:[1]

1. *Blue chip stocks*. These are stocks issued by major companies with long and unbroken records of earnings and dividend payments. They should appeal primarily to pension plans seeking safety and stability.

2. *Growth stocks*. These are stocks issued by companies whose sales, earnings, and share of the market are expanding faster than either the general economy or the industry average. They represent a higher risk, but the prospects for capital appreciation should produce a correspondingly higher total return. Because they pay relatively small dividends, they may not be attractive to pension plans with cash flow problems.

3. *Income stocks*. These are stocks that pay higher than average dividend returns. They were attractive to pension plans that bought stock for current income. However, they have taken on new importance for nontax-exempt investors since the Tax Reform Act of 1986 phased out the advantages of capital gains treatment. It remains to be seen whether the price of these stocks will be bid up to prohibitive levels.

---

[1]Jerome B. Cohen, Edward D. Zinbarg, and Arthur Zeikel, *Investment Analysis and Portfolio Management*, 5th ed. (Homewood, Ill.: Richard D. Irwin, 1987), pp. 21–29.

4. *Cyclical stocks*. These are stocks issued by companies whose earnings fluctuate with the business cycle and are accentuated by it.

5. *Defensive stocks*. These are stocks issued by recession-resistant companies. This may be an important consideration for pension plans that cannot afford major capital losses.

6. *Interest-sensitive stocks*. These are stocks whose prices tend to drop when interest rates rise, and vice versa. It is quite possible that there will be an increased demand among pension plans for these stocks as a result of FASB 87. As explained in Chapter 10, a decline in the discount rate for valuing the present value of the pension obligations will result in increased pension expenses (once the corridor is exceeded) unless there is a corresponding increase in the value of the pension assets.

Mutual Funds

For plans with assets too small to be handled by an investment manager, mutual funds may be the only choice, other than a common trust fund. Larger plans may also choose mutual funds as a relatively inexpensive way of diversifying their portfolios.[2]

Pension plans have been choosing mutual funds more frequently in recent years for the following reasons:[3]

1. Greater liquidity through ease of entry and exit.
2. Greater degree of diversification.
3. Easier means of portfolio specialization.
4. Daily update of holdings through newspaper listings.
5. Ease of meeting asset allocation or market timing goals.
6. Ease of checking past performance through published studies and indexes.

Real Estate

The enormous number of real estate investments available in today's market makes a comprehensive treatment of this topic beyond the scope of this book.[4] However, certain basic characteristics of this market provide insight as to its overall place in a pension plan portfolio. First, real estate investments (particularly ownership interests) appear to offer an adequate inflation hedge under most scenarios. Second, real estate investing does not operate in the same efficient market as stocks and bonds. Instead of having several thousand individuals bidding on the price of a homogeneous asset each day, a real estate property may be on the market for months before

---

[2]See the passive versus active management section later in this chapter for more detail.

[3]Jay M. Dade, "Mutual Funds Today: Strength through Diversity," *Pension World*, December 1986, pp. 34–36.

[4]For an excellent discussion of this topic, see *Investment Policy Guidebook for Corporate Pension Plan Trustees*, Appendix A (Brookfield, Wis.: International Foundation of Employee Benefit Plans, 1984).

any offer is made. A third point, closely related to the second, is the relative lack of marketability for many real estate investments. This feature alone would prevent most pension plans from investing the preponderance of their assets in real estate. A final point deals with the volatility of real estate investments. Although it is difficult to develop reliable estimates in the absence of an active market, the consensus opinion appears to be that the volatility of real estate investments has been significantly below that of common stocks.

Futures

A futures contract is an agreement to make or take delivery of a specified commodity (e.g., the S&P 500 index) at a specified date at an agreed-upon price. No money changes hands until the delivery date; however, a deposit is required that may be invested in Treasury securities in the interim. The account is settled each day. This means that if a pension plan made a contract to sell the S&P 500 in the future and the index declined that day, money is deposited into the pension plan's account; however, money would be withdrawn from the account if the index had increased.

Although this may appear to be a highly speculative investment when viewed in isolation, many pension plans have started to use this technique in conjunction with an existing portfolio of equities. This may serve as a useful hedge against losses in the equity portfolio. A particular type of hedging, known as portfolio insurance, is described later in this chapter.

Guaranteed Investment Contracts

Some insurance companies have developed contracts for special lump-sum arrangements designed to attract pension or profit sharing funds. These contracts, often called *guaranteed investment contracts, guaranteed interest contracts, guaranteed income contracts, guaranteed return contracts,* or just *GICs,* have proven extremely popular in recent years. Under this type of arrangement, the insurer guarantees a fairly high interest rate such as 9 to 10 percent for a number of years on a lump-sum payment.[5] Many variations exist among the GICs offered. However, two basic types of contracts are used, the so-called bullet contract and the extended guarantee contract.[6] The bullet type of GIC receives a single deposit from a plan sponsor, holds the funds for a specified period at a specified interest rate, and pays the funds at a maturity, which commonly runs from 3 to 10 years.

[5]For a number of reports on various aspects of Guaranteed Investment Contracts see *Employee Benefit Plan Review Research Reports* (Chicago, Ill.: Charles D. Spencer and Associates, Inc.), Section 150.

[6]See *Time to Renegotiate* (Meidinger Asset Planning Services, Inc., 1982), p. 3.

Under the extended guarantee type of GIC, the insurance company accepts deposits from the plan sponsor over a period of several years and credits them with the agreed-upon interest rates. Various other arrangements are possible; for example, other GICs offer an attractive minimum-interest rate, with participation features and also guarantee repayment of principal at book value over a period of years after a specified date. Still others do not specify a guaranteed interest rate in percentage terms, but guarantee payment of the insurance company's general account earned new-money rates during each year over the entire life of the contract, during both the accumulation and payout periods—whatever they turn out to be each year—and offer a variety of principal repayment methods. Almost all GICs offer many annuity or other payout options, but the contract holder docs not have to utilize such options. Moreover, many insurance companies are willing to negotiate terms and provisions to be included in larger contracts especially suited to the needs of a particular pension plan. Other forms of guaranteed investment contracts, providing for continuing deposits, have been developed for profit sharing and savings plans.

The market for GICs appears to be large for a number of reasons. Primarily, GICs presently provide a rate of return in excess of rates obtainable from most fixed income securities. In addition, the fixed income fund is the most popular account in most defined contribution pension, profit sharing, and thrift plans. GICs can provide the contract holder with a combination of protection against loss of principal if interest rates rise generally from the time of purchase either by receiving payment of principal at book value in a lump sum under some contracts, or over a period of time under others, and a call on higher guaranteed interest rates during extended payout option periods if interest rates decline from the time of purchase to the time of payout.

To trustee fiduciaries and pension fund investment managers concerned about the prudent expert standards, the guarantees provided by GICs and the insurance companies backing them up are attractive.[7] Moreover, GIC guarantees often may allow the plan's actuary to use a higher assumed interest rate in determining required contributions and reserves. As a result, the employer's contributions to a plan frequently can be reduced immediately and net earnings of the employer can be increased.

In evaluating GICs, particular attention should be paid to some of the following plan characteristics:[8]

1. The level of guaranteed interest rate return.
2. Whether the contract is on a participating or nonparticipating basis.

---

[7]See Mary E. Weims, "Guaranteed Investment Contracts: Considerations for the Pension Fiduciary," *Employee Benefits Journal*, June 1983, pp. 5–9.

[8]For a more detailed evaluation of GIC plan characteristics see Dan M. McGill, *Fundamentals of Private Pensions*, 5th ed. (Homewood, Ill.: Richard D. Irwin, 1984), pp. 469–72.

3. The length of the period over which payment of the specified interest rate is guaranteed.
4. The right of the contract holders to liquidate their contracts for cash, should cash be needed, before the maturity date.
5. Whether any penalties or risk of loss exist on cash-out or termination of a contract at or after maturity, if there is an upward movement in interest rates from the time of purchase to the time of cash-out or maturity.
6. The optional methods of obtaining maturity values and the level of expenses charged against the earnings.
7. The attractiveness of guaranteed annuity purchase rates provided under the optional methods of settlement and the time period of such guarantees.

GICs will probably continue to be very popular for many of the reasons cited here. They can be made very flexible to meet the specific objectives of the employer and employees, and they can also be used easily for profit sharing and thrift plans as well as pension plans.

SELECTING AN INVESTMENT MANAGER

The process of selecting an investment manager obviously differs from sponsor to sponsor; however, the following five steps are typical of the procedure employed by many sponsors.[9]

Review of Investment Firms

The first step is to initiate a search to screen initial candidates. This procedure is generally conducted by an individual within the plan sponsor's firm, perhaps with the aid of outside consultants. Plan sponsors can obtain outside consulting services from a number of sources, including brokerage firms, actuarial and accounting organizations, and pension consulting firms.

Although many sponsors may be inclined to perform the investment firm review solely on an in-house basis, there are several potential advantages of a consultant that should be considered. First, since the consultants have continuing exposure to the investment firms, they will probably have a better understanding of which investment firms could best serve the sponsor's objectives. Second, consultants have much more experience in the evaluation process. They are less likely to ask the investment firms vague questions that yield little, if any, useful information and they are less inclined to have their decisions swayed by ingenious presentations. On a more positive side, they can pinpoint the specific information needed from investment management candidates, frame the questionnaire, and help

---

[9]*Investment Policy Guidebook*, pp. 103–6.

organize the subsequent interviews. Third, consultants can help construct the initial list, so that firms may be screened efficiently without the search team having to waste time and effort.

Regardless of whether the plan sponsor is being aided by a consultant, there is an obvious need to obtain information on investment firms at this stage. Fortunately, several sources exist for this purpose. Included among these are top management and members of the board of directors, counterparts at other companies, pension fund actuaries, accountants and attorneys, specialized magazines (such as *Pensions & Investment Age* and *Pension World*), and senior officers of brokerage companies.

Send Detailed Questionnaires

After the original list has been reduced to a manageable size (perhaps with the aid of a consultant), a detailed questionnaire should be sent to the remaining investment firms. The questionnaire should be carefully designed to elicit specific information on several topics, including:

1. Portfolio strategies and tactics.
2. Ownership as well as employee compensation.
3. Decision-making procedures.
4. List of current clients and specific people to contact for references.
5. Names of accounts lost as well as those gained in recent years.
6. Historic performance of each class of assets managed.
7. Explanation of exactly how the firm's performance statistics have been computed.

Conduct Interviews

After the questionnaires have been reviewed and the references have been thoroughly checked, interviews should be conducted (in the presence of the sponsor's consultant, if one is used). Whether it is better to hold the initial interview at the sponsor's location or to visit the offices of candidates is debatable; however, it is argued that the latter produces a more realistic impression of the investment firm.

It is important that specific guidelines for the presentations be formulated in advance. For example, the "canned presentations" should be limited within some specific time frame. Moreover, questions should be designed to elicit specific information on:

Research procedures.
Decision-making routine.
Strategies and tactics employed.
Control disciplines.
Transaction guidelines.

Levels of salaries and other incentives for employees.
Key personnel.
Investment performance statistics and the degree of performance variation among accounts.

Final Evaluation

Before an attempt is made to analyze the information obtained from the interviews, it may be useful to review sample portfolios of the investment firms to assess whether a firm actually utilizes the methods described by its literature and representatives. At this time, the written questionnaires are often reviewed to check for inconsistencies with oral statements made during the interviews. Using the assembled information, the list of investment firms is condensed to a small group of finalists (e.g., less than five) and the information is given to the sponsor's top management.

The management of the sponsor will then meet with senior officers and relevant portfolio personnel of the finalist firms, and the decision on which firm(s) to retain to manage the pension assets is made.

Post-Selection Activity

A substantial amount of activity remains after the decisions have been made. For example, legal agreements should be reviewed, all fees and other costs should be determined, and the initiation date for performance measurement should be established.

The selection of the investment firm is not the final step in this process. Indeed, it is just the first iteration of a continuing operation. Portfolio review and evaluation using the performance measurement techniques described in Chapter 11 must be performed periodically. This will be facilitated by having the mechanics of fund and reporting systems worked out as soon as possible.

PASSIVE VERSUS ACTIVE MANAGEMENT

A passive investment strategy is characterized by a broadly diversified buy and hold portfolio aimed at replicating the return on some broad market index at minimum cost. The costs of highly trained professionals can be minimized and the transactions costs are relatively low due to the reduced amount of trading. In contrast, active investment strategies attempt to outperform the market either by selecting assets whose returns, on average, exceed those of the market, or by timing the movement of funds into and out of the market in an attempt to capitalize on swings in the prices of the assets.

Proponents of the passive strategy argue that as the stock market becomes increasingly efficient, it is more difficult for investment managers to consistently outperform the market. If actively managed funds do indeed encounter difficulties producing a gross rate of return superior to that of the market, it will obviously be even more difficult to produce a superior return on a net basis (after the effects of fees and transactions costs have been accounted for).

There are various degrees to which passive investing may be implemented. The three most popular forms — index funds, dedication and immunization techniques, and portfolio insurance — are described below.

Index Funds

Index funds represent the ultimate form of passive investing. An equity index fund replicates a particular index such as the S&P 500 and is designed to generate a beta of 1.0 (i.e., the rate of return on the fund is expected to be equal to that of the S&P 500). These funds are based on the efficient market hypothesis (EMH) that states that the securities markets are efficient in the processing of information. In other words, the prices of securities observed at any time are based on a correct evaluation of all information available at the time.

If this hypothesis were true, the value of an investment manager's services would be far less than the current level of compensation enjoyed by these professionals. However, a number of published studies have reported contrary evidence indicating at least a lack of complete efficiency in the market. Anomalous results have been found in the so-called weekend, small firms, and January effects.[10] Indeed, even the termination of over-funded defined benefit pension plans has been found to yield abnormal returns that contradict the EMH.[11]

Regardless of the merits of the EMH, more than a quarter of all institutional tax-exempt funds are indexed or managed under a similar type of passive investment strategy.[12] Some sponsors will use index funds as an investment for the core of their portfolio and allow active management of the remaining amount of the assets. This tactic possesses the advantage of freeing the investment managers from having to deal with the core

---

[10]R. Rogalski, "New Findings Regarding Day-of-the-Week Returns over Trading and Non-trading Periods: A Note," *Journal of Finance*, December 1984; M. Reinganun, "Abnormal Returns in Small Firm Portfolios," *Financial Analysts Journal*, March/April 1981; and D. Keim, "Size Related Anomalies and Stock Market Seasonality: Further Empirical Evidence," *Journal of Financial Economics* 12 (1983).

[11]Michael J. Alderson and K. C. Chen, "Excess Asset Reversions and Shareholder Wealth," *Journal of Finance*, 1986, pp. 225–41; and Jack L. VanDerhei, "The Effect of Voluntary Termination of Overfunded Pension Plans on Shareholder Wealth," *Journal of Risk and Insurance*, March 1987, pp. 131–56.

[12]Ed Christman, "Passive Portfolios Contain 26.8 Percent of Tax Exempt Assets," *Pensions & Investment Age*, May 19, 1986, p. 2.

portfoliolio and, instead, allowing them to focus their time on their specialty areas. Moreover, given a relative sense of security for the core investment, investment managers are able to pursue a higher risk strategy on their subset of the plan's assets in hopes of above-average returns.

Dedication and Immunization Techniques

Another form of passive investment of pension plan assets makes use of the bond market and has been variously referred to as dedication, immunization, and contingent immunization.[13] This technique attempts to construct a bond portfolio such that its cash flow can be used to fund specific plan liabilities; for example, to pay benefits to a group of retirees. The primary advantage resulting from this matching of pension assets and liabilities is that the plan actuary will not be forced to use a conservatively low interest rate in discounting the plan liabilities. Not only could this decrease the reported present value of the plan's liabilities, but it could also result in a decrease in the plan's minimum contribution to the funding standard account as this gain is amortized.[14]

The typical dedication program will start by modeling the expected schedule of liabilities under a particular subset of the plan. The benefits related to the retired population are often chosen due to the fact that the benefits are already determined (i.e., there is no uncertainty regarding career or final average salary) and the time horizon will be shorter than the liabilities associated with the active employee population. The model will produce a monotonically decreasing payout schedule over time, most likely reaching a negligible amount by the end of 30 years (the maximum maturity for most types of bonds). A computer program will then search for an optimal combination of acceptable bonds that will produce a cash flow over this period to meet the liability payout schedule.

Perhaps the easiest way to visualize this is to assume that all payouts will be met through principal payments (when the bonds mature) or coupon payments. This would certainly minimize the administrative complexity of the program since, if principal and coupon payments are exactly equal to the payouts each year, there would be no need to reinvest the proceeds. However, this may not produce the optimal combination of bonds in that another combination of maturities (one that assumes some proceeds need to be reinvested for a period of time before they are used to satisfy plan liabilities) may produce a lower total cost to the sponsor. It should be realized that this is a riskier undertaking, however, since the eventual cost to

---

[13]Martin L. Leibowitz, "The Dedicated Bond Portfolio in Pension Funds — Part I: Motivations and Basics," *Financial Analysts Journal*, January–February 1986, pp. 68–75.

[14]It should be noted that this scheme is not limited to the use of a bond fund. A similar effect is achieved whenever an annuity contract is purchased at a guaranteed rate in excess of the current actuarial discount rate.

the sponsor may increase if the assumed rates at which these proceeds may be reinvested proves to be too optimistic.[15]

In contrast to the cash-matching nature of dedication, an immunization program attempts to construct a portfolio of bonds whose market value equals the present value of the selected subset of liabilities and, even if the interest rate changes, whose value will always be at least as great as the value of the liabilities.[16] Although the feasibility of this approach may not be intuitively obvious, it depends upon the capital gains on the assets off-setting the decrease in reinvestment income when interest rates fall. This balancing is accomplished through a concept known as "duration," which provides a measure of the portfolio's sensitivity to interest rate changes.[17]

As opposed to the relatively simple administrative requirements involved in a dedicated portfolio, an immunized portfolio will require subsequent rebalancing. Moreover, although immunization provides more flexibility in constructing the bond portfolio (and should therefore result in a lower cost to the sponsor), it is possible for the assumptions used in the immunization model to be violated and, as a result, the sponsor may experience a shortfall from this approach.

Largely in response to the limitations of the immunization approach, a hybrid technique known as horizon matching has been recently introduced. In essence, this approach splits the liabilities into two portions. The first portion consists of all liabilities that occur up to a certain horizon (three to five years) and is handled through a dedicated portfolio. The second portion consists of liabilities beyond the horizon and is treated through immunization. Although this tactic will give up some of the cost savings of a full immunization approach, the restructuring will mitigate the effects of failing to satisfy the assumptions of the immunization approach.[18]

A major disadvantage of the immunization approaches is that the sponsor gives up the opportunity to produce additional income through active management of the bond portfolio. This is overcome, to a certain extent, through a device known as contingent immunization. Basically, this approach assumes the sponsor is willing to accept a minimum rate of return on the bond portfolio a percentage point or two below the current market rate. This differential provides a safety margin for the investment manager

---

[15]Other risks that may exist in either type of dedication include call vulnerability, quality, type of issue, and diversification across type and individual issues. See Leibowitz, "Dedicated Bond Portfolio, Part I," pp. 73–74.

[16]Martin L. Leibowitz, "The Dedicated Bond Portfolio in Pension Funds — Part II: Immunization, Horizon Matching and Contingent Procedures," *Financial Analysts Journal*, March–April 1986, pp. 47–57.

[17]The duration measure can be thought of as the average life of the liabilities when weighted by the present value of their respective cash flows. Technically, the duration match of assets and liabilities is not a sufficient condition for an "immunized" portfolio. In addition, certain second-order conditions must be satisfied. See Michael R. Granito, *Bond Portfolio Immunization* (Lexington, Mass.: Lexington Books, 1984) for more detail.

[18]Specifically, this is designed to dampen the effect of yield curve reshaping.

to adopt an active management strategy. If the safety margin is exhausted through market losses, the portfolio will be in a position such that it can be immunized at the minimum rate of return.

Portfolio Insurance

Portfolio insurance is a device used to protect the value of the portfolio in the event of a significant market decline without giving up the potential to benefit from rising markets.[19] Although numerous variations of this approach exist, it is basically implemented through one of two approaches: dynamic hedging or transactions in the financial futures markets.

It should be noted at the outset that there is nothing intrinsically unique about a device that reduces the risk of a pension plan portfolio. Indeed, this decision is often made implicitly in the asset allocation stage. An investment manager could easily decrease the riskiness of the portfolio by 50 percent by lowering the active asset allocation from 100 percent to 50 percent (and leaving the remainder in a risk-free asset such as T bills). However, this strategy would automatically result in a proportionate decrease in the portfolio's expected return. In contrast, portfolio insurance offers a combination of financial instruments that will — at least in theory — truncate the distribution of possible rates of return at some prespecified minimum floor return (e.g., no more than a 15 percent decline during the next year). There is obviously a cost associated with such a "guarantee"; although in the case of portfolio insurance, it can be conceptualized as a constant cost (as opposed to a cost that is proportional to the rate of return the portfolio would have otherwise produced) in the region above the minimum floor return.[20]

Implementation of the Process.[21]   Portfolio insurance may be created by dynamic hedging strategies that periodically adjust a portfolio's asset allocation between active and risk-free assets. Based on the level and term of protection desired, an initial active allocation is established. It is then adjusted in response to changes in portfolio values and the passage of time. Portfolio insurance is not a market-timing technique; there is no attempt to

---

[19]Hayne E. Leland, "Who Should Buy Portfolio Insurance?" *Journal of Finance* 35 (May 1980), pp. 581–94.

[20]This cost does not materialize directly; instead, it can be thought of as the opportunity cost of having a portion of the pension plan assets in risk-free assets at the time of a market increase. The cost will obviously be positively associated with the degree of protection desired. In other words, a "guarantee" that the portfolio will not decline by more than 15 percent in one year will require less activity than one that permits no decline at all in the same time period. Perhaps less obvious is that the cost should decline as the term of protection is lengthened. For more information, the mathematically inclined reader should see Simon Benninga and Marshall Blume, "On the Optimality of Portfolio Insurance," *Journal of Finance* 40 (December 1985), pp. 1341–52.

[21]John R. Meneghetti, "Portfolio Insurance: Finding the Right Balance," *Pension World*, September 1986, p. 36.

forecast returns. In rising markets, an increasing percentage of the portfolio is allocated to active assets; in declining markets, an increasing percentage is allocated to reserve assets. Under extreme conditions, the portfolio may be allocated entirely to either active or reserve assets.

Alternatively, portfolio insurance may be implemented by indirectly changing asset allocations through the financial futures markets. As the market declines, more financial futures are sold short against the equity assets insured. The profit generated from these sales is presumed to offset the losses on the pension plan assets. Conversely, as the market rises, these contracts can be removed.

Benefits of Portfolio Insurance.   Both forms of this technique offer two advantages to a plan sponsor. First, it enables pension funds to retain most of the asset gains they achieve when the markets move upwards, yet also enables them to limit their losses when the markets fall. This may be done with or without regard to timing considerations. For example, it could be used only at times of perceived market vulnerability. It also allows portfolios to be invested more aggressively.

If the process is implemented through financial futures, other advantages may also exist:[22]

1. Portfolio insurance is cheaper and easier to employ than to trade sizable blocks of stocks and bonds because the commission of futures contracts are lower than those on stocks.
2. It continues to reduce exposures to the market's vagaries as the market drops by short selling more and more futures contracts.
3. It lets pension fund portfolios remain undisturbed.

Objections to Portfolio Insurance.   It is safe to say that portfolio insurance has not been unanimously accepted in the pension investment community. The following are representative of the criticisms usually cited:[23]

1. No one really knows how much the pension fund will lag the rest of the market.
2. Portfolio insurance has not been subject to extensive testing in a bear market. For example, a catastrophic decline in the active asset might occur before the appropriate adjustment could be made.
3. If a large sum of money needs to be hedged, the investment manager must rely on S&P 500 futures. However, if the objective of portfolio insurance is to allow the investment manager to be more aggressive, the

---

[22]Ralph L. Knisley, Jr. "Portfolio Insurance: Will the New Importance of Surplus Management Change the Strategy of Fund Managers?" *FE Manual*, April 1987, pp. 82–83.

[23]Ronald Derven, "Avatar Associates Takes a Different View of Portfolio Insurance," *Pension World*, May 1987, p. 34. Although a discussion is beyond the scope of this text, another limitation of this approach is the potential calamitous effect of a whipsaw market.

insurance may not be complete. This arises since the new-found aggressiveness of the investment manager will probably lead to growth stocks and small capitalization stocks, which are not reflected to any significant extent in the S&P 500.

QUESTIONS FOR REVIEW

1. Describe the various forms of money market instruments.
2. Explain why a pension plan investment manager might invest pension assets in bonds instead of money market instruments. What are the additional risks associated with this decision?
3. Explain why pension plans have been choosing mutual funds more frequently in recent years.
4. Describe the two basic types of GICs.
5. Explain why investment managers may find GICs to be attractive pension investments.
6. Describe the plan characteristics that should be considered in the evaluation of a GIC.
7. What type of information should be elicited in questionnaires sent to prospective investment managers?
8. Explain why a passive investment strategy may be attractive to a pension plan sponsor.
9. Describe the basic objectives behind the use of dedication or immunization techniques for pension plan portfolios.
10. Explain the relative benefits and limitations of portfolio insurance.

QUESTIONS FOR DISCUSSION

1. Discuss how you would assess the cost of a portfolio insurance strategy.
2. Discuss how FASB 87 might influence an employer's decision to utilize dedication or immunization techniques.
3. Discuss how an employer should decide between active and passive investment strategies.

13

Trust Fund Plans

A qualified plan must use a funding instrument (trusts, custodial accounts, or group contracts) to hold an accumulate plan assets. This chapter deals with trust fund plans while insurance products are discussed in the next chapter. The trust fund arrangement was the first of the existing funding instruments to be used to fund private pension benefits. In addition to being the oldest of the funding instruments, trust fund plans currently account for the bulk of the employees covered and the assets held by private plans. Of the approximately 51 million participants under private plans, about 30 million are covered under trust fund plans, with about 60 percent of all pension fund assets being held by these plans. The trust fund approach is used extensively in the case of multiemployer plans, although the increased flexibility now available under group pension contracts has resulted in greater life insurance company competition for multiemployer plan business.

This chapter is concerned with those plans in which all or a substantial portion of the plan assets are accumulated and invested by the trustee. In other words, the discussion in this chapter does not pertain to plans in which a trustee is used but benefits are funded entirely through insurance company contracts (for example, a fully insured individual policy plan).

GENERAL CHARACTERISTICS

A trust fund plan is an arrangement under which employer and employee contributions, if any, are deposited with a trustee who is responsible for the administration and investment of these moneys and the income earned on accumulated assets of the fund, and who normally is responsible for the direct payment of benefits to eligible participants under the plan. If the trust fund arrangement is used in combination with an insured funding instrument, benefit payments to participants are generally made by the insurance company, with transfers from the trust fund made as required. The trustee is usually a corporate trustee (trust company). Individuals can also serve as trustees of the plan, although this practice has become less frequent because of the fiduciary requirements of ERISA.

Trust Agreement

The duties and responsibilities of the trustee are set forth in a trust agreement executed by the employer and the trustee. In the case of a negotiated multiemployer plan, the trust agreement is executed by individuals representing the unions and an equal number of individuals representing the employers, and these persons often compose the board of trustees responsible for the administration of the plan. The board of trustees may retain the task of investing plan assets, or it may choose to delegate this duty to a corporate trustee. In the latter case, a trust agreement setting forth the duties and responsibilities of the corporate trustee is executed by the board of trustees and the corporate trustee.

A typical trust agreement between an employer and a corporate trustee contains provisions regarding the irrevocability and nondiversion of trust assets; the investment powers of the trustee; the allocation of fiduciary responsibilities; the payment of legal, trustee, and other fees relative to the plan; periodic reports to the employer to be prepared by the trustee; the records and accounts to be maintained by the trustee; the conditions for removal or resignation of the trustee and the appointment of a new trustee; the payment of benefits under the plan; and the rights and duties of the trustee in case of amendment or termination of the plan.

The trust agreement, then, is concerned primarily with the receipt, investment, and disbursement of funds under a pension plan. The plan provisions may be incorporated in the trust agreement or they can be set forth in a separate plan document. The use of two separate documents is prevalent in trust fund plans and is almost always the approach used in multiemployer plans. The advantage of a separate plan document is that amendments to the plan can be made without the need to involve the trustee in frequent amendments to the trust agreement.

Administrative Duties of Trustee

The bulk of the record-keeping associated with a pension plan is normally performed by the employer under single-employer trust fund plans. If the plan is contributory, the employer generally retains responsibility for maintaining a record of employee contributions. In this case, total contributions are paid to the trustee without reference to any division of employer and employee contributions. The employer normally also assumes responsibility for the maintenance of records of earnings and credited service for each participant. In some cases, the record-keeping function is performed by the consulting actuary for the plan or a third-party administrator.

Most corporate trustees are able to relieve the employer of the burden of maintaining the necessary records associated with the plans. Corporate trustees sometimes maintain records in the case of profit sharing plans or defined contribution pension plans and, to a more limited extent, for multiemployer plans. If the trustee performs any record-keeping function, a service charge, in addition to the trustee's investment fee, is levied on an account basis, as explained later in this chapter. The advantages of specialization and the economies of size permit corporate trustees who handle a substantial volume of pension business to perform these services for a reasonable fee. The employer must decide whether it is more economical in its case to maintain these records itself or to have this service provided by the trustee or by a consulting actuary or service organization.

In the case of a negotiated multiemployer plan, the board of trustees, rather than the individual employers, is generally responsible for the maintenance of plan records. The record-keeping function is usually performed by a pension fund office created by the board of trustees. If a corporate trustee is retained to manage the assets of the fund, the plan trustees may delegate the task of record-keeping to the corporate trustee. In recent years, there has been a significant increase in the number of professional plan administrators. The function of a professional administrator is to keep all the specific records of service and earnings for individual members of the plan and to handle all routine administrative transactions.

Whether or not the corporate trustee performs the record-keeping function, it never makes any benefit distributions from the fund without authorization from the employer or retirement committee. In the case of a single-employer trust fund plan, the employer generally appoints a plan or retirement committee, usually composed of officers of the company. It is the responsibility of this committee to determine a participant's eligibility for benefits under the plan. Under multiemployer plans, authorization of benefit payments is the responsibility of the board of trustees or a committee of its members appointed by the board; but in some cases, this function is delegated to a professional administrator.

Apart from the administrative aspects of trust fund plans, a corporate trustee is always responsible for maintaining accurate and detailed records of all investments, receipts, disbursements, and other transactions involving the trust assets. In addition, the trustee is required to submit an annual statement regarding these trust transactions to the plan or retirement committee, usually within 90 days of the close of the plan's fiscal year. The trust agreement may require that statements be rendered to the committee more frequently than annually; for example, quarterly or monthly. Also, in some cases, the trustee assumes responsibility for the filing of forms for the trust as required by tax regulations.

Additionally, the trustee must make annual reports under the provisions of the Employee Retirement Income Security Act (ERISA) and the basic information must be made available in summary form to all participants and beneficiaries.

Investment Powers of Trustee

The primary function of a trustee is the investment management of trust assets.[1] The trustee invests the trust assets (including contributions and investment income) in accordance with the provisions of the trust agreement, the investment policy desired by the employer or retirement committee, and the fiduciary standards imposed by ERISA and by general trust laws. The investment power granted to a trustee by the trust agreement varies among plans; it may range from approval by the investment committee of every action affecting the fund's assets, to full discretion in investment affairs. Furthermore, the corporate trustee does maintain personal contact with the employer, and therefore the latter may influence, directly or indirectly, investment decisions. If the trust agreement fails to specify the investment powers of the trustee, the trustee is restricted to investments that are legal for trust funds in the state in which the trust is established and the federal statute governing fiduciary investments.

The trustee, until the enactment of ERISA, could invest all trust assets in the securities of the employer. Essentially, ERISA restricts investment of pension plan assets in an employer's securities to 10 percent of the fund value. The limit does not apply to profit sharing or thrift plans that explicitly permit larger investments in employer securities. Nor does it apply to stock bonus plans or employee stock ownership plans (ESOPs) that are typically invested exclusively in employer securities. Loans to the employer made from plan assets, except for ESOPs, have generally been forbidden by ERISA even though adequate security for the loan and a reasonable rate of return exist. The law considers as a possible prohibited transaction a

---

[1]However, there is a growing interest, in the case of very large plans, in the utilization of investment advisory services for the management of plan assets, with the corporate trustee serving as custodian.

loan or extension of credit between the qualified plan and a party in interest such as the employer.[2]

The trustee is required to maintain a separate accounting and an actual segregation of the assets of each trust. In other words, the assets of a trust generally cannot be commingled with the assets of other trusts or with the general assets of the trustee. Thus, under these circumstances, there is no pooling of the investment experience of a number of trusts. If the investment experience has been exceptionally favorable for a particular trust, the full benefit of that experience is credited to the trust account. On the other hand, the trust must bear the full impact of adverse investment income and capital loss experience. Therefore, a relatively small trust fund plan would be subject to the danger of inadequate diversification of its investment portfolio. To meet this problem, corporate trustees have established common trust funds. A common trust fund permits the commingling of assets of all participating trusts. Although originally established to meet the needs of smaller trusts, corporate trustees have obtained permission to allow pension trusts of any size to participate in common trusts established specifically for qualified pension plans. A trust participating in a commingled fund for investment purposes buys units or shares of the fund.[3] Dividends are paid on each unit, each dividend being a proportionate share of the total income earned by the commingled fund. These units fluctuate in value as the value of the assets of the commingled fund fluctuates.

The principal advantage of a common trust fund is that it permits any trust to enjoy the investment advantages normally available only to the very large funds. These potential advantages have been described as follows.[4]

1. Higher rate of return on fixed income investments. Commingled investment permits purchases in amounts large enough to take advantage of private placements and special offerings of securities, which generally carry higher yields than regular market offerings; and in mortgages, leaseback arrangements or other interests in real property.

2. Increased growth potential through selective stock holding. Commingled investment permits such funds to achieve a degree of selective diversification in equities that would be impossible to attain through individual investment, except in sizable funds.

3. Maximum liquidity of funds for cash requirements. Commingled investment permits redemption of units at the end of any month, at the current market value of units, so that money required for payouts is made available through use of current cash flow rather than having to sell investments, as might have to be done in a separate fund.

4. Dollar averaging on investment purchases. Current cash flow from

---

[2]For a discussion of this aspect of trust investments, see Chapter 4.

[3]Bank of New York, *Trusteed Employee Benefit Plans* (New York: Bank of New York, 1966), p. 10.

[4]Ibid., pp. 10–11.

incoming contributions, spaced as they are at intervals throughout a given year, has the effect of dollar averaging on investment purchases, which generally works to the advantage of all participating trusts.

5. Lower investment brokerage fees. A commingled trust can purchase stocks in round lots and in amounts that entail lower brokerage commissions.[5]

Most corporate trustees believe common trusts offer significant advantages to the larger plans as well as to smaller plans. In one large urban bank, approximately 55 percent of all its pension trust accounts participate in the bank's commingled pension trust. However, there is an element of inflexibility in the use of a common trust fund that should be noted; that is, the inability to transfer specific fund assets to another funding agency. Units can be liquidated, but during a period of depressed security prices the employer may prefer to transfer trust assets in kind, with the expectation that market prices will be higher at some future date.

Participation in a commingled pension trust is restricted to qualified plans. Participation by a nonqualified trust could result in loss of the qualified tax status of the entire common trust fund.

Some corporate trustees have established many common trust funds, with each fund designed to provide an investment medium having certain principal characteristics and objectives. For example, one fund may emphasize investments in bonds, notes, debentures, and other fixed income obligations. A second fund may be invested principally in private placements, mortgages, or other interests in real property. A third fund may be invested in a selection of quality common stocks with the objective of growth of principal and income over the long term. In addition, a special equity fund may be available for those trusts interested in pursuing a more aggressive investment policy. The multiple common trust funds offer the employer considerable flexibility in the proportion of trust assets to be invested in each of the classes of investments.

Investment flexibility has been an attractive feature of the trust arrangement for many employers. During the past two decades, many employers have expressed a preference for investment of a relatively large proportion of pension assets in common stocks. Insured plans were not able to offer this investment flexibility until the development of separate account funding.

BENEFIT STRUCTURE

Retirement Benefits

The trust fund arrangement offers maximum flexibility in the design of a retirement benefit formula. Since funds are not allocated, even for retired

---

[5]A small trust fund plan can also obtain the advantages of commingling through investments in mutual fund shares.

employees, any type of benefit formula can be utilized under a trust fund plan. As is true in the case of several of the insurance products described in the next chapter (deposit administration and immediate participation guarantee plans, and guaranteed investment contracts), retirement benefits based on final earnings can be provided without difficulty under trust fund plans. Likewise, benefit formulas that provide for the integration of social security benefits (including social security offset provisions) can be accommodated readily under the trust fund arrangement.

It is true that the more complex the benefit formula, the more difficult is the task of the actuary in projecting costs and calculating contribution payments under the plan. The fact remains, however, that the trust fund instrument does not of itself present any obstacles to the use of the most complex of benefit formulas. For example, provision for adjustments of retired employees' benefits in accordance with a designated cost-of-living index can be provided under this funding instrument. The actuary can include in the cost calculations an assumption regarding future price level changes, which admittedly is not readily predictable with a great degree of accuracy. However, actuarial gains and losses because of variations of actual from expected price levels can be reflected in subsequent valuations and determinations of contribution payments. Trust fund plans can also provide a retirement benefit that varies with the market value of the assets supporting the pension benefits of retired workers (variable annuities). A few trust fund plans do provide for cost-of-living adjustments and equity or variable annuity benefits.

Defined contribution formulas can also be used in trust fund pension plans. A pension plan generally provides a lifetime annuity benefit to retired employees. The law requires the plan to provide a joint and one-half survivor annuity for an employee and his or her spouse unless there is an election to the contrary. Therefore, under a defined contribution pension plan formula, at some point in time the accumulations on behalf of each participant must be expressed in terms of a lifetime monthly benefit (except in cases where lump-sum distributions are made). The monthly benefit may be calculated as each annual contribution is received, or annual contributions may be accumulated to retirement date and the determination of the level of monthly benefits may be made at that time.

In the case of some negotiated plans, particularly multiemployer plans, the employer's financial commitment is expressed as some specified cents per hour worked or as a fixed percentage of compensation. However, these plans generally are not traditional defined contribution plans in that they also provide a defined benefit. The trust fund instrument can accommodate these plans without any difficulty.

Early retirement benefits can be, and frequently are, provided under trust fund plans. The amount of early retirement benefit may be the actuarial equivalent of the participant's accrued normal retirement benefit, or, if the employer desires, a more liberal early retirement benefit may be provided. The additional cost under the latter alternative can be anticipated in computations of contribution payments required under the plan.

Death Benefits

An increasing proportion of the larger trust fund plans provide preretirement death benefits. Preretirement death benefits seldom have been provided under small-sized trust fund plans. The law requires all qualified plans to include an option providing at least a 50 percent joint and survivor annuity. As described in Chapter 6, if a participant dies before the annuity starting date and has a surviving spouse, the automatic benefit must be in the form of a qualified preretirement survivor (QPS) annuity to the surviving spouse.

The availability of postretirement death benefits depends on the normal annuity form under the plan. A pure life annuity has been the typical normal annuity form under trust fund plans or a modified refund annuity in the case of contributory plans. Once again, however, the law provides that the joint and one-half survivor annuity be the normal annuity form for a participant and his or her spouse unless an election is made to the contrary. The level of benefits under a joint and one-half survivor annuity can be greater than the actuarial equivalent of the previous normal annuity form. If the cost of this increase in benefit is not passed on to the participants and is assumed by the employer, it can be projected in the actuary's calculations of the periodic contributions required under the plan. These benefits can be provided without difficulty under trust fund plans.

Disability Benefits

Some trust fund plans provide disability benefits. Responsibility for determining whether a participant is eligible for disability benefits usually rests with a retirement committee appointed by the employer. In the case of a multiemployer plan, this function is assumed by the board of trustees or a committee composed of board members. The trustee begins payment of disability benefits on receipt of certification by the retirement committee of a participant's eligibility for benefits. The retirement committee also assumes responsibility for reviewing approved disability claims to determine whether continuance of disability exists.

Several reasons exist for the prevalence of disability benefits under trust fund plans. First, union leaders strongly favor provision of disability benefits under pension plans, and a substantial proportion of negotiated plans utilize the trust fund approach. Second, disability benefits provide employers with a desirable personnel management tool if control over the determination of disability rests with the employer. A disability pension can be used as a graceful, and often relatively economical, method of retiring unproductive employees. Third, the reluctance of insurance companies (at least until recent years) to insure long-term disability benefits encouraged the self-insuring of these benefits under trust fund plans.[6] However, in recent years, the use of insured group long-term disability plans has increased.

Vested Benefits

The rights of trust fund plan participants to benefits derived from employer contributions, as is true under other funding instruments, depend upon the vesting provisions of the plan. The vesting provisions in the plan must be at least as generous as those required under the law. If the actuarial value of the employee's vested benefit is less than $3,500, the employer may cash out the benefit. This reduces the administrative expense of keeping records of terminated employees. Additionally, if the terminating employee agrees, a vested benefit in excess of $3,500 may be cashed out under certain conditions.[7] The value of the vested benefit may be transferred to an individual retirement account (IRA) or, with the consent of the employer, to the pension plan of the employee's next employer if the new employer also consents. Of course, terminating employees are always entitled to the benefit attributable to their own contributions. Under most trust fund plans, the availability of vested benefits is deferred until the terminating employee reaches normal retirement age. If the plan is contributory, entitlement to the vested benefit has generally been conditioned on the terminating employee leaving his or her own contributions in the plan; withdrawal of the contributions results, in these cases, in the forfeiture of the portion of the vested benefit attributable to employer contributions. The law permits employees to withdraw their own contributions without having vested benefits canceled unless an employee is less than 50 percent vested. In those cases, an employer can cancel vested benefits if an employee withdraws his or her own contributions. The plan must contain a payback provision allowing employees to restore their benefits by repaying prior distributions with interest.

Since contributions to a trust fund are not allocated to specific participants under the plan (with the possible exception of a traditional defined contribution plan), vesting is always expressed in terms of benefits rather than contributions. A terminating employee's vested benefits represent a deferred claim against the assets of the trust fund. This claim is conditioned on (1) the terminating employee living to retirement age (except for his or

---

[6]It should be noted that under deposit administration and immediate participation guarantee plans, disability benefits, when provided, generally are self-insured by the employer in that these benefits are paid directly by the employer or charged directly to the unallocated account.

[7]See page 106.

her own contributions), (2) the employee making application for the benefit in accordance with plan provisions, and (3) the adequacy of the trust fund to provide the vested benefit and the protection afforded by the Pension Benefit Guaranty Corporation. In case of termination of the plan, the priority, if any, of vested benefits is dependent on plan provisions subject to the requirements of the law.

CONTRIBUTIONS

The annual contribution payments under a trust fund plan are determined by periodic actuarial valuations by the plan actuary who must be an enrolled actuary under the law. The plan actuary calculates the amount of contributions to be made to the trust fund on the basis of: (1) a given set of actuarial assumptions, (2) a particular actuarial cost method, and (3) the census data for the group of employees covered under the plan. It is the task of the actuary, as strongly reinforced by the law, to choose a set of actuarial assumptions and techniques that, based on his or her judgment and experience, appear to be reasonable for the particular plan. This obligation is imposed on all enrolled actuaries who provide actuarial services for plans covered under the law, whether such actuaries are acting in a consulting capacity or working for insurance companies. Generally, the actuary will choose assumptions more conservative than the experience actually expected under the plan, to provide a margin for contingencies. It is also the responsibility of the actuary to choose an appropriate actuarial cost method to be used in calculations of contribution payments. Since the choice of an actuarial cost method has a significant impact on the incidence of contribution payments, it is important that the employer have a clear understanding of the factors involved in the final selection of a cost method.

Under trust fund plans, the employer has some input in decisions regarding the choice of actuarial assumptions and the cost method to be used in calculations of contribution payments. Thus, the employer has maximum flexibility under a trust fund plan in directing the timing of contribution payments as long as such contributions meet the minimum funding standards of the law.

Of course, this does not mean the ultimate cost of the plan is necessarily lower under trust fund plans. The actuarial gains from turnover and mortality under allocated funding instruments eventually are recognized in the form of employer credits against premiums due in future years. Also, lower levels of contributions in the initial years of the plan must be offset by higher contribution levels in subsequent years. Actuarial assumptions and cost methods do not affect the ultimate cost of the plan, except to the extent that they influence levels of funding and, therefore, the amount of investment income earned on plan assets. The fact remains that the employer has greater control over the incidence of contribution payments under trust fund plans because of the way in which actuarial assumptions and methods are established and the unallocated nature of the funding instrument. This flexibility is also available, to almost the same degree, under most group pension contracts.

Subject to the minimum funding standards of the law, contribution payments under trust fund plans are made at the convenience of the employer. In other words, there are no fixed contribution due dates. The employer may make contribution payments on a monthly, quarterly, or annual basis. Of course, Internal Revenue Service requirements regarding the timing of contributions must be observed if deductibility of contribution payments is desired.

In addition to the contribution payments necessary to provide the benefits to participants of the plan, the employer must make some provision for the expense associated with trust fund plans. The major expenses under trust fund plans are trustee, consulting actuary, and legal fees, as well as record-keeping and other administrative expenses. Investment fees of corporate trustees usually are expressed as a percentage of the trust corpus—the percentage being graded downward with the size of the fund.

The trustee imposes additional charges if it maintains plan records, makes pension payments to retired employees, or holds insurance and annuity contracts. Because of the additional reporting and other administrative requirements of ERISA, additional fees for the additional services are probably necessary. If the employer performs the administrative functions associated with the plan, the cost of performing these duties should be recognized in determining the true cost of a trust fund plan.

With reference to legal and actuarial fees, it is virtually impossible to quote any figures that can be viewed as typical charges under trust fund plans since fees for these services vary so widely among plans. The legal services required for the plan are normally performed by the attorney who handles all other legal work for the employer, and therefore are usually incorporated into the overall legal retainer paid by the employer. A consulting actuary's fee varies with the type and amount of service rendered. The actuary may perform preliminary cost studies or special projects on a fixed-fee basis, but most of his or her services to the plan are billed on an hourly or daily rate basis. The fees for legal and actuarial services can be paid by the trustee out of trust assets or they can be paid directly by the employer. The latter approach is the procedure followed in most cases.

No guarantees are available under trust fund plans.[8] The trustee cannot guarantee a minimum rate of investment income, nor can it guarantee plan

---

[8]In order to compete with the guaranteed investment contracts (GICs) offered by insurance companies, many sophisticated techniques are being used to try to match maturities of investments with the time that specific amounts are needed to pay benefits. These include such approaches as immunization and dedicated portfolio techniques, which are discussed in Chapter 12.

assets against capital losses. Likewise, the mortality risk cannot be transferred to the trustee. The absence of guarantees is consistent with the legal nature of trust arrangements. A trustee's obligation is limited to the management of trust assets in a reasonable and prudent manner and in accordance with the duties set forth in the trust agreement and state and federal law. The adequacy of the fund to provide the benefits promised under the plan is the responsibility of the employer. The high degree of responsibility imposed on the employer under a trust fund plan is consistent with the maximum degree of flexibility available to the employer under this funding instrument. Guarantees must be minimized or eliminated if an employer desires maximum contribution flexibility and complete and immediate reflection of plan experience. Therefore, in choosing a funding instrument, the employer should consider the extent to which guarantees and flexibility are desired.

Many large employers have chosen funding instruments that offer a high degree of flexibility and immediate reflection of plan experience. In the case of a trust fund plan, the actual experience of the plan is reflected immediately in the status of the fund. For example, if investment experience has been favorable, the fund receives the full benefit of the favorable experience. Likewise, the full impact of adverse investment experience is borne by the individual trust. However, the investment risk can be spread to some extent through the use of a commingled investment fund. The use of a common trust reduces a plan's investment risk as a result of the greater investment diversification available; but it still does not offer a guarantee of principal or a minimum rate of return. The employer cannot shift the mortality risk under trust fund plans. If the plan covers a large number of employees, the employer may be willing to assume the mortality risk. The mortality risk becomes a more significant consideration as the size of the group covered decreases. Deviations of actual from expected experience for other factors (for example, turnover, disability rates, and actual retirement ages) also are immediately reflected in the status of the trust fund.

Under trust fund plans, actuarial valuations are performed periodically (usually annually, but no less frequently than every three years for regulatory purposes) to determine the adequacy of the fund. If the actual experience evolving under the plan indicates the current level of funding is inadequate, actuarial assumptions can be revised to produce higher levels of contributions in future years. Since the liabilities under a pension plan evolve over a long period of time, adequate provision for these liabilities can be made if frequent actuarial valuations are performed and if the employer is willing and able to make the necessary contributions.

TERMINATION OF PLAN

In the event of termination of a trust fund plan, the disposition of plan assets is determined in accordance with the provisions of the law.

Situations sometimes arise in which an employer desires to switch funding agencies without any intention of terminating the plan. A transfer of assets to another trustee or to an insurance company can be effected without difficulty under trust fund plans. The trust agreement contains no prohibitions against transfer of plans assets (assuming that such transfers are made in accordance with the requirements of the Internal Revenue Service). The trustee may impose a minor charge for the administrative duties associated with a termination of the trust. Of course, losses may be sustained if assets must be liquidated over a relatively short period of time. In some cases, transfers of securities and other assets may be permitted rather than requiring liquidation of investments, unless the assets are held in a commingled trust, in which case transfers of securities generally are not permitted. The freedom to transfer plan assets and the flexibility it offers in case of mergers or other circumstances is viewed by some employers as an important advantage of trust fund plans.

SPLIT FUNDING

The trust fund arrangement can be used in conjunction with group permanent contracts or individual insurance and annuity contracts as one approach in funding pension benefits. This approach is generally referred to as a combination plan. Group pension contracts also can be used in combination with the trust fund arrangement. These latter arrangements are usually referred to as split-funded plans (although the term *combination plan* can be applied to describe any plan utilizing two or more funding instruments).

Split-funded plans generally utilize group deposit administration or immediate participation guarantee or modified immediate participation guarantee contracts. The decision of the employer to split-fund its pension plan is usually motivated by a desire to obtain, at least in part, the advantages of an insurer's guarantees and a possibly favorable investment opportunity. For example, the trust agreement may provide that the trustee administer all assets held on behalf of active employees and that an immediate annuity be purchased as each employee retires. Likewise, an insurer may enjoy relatively high yields on direct placement and mortgage investments, and therefore the employer may decide to invest a portion of plan assets in a deposit administration contract, an immediate participation guarantee contract, or a guaranteed investment contract.

QUESTIONS FOR REVIEW

1. What is a trust fund plan?
2. Describe the provisions that are generally found in a trust agreement.
3. Describe the typical administrative duties and investment powers of a trustee.

4. How does the federal law restrict the trustee's investment powers?

5. What is a common trust fund?

6. What advantages does a common trust fund have over an individually managed fund?

7. It has been said that any benefit formula can be used in conjunction with trust fund plans. Explain.

8. What are the major expenses of a trust fund plan in addition to the contributions needed to pay plan benefits?

QUESTIONS FOR DISCUSSION

1. Discuss how the investment risks assumed under a trust fund plan should be treated by the employer.

2. Discuss how the mortality risks assumed under a trust fund plan should be treated by the employer.

14

Special Insurance and Annuity Products

INTRODUCTION

Originally, the majority of pension plan assets were placed with insurance companies and were protected by strong guarantees as to investment and mortality experience. Beginning with group deferred annuity contracts in the early 1920s, insurance products were designed specifically for use in pension plans. These contracts provided that a single premium would be paid to purchase a contract on each employee promising to pay (at normal retirement age) the equivalent of his or her accrued benefit for that year. Although all investment and mortality risks were transferred from the employer to the insurance company once the contracts were purchased,[1] it was difficult to provide a substantial degree of flexibility in plan design features such as past service benefits and supplemental benefits, since the price of funding a dollar's worth of monthly retirement income increases prohibitively as the employee approaches normal retirement age.

The limited flexibility of this contract, as opposed to the virtually unlimited freedom offered by the trust fund approach provided by banks, eventually led the insurance industry to develop an unallocated[2] form of instrument known as a deposit administration contract. The chief advantage

---

[1]The rates were typically guaranteed for the first five year's purchases of deferred annuities.

[2]Funding instruments are classified on the basis of whether contributions are allocated to provide benefits to specific employees prior to retirement or whether contributions are accumulated in an unallocated fund to provide benefits for employees when they retire.

of this contract was the fact that virtually any type of benefit formula or actuarial cost method could be utilized under this approach. Although deposit administration contracts also insulated the sponsor from fluctuations in mortality and investment experience to a large extent, the dividend formula provided that the sponsor's actual cost would be influenced to some degree by the actual experience under the pension plan. This was particularly true as the insurance industry started to move from a situation in which the average rate of return for the insurance company's entire portfolio of pension assets was used to accumulate the book value of the sponsor's assets to a concept known as the new-money or investment-year method, in which the interest rate credited on the sponsor's assets is a function of the year they were deposited with the insurance company.

Although the deposit administration contract improved the plan design flexibility features of an insured plan, there was still a certain amount of discontent among plan sponsors due to the delay in the receipt of plan dividends and the use of contingency funds to smooth out experience over time. In response, the insurance industry developed a new product in the 1950s known as an immediate participation guarantee contract; it determines plan costs based on the sponsor's direct experience with respect to mortality and investment experience, while still providing annuity guarantees to the retirees under the plan.

In time, some sponsors began to question the need for locking up funds for annuity purchases and many were disenchanted with the restrictions or implicit penalties imposed on the withdrawal of funds in immediate participation guarantee contracts. The insurance industry again responded to this demand by offering guaranteed investment contracts which offer a unique type of investment guarantee. No guarantees are provided with respect to mortality, however, and the insurance company provides no assurance that sufficient funds will be available to pay the accrued benefits of participants. In summary, the evolutionary process has made insurance companies another form of investment manager.

The major development in the group pension field in the last decade is the substantial increase in flexibility under insurance contracts. Insurers are now in a position to tailor the contract to the specific needs of the employer. Employer demands for greater flexibility in investment policy and in the timing of contribution payments have led to a strong preference for the unallocated type of contract in the group pension market. This demand for greater flexibility has extended to the small employer market, and insurers have accommodated this demand by making unallocated contracts available to relatively small firms. The result has been a dramatic decline in the relative importance of the group deferred annuity contract to the point where it is almost completely obsolete.

While there are some deposit administration and immediate participation guarantee contracts still active at most insurers, many policyholders have opted to convert their funds into more modern funding vehicles. A growing number of court cases challenging the viability of these contracts is perhaps the major issue confronting these contracts today. Generally, these suits call into question the insurer's fiduciary standard under the Employee Retirement Income Security Act (ERISA) in making certain interest credits or fund adjustments on contract termination.

GROUP DEFERRED ANNUITY CONTRACTS

The group annuity contract, unlike individual insurance and group permanent contracts, was devised specifically to meet the funding needs of pension plans, the first such contract being issued in 1921. The volume of these contracts grew very rapidly in the following two decades, and they constituted by far the most prevalent group insured funding instrument prior to the growth of deposit administration plans in the 1950s. However, they are rarely used today.

Group annuity contracts provide for the funding of benefits through the purchase of units of single-premium deferred annuities for each participant. However, some insurance companies offer level premium deferred annuities on a group underwriting basis.

Unlike group life insurance, group annuity contracts are subject to very little statutory regulation regarding eligible groups or minimum number of covered lives. However, insurance companies do impose, as a matter of underwriting policy, certain requirements for these contracts. Most insurers require a minimum number of eligible employees (10, for example) for an employer to be eligible for a group annuity contract. If the plan is contributory, at least 75 percent of the eligible employees must participate in the plan, 100 percent participation being required in the case of noncontributory plans. These underwriting requirements are not imposed so much to minimize adverse selection as to produce a sufficient-sized case to justify the insurer expenses incurred in setting up the plan. A minimum annual premium per participant or for the plan as a whole also is imposed to assure the above objective. Also, the insurer may impose an administrative charge if the total premium in a contract year is less than a specified amount.

GROUP DEPOSIT ADMINISTRATION CONTRACTS

The deposit administration contract, which first appeared in the 1920s, evolved from the basic group deferred annuity contract. For this reason, it is often referred to as a deposit administration group annuity contract. The deposit administration contract was developed to overcome certain of the inflexibilities associated with the group annuity contract. Although originally developed as a result of interinsurer competition, the growth in popularity of the deposit administration plan began in the early 1950s largely in response to the increased competition from the trust fund arrangement, which offers a great deal of flexibility in plan design, timing of employer contributions, and investment alternatives. Because of the other more flexible funding instruments currently available and discussed later in this chapter, group deposit administration contracts are not as popular today.

The distinguishing characteristic of deposit administration contracts, as contrasted with group deferred annuity contracts, is that employer contributions are not allocated to specific employees until retirement date. Stated differently, the actual purchase of annuities (which includes a charge for expenses) does not take place until an employee retires.

One major advantage of deposit administration contracts is the flexibility available in designing the plan's benefit provisions. Whereas group deferred annuity contracts are limited largely to unit benefit formulas, any type of retirement benefit formula can be employed without difficulty under a deposit administration contract. Also, deposit administration contracts may be used without difficulty in plans that base benefits on final average earnings. The fact that benefits cannot be precisely determined until the employee actually retires presents no problem under these contracts since annuities are not purchased until the date of retirement. Likewise, minimum retirement benefits and the most complex integrated benefit formulas can be handled readily under deposit administration plans. Furthermore, the availability of equity funding permits the use of variable annuity benefits. The absence of annuity purchases until retirement date permits considerable flexibility in the establishment of early and late retirement benefit provisions. For example, early retirement benefits may be provided on a more liberal basis than the actuarial equivalent of normal retirement benefits (subject to Internal Revenue Service limitations), while additional benefits may be permitted for service rendered after the normal retirement date.

Contributions are credited to an unallocated fund that, under a conventional deposit administration contract, is variously referred to as the deposit fund, active life fund, deposit account, or purchase payment fund. However, the dramatic growth of separate account funding[3] (which many insurance companies make available under their deposit administration plans) has led to changes in contract terminology. For example, instead of *deposit account*, some insurers now use the terms *general investment portfolio account* or *fixed dollar account*, since contributions credited to the deposit account are invested in the insurer's general investment portfolio,

---

[3]The assets held in separate accounts are not commingled with the general assets of the insurer and are exempt from state statutory investment restrictions normally applied to life insurance companies.

which in turn is composed principally of fixed income securities. The insurer offering a separate account facility must append some appropriate term to distinguish this account (or accounts, if more than one is established) from its general investment account. A variety of terms have been used to identify the separate account; for example, *equity account*, *separate account*, or *variable contract account*.

The main thrust of the separate accounts development, from the policyholder's point of view, is the broadened choice of investments between fixed dollar and equity securities. Therefore, *fixed dollar account* and *equity account* are the terms that are used when discussing the features of deposit administration contracts from the policyholder's viewpoint. The terms *general investment account* and *separate account* are used when discussing investment alternatives under these plans from the insurer's point of view.

A fixed dollar account, maintained for each policyholder, represents a record of the portion of plan funds held to be invested primarily in fixed income obligations. An equity account, also maintained for each policyholder, represents a record of the portion of plan funds held to be invested primarily in common stocks. The policyholder has complete discretion as to the proportion of plan contributions to be credited to each of these accounts. If the employer so desires, 100 percent of contributions (assuming state regulatory requirements are met) can be credited to the fixed dollar account or to the equity account, although the usual decision is to allocate some portion to each of the accounts.

The contributions credited to the fixed dollar account become part of the general assets of the insurance company for investment purposes. If the insurer has established a separate account for fixed dollar investments, plan contributions can be allocated to the general investment account or the fixed dollar separate account in accordance with policyholder instructions. The fixed dollar account is credited with the rate of interest guaranteed in the contract. Also, dividends due under the contract are credited to the fixed dollar account. As pensions become payable to retiring employees, annuities may be provided by allocations from either the fixed dollar or the equity account, although generally annuities are provided by allocations from the fixed dollar account. When an annuity is established, a certificate is issued to the retired employee describing the benefits.

The contributions credited to the policyholder's equity account are invested in one or more of the insurer's separate accounts provided under the contract. While equity account accounting procedures differ among insurance companies, the following approach is illustrative of the general concepts involved in separate account funding. Each policyholder's share of the separate account is determined on a participation unit (or variable unit) basis. The policyholder's equity account provides a cumulative record of the number of participation units credited to the account and the number of units allocated or withdrawn from the account. The balance of participation units credited to the account multiplied by the current participation unit value equals the amount of equity account assets held on behalf of the policyholder at any given point in time. The participation unit value is adjusted periodically, usually each business day, to reflect investment results under the separate account. The insurer offers no guarantee as to principal or interest on moneys credited to the equity account.

The policyholder generally has some flexibility in transferring funds between the fixed dollar account and the equity account. Generally, advance written notice to the insurer (e.g., 15 business days) is required. The advance notice requirement serves to minimize the potential problem of an undue amount of switching activity that might arise from attempts to play the market. Also, the insurer generally reserves the right to limit the amount or the percentage permitted to be transferred from the fixed dollar account to the equity account either on a per policyholder basis or on a book of business approach. For example, the total of the amounts transferred in any month may not exceed $1 million for all policyholders, or each policyholder may transfer up to 20 percent of the fixed account in any one year. The objective of this provision is to minimize potential financial anti-selection and liquidity problems arising from such transfers. Likewise, the insurer has the right—which it might exercise under some conditions, as when the stock markets are unstable—to limit transfers in a given month from the equity account according to the restrictions described above.

If the policyholder decides to place future contributions with a new funding agency such as another insurance company or a bank, the policyholder may either: (1) permit the fixed dollar and equity accounts to be used to purchase annuities until exhausted or (2) elect a transfer date for the transfer of funds credited to the fixed dollar and equity accounts. If the policyholder has elected to transfer the funds in its accounts, purchase of annuities will cease as of a specified date such as the 15th business day after the insurer receives such request. Transfer payments begin on the transfer date and are usually made on a monthly basis. The minimum amount that can be transferred monthly from the fixed income account is specified in the contract; for example, 1 percent of the amount of the account on the date annuity purchases cease, or the balance of the account, if less, with insurer permission required to transfer amounts in excess of the minimum monthly amount. Thus, the insurer reserves the right to spread transfer payments over a period of time. In other words, if the contract provides that monthly transfer payments will not be less than 1 percent of the amount of the account on the date purchases cease, the insurer has the right to stretch transfer payments over a 15- or 20-year or more period, depending on the interest rate being credited to the account. In practice, the agreed-upon transfer schedules generally are considerably shorter than the maximum permissible contractual period. The insurer generally permits lump-sum transfers, on a market value basis, although for very large accounts the insurer may reserve the right to spread payments over a period of time. With reference to the equity account, the contract generally provides that the sum transferable is the contract fund balance valued on a market value basis. Also, the maximum payout period is generally shorter than the period applicable to the fixed dollar account. For example, the contract might provide that monthly transfer payments from the equity account will not be less than (1) the greater of $1 million worth of participation units or 5 percent of the amount of the account on the date annuity purchases cease, or (2) the balance of the account, if less. In this latter case, the maximum period over which insurer transfer payments can be made is 20 months. The difference in treatment of transfers from each account is due to the differences in liquidity and marketability between fixed dollar and equity securities.

In the case of transfers to another funding agency, the insurer usually reserves the right to withhold some amount of the fund (usually up to 5 percent, the specific percentage to be determined by the insurer) to cover expenses not yet recovered and to offset possible financial antiselection (although transfers on a market value basis minimize the latter problem).

An administration charge is normally levied when annual premiums are less than a specified amount. For example, one insurer imposes an annual administration charge under its fixed dollar contracts equal to $800 less 2 percent of any amount of annual contributions paid in excess of $25,000 but not in excess of $65,000. Thus, there is no charge if the previous year's contributions were at least $65,000. If equity funding is utilized under the contract, the annual charge is somewhat higher (e.g., $1,100 less 2 percent of the amount by which the previous year's contributions exceeded $25,000 but not $80,000). The charge for the first contract year is based on the appropriate expense formula, but using as a base the contributions anticipated in the first contract year. The contract administration charge is generally allocated from the fixed dollar account.

SEPARATE ACCOUNT FUNDING

Historically, life insurance companies have invested the bulk of their assets in fixed dollar investments. The laws in most states restrict the investments of life insurance companies' general account assets in common stocks to some specified percentage (e.g., 5 percent) of the total assets of the company. This restriction is imposed because of the fixed dollar obligations and contractual guarantees provided in traditional life insurance and annuity contracts and, also, because of the relatively small surplus maintained by life insurance companies.

However, with the advent of separate accounts in 1962, insurers could offer group clients a wide range of investment choices. The assets held in separate accounts are not commingled with the general assets of the insurer and are exempt from state statutory investment restrictions normally applied to life insurance companies.

There is much variety in the manner in which separate accounts are operated by the various insurance companies. Some insurers offer accounts only on a commingled basis; others also offer accounts maintained solely for a single customer. Initially, separate accounts were invested primarily in common stocks, but other forms are now available; further major developments in the nature and form of the separate accounts available as the types of underlying investments in these accounts are broadened can be expected. For example, some insurers have established separate accounts invested primarily in mortgages, including equity participations; others have established commingled separate accounts invested primarily in the ownership of income-producing real property; and other accounts are invested in publicly traded bonds, short-term securities, direct placements and, most recently, foreign securities. One or more separate accounts may be used under the same group pension contract.

Separate accounts were developed for two reasons: (1) to compete with trust fund plans in making equity investments available to employers for funding fixed dollar plans, and (2) to fund variable annuity plans. In the first case, many employers believe the long-term rate of return on equities will be greater than the return on fixed income investments and the increased return will serve to reduce their cost of providing the fixed benefits promised under the plan. In the second case, equity-based variable annuities by definition require the assets supporting these annuities generally be fully invested in equity securities.

The insurer does not guarantee principal or interest for plan assets held in a separate account. The income and gains or losses, realized or unrealized, on separate account investments are credited to or charged against the separate account without regard to the other income, gains, or losses of the insurance company.

Separate accounts are subject to regulation by the Securities and Exchange Commission (SEC). However, exemptions from certain provisions of the acts administered by the SEC have been accorded to qualified retirement plans over the years. First, exemptions under the Securities Act of 1933 and the Investment Company Act of 1940 were provided by Rule 156 and Rule 3(c)3 for noncontributory, qualified plans covering at least 25 lives at the time the contract is issued. Later, Rule 6(e)1 extended the exemption to contributory plans, provided that certain conditions were satisfied regarding employee contributions allocated to separate accounts. Lastly, the Investment Company Amendments Act of 1970 exempts from the 1940 Act separate accounts used exclusively to fund qualified plans, and from most provisions of the 1933 Act and the Securities Exchange Act of 1934 separate accounts interests issued in connection with qualified plans (except for H.R. 10 and IRA plans). Separate accounts are also subject to state regulatory requirements. A 1980 change to the Securities Acts extended the exceptions to plans of governmental units even though not qualified. SEC Rule 180 (December 1981) provides an exception to the registration requirements of the 1933 Act for certain financially sophisticated H.R. 10 plans.

GROUP IMMEDIATE PARTICIPATION
GUARANTEE CONTRACTS

The deposit administration contract went a long way toward providing employers with the desired degree of flexibility not available under the traditional group annuity contract. In addition, the deposit administration contract offers certain interest and annuity rate guarantees. However, the insurance company is able to provide these guarantees only because it accumulates a contingency reserve and because it has control, through dividend computations, over the rate at which actuarial gains pertaining to guaranteed items are credited to the employer. Some employers object to these features of deposit administration plans. These employers prefer an immediate reflection of the actual experience under their plans and are willing to give up the guarantees of the deposit administration plan to get it. Thus, insurance companies developed the immediate participation guarantee (IPG) contract, the first contract of this type being issued in 1950.[4] In an IPG plan, the employer's account is credited with the contributions received during the contract period plus its share of actual investment income for the year according to the investment year method. There is generally no guarantee of principal or a minimum rate of interest under these contracts. The account is charged with all the expenses associated with the particular contract. As issued by many insurance companies, these contracts provide that all benefits, including annuity payments, are charged directly against the account as they are paid. In other words, annuities are not actually purchased for participants at retirement date, as is the practice under deposit administration plans. Some insurance companies do segregate from the account the gross premium for the annuities of retired workers in order to provide annuity guarantees. However, in these latter cases, the premium amount remains the policyholder's funds and does not become part of the insurer's general account as with deposit administration plans. The result is similar to that achieved by insurers that only charge to the account the annuity payments actually made. There is no charge to the account for an allocation toward building up a contingency reserve. Also, since no dividend as such is paid, all the record-keeping pertaining to a particular contract can be maintained in one account. Thus, the employer can be quickly apprised of the experience to date under the plan.

If annuity premiums are segregated from the account at retirement date,

---

[4]This type of contract is also referred to as a *pension administration contract*.

the insurer does perform periodic valuations to be certain the credit balance in the account is at least sufficient to provide the promised annuity payments to retired workers. If the credit balance approaches the amount of reserve required to provide the benefits of already retired employees, annuities are actually purchased for the retired workers.

The IPG contract also specifies a schedule of guaranteed annuity gross premium rates. However, since annuities are not actually purchased at retirement date, these guaranteed annuity rates are only of significance if the plan is terminated.

All the aspects of flexibility in contribution timing and plan design discussed under deposit administration plans are equally applicable to IPG contracts. The further reduction in insurer guarantees and the immediate reflection of actual experience under the plan bring the IPG contracts one step closer to trust fund arrangements.

Some insurance companies have developed a contract that possesses characteristics of both deposit administration and IPG contracts; it is usually referred to as a modified immediate participation guarantee contract or a direct-rated deposit administration contract. The major characteristic of this latter contract is that the unallocated account is maintained on an immediate participation basis, but single-premium immediate annuities are actually purchased for each participant on retirement.

Equity funding and variable annuity benefits generally are available under IPG contracts. The features of equity funding are basically similar to those discussed under deposit administration contracts.

There is another variation on the immediate participation guarantee concept that became prevalent in the late 70s and early 80s. There is no generic name for this product variation, as insurers increasingly moved to a brand name for this product concept. Essentially the insurer provides a one-year guarantee to the policyholder based on expectations of what the new money concept will generate for investment returns in the forthcoming year, rather than providing direct experience of the investment year method system in arrears. The policyholder receives a new one-year interest guarantee each year. Usually there are also more liberal contract features than in an immediate participation guarantee contract.

SINGLE–PURCHASE ANNUITY CONTRACTS

Group single-premium annuity contracts have been designed to provide annuities for participants in an uninsured pension or profit sharing plan that has terminated.[5]

In addition, the high level of interest rates, increasing government regu-

---

[5]For a detailed discussion of what happens when a pension plan terminates, see Chapter 23.

lations of defined benefit pension plans, and financial accounting standards have contributed to the termination of defined benefit pension plans in favor of defined contribution plans. In recent years, the accelerating pace of corporate mergers and takeovers has led to considerable interest in single-purchase group annuity arrangements. Apparently, there is sometimes concern among the officers of the corporation being absorbed that pension assets will be used by the new management for subsequent acquisitions or the rate of funding will be reduced to a point at which the security of their pension benefits will be impaired, though this should not be as much of a problem since the enactment of ERISA. If annuities are purchased, the funds are unavailable to the new management and the purchased annuity benefits are guaranteed by the insurance company.

Under a single-purchase contract, immediate annuities are provided for present pensioners and deferred annuities for those who are below retirement age. This type of contract almost always is nonparticipating. Since single-purchase situations invariably involve substantial sums of money, a great deal of competition exists among insurers for this type of business. These contracts are generally available for single purchases of $50,000 or more.

This type of contract also may be used by plans that have not terminated but wish to purchase annuities for a block of retired persons to take advantage of favorable rate guarantees.

FULLY INSURED PLAN

Under individual policy plans, the cash value under the contract as of the retirement date of the employee can be used as the single-premium sum needed to provide the annuity benefit. Thus, in theory, any permanent life insurance or any annuity contract can be used to fund a pension benefit. However, under a fully insured plan, the policy cash values at retirement must be sufficient to provide the full benefit, since no other source of funds is contemplated under the plan. To generate sufficient cash values under ordinary life policies, the face amount of the policy must be considerably in excess of 100 times the monthly retirement benefit or more than the requirement in a defined contribution plan that no more than 50 percent of the premium be used for life insurance — the maximum permitted under qualified plans. Thus, retirement income or retirement annuity contracts typically were used, since they were designed specifically by insurers to provide the proper ratio of insurance to income and to generate the cash values needed to provide a specified monthly income as of a given retirement age. Some insurers offer a variation of the conventional fully insured plans by funding pension benefits with ordinary life insurance and a fixed dollar or guaranteed annuity. The cash value of the whole life policy together with the annuity provides the retirement benefit. The preretirement benefit consists of the face amount of the whole life policy plus the death benefit under the annuity (greater of cash value or total premiums paid).

The retirement annuity contract is an individual deferred annuity contract and is expressed in units of a $10-a-month annuity benefit payable beginning at a specified age, usually the normal retirement age under the plan. The retirement income policy is expressed in terms of $1,000 of face value of life insurance for each $10-a-month annuity benefit on some stipulated annuity form.

Many insurance companies in the pension market issue a variation of the retirement annuity frequently referred to as a *flexible purchase payment annuity*. Although the contract provides for a schedule of payments, it is flexible; that is, payments can be decreased, increased, or skipped as circumstances may require as long as the amount of any purchase payment made is at least some minimum such as $15. The right to suspend or resume contributions at any time is commonly referred to as a "stop and go" feature. At retirement, the termination value of the contract may be taken as a lump-sum cash payment or it can be converted to a guaranteed income for the life of the annuitant plus the life of his or her spouse, if desired, at rates currently guaranteed in the contract. If the participant dies before retirement, the beneficiary receives an amount equal to the total purchase payments made or the guaranteed termination value of the contract, whichever is greater. As discussed in Chapter 6, if a participant dies before the annuity starting date and has a surviving spouse, the automatic benefit must be in the form of a qualified preretirement survivor (QPS) annuity to the surviving spouse. Because of the flexibilities inherent in this type of contract, it has largely replaced the more traditional retirement income and retirement annuity contracts for the funding of smaller defined contribution pension plans.

Individual policy plans require that separate contracts be issued on the life of every covered employee. In many cases, a trust agreement is executed between the employer and the trustee, and the trustee serves as custodian of the individual contracts. The trustee normally applies for the insurance or annuity contracts and pays the premiums due. The insured employee, of course, must sign the application for the contract. Legal ownership of the contracts is vested in the trustee, either through the use of an ownership clause or by attachment of an appropriate rider to each of the contracts. Generally, the use of a trustee is required under the Internal Revenue Code. There are exceptions if a nontransferable retirement income, annuity, or a life insurance contract that provides incidental life insurance is used. These requirements are imposed to preclude the possibility of the employer recovering funds that must be irrevocably committed to the plan.

The use of a trustee under individual policy plans has resulted in the use of the term *pension trust* to describe these plans. This terminology is unfortunate, since plans employing funding instruments other than individual policies quite often use a trust agreement. In the case of a noninsured plan, for example, a trust agreement is a necessary condition for qualification of the plan. Thus, the term *pension trust* should not be used unless the plan has a trustee. Indeed, it would probably be best if the term disappeared entirely from pension terminology.

COMBINATION PLANS

General Characteristics

The term *combination plan* can be used to describe any funding arrangement that employs two or more different funding instruments. However, the term is generally used in practice to describe those plans that use a combination of individual contracts and an unallocated conversion fund. The conversion fund is also sometimes referred to as the auxiliary fund or the side fund. The objective of the combination plan is to retain, in part, the guarantees and life insurance benefits associated with individual contracts, while at the same time obtaining a degree of the flexibility inherent in unallocated funding instruments.

The mechanics of the plan involve the purchase of a whole life insurance contract (or its equivalent) on the life of each participant, frequently with a face amount usually equal to 100 times the monthly expected pension benefit. Although almost any type of cash value policy can be used (including some of the newer forms such as universal life policies that provide interest-sensitive investment returns), the general practice is to purchase ordinary life contracts. Some insurance companies use an endowment-type contract that provides a relatively small fixed cash value as of age 65 regardless of the issue date of the contract; for example, $400 per $1,000 of face value. Standardization of the amount of cash value available at retirement simplifies the calculation of the amounts required in the conversion fund. Ordinary life contracts or endowment contracts generate the lowest scale of cash values of the various whole life and endowment contracts, and therefore a significant portion of the funding may be provided through the conversion fund. Thus, ordinary life contracts are favored since the flexibility inherent in the conversion fund often is a prime factor in the employer's decision to use a combination plan. On the average, the cash values of the ordinary life contract will equal about 35 percent of the net single-premium sum required at normal retirement age to provide the monthly pension benefit, the remaining 65 percent being provided out of the conversion fund. The exact proportion of the cash value to the principal sum required at retirement will, of course, vary somewhat with the age at issue, the individual insurance company employed, and the length of time that the contract is in force as of the retirement date, unless endowment-type contracts are used.

The combination plan may require the use of a trustee. If the conversion fund is administered by a corporate trustee, the latter party normally also serves as the trustee to own the ordinary life insurance contracts. The conversion fund often is held and administered by the life insurance company that issues the insurance contracts. In this case, the trustee is generally an individual — often one of the officers of the firm. Only one trust agreement is required, regardless of whether the conversion fund is administered by a corporate trustee or an insurance company.

Evidence of insurability may be required for the insurance contracts issued under a combination plan. However, most insurers are willing to issue these contracts up to some limit on a guaranteed issue basis, subject to certain underwriting restrictions.

Contributions

The periodic contributions required under a combination plan are composed of premium payments for the life insurance contracts and contributions to the conversion fund. The premium rates for purchased ordinary contracts are guaranteed and level in amount, subject to reduction through dividends. Of course, if an employee's benefits are increased, additional amounts of life insurance will have to be purchased at the rates in effect at the time the contract is actually purchased. In addition to the guarantee of premium rates, the issued contracts also carry an insurer guarantee of the annuity rates applicable at the employee's retirement date. The guaranteed annuity rates apply to the sums withdrawn at the retirement date from the conversion fund, as well as to the cash values accumulated under the life insurance contract as of that date. The extent of the annuity rate guarantee applicable to the moneys from the conversion fund normally is expressed as some multiple of the face amount of insurance; for example, at the rate of $10 to $30 of monthly income for each $1,000 of face amount. Some insurers impose a conversion charge, usually expressed as a percentage of the difference between the principal sum required at retirement age to provide the pension and the cash value of the policy as of that date. This charge is generally 2 or 2.5 percent, although a higher effective percentage may be imposed where the insurance benefit is less than 100 times the monthly benefit. The higher charge is required in the latter cases to offset the reduced amount of loading available to the insurer because of the relatively lower amounts of insurance.

If the conversion fund is held by an insurance company in a fixed dollar account, the insurer guarantees that the fund will be credited with a minimum rate of interest and that there will be no capital depreciation. In addition, most insurers pay interest in excess of the guaranteed rate, as conditions permit. The conversion fund can be administered by a trustee, if the employer desires, in which case there is no guarantee of principal or interest.

The amount of annual contribution to the conversion fund depends on the actuarial assumptions and the actuarial cost method used. Since the assets in the conversion fund are not allocated to specific employees, the employer can discount in advance for expected mortality and turnover. In practice, a mortality assumption frequently is used, but seldom is there a discount for turnover. Some flexibility also exists in its choice of a reasonable interest assumption for the conversion fund. Thus, different estimates of the amount of contribution required for the conversion fund can be generated depending upon the choice of assumptions. It should be noted however that the enrolled actuary has final control for the assumptions used to determine the amount of the conversion fund contribution.

Some flexibility also exists in the choice of an actuarial cost method to be used in calculating contribution requirements under a combination plan as long as the minimum funding standards are met. For example, an individual level cost method with supplemental liability can be used. As discussed in Chapter 9, this method generates a low annual normal cost. Employers are free to fund the supplemental liability as they see fit, subject to the limitations imposed by the Internal Revenue Code. During periods of financial difficulty, the employer may reduce contributions to the conversion fund, again within the limitations imposed by the Internal Revenue Code. Thus, the combination plan provides considerably greater flexibility as to the timing of contribution payments than is available under a fully insured plan. Furthermore, the employer has a great deal of investment flexibility with reference to the conversion fund. If the fund is administered by a trustee, the assets can be fully invested in common stocks, if such an investment policy is desired. Of course, investments must be made in accordance with the prudent expert rule established in the law. Also, in the past several years, most major life insurance companies have developed many different types of investment products in which conversion fund assets can be invested.

However, since contributions to the conversion fund do not constitute premiums as such, responsibility for the adequacy of the fund rests with the employer. If the actuarial assumptions prove to be erroneous, the assets in the conversion fund may not be adequate to provide the promised benefits. Also, it must be remembered that the choice of actuarial cost method has little effect on the ultimate cost of the plan. Lower contributions in the early years must be offset by a higher level of contribution payments in future years. Nevertheless, the flexibility in the timing of contribution payments under combination plans is offered as an important advantage of this funding arrangement over fully insured individual policy plans.

The calculation of the amounts of required periodic contributions for the conversion fund generally is performed by the insurance company, although some companies provide this service only if they hold the conversion fund. If the employer desires, a consulting actuary can be retained to perform this service. In any event, the actuarial valuation must be performed by an enrolled actuary who has the professional, educational, and experience qualifications required by law.

QUESTIONS FOR REVIEW

1. Explain why many cash value life insurance policies cannot be used by themselves to fund pension benefits.
2. Distinguish between retirement income and retirement annuity contracts.
3. What are the advantages of using a combination plan?
4. Why are ordinary life contracts favored for use with combination plans?
5. How is the annual contribution to the conversion fund in a combination plan determined?
6. Compare deposit administration contracts with group deferred annuity contracts with respect to the allocation of employer contributions.
7. What flexibility does an employer have with respect to annual contributions under a deposit administration plan?
8. Contrast the deposit administration contract with a group immediate participation guarantee (IPG) contract with respect to insurance company guarantees.

QUESTIONS FOR DISCUSSION

1. Discuss how an employer would decide between an insured funding arrangement and a self-insured, or trust fund, arrangement.
2. Discuss how an employer would decide among the various alternative insured funding arrangements.
3. Discuss how an insurance company would price the various guarantees it offers employers through its contracts.

15

Profit Sharing Plans

Profit sharing plans constitute an important component in the overall structure of employee benefit programs in the United States. The requirements imposed by ERISA as to vesting, minimum funding, and employer liabilities for plan terminations have resulted in a growing interest in money purchase or individual-account retirement programs. Profit sharing and thrift plans have considerable appeal in this regard since they embody the individual account concept without imposing on employers any fixed commitment to provide any specific level of benefits. Thus, one can expect to see greater use of profit sharing plans in lieu of pension plans or of a basic pension benefit plus a supplemental savings or profit sharing program.[1]

DEFINITION OF PROFIT SHARING

Many definitions of profit sharing have been suggested. One broad concept is that profit sharing is a plan in which the company's contributions are based upon business profits,[2] regardless of whether the benefit payments

---

[1]Over 80 percent of all new plans established since the passage of ERISA have incorporated the individual account concept.

[2]Effective for plan years beginning after December 31, 1985, contributions to the plan are no longer required to be based on profits; however, contribution formulas are still permitted to be based on profits.

are made in cash, are deferred, or are a combination of the two. This definition suggests three basic profit sharing plan approaches, which may be defined as follows: (1) current (cash)—profits are paid directly to employees in cash, check, or stock as soon as profits are determined (for example, monthly, quarterly, semiannually, or annually); (2) deferred— profits are credited to employee accounts to be paid at retirement or other stated dates or circumstances (for example, disability, death, severance, or under withdrawal provisions); and (3) combination—part of the profit is paid out currently in cash and part is deferred. This can take place under one plan with both current and deferred features or under two separate plans—one cash and the other deferred, covering, by and large, the same employee groups.

The definition of a profit sharing plan as set forth in federal income tax regulations is as follows:

> A profit sharing plan is a plan established and maintained by an employer to provide for the participation in his profits by his employees or their beneficiaries. The plan must provide a definite predetermined formula for allocating the contributions made to the plan among the participants and for distributing the funds accumulated under the plan after a fixed number of years, the attainment of a stated age, or upon the prior occurrence of some event such as layoff, illness, disability, retirement, death, or severance of employment.[3]

Qualification of profit sharing plans for tax exemption under Section 401 of the Internal Revenue Code, then, is restricted to deferred or combination type plans. Current or cash profit sharing plans, therefore, are not treated in this chapter. Also, combination cash or deferred plans, because of the unique requirements of federal tax law that apply to such plans, are treated separately in Chapter 17. Thus, this chapter relates only to tax-qualified deferred profit sharing plans.

QUALIFICATION REQUIREMENTS

The qualification requirements for profit sharing plans are, for the most part, identical to those applicable to pension plans—a detailed discussion of which can be found in Chapter 4. However, it is appropriate in this chapter to discuss these requirements in terms of their application specifically to profit sharing plans. This discussion relates only to plans that are not top heavy. The special requirements applicable to top-heavy plans are covered in Chapter 6.

Coverage Requirements

To qualify, a profit sharing plan must be for the exclusive benefit of employees or their beneficiaries. Therefore, a plan will not qualify if the

---

[3]Reg. 1.401(b)(1)(ii).

coverage requirements result in discrimination in favor of the highly compensated employees. Restriction of coverage by type of employment (for example, salaried employees, hourly employees, sales representatives) is permitted, provided that such coverage requirements do not result in the prohibited discrimination.

Relatively few profit sharing plans impose a minimum age requirement, but practically all profit sharing plans specify a service requirement as a condition for participation in the plan. The Code permits the use of a minimum age of up to 21 and a service requirement of up to one year (two years if the plan provides for full and immediate vesting).[4]

Apart from the requirements of the Code, eligibility requirements under profit sharing plans generally tend to be less restrictive than those usually found under pension plans. There are several possible explanations for this fact. First, profit sharing plans often are established to provide a direct incentive for employees to increase productivity and reduce operating costs. If this is the primary objective of the plan, it is only logical that few restrictions on participation be imposed. Second, if the employer is establishing the plan primarily for personal tax reasons, liberal eligibility requirements may produce relatively favorable results for the owners of the business. Since the nonvested accumulations of terminating employees are reallocated among remaining participants, the employer may be less concerned about the scope of coverage under the plan. Third, the cost problem of funding a defined benefit for an older entrant under a pension plan is nonexistent in the case of a profit sharing plan. Since a participant under a profit sharing plan is never entitled to any more than the accumulations credited to his or her account, there is no need to impose a maximum age requirement. Lastly, as will be seen, few profit sharing plans are integrated with social security benefits because of limitations imposed on this type of plan under federal tax law.

Contribution Requirements

The Internal Revenue Code does not require, as a condition for qualification, that a profit sharing plan include a definite predetermined contribution formula. However, the regulations require that "substantial and recurring" contributions must be made if the requirement of plan permanency is to be met.

Contributions under a profit sharing plan may be made on a discretionary basis (for example, as determined annually by the board of directors of the company) or in accordance with a definite predetermined formula. The discretionary approach offers the advantage of contribution flexibility. The board of directors can adjust contributions in view of the firm's current financial position and capital needs. Also, the discretionary basis precludes the possibility that contribution payments will exceed the maximum

---

[4]For plan years beginning before January 1, 1989, three years of service are permissible.

amount currently deductible for federal income tax purposes (to be discussed later in this chapter). If the amount of contribution is discretionary, the plan often imposes certain minimums and maximums. For example, the plan may provide that contributions cannot exceed 15 percent of profits, but it is discretionary up to that limit, or 10 to 30 percent of profits — the percentage to be determined by a board of directors, or as discretionary, but as approximately 25 percent of profits before taxes.

There are advantages in using a definite predetermined formula. A definite formula promotes increased employee morale and feelings of security. Without a definite formula, employees may feel that they cannot count on a share of what they have helped to produce. Also, the Wage-Hour Division of the Department of Labor requires a definite formula if a company wants to exclude its contributions from regular pay rates in computing overtime. In other words, failure to use a definite formula may result in the payment of extra overtime.[5]

Whether a definite formula or a discretionary contribution approach is used, management still must determine the extent to which employees are to directly or indirectly share in the firm's profits. In arriving at this decision, management must take into account such factors as the objectives of the plan, the nature of the firm's business, the pattern of profits, and the age, service, and sex composition of the employee group. Obviously, a good deal more thought must be given to this matter if a definite contribution formula is used.

The contribution commitment under definite formula plans generally is expressed as a fixed percentage or a sliding scale of percentages of profits. The specified percentages usually are applied to profits before taxes, although the base of after-tax profits is also permitted. The sliding scale formulas provide for higher percentage contributions for higher levels of profits. A percentage of compensation formula also can be used if the plan imposes conditions pertaining to levels of profits. Without this condition, a percentage of compensation plan probably would be classified as a defined contribution (money purchase) pension plan rather than a profit sharing plan.

Whether a definite formula or discretionary basis is used, the plan usually specifies some limitation on the amount of annual contribution payable. One reason is to give priority to a minimum rate of return on capital for stockholders. Limitations on contribution payments can be expressed in several different ways. For example, the plan may provide that no contribution will be made in years in which dividend payments are less than a specified amount, or unless aggregate profits exceed a stated amount, or if

---

[5] The absence of a definite formula will not automatically produce this result as, for example, in a plan that allocates the employer's contribution on a basis that takes overtime into account or in a plan that provides full and immediate vesting. In these situations, the company may exclude its contributions when calculating overtime rates even though a definite formula is not used.

profits are less than a given percentage of the firm's capital funds. Many plans also impose the limitation that contributions in any one year cannot exceed the maximum amount deductible for federal income tax purposes.

Employee Contributions

It is conceptually illogical to require employee contributions under profit sharing plans. Furthermore, in those plans that require employee contributions, the employer's contribution is based on the amount of the employee's contribution. For these reasons, contributory plans are generally referred to as thrift or savings plans to distinguish them from the traditional profit sharing plans. For a complete discussion of these plans, see Chapters 16 and 17.

Contribution Allocation Formula

It was noted above that the Internal Revenue Service does not require a plan to include a definite *contribution* formula as a condition for qualification. However, it is necessary that the plan include a definite *allocation* formula to become qualified. Since contributions to the plan are generally based on profits, a method or formula is needed to determine the amount to be credited to each participant's account.

The employer must decide the basis upon which the contributions to the plan are to be divided among the various participants. The allocation of contributions to the account of each participant is usually made on the basis of compensation or a combination of compensation and service. If compensation is used, then allocations are made on the basis of the proportion of each participant's compensation to the total compensation of all participants. For example, if employee A earns $10,000 a year and the total annual compensation for all participants is $200,000, A will be credited with 5 percent of the employer's total annual contributions. Under a formula that reflects both compensation and service, a unit of credit might, for example, be given for each year of service and an additional unit for each $100 of compensation. With 20 years of service, employee A would have 20 units of service and 100 units for compensation of $10,000 a year. Employee A's share of contributions will be determined, therefore, by the fraction of 120 over the total number of units similarly calculated for all participants.

The Internal Revenue Service requires a definite allocation formula in qualified plans so that it may determine whether contributions are shared in a nondiscriminatory manner. In general, allocations based on compensation meet the test of nondiscrimination. However, introduction of years of service into the formula may produce discrimination, since highly compensated employees often have long periods of service with the firm. If application of the allocation formula indicates that discrimination might result, the Internal Revenue Service may require modification of the formula before issuing an approval letter. The most popular allocation formulas are those based on compensation, although many plans use a combination of compensation and years of service.

The allocation formula is used to determine the employee's share of contributions for accounting or record-keeping purposes. The contribution dollars are not segregated on behalf of each participant. Contributions are received, administered, and invested by the trustee as unallocated assets. The balance in each participant's account represents the participant's share at that moment of the assets of the fund. Whether the participant is currently entitled to all or a part of the money credited to his or her account depends upon the provisions of the plan. An exception is the case where the trust permits each participant's account to be invested in "earmarked" investments, such as an insurance contract.

Finally, it should be noted that the allocation of employer contributions is subject to the contribution and benefit limitations of the Code. These limits are described in Chapter 6.

Integration with Social Security

As mentioned earlier, profit sharing plans seldom are integrated with social security benefits. However, these plans can be integrated with social security benefits, subject to the requirements for a defined contribution plan described in Chapter 6 plus the further restriction that the integrated portion cannot be withdrawn. It should be noted that the maximum deductible amount that can be allocated to each participant's account in any one year pertains to the aggregate of employer contributions and forfeitures of nonvested accumulations during the year. In nonintegrated profit sharing plans, the maximum deductible annual contribution is 15 percent of compensation. Furthermore, if the plan is not integrated, forfeitures may be reallocated among remaining participants without reducing the 15 percent maximum. Lastly, if an employer has integrated both its pension and profit sharing plans covering any of the same employees, the integration under both plans cannot exceed 100 percent of the integration capability of a single plan. The objective of this requirement is to avoid the discrimination in favor of highly paid employees that would otherwise result.

Stepped-up integration formulas can be used with profit sharing plans. Under a stepped-up formula, eligibility for participation would not be based on compensation. Furthermore, the contribution percentage applicable to earnings in excess of the social security taxable wage base can be increased by the amount of contribution applied to earnings below the taxable wage base.

Provision for Distributions

As indicated earlier, the definition of profit sharing in the regulations permits distributions "after a fixed number of years, the attainment of a stated age, or upon the prior occurrence of some event such as layoff, illness, disability, retirement, death, or severance of employment."

The primary objective of many deferred profit sharing plans is to permit the employee to build up an equity in the fund to enhance his or her economic security after retirement. The law requires that the accumulations credited to the employee's account vest in full at normal retirement age. Most plans also fully vest the amounts credited to the employee upon death, while a lesser but still significant number of plans provide full and immediate vesting upon the occurrence of total and permanent disability.

Whether an employee is entitled to a distribution from the fund upon voluntary termination of employment or upon being laid off depends upon the vesting provisions of the plan. Of course, if the plan is contributory, the employee is always entitled, at a minimum, to a return of the benefit attributable to his or her contributions upon death, total and permanent disability, or severance of employment.

The value of employer-provided contributions under a deferred profit sharing plan also must vest upon severance of employment in accordance with the requirements of the Code. Thus, the plan must satisfy one of the alternative vesting schedules.[6]

Therefore, under most profit sharing plans, there will still be some forfeited amounts that can be reallocated among remaining participants. The reallocations generally are based on the compensation of each remaining participant in relation to the total compensation of remaining participants. The Internal Revenue Service will not permit reallocations on the basis of the account balance of each of the remaining participants if such a procedure would produce discrimination. Furthermore, if this allocation approach is used, the employer must resubmit for a new determination letter each year. However, the investment income of a qualified profit sharing trust may be allocated on the basis of the account balances of participants. Thus, it is possible to have different allocation formulas for contributions, forfeitures, and investment income.

Some plans also permit participants to withdraw a portion of their vested benefits in the plan prior to separation of employment. The regulations permit distributions from a qualified profit sharing plan "after a fixed number of years." The Internal Revenue Service has interpreted this to mean that accumulations cannot be distributed in less than two years. In other words, if contributions have been credited to an employee's account for three years, he or she can withdraw an amount equal to the first year's contribution and the investment income credited in that year (assuming that the plan permits such withdrawals). Withdrawal provisions are more prevalent in thrift plans. The right to withdraw may be restricted to employee contributions, or it may apply to the vested portion of accumulations attributable to employer contributions. Of course, the participant must

---

[6]See Chapter 6 for a full discussion of these minimum vesting requirements.

report the withdrawn amount as taxable income in the year in which it is received (unless it consists of the employee's own contributions), and such amount will be taxable as ordinary income. Moreover, an additional tax of 10 percent of the taxable portion of the distribution is assessed on distributions before the participant reaches age 59½. Although a withdrawal provision may be desirable in a plan, care should be exercised, since a provision that is too liberal could result in defeating the long-term savings objective of the plan.

Loan provisions also are found in some deferred profit sharing plans. Under a loan provision, a participant generally is entitled to borrow up to a specified percentage (75 percent, for example) of the vested portion of his or her account (including any employee contributions). The loan provision has an advantage over a withdrawal provision in that repayment of the loan will permit achievement of the objective of a long-term program geared toward retirement. However, some employers may prefer the withdrawal provision, since such a provision might help in avoiding possible employee dissatisfaction that could result from the feeling that they must pay interest on the use of their "own" money. The loan provision is also advantageous in that, within limits, the sums borrowed are not subject to federal income tax. However, the interest payments are no longer deductible for federal income tax purposes.[7] The Code requires that loans be available to all participants on a reasonably equivalent basis and that a loan not be made available to the prohibited group in a percentage greater than that made available to other employees. The law also requires that the loan bear a reasonable rate of interest, be adequately secured, and be made only by the plan (and not by a third party, such as a bank, with the employee's account balance as security).

A loan to an employee will be treated as a taxable distribution unless certain requirements are met. These requirements involve the amount of the loan (or accumulated loans) and the time period for repayment. The maximum amounts that can be borrowed without being considered a distribution depend upon the amount of the employee's vested interest in his or her account balance. If it is: (1) $10,000 or less, the entire vested interest is available; (2) between $10,000 and $20,000, $10,000 is available; (3) between $20,000 and $100,000, 50 percent of the vested interest is available; or (4) $100,000 or more, $50,000 is available. The $50,000 limitation on loans from qualified plans is reduced by the excess of the highest outstanding loan balance during the preceding one-year period over the outstanding balance on the date a new loan is made.

As to the time period for repayment, the loan, by its terms, must be

---

[7] Technically, there will be a transition period as the consumer interest deduction is phased out over a five-year period: 60 percent of personal interest is nondeductible in 1988, 80 percent in 1989, 90 percent in 1990, and 100 percent in 1991 and later. Further, during the phase-in period, no deduction will be allowed for interest paid on any loan to a key employee, or for interest paid by any employee on a loan secured by elective contributions.

repaid within five years.[8] However, if the loan is used to acquire a dwelling unit (which is to be used as a principal residence of the participant) and meets the amount limitation, this time limit does not apply.

Other Requirements

Qualified profit sharing plans, like qualified pension plans, must meet the requirements of the Internal Revenue Code. Thus, they must be in writing, permanent, communicated to employees, and must preclude diversion or recapture by the employer of contributions to the plan. In the case of profit sharing plans, the regulations require that "substantial and recurring" contributions be made as evidence of the permanency of the plan. A qualified profit sharing plan must treat service as required by the Code, must permit employees to buy back their benefits under stated conditions, and must include a number of other features such as a prohibition against assignments (with the exception of certain specified events), the protection of an employee's benefits in the event of plan merger or consolidation, and the payment of benefits by prescribed times. The plan must also comply with the top-heavy provisions of the law.

The requirement that a qualified pension plan provide definitely determinable benefits obviously does not apply in the case of qualified profit sharing plans. Also, certain other provisions of ERISA are not applicable to qualified profit sharing plans—for example, the minimum funding standards and the plan termination insurance requirements.

LIMITS ON DEDUCTIBILITY OF
EMPLOYER CONTRIBUTIONS

The limits on the deductibility of employer contributions to a profit sharing plan are set forth in Section 404 of the Internal Revenue Code.

For profit sharing plans, the maximum deductible contribution is equal to 15 percent of the compensation paid or otherwise accrued during the employer's taxable year to all covered employees.[9] Carryover provisions apply in profit sharing plans when the contribution in one taxable year is greater than the deductible limit for such taxable year. This type of carryover is called a "contribution carryover." Thus, if a contribution is made in

---

[8]Effective for loans made, renewed, renegotiated, modified, or extended after December 31, 1986, a substantially level amortization of the loan is required, with payments made at least quarterly.

[9]If the contribution to the profit sharing plan is less than this amount, the difference between the amount actually paid in and the 15 percent limit (called a "credit carryover") can be contributed and deducted in succeeding years, but only if the carryover was accumulated before 1987. However, the credit carryover contribution in any later year cannot exceed 15 percent of the compensation paid or otherwise accrued during such later year. Also, there is an overall annual limitation when a credit carryover is involved. This overall limit is 25 percent of current covered payroll.

a given year in excess of the allowable deduction for such year, the employer will be allowed to take a deduction for such excess payment in a succeeding taxable year if it does not bring the deduction for the succeeding year to over 15 percent of the participating payroll for such succeeding year. However, the excess is subject to a 10 percent penalty tax.

If both a defined contribution pension plan and a profit sharing plan exist, with overlapping payrolls, the total amount deductible in any taxable year under both plans cannot exceed 25 percent of the compensation paid or accrued to covered employees for that year.[10] When excess payments are made in any taxable year, the excess may be carried forward to succeeding taxable years, subject to the limitation that the total amount deducted for such succeeding taxable year (including the deduction for the current contribution) cannot exceed 25 percent of the compensation paid or accrued for such subsequent year.

The 25 percent limitation does not eliminate the requirement that a currently deductible profit sharing contribution must not exceed 15 percent of the payroll of the participating employees and that a currently deductible pension contribution must not exceed the amount that would have been the limit had only a pension plan been in effect.

TAXATION OF DISTRIBUTIONS

The taxation of distributions from a qualified profit sharing plan is identical to the tax treatment of distributions from a qualified pension plan, discussed in detail in Chapter 22. However, the tax treatment of distributions of securities of the employer should be mentioned here because the practice of investing a portion of trust assets in the securities of the employer seems to be more prevalent under profit sharing plans than under pension plans. Securities of the employer include stocks, bonds, and debentures issued by the employer's parent or subsidiary corporations. If a total distribution (defined in Chapter 22) of the employee's equity is made under conditions qualifying for favorable tax treatment, the value of the securities of the employer for the purpose of determining the employee's gain is the lower of the cost to the trust or the fair market value of the securities. In other words, the employee is not taxed at the time of distribution on the unrealized appreciation unless he or she so elects.[11] However, the unrealized appreciation is taxed as ordinary income when sold. If the employee elects to defer taxation of this amount, this value then becomes the employee's cost basis should the securities be sold at a later date. If the

---

[10] This 25 percent limit will be increased to the extent larger contributions are required by the Code's minimum funding standards, as described in Chapter 9.

[11] Even though not subject to regular tax in the year of distribution, the net unrealized appreciation would be taken into account for purposes of the excess distributions tax. See Chapter 22.

securities of the employer are included in a distribution not subject to favorable tax treatment, only the portion of the securities attributable to employee contributions can be valued on the basis of cost to the trust.

TERMINATION OF PLAN

Although a qualified profit sharing plan must be permanent, the Internal Revenue Service does permit inclusion of a provision giving the employer the right to amend or terminate the plan. However, if the vesting schedule is changed, any participant with at least three years of service (at least five years of service are required for plan years beginning before January 1, 1989) must be given the election to remain under the preamendment vesting schedule. If the plan is terminated for reasons other than "business necessity" within a few years after its inception, this action will be considered by the Service as evidence that the plan, from its inception, was not a bona fide program for the exclusive benefit of employees in general. If business necessity exists, the employer may terminate the plan without adverse tax consequences. However, it generally will be more difficult to prove business necessity in the case of a profit sharing plan than with a pension plan, since contributions are not required under profit sharing plans during periods of financial difficulties.

If a plan is terminated, all assets in the fund are vested immediately in plan participants. Since all plan assets are allocated to specific participants, no problem exists regarding any order of priorities in the distribution of the fund. Each participant is entitled to the balance in his or her account.

Upon termination of the plan, the trustees will determine, in accordance with plan provisions, a method of distributing the plan assets. The participants' shares may be distributed in a lump sum, distributed in installments over a period of years, or used to purchase immediate or deferred annuities (either fixed or variable), or the assets may be distributed in kind.

USES OF INSURANCE

The trust agreement of a qualified profit sharing plan can be written to permit the investment of part of the trust funds in life and health insurance contracts. Also, all or a portion of trust funds can be used to purchase annuities for participants. Profit sharing funds may be used to purchase insurance on the lives of participants or key personnel.

Insurance on Participants

The Internal Revenue Service has ruled that trust funds not otherwise available for distribution may be used to purchase ordinary life insurance for participants, provided the premium payments for such insurance coverage are "incidental." The Internal Revenue Service has defined incidental as follows:

1. If only ordinary life insurance contracts are purchased, the aggregate premiums in the case of each participant must be less than one half the total contributions and forfeitures allocated to his or her account.

2. If only accident and health insurance contracts (including hospitalization, major medical, or similar types of insurance) are purchased, the payments for premiums may not exceed 25 percent of the funds allocated to the employee's account.

3. If both ordinary life and accident or health insurance contracts are purchased, the amount spent for the accident and health insurance premiums plus one half of the amount spent for the ordinary life insurance premiums may not, together, exceed 25 percent of the funds allocated to the employee's account.

In addition to the above test, the purchase of ordinary life insurance contracts by the trust will be incidental only if the plan requires the trustee to convert the entire value of the life insurance contract at or before retirement into cash, or to provide periodic income so that no portion of such value may be used to continue life insurance protection beyond retirement, or to distribute the contract to the participant.

However, these restrictions apply only when the trustee is using funds that have accumulated for less than two years and when the form of insurance purchased is ordinary life (or health insurance). If the trustee is using funds accumulated for more than two years, these restrictions are not applicable. These restrictions are also inapplicable if the life insurance purchased is of an endowment or retirement income variety because these contracts are really considered savings accumulation vehicles rather than insurance contracts.

Profit sharing trust funds are seldom used to purchase health insurance coverage for participants since no particular advantages exist in providing such insurance through the trust. The full premiums for health insurance contracts are viewed as current distributions from the trust and therefore constitute taxable income to participants as these premiums are paid. Furthermore, benefit payments under health insurance contracts owned by the trust offer no special tax advantages. Therefore, the purchase of these coverages out of personal income or through the use of a group health insurance contract outside the trust generally is preferred.

On the other hand, there are many reasons why life insurance for participants under a profit sharing plan might prove advantageous. Life insurance is a convenient method of providing substantial death benefits for participants during their early years under the plan. Over a long period of time, the accumulations in the employee's account available upon death may indeed amount to a very substantial sum. However, during the early years of participation, the accumulations will be rather modest. Also, the young employee with a limited period of participation under the plan is usually the person with substantial life insurance needs. Therefore, life insurance offers considerable flexibility in achieving an objective of substantial immediate and long-term death benefits under the plan. Insurance coverages need not be purchased for all participants to preserve the qualified status of the trust. The trust agreement should specifically grant each participant the right to direct the trustee as to the purchase of specific investments for the account of each participant. If the trust agreement authorizes the trustee to purchase investments earmarked for the accounts of participants (and all participants have the right to so direct the trustee), then any participant can instruct the trustee to purchase life insurance without disqualifying the plan.

Still another advantage in the use of whole life insurance coverage is the guaranteed annuity option available under such contracts. Furthermore, most insurance companies permit the participant to supplement the cash value at retirement with additional sums and convert the total amount to an annuity at the guaranteed rates. (For example, the insurer might guarantee to accept whatever amount is necessary to provide a monthly income at the rate of $30 for each $1,000 of face amount.) Thus, immediately prior to retirement, the participant can direct the trustee to use part or all of the remainder of his or her share to supplement the annuity benefit that can be provided by the cash value of the contract. Lastly, investments in life insurance contracts can be viewed as the fixed income portion of the profit sharing portfolio. The high degree of security of life insurance investments could permit the trustee to assume a more speculative attitude in the investment of the remainder of trust assets.

In practice, the amount used as premiums for ordinary life insurance generally does not exceed 25 to 33⅓ percent of expected average annual contributions. The reason for this practice should be apparent. If premiums approach the legal limit, the annual premium may exceed the limit if contributions fall off in future years. For the same reason, it is often preferable that insurance contracts not be purchased until the plan has been in existence for a period of time. The accumulations in the participant's account will provide a cushion if contributions should drop off in future years.

The participant has a current tax liability when life insurance contracts are purchased under a qualified profit sharing plan. The premium for the pure insurance protection (i.e., face amount less the cash value) is viewed as a current distribution from the trust and therefore currently taxable as income to the employee. The amount of reportable income, then, is calculated by multiplying the pure protection portion of the contract by the term insurance premium rate at the participant's attained age.

Any type of life insurance policy can be purchased by a profit sharing trust. A group contract can be issued, with its attendant cost advantage and absence of insurability requirements. However, group contracts seldom are used. The principal problem of using a group contract is that it might be difficult to obtain a level of participation that meets the insurer's underwriting requirements. Of the individual policies, ordinary life, life paid up at 65, or policies maturing for a fixed amount (such as $400 per $1,000 of face amount) generally are used. Of course, retirement annuity contracts can also be used. Since there is no pure insurance protection under these contracts, there is no limit on the portion of contributions applied to the purchase of these contracts. However, once again, since life insurance normally is desired if investments are made in insurance company contracts, retirement annuities are seldom purchased by a profit sharing fund except possibly at a participant's retirement date. With the favorable single-premium immediate annuity rates offered in recent years by many insurers, retiring participants may become more interested in purchasing such annuities.

The insurance contracts purchased on the lives of participants are owned by the trust. The premiums for these contracts are charged directly to the accounts of the particular participants. Likewise, upon the death of a participant, the insurance proceeds are credited in full to the account of the deceased participant or, as is generally the case, the proceeds are paid by the insurer directly to the deceased participant's beneficiary.

Upon retirement, the trustee can surrender the contract and pay the cash value sum to the participant; if the participant desires, the cash value can be converted into an annuity; and, lastly, the trustee can distribute the policy to the participant. If the insurance contract is distributed, the employee can keep the contract in force by continuing to pay the premiums required under the contract. If the contract is kept in force, the cash value as of the date of distribution is taxable income to the employee. Favorable tax treatment (described in Chapter 22) applies if the necessary conditions are met, particularly for the balance of the participant's account.

The disposition of the contract upon severance of employment before retirement depends upon the vesting provisions of the plan. If the participant's vested equity exceeds the cash value of the contract, the trustee can distribute the insurance contract, which can be kept in force if the participant so desires. If the vested value is less than the cash value: (1) the participant can acquire the contract by paying the trustee the nonvested portion of the cash value; (2) the trustee can make a loan from the insurer to the extent of the nonvested portion of the cash value and assign the contract, subject to the loan, to the participant; or (3) the trustee can surrender the contract for its cash value and pay the participant's vested interest in cash. The right to keep the insurance contract in force is, of course, quite important for employees in poor health.

Life Insurance on Key Personnel

A profit sharing trust has an insurable interest in the lives of officers, stockholder employees, and key employees of the corporation. Contributions to the plan are dependent upon the continued profitability of the business. The future profitability of a business firm may well depend, particularly in the case of small and medium-sized corporations, upon the performance of a few key employees. Therefore, a profit sharing trust may wish to protect itself, through the purchase of insurance, against reductions of future levels of contributions attributable to the death of such key employees. It would seem necessary, under most state laws, that the trust agreement give the trustee the necessary authority to make such a purchase.

Insurance contracts are purchased and owned by the trust. The trust is also named as the beneficiary under such contracts. The premiums for insurance are paid by the trustee out of trust assets. Upon the death of the insured, the insurance proceeds arc paid to the trust and usually are allocated among participants on the basis of the account balances of each participant.

The purchase of insurance on key employees creates no current tax liability for participants. Likewise, the tests regarding the incidental nature of insurance are not applicable in the case of such insurance purchases. Since the purchase is for the benefit of the trust, the percentage limitation on contributions applied as premiums will not be applicable. As a practical matter, the trust is not likely to invest the bulk of contributions in such insurance contracts. Furthermore, there may be a fiduciary issue under ERISA as to whether the application of a substantial portion of the contributions to the plan for such insurance is truly in the best interests of all participants.

PENSION VERSUS PROFIT SHARING PLANS

Qualified pension and profit sharing plans are two extremely effective methods of providing deferred compensation and economic security for employees during their retirement years. Although the broader objectives of both plans may be somewhat similar, the basic characteristics of each method are different in several important respects. Therefore, the employer must carefully evaluate the advantages of each plan in deciding on the program that best suits its needs. While the relative advantages and disadvantages of these plans were discussed at length in Chapter 3, it might be of value to review briefly the characteristics of both plans in the context of the more important factors an employer considers in choosing one over the other.

Objective of Plan

The employer must first decide on the primary objective it hopes to achieve with the establishment of the plan. If the employer is interested primarily in a plan that offers employees an incentive to perform more efficiently and productively, a profit sharing plan might be the better choice. While a pension plan may enhance the productivity of employees, the employees under a profit sharing plan are likely to recognize a closer connection between their productivity and their financial rewards under the plan.

On the other hand, if the employer believes its interests would be better served by a plan that provides a known level of retirement security for employees, then a pension plan might be best.

Also, the employer may desire a plan that permits the maximum tax advantages to accrue to key employees. In that case, the tax aspects of both plans should be reviewed with this objective in mind.

Adequacy of Retirement Benefits

The accumulations under a profit sharing plan can grow to a substantial level over a long period of years. However, for short periods of participation, the accumulations, of necessity, must be rather modest. Therefore, employees entering the plan at advanced ages cannot expect much in the way of a retirement benefit. This may be an important factor for stockholder employees, who generally are advanced in years at the inception of the plan. Although past service may be recognized in the contribution allocation formula under a profit sharing plan, this factor alone would not offset the adverse effect of a short participation period on the size of the accumulation.

Pension benefit formulas, however, can be designed to provide substantial benefits without reference to the participant's length of participation in the plan. For example, an employee age 55 at the inception of the plan may be able to retire with a lifetime benefit of, say, 40 percent of compensation. As a result of this, older employees at the inception of the plan (often the stockholder employees) will receive a greater portion of the employer's total contribution under a pension plan than they would under an equivalent contribution made to a profit sharing plan. The appeal of the pension plan for these employees, therefore, is obvious.

The impact of inflation and growth in earnings on benefit adequacy also should be considered. A profit sharing plan, in essence, is a career-pay plan, and growth in an employee's earnings, whether due to inflation or merit, will affect future contributions only. As the years remaining to retirement become fewer in number, benefits may tend to become inadequate relative to final pay. This effect is illustrated in Table 6–2, Chapter 6. This result, of course, could be offset, at least in part, if the employee's account is invested in equities and if the market value of these equities increases to reflect inflation and productivity growth. It should also be observed that the Internal Revenue Service permits integration with social security benefits under both pension and profit sharing plans. However, the integration rules are much more favorable under defined benefit pension plans than under profit sharing plans. Thus, the higher salaried employees generally fare much better under an integrated pension plan.

Death Benefits

A qualified pension plan can provide a death benefit of up to 100 times the monthly pension benefit (or the reserve under an insurance contract, if higher). Thus, a pension plan can provide a substantial amount of death benefit that may be quite appealing to stockholders and high-salaried employees.

Life insurance can also be used in conjunction with profit sharing plans. The premium for life insurance must be less than 50 percent of the contributions that have been allocated to a participant's account; however, insurance premiums paid with funds that have accumulated for at least two years are not subject to these limitations. For older employees, this limitation is likely to produce a lower level of death benefit (total of insurance proceeds and remainder of account balance) under profit sharing plans.

Timing of Distributions

Pension plans provide a retirement benefit and, in addition, may provide death and disability benefits. Profit sharing plans may permit distributions upon the occurrence of any of the above contingencies and, in addition, may permit loans or withdrawals of part of a participant's account balance while continuing to participate in the plan. Profit sharing plans, then, offer slightly greater flexibility in benefit distributions. The right to withdraw or the right to borrow to meet emergency situations or for such a need as building a home may enhance employee awareness and immediate appreciation of the true value of the plan.

The rate of vesting under profit sharing has been and may continue to be more rapid than under pension plans. The rapid vesting under profit sharing plans is an important benefit for participants.

Contribution Flexibility

An important advantage generally offered in favor of a profit sharing plan is that the employer is not committed to a relatively fixed cost under the plan. Contribution formulas can be amended or contributions to the plan can be made on a discretionary basis. However, the Internal Revenue Service does require as evidence of the permanency of the plan that substantial and recurring contributions be made.

Pension plans generally promise a definite benefit or definite contribution, and therefore the funding must be adequate to provide these benefits. The Internal Revenue Code does permit some flexibility in the timing of contribution payments, but this flexibility clearly is not as great as that available under a profit sharing plan.

However, there is also the question of the maximum limitation on the deductibility of employer contributions under these plans. Under profit sharing plans, the employer cannot deduct aggregate contributions in excess of 15 percent of aggregate compensation of participants. Under a pension plan, no percentage of aggregate compensation maximums exists on the deductibility of employer contributions. Therefore, if an employer is interested in contributing as much as possible to a plan on a tax-deductible basis, a pension plan might be more desirable.

Appreciation of Participant's Equity

A participant's share in a profit sharing plan is increased by allocations of contributions, investment earnings and appreciation, and reallocation of the forfeitures of nonvested accumulations of terminating employees. The assets of a profit sharing plan can be invested in a wide range of securities, a substantial proportion of which generally are equity investments. Investment gains and losses are reflected in the account balances of participants. In the case of a pension plan, the impact of investment gains and losses is enjoyed or borne primarily by the employer (ignoring the question of possible insurer guarantees) rather than by participants.[12]

Also, forfeitures under profit sharing plans may accrue to the benefit of the remaining participants, whereas forfeitures under defined benefit pension plans are applied to the reduction of the employer's future contributions. Nevertheless, since profit sharing plans usually provide more rapid vesting and since favorable investment experience is passed on to participants, the cost to the employer per dollar of retirement benefit generally is higher under profit sharing plans than under pension plans.

PENSION AND PROFIT SHARING PLANS

The above discussion assumes that the employer is faced with the decision of establishing one or the other type of plan. This may well be the typical situation in the small and medium-sized corporation. However, it is quite possible that an employer may wish to establish both types of plan covering essentially the same group of employees. A number of corporations actually have established both plans. The profit sharing plans in these cases are usually viewed as a supplement to the pension plan. There is no question that the advantages of both plans can be combined to offer an enviable package

---

[12] This, of course, would not be so in the case of a defined contribution pension plan or target benefit plan.

of deferred compensation for employees. As discussed in Chapter 4, however, the Internal Revenue Code imposes a combined limitation on contributions and benefits when an employer provides both a pension and a profit sharing plan.

QUESTIONS FOR REVIEW

1. What are the typical coverage requirements found in a profit sharing plan? Explain.
2. What might explain why profit sharing plan eligibility requirements are generally less restrictive than those found in pension plans?
3. What contribution requirements are imposed by the IRC on profit sharing plans?
4. What advantages can be ascribed to a definite predetermined contribution formula for a profit sharing plan?
5. Describe a common approach for allocating employer contributions that recognizes both compensation and length of service.
6. What usually happens to forfeited amounts of nonvested contributions in a profit sharing plan?
7. Is a profit sharing plan obligated to permit participants to withdraw a portion of their vested benefits prior to separation from employment? Explain.
8. Explain a typical loan provision that may be included in a profit sharing plan.
9. Can a qualified profit sharing plan be terminated? Explain.
10. What is meant by an incidental insurance benefit under a profit sharing plan?

QUESTIONS FOR DISCUSSION

1. Discuss the conditions under which an employer may desire to establish a profit sharing plan.
2. Assume that an employer has had a profit sharing plan for several years and that the reaction of the employees toward the plan has been unsatisfactory. Discuss the plan design flexibility available for a profit sharing plan that may be utilized by the employer to improve the employees' reaction without increasing the employer's annual cost.
3. Assume that a publicly held firm decides to sponsor a profit sharing plan that will incorporate a definite predetermined contribution formula. Discuss how you would establish such a formula, keeping in mind the need to be equitable to stockholders, bondholders, and employees.

16

Thrift and Savings Plans

Thrift and savings plans have become an increasingly popular form of employee benefit. Having started with the large petroleum companies, they have spread gradually to many corporations in a number of other industries. Many of the major companies in manufacturing and service industries now have such plans for their employees.

Unlike other employee benefit plans, which usually are designed with a specific purpose or objective in mind, savings plans generally meet a number of objectives and provide for the payment of benefits under several different contingencies. From an employer's viewpoint, they offer most of the advantages of profit sharing plans, but at a considerably lower cost. As a result, many employers have instituted savings plans to provide relatively low-cost supplemental benefits in the event of the retirement, death, or disability of an employee, as well as to provide meaningful benefits during active employment. It generally is recognized, however, that because of relatively lower contribution levels, savings plans do not have the same incentive value for employees as do profit sharing plans.

Under federal tax law, a savings plan may achieve a qualified status and, as a result, the employer and employees may obtain the favorable tax benefits that flow from having such a plan. For this purpose, savings plans generally are designed to meet the qualification requirements applicable to profit sharing plans.[1] Thus, with the exception of employee and employer contribution patterns, savings plans possess most of the general characteristics of deferred profit sharing plans. The significant characteristics of savings plans are as follows:

1. Employee participation in the plan is voluntary and, to participate, an employee must agree to make contributions.

2. An employee usually has the option of determining the level of his or her contributions — that is, the employee may choose to make contributions at the minimum or maximum level set by the plan or at permitted intermediate levels.

3. Employer contributions usually match or are equal to some fraction of the contributions made by employees up to a specified level. (Employer contributions sometimes are made in full or in part by means of a profit sharing formula or on a discretionary basis; however, in most savings plans the employer contributes a fixed percentage of employee contributions.)

4. Both employer and employee contributions generally are made to a trust fund.

5. Assets of the trust are usually invested in one or more investment funds, with the employee frequently having the option of choosing how his or her own contributions (and sometimes the employer contributions on the employee's behalf) will be invested. In some plans, employer contributions are invested automatically in securities of the employer, with the employee having an investment option only for his or her own contributions.

6. An employee's account is generally paid to the employee (or on behalf of the employee) in the event of retirement, death, disability, or termination of employment. Benefits on termination of employment are, of course, limited to the employee's vested interest. However, savings plans usually have relatively liberal vesting provisions.

7. Most savings plans permit an employee, during active employment, to withdraw the value of employee contributions as well as all or part of the employee's vested interest in employer contributions. Such withdrawals, however, are usually subject to some form of penalty (such as a period of suspended participation) unless they are limited to withdrawals made for specific financial needs such as those associated with illness, the purchase of a home, college education, and the like.[2]

---

[1]A contributory money purchase pension plan also could be regarded as a savings plan, particularly if it is supplemental in nature. However, such plans are relatively uncommon since they would not permit employees to withdraw funds prior to termination of employment. The discussion in this chapter relates only to savings plans that are tax qualified as profit sharing plans.

[2]Withdrawal of employee supplemental contributions — those with respect to which an employer contribution has not been made — may be made without a plan-specific penalty. However, a portion of the withdrawal will be subject to federal income tax. Specifically, an employee will be able to exclude from taxable income only the portion of the distribution that has the same ratio to the total payment as the after-tax employee contributions have to the total accrued benefit. In addition, the withdrawal could be subject to an additional 10 percent tax if it is considered to be an early withdrawal.

The balance of this chapter discusses the various objectives that may be met by savings plans, as well as their basic features.

SAVINGS PLAN OBJECTIVES

As noted earlier, a savings plan may serve a number of different objectives. It is important, when designing such a plan, to establish those objectives that are of paramount importance to the employer. This is necessary since the design of the plan will be influenced by the objectives it is to serve. For example, if a major objective of a particular plan is to provide supplemental retirement income, it is quite likely that withdrawal privileges, if permitted at all, will be relatively restricted; otherwise, an employee could defeat the employer's basic objective by making substantial withdrawals from his or her account prior to retirement.

Savings plans usually serve one or more of the following objectives:

1. To attract and retain employees.
2. To provide deferred compensation on an advantageous tax basis.
3. To encourage employee thrift and savings.
4. To provide benefits to supplement other employee benefit plans in the event of illness, disability, death, retirement, or termination of employment.
5. To accumulate funds for other purposes.
6. To foster a greater sense of company identification through the purchase of company securities.

Each of these objectives and its influence on plan design is discussed below.

Attracting and Retaining Employees

Generally speaking, most employee benefit plans serve the broad purpose of attracting and retaining employees. In that sense, then, savings plans are the same as other benefit programs. However, savings plans (and profit sharing plans) have a somewhat greater appeal to younger employees, since they offer immediate and tangible benefits during the early years of employment. For this reason, savings plans can be particularly effective in attracting new employees.

Where this is a primary objective of a savings plan, it generally would indicate that the plan should be designed with minimum eligibility requirements, a definite formula for determining employer contributions, relatively generous benefits, and liberal vesting requirements.

Deferred Compensation

As noted earlier, a savings plan, if it meets the necessary requirements, may be considered a qualified plan under federal tax law. Employer contributions made on behalf of the employee are not taxable (even though the employee has à vested right to such contributions) until they are distributed. Moreover, investment income earned on both employer and employee contributions qualifies for the same deferred tax treatment. Distributions to an employee may be taxed at a relatively low rate, particularly when they begin after age 59½. For these reasons, a significant objective of many savings plans is to provide tax-deferred compensation.

Where deferred compensation is a key objective, the plan generally is designed to permit maximum employer and employee contributions.

Employee Thrift and Savings

Even though they are called thrift and savings plans, the specific objective of encouraging employees to be thrifty and to save is not always a primary consideration in the establishment of such a plan. Nevertheless, many employers believe that employees should plan on meeting at least part of their own economic security needs without relying fully on government and employer-provided benefits. A savings plan is a most efficient vehicle in meeting such an objective.

A savings plan to further such an objective is generally designed with liberal eligibility requirements and with maximum flexibility in terms of the levels at which an employee may contribute. The plan also may permit employees to contribute additional amounts (without a matching employer contribution) up to the maximum permitted by federal tax law. Also, to overcome any reluctance on the part of an employee to tie up savings until some future event such as retirement, death, or termination of employment, the plan probably should permit loans and, possibly, withdrawals during active employment—at least to the extent of the employee's own after-tax contributions.

Supplemental Benefits

The vested portion of an employee's account under a savings plan is paid to the employee (or on behalf of the employee) in the event of retirement, death, disability, or termination of employment. As a result, a savings plan can provide meaningful benefits to supplement an employer's other benefit plans that deal with these contingencies. It is common for an employer to adopt a savings plan for the specific purpose of supplementing another such plan, rather than making direct improvements in the plan itself. For example, an employer might feel that the level of benefits provided under its pension plan is not adequate. Rather than improving the benefit formula under its retirement plan, the employer might seek to remedy the inadequacy of the retirement plan by instituting a savings plan. The two plans together could meet the employer's objectives in terms of total retirement income and, at the same time, create the additional advantages that could accrue from the savings plan itself.

If supplementing other employee benefit plans is an important objective of a savings plan, this will have a material influence on the design of the plan as it relates to employer contributions. Also, this objective generally suggests that employees be given limited, if any, withdrawal privileges during active employment, since to do otherwise could defeat a major plan objective.

Company Identification

It is quite possible, in the case of a publicly held corporation, that a major objective of instituting a savings plan might be to promote a greater sense of company identification by having employees become corporate shareholders. While this also may be accomplished with other plans, a savings plan under which part of the assets is invested in employer securities can assist in achieving this employer objective. On occasion, the assets of a savings plan of a privately held firm are invested in the same fashion; however, this is relatively uncommon.

If assets are to be invested in employer securities, a common plan provision is to require that all employer contributions be invested in this manner, while employees have the option of having their own contributions invested in fixed income or equity investments. Employees are sometimes given the option of having their own contributions invested in employer securities. Some plans, rather than mandating that employer contributions be invested in employer securities, give the employee complete investment options for both employer and employee contributions.

BASIC FEATURES   — *after-tax dollars (not 401k)*

The preceding discussion has touched generally upon the basic features of savings plans. The balance of this chapter discusses each of the following major plan provisions in greater detail: eligibility requirements, employee contributions, employer contributions, allocation to employee accounts, investment of funds, vesting, withdrawals and loans, and the distribution of benefits. This material relates primarily to plans where employee contributions are made on an after-tax basis. Savings plans where employees contribute by way of salary reduction—so-called Section 401(k) plans—are discussed in Chapter 17. Also, this chapter deals only with plans that are not top heavy. The special requirements applicable to top-heavy plans are discussed in Chapter 6.

Eligibility Requirements

Savings plans are subject to the same requirements of the Code as are pension and profit sharing plans. Typically, an employee will be required to meet some minimum service requirement and to have attained some minimum age before being given the opportunity to join the plan. Under federal tax law, the service requirement cannot exceed one year (two years if the plan provides for full and immediate vesting[3]), and the minimum age cannot be higher than 21.

It is also possible to use other eligibility requirements such as an employment classification. Such requirements, however, are relatively rare in savings plans.

If a savings plan is to be considered a qualified plan under federal tax law, it must not discriminate in favor of the highly paid employees. Thus, the eligibility requirements chosen must not result in discrimination in favor of this group.

Nondiscrimination Requirements

The same nondiscrimination tests that apply to cash or deferred arrangement (CODA) salary deferrals are applied to employee after-tax contributions and employer matching contributions to a thrift or savings plan. Although these tests are described in considerable detail in Chapter 17, the following description provides a brief summary of the operation of the average contribution percentage (ACP) test in general and the specific manner in which it is applied to a thrift or savings plan.

The contribution percentage for highly compensated employees cannot exceed the greater of (1) 125 percent of the contribution percentage for all other eligible employees, or (2) the lesser of 200 percent of the contribution percentage for all other eligible employees, or such contribution percentage plus 2 percentage points. The contribution percentage for a group of employees is the average of the contribution ratios computed separately for each individual employee in the group. The contribution ratio for an individual is the sum of the employer matching and employee contributions made on behalf of each employee, expressed as a percentage of the employee's compensation for the year.

An employer may elect to take elective contributions and qualified nonelective contributions under the plan or any other plan into account for purposes of the special nondiscrimination test. Again, these terms are discussed in considerable detail in Chapter 17 but, for purposes of this chapter, they can be defined in the following manner. Elective contributions are amounts contributed in accordance with an employee's election under a qualified CODA. Qualified nonelective contributions are any employer contributions (other than matching contributions) that are nonelective but are subject to the vesting and withdrawal requirements applicable to CODAs.

---

[3]For plan years beginning before January 1, 1989, three years of service are permissible.

If two or more plans of an employer need to be treated as one plan to meet the coverage rules, the plans also must be aggregated for purposes of the special nondiscrimination rules for matching and employee contributions. Also, any highly compensated employee who participates in two or more plans of an employer to which after-tax, elective CODA, or matching contributions are made, will have all such amounts aggregated and used as his or her contribution percentage under both plans.

Employee Contributions

As noted earlier, most savings plans are contributory. Thus, an eligible employee must agree to make contributions to participate. While it is possible to have a single-employee contribution rate, it is customary to permit an employee to elect to contribute at any one of several different levels. Thus, for example, the plan may permit an employee to contribute 1, 2, or 3 percent of compensation. Another common provision is to permit the employee contribution rate to be any whole percentage of from 1 to 6 percent. Employee contributions also can be established as flat dollar amounts or by the use of earnings brackets.

Many savings plans permit supplemental employee contributions to be made. Any such contributions would become part of the employee's account and, until distributed, investment income on such contributions would not be subject to federal income tax. Employee contributions (both basic and supplemental) are considered for the contribution test referred to above and as part of the maximum annual addition that may be made on an employee's behalf under federal tax law.

Permitting an employee to elect the level at which he or she wishes to participate is generally desirable, since each employee can select the pattern best fitted to individual needs. This flexibility is continued by permitting the employee to change contribution rates from time to time after becoming a participant. Thus, for example, an employee who initially contributed at a rate of 3 percent might, after participating for a year or so and finding that personal circumstances have changed, reduce the contribution rate to 2 percent or increase it to 6 percent, assuming that these rates are permitted by the plan. By the same token, the employee is usually granted the privilege of suspending contributions for some period of time.

The right to change contribution rates or to suspend contributions usually may be exercised, after reasonable notice, at various times during the plan year. Some plans restrict these rights so that they may be exercised only at the beginning of each quarter; others are more flexible and permit change at the beginning of any pay period following the required notice. For administrative reasons, most plans do impose some form of limitation on the number of times such changes might be made. For example, the right to change or suspend contributions, might be limited so that the right can be exercised only once in any 12-month period. Also, for administrative reasons, most plans require that if an employee suspends contributions this must be done for a minimum period, such as six months or one year.

Consistent with these requirements, most savings plans do not impose any penalty on employees who do not elect to participate when first eligible. Any such employee is usually permitted to join the plan on any subsequent entry date.

Employer Contributions

Under federal tax law, savings plans are generally designed to be profit sharing plans. As a practical matter, however, most such plans contemplate that employer contributions will be made on a fixed basis related to employee contributions, even though the plan contains a nominal provision that conforms to the concept that it is a profit sharing plan.[4]

The basic approach used by most savings plans is to provide for an employer contribution equal to some percentage of the employee's contribution. Typical employer contribution schedules would call for an employer contribution of 25 or 50 percent of the employee's contribution.[5] One variation of this basic approach is to increase the employer's contribution as the employee's length of participation increases. The plan, for example, could provide for an employer contribution rate of 50 percent during the first 10 years of the employee's participation, 75 percent during the next 10 years, and 100 percent for participation in excess of 20 years. However, this type of plan may have difficulty satisfying the nondiscrimination tests described earlier, particularly if there is a substantial correlation between service and pay level.

Another variation in determining employer contribution levels is to provide for a basic contribution related to employee contributions, such as that described, plus a supplemental contribution related to current profits. Such a supplemental contribution might be made in accordance with a predetermined formula, or it could be made on a discretionary basis. It is also possible to design a plan so that the entire employer contribution is determined on a current profit basis; such a provision, however, is relatively uncommon in savings plans.

As is the case with profit sharing plans, forfeitures that arise when participating employees terminate without full vesting may be reallocated among employees or may be used to reduce employer contributions. While the majority of profit sharing plans reallocate such forfeitures among employees, the common provision in savings plans is to use them to reduce employer contributions.

---

[4] The Internal Revenue Code does not recognize savings plans as a separate category of deferred compensation plans. Since savings plans possess many of the characteristics of profit sharing plans, they have generally been considered in that category.

[5] This would apply only for the employee's basic contribution. A corresponding employer contribution is not made for supplemental employee contributions.

Allocations to Employee Accounts

An individual account is maintained for each participating employee under a savings plan. An employee's account is credited with the employee's own contributions, including any supplemental contributions, along with employer contributions made on the employee's behalf. The employee's account is also credited with its proportionate share of the investment income (or loss) of the trust fund. In this regard, the employee's account might be subdivided to reflect the different investment funds available under the plan and the different investment results that these funds might have achieved.

If the plan so provides, the employee's account is also credited with the employee's share of any forfeitures that might arise. When this is the case, forfeitures are usually allocated among employees based on the compensa tion of each participating employee in relation to the total compensation of all participating employees. While it is possible to reallocate forfeitures on the basis of account balances, this practice could produce discrimination in favor of the highly compensated employees. To insure that the prohibited discrimination will not occur, the Internal Revenue Service will not approve the account balance method of reallocation for more than one year at a time.

Investment of Funds

Although individual accounts are maintained for each participating employee for record-keeping purposes, contributions and actual trust funds are not segregated on behalf of each individual participant. Such contributions are turned over to a trustee (or trustees) and/or insurance company who invests these contributions for the benefit of the participating employees.

Many savings plans are structured so that all contributions are held and invested as a single investment fund. This is particularly so when the size of the fund is relatively small. Under such an arrangement, the employee has no choice as to how his or her account will be invested.

A growing number of savings plans provide for two or more investment funds and give the employee a choice as to the investment of account values.[6] For example, the plan might provide for two funds, one consisting primarily of fixed income securities and the other consisting of equity-type investments. The employee would then be permitted to have all of the account values invested in either fund or to have part of such values invested in each fund.

---

[6]Because of the fiduciary requirements of the law, many plans permit such a choice by employees. By doing this, employees have some voice in the investment of their funds, thus reducing some of the criticism that might otherwise be addressed to the plan fiduciaries in the event of poor investment performance of one or more of the funds held under the plan.

Other investment variations are possible, of course. Some savings plans also give employees the opportunity of investing in more than one equity-type fund, each having a varying degree of potential risk and return. Also, if employer securities are involved, a separate fund usually is established for this purpose.[7] A further investment variation is to give an employee the opportunity to direct that a portion of the account be invested in life insurance. Insurance company contracts providing a guarantee of principal and interest are becoming increasingly popular as an employee investment option.

A number of plans give an employee additional investment opportunity, as the employee approaches retirement age, by permitting the employee to transfer all or part of his or her account to an account not subject to market value fluctuations. Such a provision enables an employee to exercise some degree of control over the timing of the liquidation of account values and protects the employee from being forced to accept the market conditions that might exist at the time of retirement.

Regardless of the number of investment funds involved, there remains the further question of the investment powers of the trustee. Under some plans, the trustee is granted full authority for the investment of the fund; under others, the trustee is subject to control that ranges from broad directives to the approval of each investment. In some situations, the employer might retain investment counsel to be responsible for the investment of plan assets, with the trustee acting primarily as a custodian. In making investments, the trustee might maintain an individually managed portfolio or might utilize one or more common trust funds.[8]

If an employee is given investment options, usually some restrictions are imposed upon the employee's right to make and change investment elections. Generally speaking, if more than one fund is available, the employee will be limited in terms of the percentages of the account that can be so invested. For example, the plan may permit the employee to invest 100 percent of account values in either of two available funds—50 percent in each fund, or 25 percent in one fund and 75 percent in the other. Another similar restriction would be that the employee can exercise investment options only in multiples of 10 percent.

An employee is generally permitted to change investment elections only as of a date that the funds are being valued. Some savings plans are valued quarterly, with the result that there are only four times a year that an

---

[7] If the employee has the option of having any portion of his or her account invested in employer securities, it may be necessary to register the plan with the Securities and Exchange Commission; it is then necessary that requirements of the SEC be observed, with particular reference to any descriptive or enrollment material given to employees. Also, it will be necessary that employees be given a prospectus. However, it may be possible to apply for and receive exemption from registration under Regulation A, depending upon the aggregate employee contributions that are available for investment in employer securities.

[8] The manner in which investment responsibilities are handled can have a significant effect on the fiduciary responsibilities of the parties involved. These fiduciary responsibilities are discussed in Chapter 21.

employee could make such a change. Still other plans are valued only once a year.[9] Even if a plan is valued more frequently than quarterly, the employee's right to make changes might still be restricted to a limited number of valuation dates during the year. Again, for administrative reasons, it is customary to limit the employee's rights so that such a change cannot be made more than once in any 12-month period.

A further aspect of changing investment elections relates to the question of whether the change will apply only to prospective contributions to be added to the employee's account, to the value of prior contributions, or to both. It would seem reasonable that the right to change investment direction should apply both to prior and future contributions. A number of plans, however, grant this privilege only for future contributions or grant only limited rights of change for the value of prior contributions.

Vesting

All savings plans provide that 100 percent of the value of an employee's account is paid to the employee (or on behalf of the employee) in the event of retirement, disability, or death. For this purpose, retirement is usually defined as retirement in accordance with the employer's retirement plan. The definition of disability is more varied, but frequently is the same as that applicable to the employer's disability income plan.

A few savings plans also provide for 100 percent vesting in the event of severance of employment. However, most plans require that the employee must have completed some period of service before being entitled to full vesting of the value of employer contributions.[10] While plans vary considerably as to the degree of service or participation required for vesting, the general pattern is that full vesting is achieved after a relatively short time. Savings plans frequently develop more liberal vesting provisions than those found in profit sharing plans intended as the basic plan for retirement income. A typical vesting provision might provide that an employee will be vested at the rate of 20 percent for each year of service (or participation), so that full vesting is achieved after five years. In any event, a savings plan must meet the requirements of federal tax law and satisfy one of the alternative vesting schedules described in Chapter 6.

Withdrawals and Loans

A most valuable aspect of a savings plan is that it can be designed to permit the distribution of benefits during active employment. Such a distribution may be made by permitting employees either to make withdrawals or to make loans.

---

[9]Internal Revenue Service regulations require that the assets of a profit sharing plan be valued at least once a year at fair market value.

[10]The value attributable to the employee's own contributions is, of course, always vested.

Withdrawal Provisions.   When a savings plan has been designed to be a profit sharing plan under federal tax law, it is possible to make distributions to employees after a fixed number of years. This provision has been interpreted by the Internal Revenue Service to be a period of at least two years. Thus, it is possible to permit the withdrawal of funds that have been held in the fund for at least two years.

Withdrawal provisions vary widely and reflect the desires and objectives of individual employers. For example, some plans permit withdrawal rights only for the value of employee contributions. Others permit withdrawal of the value of vested employer contributions, but only after the value of employee contributions has been withdrawn. It is common to limit the right of withdrawal so that only 50 or 100 percent of the value of the employee's contributions may be withdrawn and, if a right to withdraw employer contributions also is granted, a similar percentage restriction also might apply.

Withdrawals are usually permitted only on a date the fund is otherwise being valued (often at the end of each quarter). Also, despite other provisions, there usually is a requirement that the minimum amount withdrawn be at least some dollar amount, such as $300. Further, once a withdrawal has been made, the employee is usually not permitted to make a second withdrawal until some period of time has expired. A typical provision would be to restrict withdrawals to not more than one in any 12-month period.

There are other approaches to establishing the withdrawal rights of an employee. Some plans, for example, might grant a withdrawal privilege for the contribution made each year at some stated time at least two years after the contribution was made. For example, an employee might be given the right, each year, to withdraw the value of the employer contribution that was made the third year preceding the year of the withdrawal. If the employee fails to make a withdrawal of a particular year's contribution within the time designated, the value of this contribution will remain in the employee's account to be distributed at some future event such as retirement, death, or severance of employment.

It is common practice to impose a penalty on any employee who makes a withdrawal. One such penalty would be to suspend an employee's participation in a plan for a period of time following withdrawal. The suspension operates as a penalty, since it automatically results in the employee's forgoing some amount of future employer contributions.[11]

Another approach is to permit withdrawals only with the consent of a plan committee and only upon proven financial need in the event of financial emergency. Presumably, this would apply to matters such as the edu-

---

[11]As mentioned earlier in this chapter, a portion of the withdrawal will be subject to federal income tax. Moreover, a 10 percent penalty tax will apply to distributions (other than those that are not subject to the regular federal income tax because they are returns of employee contributions) made before the participant's death, disability, or attainment of age 59½. See Chapter 22 for a detailed discussion.

cation of children, the purchase of a home, severe illness, and the like. Under such a withdrawal provision, a penalty is usually not established.

Loans.   A less popular but still common provision permits an employee to utilize the value of his or her account during active employment by making a loan from the plan. Under a loan provision, an employee is usually allowed to borrow up to a specified percentage (such as 75 percent) of the vested portion of the employee's account.

A loan to an employee will be treated as a taxable distribution unless certain requirements are met. These requirements involve the amount of the loan (or accumulated loans) and the time period for repayment. The maximum amounts that can be borrowed without being considered a distribution depend upon the amount of the employee's vested interest in his or her account balance. If it is: (1) $10,000 or less, the entire vested interest is available; (2) between $10,000 and $20,000, $10,000 is available; (3) between $20,000 and $100,000, 50 percent of the vested interest is available; or (4) $100,000 or more, $50,000 is available. The $50,000 limitation on loans from qualified plans is reduced by the excess of the highest outstanding loan balance during the preceding one-year period over the outstanding balance on the date a new loan is made.

As to the time period for repayment, the loan, by its terms, must be repaid within five years.[12] However, if the loan is used to acquire a dwelling unit (which is to be used as a principal residence of the participant) and meets the amount limitation, this time limit does not apply.

Also, the loan provision must be available to all participants on a reasonably equivalent basis and must not be made available to the prohibited group in a percentage amount greater than that made available to other employees. The law also requires that the loan bear a reasonable rate of interest, be adequately secured, and be made only by the plan (and not by a third party, such as a bank, with the employee's account balance as security).

Distribution of Benefits

Most savings plans provide that the value of an employee's account be distributed in the form of a cash payment. Usually, there is also a provision that allows an employee to elect to have distribution in the form of installments over a period of time or to have all or part of the account applied to the purchase of an annuity contract. If the possibility exists that the benefit could be paid out in the form of a life annuity, federal tax law requirements with respect to joint and survivor annuities for married employees will apply.

---

[12]Effective for loans made, renewed, renegotiated, modified, or extended after December 31, 1986, a substantially level amortization of the loan is required with payments made at least quarterly.

When any part of the employee's account is invested in employer securities, it is customary to provide that this portion will be distributed in the form of securities rather than in cash. This could produce a tax advantage to an employee who receives a distribution of such securities purchased by employer contributions upon severance of employment or after age 59½ and under circumstances when the entire value of his or her account is distributed within one year. Under such circumstances, the value of the securities is the lower of their cost to the trust or their fair market value. Thus, if the employee so elects, he or she would not be taxed, at the time of distribution, on any unrealized appreciation that has taken place since the time the securities were acquired by the trust.[13] If the employee should subsequently sell the securities, the gain would then be taxable. If securities purchased by employee contributions are distributed, deferral of the tax on any unrealized appreciation is available without the requirement that the employee receive the distribution upon severance of employment or after age 59½, or that it be part of a total distribution within one year.

QUESTIONS FOR REVIEW

1. Explain the significant characteristics of savings plans.
2. Explain the basic objectives of savings plans.
3. What eligibility requirements typically are found in thrift and savings plans? Explain.
4. How is flexibility incorporated into a savings plan with respect to employee contributions?
5. What approaches are used for determining the extent of an employer's contribution to a savings plan?
6. How are savings plan assets invested? Explain.
7. Explain vesting as it pertains to thrift and savings plans. How do the vesting requirements compare with those typically found in profit sharing plans?
8. Explain the approaches that are used in providing withdrawal benefits.
9. Does the federal tax law impose any restrictions on loan provisions in a savings plan? Explain.
10. What alternative ways may benefits be distributed in a savings plan?

QUESTIONS FOR DISCUSSION

1. Discuss the conditions under which an employer may desire to establish a thrift and savings plan.

---

[13]Even though not subject to regular tax in the year of distribution, the net unrealized appreciation would be taken into account for purposes of the excess distribution tax. See Chapter 22.

2. Assume that an employer has had a thrift and savings plan for several years and that the reaction of the employees toward the plan has been unsatisfactory. Discuss the plan design flexibility available for a thrift and savings plan that may be utilized by the employer to improve the employee's reaction without increasing the employer's annual cost.

3. Discuss how the new nondiscrimination requirements for matching contributions and nondeductible employee contributions are likely to affect plan design for thrift and savings plans.

17

Cash or Deferred Plans

4.01(k)

Conventional deferred profit sharing plans, along with thrift and savings and employee stock ownership plans, are discussed in Chapters 15, 16, and 18. This chapter deals with a variation of these plans—one where the employee is given a choice of receiving an amount in the form of currently taxable compensation (for federal tax purposes) or of deferring this amount to be taxed at a future time. More specifically, the employee has the choice of receiving an employer contribution in cash or having it deferred under the plan, and/or the choice of making his or her own contribution to a plan from before-tax income, thus avoiding any federal tax on this amount until it is received in the form of a plan distribution.

Cash or deferred arrangements (CODAs) are not an entirely new concept. They have existed since the 1950s. However, they were beset with legislative and regulatory doubt during the middle 1970s. The Revenue Act of 1978, along with proposed regulations issued by the Internal Revenue Service in 1981, has opened the way for these plans. Their growth, since 1981, has been significant.

This chapter reviews the legislative history of these plans, the technical requirements they must meet, some special considerations that must be taken into account (including some still unresolved issues), and their relative advantages and disadvantages—both to employers and employees. General matters of plan design and tax qualification that apply equally to

CODAs as to other tax-qualified plans are not discussed in this chapter since they are covered elsewhere.

LEGISLATIVE HISTORY OF CODAs

Before 1972, the Internal Revenue Service provided guidelines for qualifying cash option CODAs in a series of revenue rulings. In essence, more than half of the total participation in the plan had to be from the lowest paid two thirds of all eligible employees. If this requirement was met, employees who elected to defer were not considered to be in constructive receipt of the amounts involved even though they had the option to take cash. Salary reduction plans satisfying these requirements were also eligible for the same favorable tax treatment.

In December 1972, the Internal Revenue Service issued proposed regulations stating that any compensation that an employee could receive as cash would be subject to current taxation even if deferred as a contribution to the employer's qualified plan. Although primarily directed at salary reduction plans, the proposed regulations also applied to cash option profit sharing plans.

As the gestation period for ERISA was coming to an end, Congress became increasingly aware of the need to devote additional time to the study of the CODA concept. As a result, ERISA included a section providing that the existing tax status for CODAs was to be frozen until the end of 1976. Plans in existence on June 27, 1974 were permitted to retain their tax-favored status; however, contributions to CODAs established after that date were to be treated as employee contributions and, as a result, were currently taxable.

Unable to meet its self-imposed deadline, Congress extended the moratorium on CODAs twice; the second time the deadline was extended until the end of 1979.

The Revenue Act of 1978 enacted permanent provisions governing CODAs by adding Section 401(k) to the Internal Revenue Code, effective for plan years beginning after December 31, 1979. In essence, CODAs are now permitted, as long as certain requirements are met.

This legislation, in itself, did not result in any significant activity in the adoption of new CODAs. It was not until 1982, after the Internal Revenue Service issued proposed regulations in late 1981, that employers began to respond to the benefit-planning opportunities created by this new legislation. By providing some interpretive guidelines for Section 401(k), and by specifically sanctioning "salary reduction" plans, the Service opened the way for the adoption of new plans and for the conversion of existing, conventional plans. For example, many employers converted existing after-tax thrift plans to CODAs to take advantage of the Section 401(k) tax shelter on employee contributions.

The Tax Reform Act of 1984 provided some subtle modifications to Section 401(k). The original specification of the nondiscrimination standards for cash or deferred plans appeared to permit integration with social security. This ambiguity was resolved by applying both the general coverage tests (described in Chapter 4) and a special actual deferral percentage (ADP) test (described later in this chapter) to all CODAs. The 1984 legislation also extended cash or deferred treatment to pre-ERISA money purchase plans, although contributions were limited to the levels existing on June 27, 1974.

The changes imposed by the Tax Reform Act of 1986 were much more substantive. In addition to reducing the limit on elective deferrals, this legislation provided a new definition of highly paid employees, restricted the ADP test, imposed an additional tax on early distributions, and reduced the employer's flexibility in designing eligibility requirements for these arrangements.

At the time this text was written, the Service had not issued final regulations. Thus, this chapter is based on the proposed regulations and the statement by the Internal Revenue Service that they can be relied on for plan qualification purposes until final regulations are published.

TECHNICAL REQUIREMENTS

Section 401(k) states that a qualified CODA is any arrangement that:

1. Is part of a profit sharing or stock bonus plan, a pre-ERISA money purchase plan, or a rural electric cooperative plan[1] that meets the requirements of Section 401(a) of the Code.
2. Allows covered employees to elect to have the employer make contributions to a trust under the plan on behalf of the employees, or directly to the employees in cash.
3. Subjects amounts held by the trust that are attributable to employer contributions made pursuant to an employee's election to certain specified withdrawal limitations.
4. Provides that accrued benefits derived from such contributions are non forfeitable.
5. Does not require, as a condition of participation in the arrangement, that an employee complete a period of service with the employer maintaining the plan in excess of one year.

As a tax-qualified plan, a CODA must meet all of the nondiscriminatory requirements applicable to such plans. The special requirements for CODAs are covered in the following material. Before discussing these

---

[1]For purposes of IRC Section 401(k), the term *rural electric cooperative plan* means any pension plan that is a defined contribution plan and that is established and maintained by a rural electric cooperative or a national association of such cooperatives. For further details see IRC Section 457(d)(9)(B).

requirements, however, it is important to understand the difference between *elective* and *nonelective* contributions. Elective contributions are amounts that an employee could have received in cash but elected to defer. Nonelective contributions are employer contributions that are automatically deferred under the plan.

Type of Plan

As noted, a CODA may be part of a profit sharing or stock bonus plan. This, of course, includes thrift and savings plans. The only qualified, defined contribution plan that cannot be established as a CODA is a post-ERISA money purchase or defined contribution pension plan.[2]

As a practical matter, most CODAs fall into one of two categories—either cash or deferred profit sharing plans or thrift and savings plans. CODAs can also be subdivided into plans that involve employer contributions only, both employer and employee contributions, and employee contributions only. Plans involving only employee contributions are not expected to be used to a great extent, largely because of the difficulty these plans will experience in satisfying the special tests which are described later.

Individual Limitations

There is a $7,000 limitation on exclusion for elective deferrals for any taxable year. Any excess amounts are included in the employee's gross income. This limitation applies to the aggregate elective deferral made in a taxable year to all CODAs and simplified employee pensions (SEPs). The limit is reduced by any employer contributions to a tax-deferred annuity (described in Chapter 20) under a salary reduction agreement; however, the limitation is increased (but not to an amount in excess of $9,500) by the amount of these employer contributions. This limit is indexed to the Consumer Price Index (CPI) beginning in 1988.

A second limit, effective in 1989, caps the amount of pay that can be taken into account for most qualified plan purposes, including the determination of contributions and benefits, at $200,000. This limit is also indexed to changes in the CPI.

Nondiscrimination in Coverage and Contributions

A CODA will not be qualified unless the employees eligible to benefit under the arrangement satisfy the coverage provisions described in Chapter 4 and the contributions under the plan are deemed to be nondiscriminatory. To satisfy the nondiscrimination in contributions requirement, an actual deferral percentage (ADP) test must be met.

---

[2] CODAs are not available to tax-exempt organizations unless adopted before July 2, 1986, or to states or local governments unless adopted before May 6, 1986.

The ADP test is a mathematical test that must be satisfied by the close of each plan year. The first step in applying this test is to determine the actual deferral percentage for each eligible employee. This is done by dividing the amount of contribution deferred at the employee's election (plus, at the election of the employer, any matching or nonelective contributions that satisfy the CODA withdrawal limitations and nonforfeitability requirements and rules to be prescribed by the secretary of the treasury) by the amount of the employee's compensation. For this purpose, compensation means compensation for service performed for the employer that is currently includable in gross income. An employer may elect to include as compensation any amount that is contributed by the employer to a CODA, tax-sheltered annuity, or simplified employee pension (SEP) by means of a salary reduction agreement. The secretary of the treasury is directed to prescribe regulations to provide for alternative methods of determining compensation that may be used by an employer, provided that the employer may not use an alternative method if discrimination in favor of highly compensated employees results. Also, it should be noted that this percentage is determined for all eligible employees, whether or not they are actually participating. Thus, the ADP for a nonparticipating but eligible employee is zero.

The next step is to divide the eligible employees into two groups — the highly compensated employees[3] and all other eligible employees. For each of these groups, the actual deferral percentages are mathematically averaged. If the average ADP for the highly compensated employees does not exceed the average ADP for the nonhighly compensated employees by more than the allowable percentage, the test is satisfied for the year. The allowable percentages are set forth in Table 17–1.

TABLE 17–1: Allowable ADP Percentages for Highly Compensated Employees

If Average Deferral among Nonhighly Compensated Employees (ADP_{NHC}) Is:	Then Average Deferral Percentage among Highly Compensated Employees May Not Exceed:
Less than 2 percent	2 times ADP_{NHC}
At least 2 percent but less than 8 percent	ADP_{NHC} plus 2 percent
8 percent or more	1.25 times ADP_{NHC}

A few examples will help clarify this table. If the ADP for the nonhighly compensated employees is determined to be 4 percent, then the ADP for the highly compensated employees can be as much as 6 percent (4 percent plus 2 percent). Similarly, if the ADP for the nonhighly compensated employees is 10 percent, the ADP for the highly compensated employees can be as much as 12.5 percent (10 percent × 1.25).

It should be noted that the ADP test determines a maximum *average* deferral percentage for the highly compensated employees. It does not

---

[3]See page 50 for the definition of a highly compensated employee.

necessarily indicate the maximum deferral percentage for an individual in this group. As long as the average deferral for the highly compensated employees is less than or equal to the maximum allowed, it will be permissible for an individual in this group to defer an amount in excess of that limitation.

If any highly compensated employee is a participant under two or more CODAs of the employer, all such CODAs will be treated as one CODA for purposes of determining the employee's deferral percentage.

A similar test, referred to as the average contribution (ACP) test, applies to any after-tax contributions and nonelective contributions. The 2 percent spread implicit in Table 17–1 may be used only once to satisfy both tests, although if it is only partly used for the ADP test, the balance may be used for the ACP test.

Nondiscrimination Rules for Combined Plans

If a CODA consists of both elective contributions and nonelective contributions, the nonelective portion of the plan must satisfy the general coverage tests and the general nondiscrimination requirements with regard to contributions (both concepts are described in Chapter 4). Elective deferrals under a CODA may not be taken into account for purposes of determining whether a plan has met these requirements.

Combined plans can satisfy the nondiscrimination requirements by one of two methods. In both cases the nonelective portion must satisfy the general rules mentioned above; however, the special rules that must be met by all qualified CODAs may be met either by the elective portion of the plan alone, or the combined elective and nonelective portions of the plan. The nonelective portion of the plan may also be considered in applying the special rules in the second alternative if the contributions satisfy the regulations to be issued by the secretary of the treasury.

Failure to Meet the ADP Test.   The consequence of not satisfying the ADP test is that elective contributions in excess of the maximum will be included in the taxable income of the employees involved.

There are several ways in which an employer can minimize or eliminate the possibility that a plan will not meet the ADP test. The following lists some of the techniques that might be used for this purpose.

1. The plan can be designed so that it is in automatic compliance. For example, the employer might make an automatic 5 percent contribution for all employees that satisfies the CODA withdrawal limitations and nonforfeitability requirements and the requirements to be prescribed by the secretary of the treasury. Employees may then be given the option of contributing up to 1.5 percent of pay by way of salary reduction. The plan will always satisfy the ADP test since the ADP for the highly compensated employees could be as much as 7 percent (5 percent plus 2 percent) but, in fact, will never exceed 6.5 percent.

2. The plan also could be designed to encourage maximum participation from the nonhighly compensated employees. This could be done under a savings plan, for example, by providing for higher levels of employer contributions with respect to lower pay levels or with reference to lower rates of contribution.

3. Limits may be placed on the maximum amounts that might be deferred.

4. A mandatory minimum deferral may be required from all participating employees.

5. The plan could include a provision allowing the employer to adjust deferrals (either upward or downward) if the plan is in danger of failing to meet the ADP test.

6. The employer may make additional nonelective contributions at the end of the plan year to the extent necessary to satisfy the test. (Such contributions, of course, would have to satisfy the CODA withdrawal limitations and nonforfeitability requirements and the requirements to be prescribed by the secretary of the treasury.)

9. Contributions for a plan year could be determined in advance of the plan year and, once established on a basis that satisfies the ADP test, could be fixed on an irrevocable basis (except, possibly, that nonhighly compensated employees could be given the option of increasing their contributions).

Nonforfeitability Requirements

The value of all elective contributions to a CODA must be fully vested at all times. The value of nonelective contributions must vest in accordance with one of ERISA's prescribed vesting standards. It should be noted, however, that the vested amount of elective contributions cannot be considered for this purpose. Thus, the vesting of nonelective contributions must be accomplished independently.

As mentioned previously, if nonelective contributions are fully vested from the outset (and if they are subject to the same restrictions on withdrawals as are elective contributions), the secretary of the treasury is authorized to prescribe regulations permitting them to be taken into account when applying the ADP test.

Limitations on Withdrawals

A common provision in many profit sharing and savings plans is one that permits an employee to make a withdrawal of some part of the vested account balance while still actively employed. Sometimes, this withdrawal right is limited to hardship situations; more often than not, however, a withdrawal can be made for any reason, subject to some period of suspension from plan participation.

In the case of a CODA, the ability to make in-service withdrawals is severely limited. The value of elective contributions may be distributable only upon death, disability, separation from service, the termination of the plan (provided no successor plan is established), the sale of substantially all of the assets used by the corporation in a trade or business if the employee continues employment with the corporation acquiring the assets, or the sale of a corporation's interest in a subsidiary if the employee continues employment with the subsidiary. Distributions will be permitted at age 59½, or before 59½ for hardships (hardship withdrawals will be limited to the amount of an employee's elective deferrals, without investment income).[4] These distribution rules also apply to nonelective contributions that are aggregated with elective contributions to meet special CODA nondiscrimination rules.

Limiting the withdrawal of elective contributions to hardship cases only can be of significance to many employers, since it could have a negative effect on the participation of lower paid employees, thus creating problems in meeting the ADP test. The proposed regulations define hardship in a very narrow way. Specifically, these regulations require that the hardship be caused by immediate and heavy financial needs of the employee. Further, they require that the withdrawal not exceed the amount required to meet the immediate financial need created by the hardship and not reasonably available from other resources of the employee. Finally, they require that the determination of financial need and the amount of money necessary to meet it must be made in accordance with uniform and nondiscriminatory standards set forth in the plan.

The language of the proposed regulations raises a host of questions about the design and administration of a hardship provision. For example, what is meant by a "heavy financial need"? Will this include the cost of educating children or the purchase of a residence? What is meant by "not reasonably available from other resources of the employee"? Will this require that the employee utilize all available lines of credit before a withdrawal can be made? Of equal importance are questions concerning the employer's role in administering the provision. How deeply must the employer probe into the employee's personal financial situation in order to comply with the regulations? Is such personal involvement desirable from an employee relations viewpoint?

It is hoped that final regulations will liberalize this provision and provide some meaningful rules on which to base hardship withdrawals. In the

---

[4]If after-tax employee contributions are made to the CODA, a portion of the withdrawal will be subject to federal income tax; otherwise, the entire withdrawal will be taxable. Moreover, a 10 percent penalty tax will apply to distributions (other than those that are not subject to the regular federal income tax because they are returns of employee contributions) made before the participant's death, disability, or attainment of age 59½. See Chapter 22 for a detailed discussion.

meantime, some relief might be provided by including a loan provision in the plan.[5] Such a provision would make some moneys available to participants during active employment, although it would add to the administrative complexities of the plan.

It should be noted that some amounts might still be available for non-hardship, in-service withdrawals. As already noted, nonelective contributions may be withdrawn (unless they are designated to be part of the ADP test). Also, the value of any after-tax employee contributions may be withdrawn, as may the value of any contributions (employer and employee) made to a plan before it became a CODA. Finally, even elective contributions may be withdrawn from a profit sharing or stock bonus plan on a non-hardship basis after the employee attains age 59½.

Time When Contributions Credited

For purposes of applying either the general or special CODA discrimination rules, the proposed regulations require that any elective contributions for a plan year actually be made no later than 30 days after the end of the plan year. Nonelective contributions, however, may be made until the due date (including extensions) for the filing of the employer's tax return for the taxable year in which the plan year ends.

Separate Accounting

The proposed regulations state that all amounts held by a plan that has a CODA will be subject to the CODA nonforfeitability and withdrawal requirements unless a separate account is maintained for benefits specifically subject to these requirements. Included are amounts contributed for plan years before 1980, contributions not subject to a deferral election, and contributions made for years when the CODA is not qualified.

OTHER CONSIDERATIONS

The preceding has dealt with the requirements of federal tax law for the qualification of CODAs and the income tax treatment of elective contributions. There are, however, other issues that must be addressed. The following section discusses the status of elective contributions for purposes of social security, other employer-sponsored plans, and state and local taxes. It also discusses the express limits on 401(k) contributions, the treatment of excess deferrals, and the effect of such contributions on deduction limits.

---

[5]Loan provisions are discussed in Chapter 15.

Social Security

Originally, elective contributions to a CODA were not considered to be wages for purposes of social security. Thus, they were not subject to social security (FICA) tax, nor were they taken into account when calculating social security benefits.

This was changed by the 1983 social security amendments. Beginning in 1984, elective contributions will be considered as wages for social security (and federal unemployment insurance) purposes. Thus, FICA taxes will be paid on such amounts (if they are under the taxable wage base) and they will be taken into account when calculating an employee's social security benefits.

Other Employer-Sponsored Plans

A matter of some concern to employers was the question of whether an employee's elective contributions could be considered as part of the compensation base for purposes of other tax-qualified plans. This uncertainty was resolved in 1983 when the Internal Revenue Service ruled that the inclusion (or exclusion) of elective contributions under a CODA as compensation in a defined benefit pension plan does not cause the pension plan to be discriminatory. The Service also noted that the inclusion of nonelective contributions will still be subject to the discrimination standards.

Employers also maintain other pay-related employee benefit plans. These include short- and long-term disability income plans, group term life insurance, survivor income benefits, and, in some cases, medical expense benefit plans. There appear to be no legal reasons why pay, for the purpose of determining benefits under these plans, cannot be defined to include elective contributions made under a CODA. If such contributions are to be included, care should be taken to make sure that necessary plan and/or insurance contract amendments are made so that compensation is properly defined.

A CODA will not be qualified if any other benefit provided by the employer is conditioned, either directly or indirectly, on the employee electing to have the employer make or not make contributions under the arrangement in lieu of receiving cash.[6] This does not apply to any matching contribution made by reason of such an election.

State and Local Taxes

Unfortunately, the treatment of elective contributions under state and local tax laws is less than clear. For years, many states followed principles of

---

[6] This prohibition is subject to a special rule under which a qualified offset arrangement was maintained by the employer on April 16, 1986 and satisfied certain conditions thereafter. For purposes of applying the special participation and discrimination standards described earlier in the chapter, the benefit under the defined benefit plan conditioned on initial elective deferrals may be treated as matching contributions under rules to be prescribed by the secretary of the treasury.

federal tax law in the treatment of employee benefits. This practice was also followed by many local governments that impose some form of income tax.

With the increased use of individual retirement accounts (IRAs) in recent years, and with the publicity that CODAs have received, there has been growing concern among state and local tax authorities over the potential loss of tax revenue. As a result, the question of state and local taxation of elective contributions has become an important issue.

At this time, the tax treatment of these amounts is uncertain in many jurisdictions. Some state and local authorities have indicated that they will follow federal tax law. However, a few already have announced that elective contributions will be taxable and subject to employer withholding. It seems reasonable to expect that many more state and local authorities will adopt this latter position.

Treatment of Excess Deferrals

Excess deferrals due to the limit on excess deferrals may be allocated among the plans under which the deferrals were made by March 1st following the close of the taxable year, and the plan may distribute the allocated amount back to the employee by April 15th. Although such a distribution will be includable in the employee's taxable income for the year to which the excess deferral relates, it will not be subject to the 10 percent excise tax that may otherwise apply to distributions prior to age 59½. Any income on the excess deferral will be treated as earned and received in the taxable year in which the excess deferral is made. Any excess contribution not distributed by this date will remain in the plan, subject to all regular withdrawal restrictions. Moreover, the amount will again be treated as taxable income when it is later distributed.

Excess deferrals due to the ADP test may be returned within 2½ months. If so, the excess deferrals will be taxable for that year, however, they will not be subject to the 10 percent excise tax. If they are returned after 2½ months but before the end of that year, they will be taxable in that year and the *employer* must pay a 10 percent tax. If they are not distributed by the close of that year, the plan is disqualified.

Deduction Limits

Section 404 of the Code imposes limits on the amount an employer can deduct for contributions made to qualified plans. For profit sharing plans, this limit is expressed as 15 percent of the payroll of the employees covered. If the employer has both a defined benefit plan and a defined contribution plan, the combined limit is 25 percent of the covered payroll.

Elective contributions affect the maximum deduction in two ways. First, they will reduce the amount of the covered payroll to which the percentage limitations apply, thus reducing the dollar amount available as a maximum deduction. Second, they are considered to be employer contributions and thus reduce the amount otherwise available for the employer to contribute and deduct.

As a practical matter, the effect of CODAs on these limits should not be of great concern to most employers. For those who maintain liberal plans, however, the level of elective contributions permitted might have to be limited in order to preserve deductions for regular employer contributions.

ADVANTAGES AND DISADVANTAGES OF CODAs

The advantages of CODAs are significant, although most of these accrue to employees rather than employers. Nevertheless, the advantages to employers are important.

From an employer's viewpoint, CODAs have all the advantages normally associated with any employee benefit plan. Thus, they should be of material value in the attraction and retention of employees, in improving employee morale, in achieving a better sense of corporate identification (when employer securities are involved), and so forth. In addition, they can serve specific corporate objectives such as increasing the level of participation in an existing plan that has had conventional after-tax employee contributions. For some employers, converting a conventional savings plan to a CODA, and thus increasing take-home pay for participating employees, could minimize pressures for additional cash compensation.

From the viewpoint of employees, the first and foremost advantage involves taxes. If a conventional savings plan is converted to a CODA, the participating employees can realize an immediate increase in take-home pay. But of more importance is the fact that contributions are accumulating under a tax shelter. This means that an employee can receive investment income on amounts that otherwise would have been paid in taxes. Over a period of years, the cumulative effect of this can be quite substantial. Finally, when amounts are distributed and subject to tax, the actual amount of tax paid might be considerably less than would otherwise have been the case. Installment distributions could be taxed at a lower effective tax rate (due to lower levels of taxable income, extra tax exemptions, and indexed tax brackets). And lump-sum distributions also may qualify for favorable five-year averaging tax treatment.

Employees also have the flexibility of determining, on a year-to-year basis, whether to take amounts in cash or to defer these amounts under the plan. Since employee needs and goals change from time to time, this element of flexibility could be quite important.

The disadvantages of CODAs also should be recognized. From the employer's viewpoint, these plans involve complex and costly administration. Also, the employer must be prepared to deal with employee relations and other problems that can occur in any year that the plan fails to satisfy the ADP and ACP tests. These plans also will involve more communications efforts than are associated with conventional employee benefit plans.

From the viewpoint of employees, the disadvantages of CODAs are not as great. In fact, the only significant disadvantage is that elective contributions are subject to the previously mentioned withdrawal limitations and the possible application of the early distribution tax (described in Chapter 22). This could be of major importance to some employees, particularly those at lower pay levels, and could be a barrier to their participation in the plan.

THE FUTURE

Despite the uncertainties that currently surround CODAs, they have already become an important part of the employee benefit planning process. In due time, the Internal Revenue Service will issue final regulations and further guidance to the requirements for these plans. And, in due time, the situation with respect to state and local taxation will be clarified.

Many organizations already have established CODAs or have converted existing plans to CODAs. Many others are actively moving in this same direction. There is every reason to believe that the growth of these plans will continue, although perhaps at a slower pace than that expected during the early 1980s.

CODAs are an interesting and tax-efficient way of providing employee benefits. They are consistent with the growing concept that employee benefit plans need to be flexible and need to address the varying needs of employees at different times during their careers. There seems little doubt that, barring legislative or regulatory interference, they will be a major factor in the employee benefit planning process of the future.

QUESTIONS FOR REVIEW

1. What requirements must be satisfied by a CODA for it to be qualified under the IRC?
2. Explain the steps involved in the ADP test.
3. May contributions (expressed as a percentage of compensation) for the higher paid employees under a qualified CODA be larger than contributions for their lower paid counterparts? Explain.
4. Explain the vesting requirements for contributions to a qualified CODA.
5. Describe the impact of CODA deferrals on social security taxes and benefits.
6. May elective contributions to a CODA be considered as part of the compensation base for purposes of other tax-qualified plans? Explain.
7. Describe how elective contributions to a CODA will affect the employer's deduction limits.
8. Explain the advantages and limitations of a CODA from the viewpoint of employees.
9. Explain the disadvantages of a CODA from the viewpoint of the employer.

QUESTIONS FOR DISCUSSION

1. Discuss the conditions under which an employer may desire to establish a CODA.
2. Assume that an employer has had a CODA for several years and that the reaction of the employees toward the plan has been unsatisfactory. Discuss the plan design flexibility available for a CODA that may be utilized by the employer to improve the employees' reaction without increasing the employer's annual cost.
3. Discuss how the new $7,000 limit on elective contributions is likely to affect plan design for CODAs.

18

Employee Stock Ownership Plans

E mployee stock ownership plans (ESOPs) have existed for many years. However, it was not until the 1970s that these plans began to grow in popularity. This increased interest had been focused primarily on two types of ESOPs—the so-called leveraged ESOP (where the plan is used in conjunction with debt financing) and the tax credit plan (where the plan is financed with an employer tax credit and, typically, where there is no additional employer contribution). Although the tax credit for the second type of plan expired on January 1, 1987, the tax credit rules are still viable for ESOPs that utilized the tax credit before this date.

As a result of the Tax Reform Acts of 1984 and 1986, leveraged ESOPs offer several significant tax advantages not available to other types of qualified retirement plans. In exchange for these privileges, however, a unique set of qualification rules applies to these plans. This chapter begins with a discussion of the corporate finance aspects of ESOPs and then describes the other unique considerations associated with this type of plan. The chapter then focuses on qualification requirements and tax benefits associated with ESOPs. The special rules for tax credit plans are discussed in the appendix to this chapter.

CORPORATE FINANCE ASPECTS

Under a leveraged ESOP, the trustee of the trust created under the plan arranges for a loan from a lending institution and uses the loan to purchase employer stock—usually newly issued. The employer stock so obtained is held by the trustee and allocated gradually to participants as contributions are made on their behalf under the plan. The stock is pledged as collateral for the loan. Because the trust cannot generate income on its own, the corporation is usually required to guarantee the loan. The loan (including interest) is repaid by the trustee from the contributions of the employer. This type of loan under an ESOP is exempt from the prohibited transactions provisions of ERISA provided that the loan is made primarily for the benefit of participants in the plan and the interest is not in excess of a reasonable rate. The regulation (54.4975-7(b)(2)) notes that these loans "will be subject to special scrutiny by the Department of Labor and the Internal Revenue Service to ensure that they are primarily for the benefit of plan participants and beneficiaries." Advocates of the ESOP claim that since the employer's contributions are tax deductible, the debt created in conjunction with the ESOP is retired with pre-tax dollars and, as a result, the ESOP is a tax-efficient way to raise capital (as contrasted with conventional debt and equity financing).

This claim is, at best, an oversimplification. Technically the trust, not the employer, incurs the debt, with the employer having contingent liability as the guarantor of the loan. The debt is retired by the trust with contributions made by the employer. However, the employer is entitled to the deduction only because its contributions are being made to a qualified employee benefit plan. Thus, while the debt is retired indirectly with pre-tax dollars, it must be understood clearly that the way in which it is being done is a charge to earnings. A careful financial analysis will indicate that, all other things being equal, the employer contributions to an ESOP will result in lower net income and lower earnings per share. Cash flow under an ESOP would be less favorable than under equity financing. The comparison of cash flow under debt financing is somewhat more complicated, but initially the ESOP should have a more positive cash flow; however, this advantage is offset by dividends paid on the increase in outstanding shares and the opportunity cost of the increase in market value of the shares sold to the trust. Also, it must be remembered that employer contributions (and resulting expense) should be expected to continue under the ESOP long after this debt has been retired.

OTHER CONSIDERATIONS

An ESOP, of course, can be considered for other very good reasons. First and foremost, it can be a very effective employee benefit plan that is capable of satisfying several important employer objectives. It can also be an effective device for converting a public company to a private organization, for disposing of a division of the corporation (the selling corporation would establish a new corporation that, in turn, would establish an ESOP for the purpose of raising capital and purchasing the division), and for providing estate liquidity to a major shareholder.

In any event, if an organization is considering the adoption of an ESOP, there are several legal and tax issues that must be given careful consideration:

1. The first of these concerns the fiduciary provisions of ERISA. ESOPs are exempt from the diversity requirements of this law; however, they are not exempt from the prudency requirements, nor are they exempt from the requirement that fiduciaries must act solely for the exclusive benefit of employees and their beneficiaries.

2. Another problem involves the possible application of "unrelated business income" concepts to an ESOP. Some authorities have voiced the opinion that increases in the value of unallocated employer stock may be considered as unrelated business income and, thus, subject to tax.

3. In the case of a public corporation, there are further issues relative to Securities and Exchange Commission requirements regarding registration, resale restrictions, and insider trading. Further, Federal Reserve Board borrowing limits may apply when margined stock is held by the lender as collateral.

4. If an ESOP acquires employer securities without recognition of gain to the selling shareholder, a nondeductible 10 percent premature disposition excise tax is imposed on the employer for certain distributions within three years of receipt.[1] The tax is 10 percent of the amount realized on the disposition. The penalty tax does not apply with respect to any distribution of qualified securities (or sales of such securities) that is made by reason of the death of the employee, the retirement of the employee after attaining age 59½, the disability of the employee, or the separation of the employee from service for any period that results in a one-year break in service. In addition, the exchange of qualified securities in certain reorganizations will escape the 10 percent penalty tax.

An ESOP presents advantages and disadvantages, both to the employer and to its employees. On the one hand, the employer gains the advantage of avoiding some of the expenses and complexities of selling stock to the public and/or existing shareholders. Also, the plan creates a proprietary interest on the part of employees and can supplement existing compensa-

---

[1]Specifically, the tax is imposed if either of the following occurs as a result of a distribution within three years of the nonrecognition sale: (1) the total number of shares held by the ESOP after the distribution is less than the total number of employer securities held immediately after the nonrecognition sale, or (2) the value of qualified securities held by the ESOP after the distribution is less than 30 percent of the total value of all employer securities as of the distribution.

tion and benefit plans. From the employee's viewpoint, the plan is similar to profit sharing, but with greater assurance of employer contributions. On the other hand, there is the disadvantage that no portion of the stock held in the unallocated trust account can revert to the employer if the trust is terminated prematurely. Also, from the employer's viewpoint, there may be some risk of disqualification because of failure to meet the "exclusive benefit" requirements of the law. Another potential drawback to the employer is that an ESOP could be an inefficient compensation tool if the stock appreciates in value because the company forgoes a tax deduction for capital appreciation on shares that under a typical nonleveraged plan would have been made in future years. A disadvantage to employees of an ESOP is that their financial security may be too closely tied to the fortunes of the employer.

Like any other employee benefit plan, careful consideration should be given to the employer's objectives and the plan's relative advantages and disadvantages before it is adopted. If all such considerations are favorable, an ESOP can be a very attractive employee benefit plan that also serves other employer objectives.

QUALIFICATION REQUIREMENTS

ESOP Defined

In a broad sense, an ESOP could be defined as any type of qualified employee benefit plan (including profit sharing and thrift) that invests some or all of its assets in employer securities. The definition of an ESOP contained in ERISA, however, is much narrower in scope. Specifically, ERISA defines an ESOP as a qualified stock bonus plan or a combination qualified stock bonus plan and defined contribution (money purchase) plan designed to invest primarily in employer securities. Regulations of the Internal Revenue Service, in turn, define a stock bonus plan as a plan established and maintained by an employer to provide benefits similar to those of a profit sharing plan, except the contributions by the employer are not necessarily dependent upon profits and the benefits are distributable in the stock of the employer company. Cash distributions are permitted; however, the employee must have the right to demand a distribution in the form of employer securities. Effective for distributions attributable to stock acquired after December 31, 1986, ESOPs must provide that, unless the participant elects otherwise, the distribution of the participant's account balance will commence not later than one year after the close of the plan year in which the participant separates from service by reason of the attainment of normal retirement age under the plan, disability, or death, or which is the fifth plan year following the plan year in which the participant otherwise separates from service (unless the participant is reemployed). The account balance will not include any employer securities acquired with the proceeds of the loan until the close of the plan year in which such loan is repaid in full. The plan must also provide that, unless the participant elects otherwise, the distribution of the participant's account balance will be in substantially equal periodic payments (not less frequently than annually) over a period not longer than five years.[2]

Plan Design

As the above definition suggests, the plan design aspects of ESOPs closely resemble those of a typical deferred profit sharing plan. Participation, forced distribution rules, and joint and survivor provisions must meet the requirements of the Code and, while the contribution formula may be based on profits, it generally requires a contribution that is a specified percentage of compensation. However, integration with social security benefits or contributions is not permitted for ESOPs established on or after November 1, 1977. Vesting requirements must also be satisfied, although leveraged ESOPs may not allocate qualifying employer securities acquired with exempt-loan proceeds until all other forfeited assets in a participant's account have been allocated.

ESOPs are also subject to the same provisions of the Code as to the deductibility of contributions and the limitation on benefits and contributions for individuals as are other qualified plans. However, certain qualification rules are relaxed for ESOPs that allocate no more than one third of contributions to highly compensated employees. If these conditions are satisfied, the plan may accept contributions up to twice the dollar limit on defined contribution plan additions per participant otherwise imposed by the tax code. Thus, in 1988, contributions of up to $60,000 or 25 percent of compensation can be made to an ESOP for any plan participant. This higher limit is available only if the added funds are used for employer securities contributed to or purchased by the ESOP. Moreover, if no more than one third of the deductible employer contributions for a year are allocated to highly compensated employees, the Section 415 limitations do not apply to (1) forfeitures of employer securities under an ESOP if the securities were acquired with the proceeds of a loan, or (2) deductible employer contributions to an ESOP that are charged against the participant's account.[3]

Contributions to an ESOP may be made in cash or by transferring qualifying employer securities to the trust.[4] While such securities could include marketable obligations of the employer, the typical employer security used

---

[2]In the case of a participant with an account balance greater than $500,000, the five-year period is extended by one year (up to a total of five additional years) for each $100,000 or fraction thereof by which the balance exceeds $500,000. The dollar amounts will be subject to cost-of-living adjustments in the same fashion as the Section 415 limits.

[3]Certain leveraged ESOPs may run afoul of the Section 415 maximum annual addition limitations because both employer contributions earmarked for loan repayment and allocations of securities released from the suspense account are deemed annual additions.

[4]The term *qualifying employer securities* is described in Chapter 3.

is stock. The number of shares of stock contributed would be a function of the application of the contribution formula and the fair market value of the stock. For example, if the formula required a contribution of $150,000, the number of shares contributed would be determined by dividing $150,000 by the stock's fair market value. If the stock is traded regularly on a stock exchange, determination of fair market value should present no difficulty. If the stock of the corporation is closely held or not publicly traded, an acceptable procedure must be developed for appraising and determining the fair market value of the stock. Generally, determination of fair market value must be on at least an annual basis and independently arrived at by a person who customarily makes such appraisals and who is independent of any party to a transaction involving a right of first refusal or a put option.[5] In the case of a transaction between a plan and a disqualified person, this value must be determined as of the date of the transaction. This procedure for determining fair market value is also used for all other purposes of the ESOP (put options, right of first refusal, and so on).

Right of First Refusal

Stock (or convertible debt securities) may be made subject to a right of first refusal in favor of the employer, the ESOP, or both. However, the security must be publicly traded at the time the right may be exercised. Also, the selling price and other terms under the right must not be less favorable to the seller than the greater of the value of the security or the purchase price and other terms offered by a buyer, other than the employer or ESOP, making a good faith offer to purchase the security. The right of first refusal must lapse no later than 14 days after the security holder gives written notice that an offer by a third party to purchase the security has been received.

Put Options

If the employer securities are not traded publicly when they are distributed or are not then subject to trading limitations, and if they were acquired with the proceeds of an exempt loan after September 30, 1976, they must be subject to a put option. This put option must be exercisable only by the employee (or his or her donee, the employee's estate, or a distributee from the employee's estate), and must allow the employee to put the security to the employer. The put option may not bind the ESOP, but it may grant the ESOP the option to assume the rights and obligations of

---

[5]For stock acquired after December 31, 1986, the value of employer securities that are not readily tradable on an established securities market must be made by an independent appraiser as defined in the regulations prescribed under IRC Section 170(a)(1).

the employer at the time it is exercised. If an employer is required to repurchase employer securities that are distributed to the employee as part of a total distribution,[6] the amount may be paid in substantially equal periodic payments over a period not exceeding five years. The payment may not be made less frequently than annually and must begin not later than 30 days after the exercise of the put option. In addition, adequate security must be provided and reasonable interest must be paid on the unpaid amounts. If an employer is required to repurchase employer securities as part of an installment distribution, the amount to be paid for the employer securities must be paid within 30 days after the exercise of the put option.

Voting Rights

If the employer securities are traded publicly, employees must be entitled to direct how the securities allocated to their accounts are voted. If not publicly traded, an employee must be allowed to direct how the plan will vote the securities allocated to his or her account on matters which, by law or charter, must be decided by more than a majority of outstanding common shares.[7]

Diversification Election

An employee who is at least 55 years old and has completed 10 years of ESOP participation must be permitted to diversify up to 25 percent of his or her account balance at the end of the year less amounts previously diversified. After five additional years he or she must be permitted to diversify up to 50 percent less amounts previously diversified. This provision is effective for stock acquired after December 31, 1986.

An employee is entitled to make this election during a five-year period. This period begins with the plan year of the ESOP following the later of (1) the plan year in which the employee attains age 55 or (2) the plan year in which the employee completes 10 years of participation in the ESOP. The election period ends in the plan year following the fifth such plan year. The ESOP is required to allow participants to make the diversification election within 90 days following the end of the plan year.

The ESOP will either have to provide at least three investment options that are not inconsistent with regulations to be issued or elect to distribute an amount to the participant not in excess of the maximum amount that the

---

[6]A total distribution is defined as the distribution within one taxable year to the recipient of the balance to the credit of the recipient's account.

[7]Certain closely held newspapers are permitted to establish ESOPs using nonvoting stock after December 31, 1986. However, these nonvoting shares would be treated as qualified employer securities only if the employer has that class of nonvoting stock outstanding and the specific shares acquired were outstanding for at least 24 months.

participant could elect to have diversified. Such a distribution must be made within 90 days following the end of the diversification election period.

ESOP TAX BENEFITS

The Deficit Reduction Act of 1984 and the Tax Reform Act of 1986 have introduced several provisions into the Internal Revenue Code designed to encourage ESOPs. The following section provides a detailed discussion of the following topics: nonrecognition of gain on employer securities sold to ESOPs, the dividends paid deduction, the interest income exclusion, and the unique estate tax provisions applicable to ESOPs. In addition to these benefits, distributions from an ESOP before 1990 are not subject to the 10 percent additional tax on early distributions (described in Chapter 22) if, on average, a majority of plan assets has been invested in employer securities for five years preceding the distributions.

Nonrecognition of Gain on Employer Securities Sold to ESOPs

Under certain conditions, a gain with respect to the sale of qualified securities to an ESOP that would be recognized as long-term capital gains will be recognized by the taxpayer only to the extent that the amount realized on the sale exceeds the cost of qualified replacement property. Obviously, the basis of the taxpayer in the qualified replacement property is reduced by the amount of gain not recognized by reason of the purchase. The term *qualified securities* means employer securities that are issued by a domestic corporation that has no stock outstanding that is readily tradable on an established securities market. The term *qualified replacement property* means any security issued by a domestic operation corporation that did not have passive investment income in excess of 25 percent of the gross receipts for the preceding taxable year and is not the corporation that issued the qualified securities.[8]

To qualify for nonrecognition, the ESOP must own, immediately after the sale, at least 30 percent of each class of outstanding stock of the corporation that issued the qualified securities, or 30 percent of the total value of all outstanding stock of the corporation.

Dividends Paid Deduction

An employer is allowed a deduction for cash dividends paid on ESOP stock if the dividends are paid to participants or beneficiaries, distributed from

---

[8]Passive investment income is defined in IRC Section 1362(d)(3)(D); an operating corporation is defined in IRC Section 1042(c)(4)(B). Special rules apply to controlling and controlled corporations to treat them as a single corporation.

the plan within 90 days of the plan year end, or used to repay indebtedness incurred to acquire employer stock. The deduction is allowed in the employer's taxable year in which the dividend is used to prepay the loan or in the year in which it is paid or distributed to participants.

Interest Income Exclusion

A bank, insurance company, or corporation actively engaged in the business of lending money, or a regulated investment company may exclude from its gross income 50 percent of the interest received with respect to a securities acquisition loan to a corporation or an ESOP to the extent that the proceeds are used to acquire employer securities for the plan or are used to refinance such a loan. The exclusion is also available for any loan to a corporation to the extent that, within 30 days, employer securities are transferred to the plan in an amount equal to the proceeds of the loan and securities are allocable to accounts of plan participants within one year of the date of the loan, provided that the commitment period of the loan does not exceed seven years.

The implications of this provision for the continued growth of ESOPs are obvious. With half of the interest income excluded from taxable income, any of the lenders enumerated above that are tax-paying entities will have a clear interest in pursuing ESOP clients. Indeed, this increased demand for ESOP clients may lead to a situation where lower interest rates are provided for these transactions. This is thought to be particularly important for leveraged buyouts.[9]

Estate Tax

If employer securities are acquired from or on behalf of the decedent by an ESOP, the executor will be relieved of liability for payment of the portion of estate tax that the ESOP is required to pay. The executor is required to elect application of this treatment and file two agreements before the due date (including extensions) for filing the estate tax return. The first agreement must be signed by the plan administrator consenting to the payment of the tax by the ESOP. The second agreement must be signed by the employer guaranteeing the payment of any amount the plan is required to pay, including attributable interest.

Also, there is now an estate tax exclusion of up to 50 percent of the proceeds of a sale of qualified employer securities to an ESOP before 1992 if the stock was not acquired from a qualified plan or through a restricted stock plan, an ISO, or a qualified or restricted stock option. Additional

---

[9]For a detailed discussion, see Ira J. Wagner and Corey Rosen, "New Incentives for Employee Stock Ownership Plans," *Journal of Commercial Bank Lending*, November 1984, pp. 56–58.

restrictions on the availability of the deduction are provided in Section 2057 of the Internal Revenue Code.

APPENDIX — TAX CREDIT EMPLOYEE STOCK OWNERSHIP PLANS

Congress has periodically encouraged capital investments by making available an incentive in the form of an immediate tax credit. This tax credit is allowed only by placing in service each year depreciable, tangible personal property and certain limited depreciable real property with a useful life of three or more years. The Tax Reduction Act of 1975 established this credit at 10 percent for the taxable years 1975 and 1976. Moreover, a corporation was permitted an additional 1 percent credit (for a total of 11 percent) if it established an employee stock ownership plan and transferred to the plan an amount equal to the 1 percent credit. These plans came to be known as TRASOPs. The Tax Reform Act of 1976 extended this additional credit through 1980 and provided for an additional 0.5 percent credit if matched by employee contributions. The Revenue Act of 1978 extended this credit through 1983.

TRASOPs appealed primarily to capital-intensive companies. Many labor-intensive organizations did not establish such plans since the average amount allocated to each employee did not compensate for the complexities of plan administration or potential problems with employee understanding and appreciation of the program.

The Economic Recovery Tax Act of 1981 (ERTA) made substantial changes in the law as it related to tax credit employee stock ownership plans. The most significant was to change the tax credit to one that is based on payroll, rather than investments, thus broadening the appeal of this type of plan to almost all employers. ERTA also eliminated the employee contribution option as well as the additional tax credit associated with employee contributions, but extended the employer tax credit through 1987. The Tax Reform Act of 1986 moved the expiration date up a year, thereby eliminating tax credit contributions to these plans after 1986.

Plans under these new provisions of federal tax law have come to be known as PAYSOPs. This appendix discusses the general requirements of the law for PAYSOPs, requirements relating to employer securities, and specific design considerations.

General Requirements

Type of Plan. A PAYSOP is a defined contribution plan designed to invest primarily in employer securities, and the plan must so state. The plan must meet the qualification requirements of the Code.

Establishment of the Plan.   A corporation must have adopted the plan on or before the due date (including extensions) for filing its federal income tax return for the taxable year for which the tax credit was claimed. The corporation must also have attached to its tax return a statement to the effect that an election of the extra tax credit was being made and that securities (or cash) equal to the additional tax credit were being transferred to the PAYSOP.

The corporation must have transferred securities to the PAYSOP (or cash received by the PAYSOP must have been used to purchase employer securities) equal in value to the extra tax credit on or before the 30th day following the due date (including extensions) for filing its federal income tax return.

Contributions to the PAYSOP may have been conditioned specifically upon Internal Revenue Service approval provided application for a determination letter was filed with the Service within 90 days after the corporate income tax return was filed and if contributions were returned within one year following the Service's notification of failure to meet PAYSOP requirements.

If an employer claimed the additional tax credit but failed to make a timely contribution, a penalty may have been assessed by the commissioner of internal revenue if the employer failed to take corrective action within 90 days of notification by the commissioner.

Administrative Expenses.   The Code permits corporations to apply a portion of the tax credit to the cost of establishing the plan (10 percent of the first $100,000 and 5 percent of the excess credit for the first year). It also permits the apportionment of some of each year's dividends on employer stock to administrative expenses (10 percent of the first $100,000 and 5 percent of the excess of dividends paid during the year ending in the tax year of credit), to a maximum of $100,000.

Employer Securities

The employer securities transferred to or purchased under a PAYSOP must be existing or newly issued common shares (or noncallable preferred shares that are readily convertible to common shares). These securities may include the stock of corporations within a controlled group, including "second-tier" subsidiaries. Generally, they may not be subject to a call or right of first refusal.

If the corporation stock is traded publicly, the number of shares to be contributed is based on the average of the closing prices for the 20 consecutive trading days immediately preceding the election of the tax credit. If not publicly traded, the number of shares to be contributed must be based on the fair market value of the shares, and an acceptable procedure for determining fair market value must be established.

The stock must have unrestricted dividend rights, the only permissible dividend restrictions being those imposed on the employer by the law of the state of incorporation. Dividend rights must be no less favorable than those of any other common stock issued by the corporation. Dividends may be paid to employees currently, or they may be accumulated in the trust for later distribution.

As in the case of a leveraged ESOP, employees must be given the right to direct how publicly traded shares allocated to their accounts will be voted. If not publicly traded, an employee must be allowed to direct voting of his or her shares on matters which, by law or charter, must be decided by more than a majority of outstanding shares. Also, if not publicly traded, the shares must be subject to a mandatory put to the employer.

Design Requirements

Plan Year. The plan year of a PAYSOP must coincide with the employer's fiscal year.

Eligibility Requirements. The plan must also satisfy the minimum participation standards of the Code as they apply to qualified pension and profit sharing plans. However, two important differences exist. First, the plan cannot require employee contributions as a condition for participation. Second, there cannot be a minimum compensation level for entry into the plan. The plan may use a minimum age of 21, and since full and immediate vesting is required, up to two years of service may be required as an eligibility requirement. A maximum age may not be used.

Employer Contribution. The PAYSOP tax credit for the years 1983 through 1986 is one half of 1 percent of the eligible payroll. No tax credit was permitted if more than one third of this employer contribution was allocated to officers, shareholders, or individuals whose annual compensation was in excess of twice the annual contribution limit under Section 415 of the Code. If the employer's current tax liability was insufficient to absorb the entire credit, a 3-year carryback and a 15-year carryforward were permitted.

Allocation of Contributions. The allocation of the credit to participants must be in proportion to their total compensation (including items such as moving expenses), but compensation in excess of $100,000 in any year must be excluded. Integration with social security is prohibited and the amount of the tax credit transferred to the PAYSOP must be accounted for separately from any other amounts contributed to the plan.

Limitation on Contributions.   The amount allocated on a participant's behalf under a PAYSOP is subject to the limitations imposed by the Code on the annual additions made to any individual participant (25 percent of compensation or a stipulated dollar amount, whichever is less). This limitation applies, in the aggregate, to all defined contribution plans maintained by the employer. However, for PAYSOP purposes only, the stipulated dollar amount is doubled. Amounts contributed to the PAYSOP are also subject to the combined plan limitations.

Vesting.   As noted earlier, each participant must be fully and immediately vested in his or her account balance at all times. In addition, vesting must also be unconditional.

Distributions.   As a general rule, distribution of benefits (including matching employee contributions) may not take place until 84 months following the allocation or the termination of the plan, whichever occurs first. However, in the case of a sale or "spin-off" distributions may be made to individuals continuing in the employ of the affected subsidiary even though the 84-month period has not expired. Also, benefits may be distributed in the event of death, disability, retirement, or other termination of employment. Dividends and other investment income are not subject to the 84-month delay. As noted earlier, dividends may be paid immediately to plan participants. Distributions may be in the form of cash or employer securities, but the employee must have the right to demand distribution in the form of employer securities. If the securities distributed are not traded publicly, they must be subject to a put to the employer, as described earlier.

QUESTIONS FOR REVIEW

1. How are ESOPs defined under ERISA? Explain.
2. How does an ESOP resemble a typical profit sharing plan?
3. In what form are contributions to an ESOP made? Explain.
4. How is the value of stock determined for purposes of an ESOP? Explain.
5. Do employees vote the shares of stock that are included in an ESOP? Explain.
6. Explain how a leveraged ESOP operates.
7. What useful purposes can an ESOP serve?
8. What matters should be given careful consideration by a firm before adopting an ESOP? Explain.
9. Explain the advantages and limitations of an ESOP.
10. Describe the diversification election available to ESOP participants.

QUESTIONS FOR DISCUSSION

1. Discuss the conditions under which an employer may desire to establish an ESOP.

2. Assume that an employer has had an ESOP for several years and that the reaction of the employees toward the plan has been unsatisfactory. Discuss the plan design flexibility available for an ESOP that may be utilized by the employer to improve the employees' reaction without increasing the employer's annual cost.

3. Discuss how the new diversification election is likely to affect plan design for ESOPs.

19

Individual Retirement Arrangements and Simplified Employee Pensions

Despite the rapid growth of the private pension system, more than 40 million American workers were not covered by qualified pension or profit sharing plans at the beginning of 1974. Congress, in recognition of this fact, included provisions in ERISA that would enable such individuals to establish their own retirement plans on a tax-deferred basis beginning in 1975. An eligible individual could make tax-deductible contributions (up to prescribed limits) under such a plan, and the investment income earned on the contributions generally would be currently sheltered from income tax. Such contributions and investment income would be taxed as ordinary income as they were received or made available. The law was later extended to provide that if a married individual had a spouse who received no compensation and neither party was an active participant in a qualified plan, a separate individual retirement account (IRA) could be set up for each individual. With the enactment of the Economic Recovery Tax Act of 1981 (ERTA) and the Tax Equity and Fiscal Responsibility Act of 1982 (TEFRA), IRAs became available to just about everyone; however, the Tax Reform Act of 1986 reduced the number of taxpayers that are eligible to make IRA contributions on a *deductible* basis.

Some employers (both incorporated and unincorporated) also are utilizing or sponsoring individual retirement savings plans in lieu of the more traditional qualified plans because, under present law, the requirements that must be met by a qualified pension plan are considerably more complex than the requirements applicable to IRA accounts. Under the provisions for simplified employee pensions (SEPs), for tax years beginning after 1978, greater simplicity may be obtained by using IRAs instead of a qualified pension plan. ERTA, TEFRA, and the Tax Reform Act of 1986 also expanded the amounts and potential future role of SEPs in retirement planning.

The material in this chapter discusses eligibility to participate in an individual retirement savings plan, the deductible contribution limits, and how such plans may be funded. Also discussed are requirements relative to the distributions and rollover provisions, and the concept of the simplified employee pension plan.

ELIGIBILITY AND CONTRIBUTION LIMITS

Eligibility

A key requirement that must be met before an individual is eligible to establish an individual retirement savings plan is that such individual must have earned income from personal services — investment income will not qualify for such a plan.[1] While the original ERISA legislation limited individual retirement arrangements to persons not covered by a qualified employer-sponsored plan, the eligibility requirements were expanded by ERTA to include any person under the age of 70½ regardless of whether he or she is covered under such a plan. In other words, any individual under the age of 70½ who has earned income is eligible to establish an individual retirement savings plan.

If an individual and spouse both have compensation or self-employment income during a taxable year, each spouse may establish an individual retirement savings plan. Community property laws do not apply to such plans. If an individual is married and otherwise eligible for an IRA and has a nonworking spouse, two IRAs may be established, but subject to certain limitations to be discussed in the next section.

In any event, an individual will cease to be eligible to make contributions to an individual retirement savings plan on and after the taxable year in which the individual attains age 70½.

Amount of Deductible and Nondeductible Contributions

As mentioned previously, the Tax Reform Act of 1986 disallowed tax-deductible IRA contributions for many taxpayers. A person may still make

---

[1]All alimony and separate maintenance paid under a divorce or separation instrument and includable in gross income is a compensation substitute for IRA purposes.

an IRA contribution each taxable year of $2,000 or 100 percent of income, whichever is less. However, beginning in 1987, if either the taxpayer or his or her spouse is an active participant[2] in an employer-maintained plan for any part of a plan year ending with or within the taxable year, the $2,000 figure is reduced (but not below zero) based on adjusted gross income (AGI), calculated without regard to any IRA contributions, in the following manner:[3]

1. In the case of a taxpayer filing a joint return, the maximum deductible amount is equal to $2,000 − .2(AGI − $40,000).
2. In the case of a married individual filing a separate return, the maximum deductible amount is equal to $2,000 − .2(AGI).
3. In the case of any other taxpayer, the maximum deductible amount is equal to $2,000 − .2(AGI − $25,000).

Whether or not a spouse is an active plan participant is not taken into consideration in the case of a married individual filing a separate return for the taxable year.

Nondeductible contributions also may be made to an IRA if they are designated as such on the taxpayer's return. Although these contributions will be made from after-tax income, they will benefit from tax-sheltered investment income during the time they remain in the IRA. Nondeductible contributions cannot exceed the difference between $2,000 ($2,250 in the case of a spousal IRA, described below) and the deductible contribution made for that year. Taxpayers may elect to treat contributions as nondeductible even though they are eligible to make deductible contributions.

If an individual and spouse both have compensation, then each spouse may establish a separate IRA if each is eligible up to the lesser of 100 percent of income or $2,000. An otherwise eligible individual also may set up an IRA for a nonworking spouse or a spouse who elects to be treated as having no compensation for the year for purposes of the IRA maximum deduction amount. Under a spousal IRA plan of this type the spouses must file a joint income tax return, no more than $2,000 can be contributed to the account of either spouse, and the maximum tax deduction (after application of the AGI test described above) is limited to the lesser of 100 percent of earned income, or $2,250. Contributions to spousal accounts are not permitted after the elder spouse reaches age 70½. If the employee-spouse is younger, he or she can continue only his or her own IRA after the other spouse reaches age 70½. Since the deduction is against gross income, it may be taken even though the individual does not itemize deductions. If the individual's employer makes the contribution directly to the plan on behalf of the individual, it must still be reported and taken as a deduction

---

[2]The determination of whether an individual is an active participant is made without regard to whether the individual's rights under the plan are nonforfeitable.

[3]No dollar limitation will be reduced below $200 until the limitation is completely phased out.

against gross income. This contribution will be subject to FICA (social security tax) and FUTA (Federal Unemployment Tax Act) but not to withholding taxes.

The contribution must be made in cash before the due date for the individual's filing of the federal income tax return for the taxable year in which the deduction is claimed. Thus, the contribution of existing property (e.g., an insurance policy) will not be permitted.

Any excess contribution is subject to a nondeductible 6 percent excise tax in addition to current taxation. The excise tax continues to be applied each year until the excess contribution is withdrawn from the IRA. For example, if an individual makes an excess contribution of $100 to an IRA in 1985, an excise tax of $6 is imposed for 1985 and for each year thereafter until the excess contribution is withdrawn.

Because of the restrictions on distributions from an IRA (discussed in a later section of this chapter) the question arises whether the withdrawal of an excess contribution is itself a taxable event. If the excess contribution is withdrawn before the tax return filing date for the year for which the contribution was made, the withdrawn amount is not included in taxable income, and the 10 percent premature distribution tax is not applied.

Any excess contributions not taken as a distribution may be eliminated in later years by contributing less than the maximum allowable deduction in such years. For example, if an individual contributed $2,100 in one year, the situation can be remedied by contributing only $1,900 the following year. If excess contributions are not eliminated through these steps, the excess amounts will be subject to a cumulative 6 percent excise tax each year until they are eliminated.

FUNDING

An individual may establish an individual retirement savings plan by making contributions to one or more of the following:

1. An individual retirement account.
2. An individual retirement annuity.
3. A U.S. retirement bond (permitted prior to May 1, 1982).

The following material discusses each of these approaches in greater detail, as well as the restrictions of the Internal Revenue Code for prohibited transactions and unrelated business income.

Individual Retirement Account

This type of plan entails the establishment of a trust or a custodial account and is by far the most popular type of IRA account. The trustee or custodian may be a bank, another person, or an organization that demonstrates to the satisfaction of the Internal Revenue Service that the individual retirement account (IRA) will be administered in accordance with the law.

The only restriction on investments in such an IRA is that the assets cannot be invested in life insurance contracts except for endowment contracts with incidental life insurance features, and ERTA effectively eliminates investments in collectibles such as antiques, works of art, stamps, coins, and the like.[4] Most IRAs are invested in assets such as bank-pooled funds, savings accounts, certificates of deposit, savings and loan association accounts, mutual fund shares, face-amount certificates, and insured credit union accounts.

The key requirements of an individual retirement account are as follows:

1. The annual contribution must be made in cash and cannot exceed $2,000, or $2,250 if a nonworking spouse is included.
2. The entire value of the account must be nonforfeitable.
3. No part of the funds may be invested in life insurance contracts or collectibles, other than legal tender gold and silver coins minted by the United States.
4. The assets in the account cannot be commingled with any other property (except the assets of other qualified trusts).
5. Distributions must be made in accordance with the restrictions imposed by the law.

The Internal Revenue Service has issued prototype trust and custodial agreements (Forms 5305 and 5305A). If these prototypes are used, the plan is considered as automatically approved by the Internal Revenue Service. If the trustee or custodian wishes to utilize its own agreement, it may do this and submit the agreement to the Internal Revenue Service for approval on Form 5306. An individual who utilizes such approved plans does not need to submit his or her individual plan for Internal Revenue Service approval.

Individual Retirement Annuity

Under this type of plan, the individual's contribution is invested through the device of purchasing a flexible premium annuity IRA from a legally licensed life insurance company.

The annuity contract must involve flexible premiums and may be participating or nonparticipating. Also, the annuity may be fixed or variable. The key requirements of a flexible premium annuity plan are as follows:

1. The annual premium cannot be fixed and cannot exceed $2,000, or $2,250 for a spousal IRA.

---

[4]Under the Tax Reform Act of 1986, an exception to the prohibition against investments in collectibles is made for investments in legal tender gold and silver coins minted by the United States.

2. The contract must be nontransferable.
3. The individual's interest in the contract must be nonforfeitable.
4. Dividends must be used before the end of the next year to purchase additional benefits or to reduce future premiums.
5. Distributions must be made in accordance with the restrictions imposed by law.

An insurance company may utilize a prototype plan or use special editions of their standard contracts that contain the specific requirements of the law. By using Internal Revenue Service Form 5306, the insurance company may secure Internal Revenue Service approval of its prototype plan or modified contracts. Any individual who uses such an approved arrangement need not submit his or her individual plan for Internal Revenue Service approval.

Selection of Funding Arrangement

No restrictions exist on the number of individual retirement savings plans an individual may establish; however, the aggregate contributions made to all plans in a given year cannot exceed the allowable contribution limits. Also, as a practical matter, the combination of the maximum permissible contribution and the minimum contribution requirements of the institutions offering such plans effectively limits the number of plans that can be operated at the same time.

Selection of the appropriate funding arrangement involves many of the same considerations taken into account in the selection of a funding instrument for a qualified pension plan. Thus, the individual must give consideration to potential investment return as well as investment risk. The expenses associated with the particular funding arrangement also must be taken into account, as must benefit security and services provided.

PROHIBITED TRANSACTIONS

Individual retirement savings plans are subject to the prohibited transactions provisions of ERISA. If the individual engages in a prohibited transaction, the plan will be disqualified as of the first day of the taxable year in which the transaction occurred. The individual must then include the fair market value of the assets of the plan (determined as of the first day of such year) in ordinary income. In addition, if the individual has not attained age 59½ (or is not disabled), an additional 10 percent tax will be levied since this is treated as a premature distribution. Generally speaking, fiduciaries and parties in interest are prohibited from engaging in the following:

1. Selling, exchanging, or leasing property.
2. Lending money or extending credit.

3. Furnishing goods, services, or facilities.
4. Transferring to or using plan assets.

There are, of course, exceptions to the prohibited transaction rules. One of the more significant exceptions permits a financial institution to provide ancillary services where this is done without interference with the interests of the participants and beneficiaries, where not more than reasonable compensation is charged, and where adequate internal safeguards exist to prevent providing services in an excessive or unreasonable manner.

Except for the individual (and his or her beneficiary), a party in interest who engages in a prohibited transaction will be subject to an excise tax of 5 percent of the amount involved. If the situation is not corrected within the time allowed (90 days unless extended by the Internal Revenue Service), a further excise tax of 100 percent of the amount involved will be levied.

UNRELATED BUSINESS INCOME

An individual retirement savings plan is subject to federal income tax on any unrelated business income that arises from the conduct of any trade or business that is not substantially related to the exempt purpose of the plan. If a plan develops such unrelated business income, the plan will not be disqualified; however, such income will be subject to tax.

DISTRIBUTIONS

The law contains very specific provisions that relate to distributions from individual retirement savings plans. In general, these provisions are designed to support the basic purpose of such plans—that they should provide retirement income. Thus, premature and lump-sum distributions are discouraged. On the other hand, the individual is expected to begin receiving payments by age 70½ and is encouraged to draw down benefits over his or her remaining lifetime (or the joint lifetimes of the individual and his or her spouse).

The following material discusses the law's basic limitations on payments, the taxation of distributions, and the treatment of premature distributions.

Limitation on Distributions

Except in the event of the individual's death or disability, distribution from an individual retirement savings plan may not be made prior to age 59½ without incurring additional tax liability. For purposes of the law, an individual is considered to be disabled "if he is unable to engage in any substantial gainful activity by reason of any medically determinable physical or mental impairment which can be expected to result in death or to be of long-continued and indefinite character."

In any case, distribution must commence prior to the end of the year in which the individual attains age 70½. These distributions may be in the form of a lump sum or in periodic payments not to exceed the life expectancy of the individual or the joint life expectancy of the individual and a designated beneficiary.[5] If an individual entitled to benefits dies before the entire interest is distributed, the required distribution to the beneficiary depends upon whether distributions to the IRA owner had already started by the date he or she dies. If they have, the remaining portion of the interest is distributed at least as rapidly as under the method of distribution being used at the date of death. If they have not, the entire interest of the employee will be distributed within five years after the death of the employee. However, there is an exception to the five-year rule for certain amounts payable over the life of the beneficiary. If any portion of the employee's interest is payable to (or for the benefit of) a designated beneficiary, such portion may be distributed over the life of such designated beneficiary (or over a period not extending beyond the life expectancy of such beneficiary) if such distributions begin no later than one year after the date of the IRA owner's death. If the designated beneficiary is the surviving spouse of the IRA owner, additional flexibility exists. In this case, distributions do not have to begin prior to the time the IRA owner would have attained age 70½.

If plan assets are not distributed at least as rapidly as described above, an excise tax will be levied. This excise tax will be 50 percent of the "excess accumulation." The excess accumulation is the difference between the amount that was distributed during the year and the amount that should have been distributed under the rules described above.

Taxation of Distributions

Distributions from an individual retirement savings plan (whether to the individual or his or her beneficiary) are taxable under IRC Section 72 (i.e., if nondeductible contributions have been made, a portion of each distribution is treated as a return of basis). Lump-sum distributions do not qualify for long-term capital gains treatment nor do they qualify for the special five-year averaging treatment made available to corporate qualified plans.

As described in Chapter 22, a portion of an IRA distribution may be subject to a 15 percent excise tax. This results if the aggregate taxable distribution to an individual in any year for all tax-favored plans — IRAs as well as pensions, savings and stock bonus plans, CODAs, and tax-sheltered annuities — exceeds the greater of $150,000 or $112,500 (indexed to the CPI beginning in 1988).

---

[5]The life expectancy of an individual, or the joint life expectancy of the individual and beneficiary, may be recomputed as frequently as once a year. For distributions to an individual and a designated beneficiary other than the individual's spouse, IRS regulations will provide a method of taking into account changes in the individual's life expectancy, but not that of the beneficiary.

For estate tax purposes, the entire value of a lump-sum distribution is included in the decedent's gross estate.

Premature Distributions

If an individual is not disabled and receives a taxable distribution from an individual retirement savings plan before attaining age 59½, this will be considered to be a premature distribution. The amount of the premature distribution will have to be included in the individual's gross income in the year of receipt. There will also be an additional nondeductible tax of 10 percent of the amount of the premature distribution.

If an individual has an individual retirement *annuity* and borrows any money under or by use of that annuity contract, the annuity will lose its tax-exempt status as of the first day of the taxable year in which the transaction occurred. The fair market value of such annuity (as of the first day of such taxable year) will have to be included in the individual's gross income for such year. If the individual has not attained age 59½ or is not disabled at such time, this also will be considered to be a premature distribution and the additional tax of 10 percent of the amount involved will be levied.

If an individual has an individual retirement *account* and uses all or any portion of the account as security for a loan, the portion so used will be treated and taxed as a distribution. Again, if the individual has not attained age 59½ or is not disabled, the 10 percent additional tax also will be levied.

ROLLOVERS

The rollover provisions of the law permit the tax free transfer of assets from one individual retirement savings plan to another and permit an employee who receives a lump-sum distribution from a qualified pension or profit sharing plan to transfer the distribution so received into an individual retirement savings plan. The following first discusses rollovers that occur between individual plans and then rollovers that involve qualified plans.[6]

In general, an individual may withdraw all or part of the assets from one individual retirement savings plan and transfer the withdrawn amount to another individual retirement savings plan without unfavorable tax treatment. To qualify as a tax-free rollover, the following conditions must be met:

1. The amount of the distribution must be transferred to the new plan within 60 days after the distribution is made.
2. The new individual retirement savings plan must contain no assets other than those received from the distributing plan.

---

[6]The authors wish to thank John J. McFadden, J.D.,Assistant Professor of Taxation at The American College in Bryn Mawr, Pa. Much of the material in this section is based on material he wrote for the Study Guide for CLU Course 308, Pension Planning.

3. After such a rollover is made, no additional rollover between individual retirement savings plans may be made for a period of one year.

No limitations are imposed on the amounts transferred and the transfer may be made prior to age 59½ without being considered a premature distribution. A rollover also may be made at a time when the individual is not otherwise eligible to make a tax deductible contribution to an individual retirement savings plan. Rollovers also may occur after age 70½, although in this event the rollover to the new plan must provide for distributions in accordance with the rules previously described.

Another rollover provision allows an IRA to be used to receive proceeds of a distribution from a corporate qualified plan or a Section 403(b) tax-deferred annuity plan, thereby avoiding immediate income taxation on the distribution. To be rolled over into an IRA, the distribution from the plan may qualify as a lump-sum distribution, or may be a distribution made upon termination of a qualified or tax-deferred annuity plan. The maximum amount that can be rolled over is the amount of the distribution less nondeductible employee contributions. Any part of the remainder can be rolled over into the IRA. If the distribution is noncash property, all the property must be transferred. But the property may be sold and any part of the sales proceeds may then be transferred to the IRA. The rollover contribution must be made on or before the 60th day after receipt of the distribution. An existing IRA can be used or a new one may be set up.

Tax-free rollover treatment is also available for distributions of 50 percent or more of the balance to an employee's credit under a qualified pension or profit sharing plan, or Section 403(b) annuity; however, partial distributions may not be rolled over to a second qualified plan. Moreover, once a partial distribution is taken, the balance to the employee's credit that remains in the plan loses tax-favored treatment.

The part of the distribution rolled over into the IRA will not be subject to current income tax for the recipient. The usual rules for taxation of IRA distributions will apply when this amount is withdrawn subsequently.

A spousal rollover also is permitted. If any portion of a lump-sum distribution from an employer's plan is paid to a spouse of an employee who has died, the spouse may roll over any portions of the distribution to an IRA. In deciding whether to roll over all or part of the proceeds of a lump-sum distribution from a qualified plan to an IRA, the advantages of alternative tax treatments must be considered. A lump-sum distribution from a qualified plan could qualify for favorable tax treatment. Thus, even though a distribution that is not rolled over is taxable immediately, it could be taxable under advantageous provisions. A distribution rolled over will not be taxed immediately; taxation will be deferred to the time when it is withdrawn from the IRA. However, this subsequent distribution, like any IRA distribution, is not eligible for the favorable tax treatment if received as a lump sum; rather, the entire amount is taxable. Furthermore, the distribution cannot be made without penalty until age 59½, although it can be deferred as late as age 70½. Also, the $5,000 income tax exclusion for employee death benefits is not available for a distribution from an IRA.

However, the deferral of income taxes under a rollover may still be advantageous. Furthermore, taxes on investment earnings of the IRA also are deferred until the rollover amount is distributed. These advantages also may be obtained without an IRA through the purchase of a nontransferable deferred annuity contract with the proceeds of the lump-sum or termination distribution from the qualified plan. The various IRA restrictions would not apply to such an annuity contract.

Rollover provisions also exist whereby an IRA may be used as a conduit to carry out a tax free transfer of cash or property from one corporate qualified plan to another.[7] Basically, if the amount received from the qualified plan is a lump-sum distribution or a termination distribution, and if it is transferred within 60 days to an IRA, the transfer is tax free as described above. In addition, if the IRA plan contains no assets other than those attributable to the distribution from the qualified plan, the amount in the IRA subsequently may be transferred tax free to another corporate qualified plan if the transfer is made within 60 days after the property is received. Similar provisions allow an IRA to be used as a conduit between two Section 403(b) annuity plans.

Finally, distributions made pursuant to qualified domestic relations orders (QDROs) may be eligible for tax-free rollover treatment. If the balance to the credit of the recipient is distributed within one taxable year and the recipient transfers any portion of the property received to an IRA, the portion of the distribution transferred to the IRA will be treated as a tax-free rollover. In the case of a distribution of property other than money, the amount transferred to the IRA must consist of the property distributed.

EMPLOYER-SPONSORED IRAs

Although the IRA is viewed primarily as a device for facilitating individual retirement savings, an employer—including a self-employed person—may sponsor an IRA for some or all employees. A labor union also may sponsor an IRA plan for its members. No requirement exists that the employer-sponsored IRAs be available to all employees or be nondiscriminatory in benefits. The contributions to the IRA may be made as additional compensation or by payroll deduction. Any amount contributed by an employer to an IRA is taxable to the employee as additional compensation income. The employee is then eligible for the IRA tax deduction up to the $2,000 limitation. The amounts contributed are additional compensation

---

[7]This conduit rule does not apply to a death payout to an employee-participant's beneficiary other than a surviving spouse.

and subject to FICA (social security) and FUTA (Federal Unemployment Tax Act) taxes. No federal income tax withholding is required if the employer believes the employee will be entitled to the offsetting IRA tax deduction.

An employer-sponsored IRA may use separate IRA trusts or annuity plans for each employee, or a single account may be used. However, the single account must provide a separate accounting for each participant's interest. Either a commingled trust fund or a nontrusteed group annuity contract with individual certificates may be used. In an employer-sponsored IRA, the prohibited transaction rules apply to transactions between the employer or other disqualified person and the IRA itself. Such prohibited transactions are subject to the ERISA penalties. The entire IRA plan or trust will not be disqualified as a result of a prohibited transaction involving an individual participant. If the individual participant engages in a prohibited transaction with the employer-sponsored IRA, only his or her individual portion of the IRA becomes disqualified, much as if he or she maintained the IRA separately.

An employer sponsoring an IRA may request a determination letter from the IRS. Furthermore, the same reporting, disclosure, and fiduciary requirements applicable to qualified plans under ERISA may apply to an employer sponsoring an IRA plan, if the employer endorses the IRA.[8] The participation, funding, and vesting rules of ERISA do not, however, apply. The funding and vesting rules are really irrelevant since the IRA plan may be funded only through the permitted IRA funding vehicles previously discussed, and each participant always is 100 percent vested. If an employer makes no actual contribution to employee IRAs, but merely provides certain facilities such as payroll deduction or checkoff, or allows the actual sponsor (e.g., an insurer or labor union) to publicize the program among employees, the reporting and disclosure requirements will not apply to the employer.

REPORTING AND DISCLOSURE

An individual having an IRA is not subject to any reporting and disclosure requirements except in years in which a rollover has occurred, or one of the penalty taxes is payable. An employer sponsoring an IRA may be subject to the reporting, disclosure, and fiduciary requirements described above.

SIMPLIFIED EMPLOYEE PENSIONS

Beginning in 1979, employers (whether incorporated or not) could establish a simplified employee pension (SEP) for their employees and, utilizing an

---

[8]The criteria for an employer endorsement are found in DOL Regulation Section 2510.3-2.

individual retirement arrangement (IRA) contract, make tax-deductible contributions up to 15 percent of total compensation or $7,500, whichever was less. ERTA raised the $7,500 limit on contributions to $15,000 for the years 1982 and 1983. TEFRA increased the limits beginning in 1984 to the lesser of 15 percent or $30,000. These limits will be increased for inflation after 1988. The Tax Reform Act of 1986 added a special elective deferral feature available only to small employers. The SEP is intended to reduce much of the paperwork required for corporate plans that cover common-law employees.

If the employer contribution to a SEP in any calendar year is less than the normal IRA limit of $2,000, the employee may contribute the difference up to $2,000. The employee contribution may be made either to the SEP or to an IRA of his or her own choice.

For the employer, a simplified employee pension is a written plan utilizing individual retirement accounts or annuities to provide retirement benefits for employees. The SEP must be a formally adopted program having the following characteristics:

1. It must be in writing; it must specify the requirements for receiving a contribution; and it must specify how each eligible employee's contribution will be computed.
2. The employer must make contributions to a SEP for any employee who has received any compensation for service during the current calendar year, is 21 years of age, has worked for the employer during any three of the last five calendar years, and received at least $300 in compensation from the employer for the year.
3. Contributions may not discriminate in favor of any highly compensated employee.
4. The program may not restrict the employee's right to withdraw funds contributed to his or her SEP at any time.
5. The employer may not require that an employee leave some or all of the contributions in the SEP as a condition for receiving future employer contributions.

The employer's program must satisfy these five conditions for the employee to be able to exclude the employer's SEP contribution, within the limits imposed by IRC Section 415 (described in Chapter 6).

SEPs are subject to the defined contribution pension plan top-heavy rules described in Chapter 6. However, a special provision lets employers elect to measure aggregate employer contributions, instead of aggregate account balances, to test if the SEP has exceeded the 60 percent limit.

Eligibility

For an IRA funded by employer contributions to be treated as a SEP, the employer must contribute to the SEP for all eligible employees. As long as the employee satisfies the eligibility criteria mentioned above, he or she must receive a contribution, with the following exception: The employer does not have to make contributions for (1) members of a collective bargaining unit if retirement benefits were the subject of good-faith bargaining, and (2) certain nonresident aliens not working in the United States.

Finally, controlled group rules apply, and if the employer is a member of a controlled group, SEP contributions must be made for all eligible employees of each one of the businesses that comprise the group.

Contributions

During any calendar year, an employer's contribution to a SEP may be in any amount up to 15 percent of the employee's compensation, but not in excess of $30,000. Like a regular IRA, contributions made up to April 15 of the following calendar year are treated as being made on the last day of the prior calendar year if they are made on account of that year.

For example, the XYZ Company has a SEP that provides for a contribution of 15 percent of an employee's compensation to a SEP each year. In 1983 employee A earns $20,000 and the maximum permissible contribution under the tax law is $3,000. The XYZ Company makes a $1,500 contribution on December 31, 1983, for A and contributes the remaining $1,500 on March 15, 1984. The entire $3,000 contribution is treated as being made on December 31, 1983.

Contributions must be made for all eligible employees in a manner that does not discriminate in favor of any highly compensated employee. Unless employer contributions represent a uniform percentage of each eligible employee's total compensation, they are considered to be discriminatory. An employer is able to integrate nonelective SEP contributions with social security contributions made on behalf of the employees under the same rules that apply to defined contribution pension plans (described in Chapter 6). Only the first $200,000 of compensation received from the employer is used in determining if the percentage is uniform and thus not discriminatory.

For example, if an employee earns more than $200,000 and the maximum deductible contribution of $30,000 is made, the applicable percentage of compensation that must be contributed for all other employees is 15 percent determined as follows:

$$30,000 \div 200,000 = 15 \text{ percent}$$

Employers may cut off all contributions to employees at the maximum contribution limit or at some lower figure. Although this could cause contributions to be discriminatory, they will not discriminate in favor of the prohibited group since contributions for higher paid employees represent a smaller percentage of their earnings.

Deductions

The employer's contributions are deducted in the tax year that begins in the calendar year during which the contributions are made or treated as being made. The deduction may not exceed 15 percent of compensation paid to employees during that calendar year. If the employer contributes more than the amount deductible, the employer can carry over the excess deduction to succeeding taxable years.

If both a qualified profit sharing plan and a SEP exist, the maximum deduction permitted for contributions to the qualified profit sharing plan (15 percent of compensation paid during the current tax year to employees who were participants in the plan) must be reduced by the amount of the deduction permitted for contributions to the SEP.

Salary Reduction Agreements

In the case of a SEP maintained by an employer with 25 or fewer employees throughout the entire preceding year, an employee may elect to have the employer make payments as elective employer contributions to the SEP on behalf of the employee, or to the employee directly in cash. At least 50 percent of the employees must elect a salary reduction and the average deferral percentage for all eligible highly compensated employees during the year may not exceed 125 percent of the average deferral percentage of all other eligible employees.

The definition of excess contributions and the rules for their distribution are similar to those described in Chapter 17 for cash or deferred arrangements. Thus, elective deferrals under a SEP are subject to the $7,000 (indexed) cap.

QUESTIONS FOR REVIEW

1. Can an individual be covered by a corporate qualified pension plan and also by an IRA? Explain the consequences with respect to the deductibility of the IRA contribution.
2. What is a prohibited transaction? Explain why this concept is important for IRAs.
3. Are there any restrictions on the period of time over which distributions from an IRA can be made? Explain.
4. Describe a premature distribution and explain the tax penalties that could result from a premature distribution.
5. What are the conditions that must be met before an individual retirement account plan rollover will qualify as a tax-free rollover?
6. Is it possible for a person to receive a lump-sum distribution from a qualified pension or profit sharing plan and transfer the funds tax free to an individual retirement savings plan? If so, what are the federal income tax results?

7. May any individual retirement savings plan be used to transfer property from one type of qualified pension plan to another? Explain.
8. Describe the operation of a simplified employee pension (SEP).
9. Identify the essential characteristics of a SEP.
10. Is it possible for both husband and wife to set up an IRA? Explain.

QUESTIONS FOR DISCUSSION

1. Discuss the conditions under which an employer may desire to establish a SEP.
2. The new IRA deduction limitation will undoubtedly decrease the participation of employees in this arrangement. Discuss how this is likely to affect plan design for qualified plans.
3. Discuss how the new salary reduction agreements are likely to affect plan design for SEPs.

20

Tax-Deferred Annuities

The motive of income tax deferral is as applicable to tax-deferred annuities (TDAs) as it is to other qualified retirement plans. And, while the potential use of tax-deferred annuities is considerably more limited, where they do apply they offer significant advantages.

STATUTORY ASPECTS

Background

Ever since 1942, the Internal Revenue Code has contained a provision that permitted certain tax-exempt charitable employers to purchase annuity contracts for their employees without current income tax liability to the employees. ERISA, for the first time, authorized funds to be placed in a custodial account for the purchase of shares of a regulated investment company (mutual fund). Eligible employers are those that qualify under Section 101(6) of the 1939 Code, or Section 501(c)(3) of the 1954 Code. Under the original statutory provision: "if an annuity contract is purchased for an employee by an employer exempt under Section 101(6), the employee shall include in his income the amounts received under such contract for the year received." In the absence of such a statutory provision, taxable income would rise as premiums are paid.

As the public became aware of this provision in the Code, some individuals began to avail themselves of this tax advantage to a far greater extent than the commissioner of internal revenue felt proper. Thus, the commissioner attempted to limit the circumstances under which, and the extent to which, the statutory provision would be deemed applicable.

The Internal Revenue Code of 1954 made no modification in the statutory provisions. However, by the Technical Amendments Act of 1958, a considerably more detailed provision, Section 403(b), was enacted, which established the concept of a 20 percent exclusion allowance. Then, by the Revenue Act of 1961, Section 403(b) was amended to extend tax deferral for such annuity purchases to employees of public school systems. After a number of years, regulations were promulgated interpreting the new provision. ERISA also made certain changes affecting tax-deferred annuity plans, as did the Revenue Act of 1978.[1] Further changes were made by the Tax Equity and Fiscal Responsibility Act of 1982 (TEFRA).[2]

The Tax Reform Act of 1986 drastically altered the fundamental design considerations for tax-deferred annuities in several respects. First, tax-deferred annuities will be subject to the same coverage and nondiscrimination requirements as qualified plans. Under prior law, there were no such requirements. Second, an annual limit initially set at $9,500 was placed on elective deferrals to tax-deferred annuities. Prior law did not provide any specific limitations for elective deferrals to tax-deferred annuities; instead, the maximum amounts were determined as part of the overall exclusion allowance or Section 415 limitation applying to defined contribution plans. Third, certain catch-up provisions were extended to employees with at least 15 years of service. These provisions, which are detailed later in this chapter, permit employees to temporarily circumvent the constraints on the maximum elective deferrals. Fourth, a tax-deferred annuity program allowing elective deferrals must extend this option to virtually all employees of the sponsoring organization. Fifth, distributions attributable to contributions made under a salary reduction agreement are subject to withdrawal restrictions. Finally, the required distribution rules and penalty taxes for early and excess distributions described in Chapter 22 apply to tax-deferred annuities.

---

[1]The Revenue Act of 1978 provided for specific distribution requirements for a tax-deferred annuity funded with mutual fund shares under a custodial account. Under these provisions, no amount may be made available to a distributee until the employee dies, attains age 59½, separates from the employer's service, becomes disabled, or encounters financial hardship.

[2]The Tax Equity and Fiscal Responsibility Act of 1982 (TEFRA) affected tax-deferred annuities in three basic ways: (1) a reduction of the dollar limit to which the maximum exclusion allowance is subject; (2) a reduction of the overall maximum contribution that can be calculated under two of the "catch-up" exceptions (that prior to TEFRA were available only to employees of educational institutions, nonprofit hospitals, and home health service agencies, but that now apply to employees of tax-exempt religious organizations as well); and (3) substantial additional changes pertaining to employees of tax-exempt religious organizations. These changes have been incorporated into this chapter.

The Present Statute

Section 403(b) of the Code, as amended, now provides in part that:

> If an annuity contract is purchased for an employee by an employer described in Section 501(c)(3)...or for an employee...who performs services for an educational institution (as defined in Section 151(e)(4), by an employer which is a State, a political subdivision of a State, or an agency or instrumentality of any one or more of the foregoing... the employee's rights under the contract are nonforfeitable, except for failure to pay future premiums, and except in the case of a contract purchased by a church, such contract is purchased under a plan which meets the nondiscrimination requirements...then amounts contributed by such employer for such annuity contract...shall be excluded from the gross income of the employee for the taxable year to the extent that the aggregate of such amounts does not exceed the *exclusion allowance* for such a taxable year.[3]

ERISA amended Section 403(b) of the Code to add Section 403(b)(7), which states in part:

> For purposes of this title, amounts paid by an employer...to a custodial account...shall be treated as amounts contributed to an annuity contract for the employee if the amounts...are to be invested in regulated investment company stock to be held in that custodial account.

Thus, the essential requirements to achieve the desired tax shelter are as follows:

1. The participant must be employed by a duly qualified charitable organization or by a public school system.
2. The participant must be a bona fide employee.
3. The annuity contract must be purchased by such employer or the employer must make a deposit to a custodial account that will purchase mutual fund shares.
4. The participant's rights under the contract must be nonforfeitable.
5. The amount paid in any year should not exceed the exclusion allowance for the year in question (and will be currently taxable to the extent that it does exceed such allowance).
6. The plan must meet the nondiscrimination requirements.

While these are the essential ingredients of a tax-deferred annuity, each of these requirements calls for further examination. The next section analyzes each of these requirements in addition to the new Tax Reform Act of 1986 provisions dealing with elective deferral limitations, expansion of withdrawal restrictions, and minimum distribution rules.

---

[3]Emphasis added. The exclusion allowance will be examined in greater detail subsequently in this chapter.

REQUIREMENTS OF A TAX-DEFERRED ANNUITY

Qualified Employers

If the employee is to qualify for tax-deferred annuity treatment, his or her employer must be either:

1. A charitable organization qualified under Section 501(c)(3) of the Internal Revenue Code (for example, a tax-exempt hospital, church, school, or other such organization or foundation).
2. A public school system (for example, one operated by the state, or by a county, city, town, school district, or other political subdivision or agency of a state).

Note that not every tax-exempt organization is a qualified employer, but only those that qualify under Section 501(c)(3).

Note also that not all types of publicly operated facilities can qualify, only public school systems. Certain other publicly operated facilities (hospitals or other charities, for example) may or may not qualify. For the qualification of such organizations, a ruling should be obtained from the Internal Revenue Service.[4]

Eligible Employees

To be eligible for the tax shelter, the individual must be an employee of a qualified charitable organization or of a public school system. The individual may be the top executive or the lowest paid clerk. He or she may be a seasonal, part-time, or full-time employee, but he or she must be an employee — not an independent contractor. This point requires particular attention in connection with certain professional people (such as radiologists, pathologists, and anesthesiologists) who may or may not, in a given set of circumstances, in fact be employees.[5] Clerical, administrative, supervisory, and custodial employees of public school systems as well as teachers qualify.[6]

---

[4]If the activity of the facility is such that if it were not publicly operated it could qualify under Section 501(c)(3), and if it has sufficient independence from the state, and so on, it may be able to obtain a ruling that it is a counterpart of a Section 501(c)(3) organization.

[5]Some professionals in the service of tax-exempt organizations may be barred by ethical or legal considerations from meeting the tests for the required employer-employee relationship. See Revenue Ruling 66–274, 1966–2 CB 446 for an outline of criteria for determining the relationship between a physician and a hospital. Also, see *Ravel* v. *Comm'r.*, 26 TCM 885 (1967) and *Azad* v. *U.S.*, 388 F. 2d 74 (1968).

[6]In addition, the regulations provide that one who is elected or appointed to certain public offices may qualify if there is a requirement that to hold the office such person must be trained or experienced in the field of education. For example, a regent or trustee of a state university or a member of a board of education is not eligible. But a commissioner or superintendent of education will generally be eligible. Reg. 1.403(b)–1(b)(5).

Annuity Contract Purchased by an Employer

In speaking of "an annuity...purchased...by an employer," the statute gives no indication of what constitutes an annuity contract or a purchase by an employer. However, the IRS has stated that tax-deferred annuities must be purchased from insurance companies or mutual funds.[7] It would appear to make no difference whether such a contract is a single-premium or annual-premium contract or whether it provides for fixed or variable annuity payments, immediate or deferred, with or without a refund provision.

For many years the Internal Revenue Service took the position that a contract that provided a life insurance benefit would not qualify as a tax-deferred annuity. But the regulations now provide that "an individual contract issued after December 31, 1962, or a group contract which provides incidental life insurance protection may be purchased as an annuity contract" to which Section 403(b) applies. The expression *incidental life insurance protection* presumably has the same meaning as it has with respect to insurance purchased under qualified trusts.[8] The Internal Revenue Service also has ruled that a modified endowment policy with an annuity rider providing a preretirement death benefit with an actuarial value of less than that of a typical retirement income policy meets the incidental death benefit test.[9]

Also, after December 31, 1962, the term *annuity* includes a so-called face-amount certificate, but does not include a contract or certificate issued after that date that is transferable.[10] The regulations spell out in some detail what is meant by the term *nontransferable*, and their language has been used as a guide by insurers in appropriately endorsing their contracts.

Thus, any annuity contract, individual or group, ordinarily issued by an insurance company may be used to provide a tax-deferred annuity, provided it contains an appropriate restriction respecting transferability.

Contracts have been developed to accommodate the needs of the tax-deferred annuity market. One can now find contracts with premiums payable for only 9 or 10 consecutive months during a year, in order to meet the needs of payroll schedules of educational institutions. Contracts also are available that permit variations in the amount of premiums paid each year

---

[7]Revenue Ruling 82-102.

[8]For a discussion of the meaning of incidental life insurance under qualified plans, see Chapter 6.

[9]Rev. Rul. 74–115, IRB. 1974–11,9.

[10]IRC 401(g), which reads in its entirety as follows:

For purposes of this section and sections 402, 403, and 404, the term "annuity" includes a face-amount certificate, as defined in section 2(a)(15) of the Investment Company Act of 1940 (15 U.S.C. sec. 80a–2); but does not include any contract or certificate issued after December 31, 1962, which is transferable, if any person other than the trustee of a trust described in section 401(a) which is exempt from tax under section 501(a) is the owner of such contract or certificate.

and therefore are readily adaptable to varying incomes (hence, varying annual exclusion allowances).

It would appear that payment of premiums will satisfy the "purchase" requirement of the statute. Thus, a qualified employer may assume the payment of premiums on an individual annuity contract already owned by one of its employees and will be considered as having purchased a tax-deferred annuity for the employee in each year that premiums are so paid, to the extent of the available exclusion allowance and provided that the contract contains the requisite restriction as to transferability.

ERISA, as mentioned previously, substantially expanded the range of permissible investments and terminated the statutorily sanctioned insurance company monopoly in the field of tax-deferred annuities. Amounts paid by an employer can be placed in a custodial account on behalf of an eligible employee for the purpose of purchasing shares of a regulated investment company (mutual fund).

Employee's Rights Nonforfeitable

Attempted definitions of nonforfeitability are elusive. Without a trust, the employee's rights under the contract would appear to be nonforfeitable if ownership of the contract is vested solely in him or her. The same would appear to be true if there is some form of joint ownership of the contract, together with an agreement between employer and employee whereby the employee could not be deprived of benefits provided by annuity premiums previously paid, even though the employer could exercise control over the time of enjoyment of those benefits.

As a practical matter, it would appear that ownership ordinarily is vested solely in the employee, thus leaving him or her free of any restrictions or problems that might arise by virtue of insolvency or change of management of the employer. As sole owner of the contract, the employee is free to exercise any of his or her contractual rights, subject, of course, to restrictions on transferability. Thus, where an insurance company product is involved, the employee may be free to elect a reduced paid-up annuity, to change the contract for a reduced annuity with an earlier maturity date, to surrender the contract, or to borrow against its cash value from the insurer.

Exclusion Allowance

The exclusion allowance for an employee for the taxable year is defined in IRC §403 (b)(2) as:

an amount equal to the excess, if any, of—
A.–the amount determined by multiplying (i) 20 percent of his or her includable compensation, by (ii) the number of years of service over
B.–the aggregate of the amounts contributed by the employer for annuity contracts and excludable from the gross income of the employee for any prior taxable year.

Thus, in general, the measure of the amount that an employer may pay for an employee — without current income tax to the employee — is determined in the following manner. First, 20 percent of the current year's includable compensation is multiplied by the total period of employment (expressed in years).[11] From the product is deducted the sum of prior amounts so expended and certain other similar employer expenditures.

ERISA established that a Section 403(b) tax-deferred annuity is a defined contribution plan, and therefore the annual contribution was subject to a limitation of the lesser of $25,000 or 25 percent of the participant's annual compensation adjusted for changes in the cost of living after 1974. In 1982 the limit had reached $45,475. However, TEFRA reduced the maximum exclusion allowance to $30,000. This limit will be adjusted for cost-of-living changes when the defined benefit pension plan dollar limit reaches $120,000. However, the act does not repeal the exclusion allowance limitations under prior law. The excess difference is the permitted tax-deferred amount for the current year subject, of course, to the Section 415 limitations.

The computation involved in this process is greatly simplified if it is assumed that an employee's compensation remains constant. In that case, if the maximum exclusion allowance is utilized fully in the current year (for example, by purchase of a single-premium annuity), the exclusion allowance available for future years will be merely 20 percent of the compensation.

Any contributions of the employer to any other tax-deferred annuity; qualified pension, profit sharing, or annuity plan; qualified bond purchase plan; and so on would be charged against the current year's exclusion allowance — if the employee has previously not been taxed thereon for any reason. Thus, for example, if contributions are being made by the same employer to a qualified plan, the amounts so contributed would reduce the amount available under Section 403(b).

If the employer has never made any prior tax-deferred payments for a particular employee (whether by payment of annuity premiums, by contributions to a qualified plan, or otherwise), the amount described on page 344 will be zero. If this is the employee's first year of employment, the exclusion allowance will be merely 20 percent of his or her includable compensation for the current year.

The computation of the exclusion allowance can be an exceedingly easy or an exceedingly difficult matter, depending upon the complexity of the facts involved. Complicating factors may be introduced by part-time employment, salary reduction agreements, or other benefit plans being

[11]This employment is only employment with the current employer. Prior employment with another qualified employer may not be taken into account. Rev. Rul. 69–629, IRB 1969–51. Also, includable compensation does not include any cost of life insurance under a typical retirement income contract, even though such amount is otherwise reportable as taxable income. Rev. Rul. 68–304, IRB 1968–24.

currently funded by the same employer that provide tax-deferred compensation. Such complicating factors will be considered subsequently in this chapter.[12]

The initial application of the exclusion allowance formula for an employee with past service may produce a very large exclusion allowance.[13] Ordinarily, a single-premium annuity intended to fully utilize this allowance immediately is not feasible. If less than the full allowance is used, the unused portion will increase the allowance available in future years over what it would have been had the entire past service allowance been fully used subject, of course, to the Section 415 limits.[14]

As a practical matter, it is frequently desirable to purchase an annual-premium annuity, selecting the amount of gross annual premium so that: (1) by the normal retirement date, full benefit will have been taken of the past service allowance, and (2) in each year, the available exclusion allowance will be equal to or greater than the premium payable. In other words, we wish to determine the maximum level amount that may be paid by the employer each year that will take full advantage of the past service allowance over the remaining years of employment.

To do so, first determine the total number of years that will have elapsed between the employee's date of employment and his or her projected retirement date and assume that this present rate of annual includable compensation will continue until retirement.[15] The maximum annual premium will then be 20 percent of includable compensation times total years of service (past and future) divided by future years of premium payments. This may be expressed algebraically as:

$$P = \frac{0.20 \times S \times T}{F}$$

where P is the maximum annual premium (in addition to salary and not a salary reduction), S represents salary, T is total years of service (both past

---

[12]See the section on "Arithmetic of the Exclusion Allowance" later in this chapter.

[13]For example, with $10,000 of current includable compensation and 10 years of past service, the exclusion allowance is $0.20 \times \$10,000 \times 10 = \$20,000$.

[14]No reference to "past service allowance" is made either in Section 403(b) or in the regulations. However, use of such an expression will be helpful in examining the operation of the exclusion allowance. It refers to the exclusion allowance that would be available to an employee as a consequence of past service with the same employer that has not otherwise been utilized.

If the full $20,000 exclusion allowance was used after the 10th year of employment, the 11th-year exclusion allowance (assuming includable compensation continues at $10,000) is $(0.20 \times \$10,000 \times 11) - \$20,000 = \$22,000 - \$20,000 = \$2,000$. However, if only $15,000 of the initial exclusion allowance had been used, then the 11th-year exclusion allowance would be $(0.20 \times \$10,000 \times 11) - \$15,000 = \$22,000 - \$15,000 = \$7,000$. However, the law would limit the deductible amount to $2,500, that is, 25 percent of the individual's $10,000 compensation.

[15]This assumption will prove to have been too conservative if compensation is subsequently increased. Conversely, it will have been too liberal if compensation decreases. See the section "Caveat about Future Salary Reductions" later in this chapter.

and future), and F is future years of premium payments.[16] This may be simplified to:

$$P = \frac{S \times T}{5F}$$

If premiums are paid other than annually, the sum of the periodic premiums should not exceed the level premium so determined.[17] If the years of service are actually less than one, the number of years of service should be taken as one.

Special consideration was given in ERISA to certain categories of employees (educational institutions, tax-exempt religious organizations, nonprofit hospitals, health and welfare service agencies, and home health service agencies) to allow those employees who have made less than the maximum allowable contributions in their early careers to make larger catch-up contributions. The three alternatives allowed are as follows:

1. *The $30,000 maximum rule*. Under this approach, an eligible employee terminating employment can, on a one-time-only basis, make up the contributions that could have been made, but were not, during the 10-year period ending on the date of separation. (This amount is 20 percent of the employee's includible compensation multiplied by the number of years of service for the employer not exceeding 10, minus employer contributions already made during the relevant period.) Although no percentage limitation applies, this one-shot catch-up contribution is limited to a maximum of $30,000.

2. *The $15,000 maximum rule*. Under this alternative, annual contributions can be made, at any time, equal to the lesser of 25 percent of includible compensation plus $4,000 or the exclusion allowance normally allowed under Internal Revenue Code Section 403(b). The maximum annual deduction allowable under this approach is $15,000.

3. *The 25 percent/$30,000 rule*. In this approach, the maximum contribution is limited to the lesser of $30,000 or 25 percent of compensation. However, the tax-deferred annuity contribution must be aggregated with other qualified plan contributions to meet this test and any employer contributions to a qualified defined benefit or defined contribution plan must be subtracted from the TDA contribution. Since, in a defined benefit plan, the employee does not know the amount contributed by the employer, the IRS has provided a rule to estimate the value of the employer's contribution.

Any election made under one of these special rules will be irrevocable. This is understood to mean that an employee electing to contribute under a special rule must continue to use the same rule in future years.

---

[16]Thus, in effect, we are finding the employee's total working lifetime exclusion allowance and prorating it over his or her remaining working years.

[17]It is the sum of the periodic premiums actually paid by the employer during a year that should be kept within the limits of the year's exclusion allowance. So if premiums are to be paid, for example, monthly, the size of the annuity or insurance contract will be slightly smaller than if premiums were paid annually.

Limits on Elective Deferrals

The maximum amount of elective deferrals an individual may make to a tax-deferred annuity in a taxable year is $9,500. The maximum amount will increase with the cost-of-living adjustments in future years, but only after the limit for cash or deferred arrangement (CODA) elective deferrals (see Chapter 17) reaches the $9,500 level. The limit applies to the sum of all the employee's elective deferrals for the taxable year, including CODAs and salary reduction SEPs.

If the employee makes an elective deferral in excess of the dollar limit for a taxable year, then the excess must be allocated among the plans under which the deferrals were made by March 1 of the following year, and the plans must distribute the excess to the employee by April 15. Such distributions (and investment income) will be included in the employee's taxable income for the year in which the excess deferral was made; however, if the excess is removed prior to the April 15 deadline, it will not be subject to the 10 percent penalty for premature distributions.

In the case of an employee who has completed 15 years of service with any educational organization, hospital, home health service agency, health and welfare service agency, church, or convention or association of churches, the $9,500 limit may be increased through a catch-up provision. The increase is limited to the lesser of:

1. $3,000.
2. $15,000 less prior catch-up contributions.
3. The excess of $5,000 times years of service, over prior salary reductions.

Nondiscrimination Requirements

For plan years beginning after 1988, a tax-deferred annuity arrangement will be subject to one set of nondiscrimination requirements for nonelective contributions and another set for elective deferrals. If an employer makes nonelective contributions, they must satisfy the nondiscrimination and coverage rules for qualified plans (described in Chapter 4). If an employer permits elective deferrals, this opportunity must be available to all employees other than certain nonresident aliens and those covered by a Section 457 plan or a qualified CODA. However, the employer can require employees to make at least a $200 deferral.

The nondiscrimination rules do not apply to tax-deferred annuity arrangements sponsored by churches. Furthermore, students working fewer than 20 hours per week may be excluded for the nondiscrimination rules.

Also included among these rules is the requirement that employer and employee contributions meet the average contribution percentage (ACP) test described in Chapter 16.

Withdrawal Restrictions

Withdrawal restrictions are imposed on tax-deferred annuities in two specific circumstances. Under a custodial account for regulated investment company stock (mutual fund), no amount may be paid before the employee dies, attains age 59½, separates from service, or becomes disabled. If contributions are made to a custodial account under a salary reduction agreement, withdrawals are also allowed if the employee encounters a financial hardship. The other restriction applies to any annuity contract distributions attributable to contributions made under a salary reduction agreement. In this case, distributions may be paid only when the employee attains age 59½, separates from service, dies, becomes disabled, or in the case of hardship. However, income attributable to contributions made under a salary reduction agreement may not be provided in the case of hardship.

In either circumstance, the employee may be subject to an additional 10 percent tax for early distributions if the distributions are received before age 59½. Several exceptions apply to this general rule and they are described in Chapter 22.

Minimum Distribution Rules

The uniform commencement date and minimum distribution rules applicable to qualified plans will be imposed on all tax-deferred annuities, beginning after 1988.

INCOME TAXATION OF BENEFITS

Income Tax Consequences during Lifetime

During his or her lifetime, and prior to actual receipt of any benefits under the contract, the employee will incur no income tax liability if (1) the annuity contract contains no element of insurance protection and (2) all premiums paid by the employer in each year are within the exclusion allowance available for the particular year.

Where the contract provides an incidental insurance benefit, the employee will be taxed in each year on the value of such incidental benefit.[18]

Also, any premiums will be taxable currently to the employee to the extent that they exceed the exclusion allowance for the particular year.[19]

Where a Section 403(b) program permits contributions to a custodial

---

[18]IRC 72(m)(3)(B); Reg. 1.403(b)–1(c)(3), and 1.72–16(b). The so-called PS 58 (term) costs of the amount at risk under the contract (expected proceeds minus cash value) will be the appropriate measure of the employee's currently taxable benefit. Rev. Rul. 68–304, IRB 1968–24.

[19]If a maximum tax-deferred annuity using a contract providing an incidental insurance benefit is desired, the premium may exceed the exclusion allowance by the (PS 58) cost of the insurance benefit for the year in question. Rev. Rul. 68–304, IRB 1968–24.

account for the purpose of purchasing mutual fund shares, a 6 percent tax is imposed on excess contributions. For the purposes of the imposition of this tax, "excess contributions" means the sum of (1) the contributions made for a taxable year to the extent that they exceed the lesser of the amount excludable under Section 403(b) or under Section 415, and (2) the amount determined under the same provision for the preceding taxable year, reduced by certain allowable but unused deductions and the sum of the distributions out of the account that have been included in gross income under Section 72(e) of the Internal Revenue Code.

In connection with 403(b) plans, loans within limits are provided on the same basis as from qualified retirement plans.

When the employee actually begins receiving benefits, the amounts received are taxable to him or her under Section 72 of the Internal Revenue Code. However, neither capital gains treatment nor the five-year averaging rule is available for any lump-sum payments. If the employee contributed nothing to the cost of the contract, and if all contributions of the employer were within the limits of the exclusion allowance in each year so that the employee previously was subject to no income tax on such contributions, everything received by the employee will be includable in his or her gross income as received.

If the employee made any contributions (or is deemed to have made contributions), he or she will be entitled to a tax-free recovery of such contributions. The employee will have made, or will be deemed to have made, contributions to the extent that (1) he or she actually made such contributions out of after-tax money, (2) employer contributions were taxable to the employee by virtue of having exceeded the exclusion allowance for one or more years, or (3) incidental insurance costs were taxable to the employee.

If the benefits are received in one sum, the employee will have ordinary income to the extent of the excess of the amount received over the aggregate contributions. If the employee receives installment payments, an exclusion ratio will be determined, and a portion of each payment proportional to the employee's contributions will be excludable from gross income. However, once the cost basis has been entirely recovered, the entire payment will be taxable. The balance of each payment is includable in gross income as received.

As described in Chapter 22, a portion of a tax-deferred annuity distribution may be subject to a 15 percent excise tax. This results if the aggregate taxable distribution to an individual in any year for all tax-favored plans — tax-deferred annuities, as well as pensions, savings and stock bonus plans, CODAs, and IRAs — exceeds $150,000 or $112,500 (indexed to the CPI beginning in 1988).

Income Tax Consequences after Death

In the case of a true annuity contract, taxation of benefits paid after the employee's death depends upon whether the employee had actually begun receiving annuity payments prior to death. If such payments had not already begun, the beneficiary would be taxed as if he or she were the employee in the manner described above.

If the employee had already begun to receive payments, taxation of the beneficiary depends upon the particular mode of payment applicable at the employee's death. If the only amounts payable after death are in the nature of refund payments, such amounts will be taxable as ordinary income, but only after the amounts so received by the beneficiary (together with all amounts received tax free by the employee during his or her lifetime) exceed the aggregate contributions of the employee. On the other hand, if the amounts payable to the beneficiary are a continuation of installment certain payments (without life contingency), or are payments to a surviving annuitant under a joint and survivor annuity, the beneficiary continues to exclude a portion of payments received each year in accordance with the exclusion ratio determined for the employee.

Beneficiaries under contracts that provide an incidental insurance benefit are taxed in virtually the same manner as beneficiaries of a deceased insured under a qualified pension plan; but capital gains treatment and the five-year averaging rule are not available for lump-sum payments. The death benefit is composed of Section 101 and Section 72 proceeds, the former being the amount at risk under the insurance contract as of the date of death and the latter being the cash value of the contract determined as of that date.

The Section 101 proceeds will be treated the same as regular personal life insurance: income tax free if received in one sum; or, if received in installments, taxable to the extent that installment payments in any year exceed a pro rata portion of the one-sum proceeds.

The Section 72 proceeds (i.e., the cash value as of the date of death) will be taxable in the same manner and to the same extent as if the employee had received such proceeds during his or her lifetime, with the single exception that the $5,000 employee death benefit exclusion of Section 101(b) will be applicable under certain circumstances. To the extent applicable, the $5,000 death benefit is deemed to increase the employee's contributions for purposes of determining the beneficiary's taxable income.

The $5,000 death benefit exclusion applies to tax-deferred annuities only under the same circumstances that it would be available with respect to deceased participants of qualified plans. The benefit must be paid, by reason of the employee's death within one taxable year of the distributee. But this tax-free death benefit is not available for employees of public school systems, nor is it available for employees of every Section 501(c) (3) organization, but only to a certain subclass.[20] If the individual was employed by

---

[20]That subclass consists of those Section 501(c) (3) organizations exempt from tax under Section 501(a) that are referred to in Section 503(b) (1), (2), or (3): namely, schools (not publicly operated) having a student body in attendance; churches, or conventions or associations of churches; or organizations receiving a substantial part of their support from the general public or from some governmental body.

an organization of the latter type, the choice of how death benefits best may be received will involve a balancing of factors.[21]

SALARY REDUCTIONS

Current Salary Reductions

At one time the commissioner of the internal revenue service took the position that the postponing of tax liability would apply only where the annuity is "merely a supplement to past or current compensation," and that, therefore, there would be no postponing of tax liability if the annuity premiums were paid in lieu of existing salary, or even "in lieu of an increase in current compensation" if this were done at the employee's request.

Under the regulations, this position still stands for amounts paid by an employer during taxable years beginning before January 1, 1958. But for taxable years beginning thereafter, a salary reduction in the amount of the payment permitted, and the funds paid out of what would otherwise have been paid as salary, will not be received constructively, provided only that:

1. There is an agreement between employer and employee for the latter "to take a reduction in salary, or to forgo an increase in salary, but only to the extent that amounts are earned by the employee after the agreement becomes effective." Such an agreement must be legally binding and irrevocable for amounts earned while the agreement is in effect.

2. The employee must not be permitted to make more than one such agreement with the same employer during any taxable year of the employee.[22]

3. "There may be no substitution of annuity premium or mutual fund contribution for salary already earned."

Also, it is now clear that the arrangement may be instigated at the request of the employee.

Salary Reduction Agreement

While from the tax viewpoint the employee may instigate a salary reduction, there must be a real reduction in his or her compensation. For the employee to merely request that the employer deduct a specified amount

---

[21]If proceeds are not taken in one sum, any otherwise available $5,000 exclusion will generally be lost, but the tax liability of the beneficiary is spread out over the years of payment. If proceeds are taken in one sum (provided the employer was a member of the subclass), tax liability will all arise in one year, but an amount of up to $5,000 may entirely escape taxation.

[22]The reduction may be expressed as a percentage of compensation rather than as a fixed dollar amount. Thus, while the percentage cannot be changed for the balance of the taxable year, the dollar amount actually contributed may change due to changes in compensation. Rev. Rul. 68–58, IRB 1968–6. Also, a change in insurers during a year will not constitute a new agreement. Rev. Rul. 68–179, IRB 1968–16.

from his or her compensation to be applied to a tax-deferred annuity will not suffice. The distinction between a reduction and a deduction cannot be overemphasized. The former produces the desired tax deferral. The latter will not.

Thus, the employer must enter into a written agreement with the employee for the salary reduction, such agreement to be applicable to compensation for services thereafter rendered until such time as the agreement shall have been terminated by either party.

Caveat about Future Salary Reductions

In the normal course of events, it is unlikely that an employee's compensation will continue without change until retirement, although such an assumption might be made for purposes of determining the maximum annual amount that may be paid without exceeding the employee's projected exclusion allowances. No difficulty is encountered (with respect to the adequacy of exclusion allowances for future years to cover fully level annual premiums) if the employee receives periodic increases in compensation.[23]

In the remote event, however, that an employee should in the future find it necessary to take a cut in compensation, the situation requires a careful review in the first year such a reduction occurs to ascertain the effect upon the current year's (and, perhaps, subsequent years') exclusion allowance.

When and if the reduced compensation problem arises, there would appear to be three possible alternatives: (1) the employee may take a reduced paid-up annuity; (2) the employee may have the employer continue to pay the annuity premium or mutual fund payment, recognizing that the amount paid will be taxable currently to the employee (but only to the extent that it exceeds the exclusion allowance for the year in question); or (3) the employee may pay the premium. The possibility that the reduced compensation problem will arise is not serious, and, if it does arise, satisfactory solutions are available. It would, therefore, seem that this possibility should never discourage one from taking advantage of this provision of the law. However, the possibility should be recognized.

ARITHMETIC OF THE EXCLUSION ALLOWANCE

The problem of determining the maximum amount, P, that may be safely paid by the employer each year to take full advantage of the past service

---

[23]As a matter of fact, it may be well to review the picture from time to time to see whether the increase in compensation is sufficient to warrant the purchase of an additional annuity.

allowance over the remaining years of employment previously has been considered. It was noted that:

$$P = \frac{S \times T}{5F} \tag{1}$$

where S represents salary, T total years of service (past and future), and F future years of payments.

But two major assumptions have been made that may not be valid in a given situation, namely (1) that the annual amount is paid from the employer's own funds without reduction to the employee's current compensation, and (2) that no other tax-deferred contribution (for example, to a qualified pension plan) is currently being made by the employer for the employee. Now, consider the situation when one or both of these factors is present.

Maximum Amount—Negotiated Salary Reduction

One important caution must be observed where there is to be a salary reduction while attempting to take advantage of the maximum exclusion allowance. In addition to the dollar limit on elective deferrals mentioned earlier, the exclusion allowed is based on 20 percent of the employee's includable compensation; that is, his or her compensation exclusive of amounts received tax free. Therefore (ignoring past service for the moment), one cannot take a 20 percent reduction in salary and have the reduction applied to tax-deferred payments, since this would produce a consideration equal to 25 percent of the remaining includable compensation. If, however, the salary reduction is limited to one sixth of that paid prior to reduction, then that one sixth of salary will give the maximum excludable annual amount for a future service annuity.[24]

Suppose that an employee (with independent income sources) wishes to take the maximum reduction in salary possible to have the largest possible future annual amount that would utilize his or her exclusion allowance, based on both past and future service, up to the limit.

Assume there are no prior contributions to be deducted (or future contributions to any other tax-deferred plan or trust for the employee's benefit) and that the salary prior to any reduction, S, would (except for the negotiated reduction) remain constant throughout his or her remaining years of employment. Then the maximum annual amount, P, that can be paid and still be excludable, ignoring the possible application of one of the catch-up provisions, can be expressed as the lesser of the dollar limit on elective deferrals or:

$$P = \frac{0.20 \times (S - P) \times T}{F}$$

---

[24]Since one sixth of salary before reduction is equal to 20 percent of the five sixths of salary which remain after the reduction.

(noting that $(S - P)$ represents includable compensation after S has been reduced by P). This may be simplified to:[25]

$$P = \frac{S \times T}{5F + T} \qquad (2)$$

Maximum Amount—Other Tax-Deferred Contributions

Where the amount is paid solely from the employer's own funds—that is, no salary reduction is involved, but other tax-deferred contributions are involved (for example, pension contributions)—the maximum annual amount, P, is determined by subtracting the aggregate amount of past, present, and future tax-deferred contributions, C, from 20 percent of includable compensation times total years of service, and dividing the difference so determined by future years of payments.[26] Thus,

$$P = \frac{0.20 \times S \times T - C}{F}$$

This may be simplified to:

$$P = \frac{S \times T - 5C}{5F} \qquad (3)$$

Suppose that the ratio of the employer's pension contributions to the employee's salary prior to reduction is known, as in the case of a defined contribution (money purchase) pension plan. Designate this ratio as Q. Then, if $C = Q \times S \times T$ (i.e., if the aggregate of pension contributions during the working years equals a constant percentage of S times total years of service and the dollar limit on elective deferrals), the formula (3) may be expressed in the form:

$$P = \frac{S \times T - 5(Q \times S \times T)}{5F}$$

that is:

$$P = \frac{(1 - 5Q)ST}{5F} \qquad (4)$$

---

[25]To illustrate the application of the formula, assume a 55-year-old male employee with a 1987 salary of $15,000. Suppose that he has 10 years of future service and 30 years of past service. Thus, $S = \$15,000$, $T = 30 + 10 = 40$, and $F = 10$. Therefore, the maximum amount again, of course, subject to Section 415 limits and the $9,500 limit on elective deferrals, would be:

$$P = \frac{S \times T}{5F + T} = \frac{\$15,000 \times 40}{(5 \times 10) + 40} = \$6,666.66$$

Section 415, however, would impose the 25 percent/$30,000 limitation, so that the maximum amount in this case would be 25 percent of the employee's salary after the reduction.

[26]Thus, in effect, the employee's total working lifetime exclusion allowance is determined by first subtracting the total of other tax-deferred contributions and then prorating it over the remaining working years.

Salary Reduction and Other Tax-Deferred Contributions

It will be recalled that in cases where there is to be a salary reduction (and ignoring past service), the employee's current cash compensation should be reduced by not more than one sixth if the amount paid via the salary reduction is not to exceed 20 percent of includible compensation after salary reduction.

Suppose that the employer is making current pension contributions for the employee (but has not previously done so). If the ratio of the employer's pension contribution to the employee's salary prior to reduction is Q, then the maximum permissible salary reduction, P, to be devoted to the tax-deferred annuity must be such that:

$$P + Q \times S = 0.20(S - P)$$

that is, the sum of tax-deferred contributions equals 20 percent of includible compensation (after salary reduction). Solving for P, this may be reduced algebraically to the formula:[27]

$$P = \frac{(1 - 5Q)S}{6} \tag{5}$$

In Formula (5), no past service was taken into account. In Formula (4), no salary reduction is involved. Where both such factors must be considered:

$$P = \frac{0.20(S - P)T - Q \times S \times T}{F}$$

that is:

$$P = \frac{(1 - 5Q)ST}{5F + T} \tag{6}$$

Employer Pension Contributions Unknown

Frequently, the actual amount previously contributed by the employer to provide pension benefits for a specified employee is not known. The plan may expressly describe the retirement benefits to be furnished, leaving the amount necessary to fund the plan to be actuarially determined, without allocation of actual contributions among individual employees. For such situations, the regulations provide explicit rules for the computation of the excludable amounts to be charged against the employee's annual exclusion allowance.

---

[27]It will be observed that if $Q = 0$ (i.e., if there is no employer contribution to a qualified plan with respect to the employee), we would have:

$$P = \frac{(1 - 0)S}{6} = \frac{S}{6}$$

In other words, we arrive at the familiar salary reduction of one sixth.

Part-Time Employees

If an employee is a part-time employee or is a full-time employee for only part of a year, he or she is allowed only an appropriate fraction of a year in computing the number of years of service. The fraction to be used is the ratio of the time spent by the employee in the employer's service during that year to the time that would be spent on a similar job for the same employer by a full-time employee.

For example, a full-time instructor at a college with the usual nine-month year is a full-time employee; but a librarian employed by an organization whose employees normally work the year round is a three-quarter-time employee if he or she works for the organization for only nine months during the year. If the normal teaching load at a college is 12 hours per week, a part-time instructor carrying a 9-hour load for the nine-month academic year would be a three-quarter-time employee. If the instructor carries a nine-hour load for only four and one half months during the year, he or she is a three-eighths-time employee.

These fractional years of service are then aggregated to find the number of years of service.[28] This is then multiplied by 20 percent of annualized includable compensation to arrive at the exclusion allowance. But if the part-time work is constant — for example, if the employee works one quarter of a year every year, and has a salary in that one quarter of a year that is the same as it was for at least the previous four years, or as many years as are necessary to aggregate one full year of employment, the part-time status can be ignored and, for purposes of the formulas, the employee can be treated as a full-time employee.

SOME FURTHER TAX CONSIDERATIONS

Social Security Taxes and Benefits

In 1953, the Internal Revenue Service ruled that the payment of a premium by the employer on a tax-deferred annuity for an employee does not constitute "wages" as defined under the Federal Insurance Contributions Act (FICA) and, therefore, that such payment was "not subject to withholding for federal employment or income tax purposes." This ruling also held that the employer was not required to file an information return Form 1099 for such payment.

However, for salary reduction type 403(b) plans, the 1983 social security amendments affirmed earlier rulings that tax-deferred annuity plan contributions under individually negotiated salary reduction plans are considered as wages similar to any other form of compensation for social security taxes up to the social security taxable wage base for that particular year.

---

[28]But if the number of years of service thus computed for a part-time employee is less than one whole year, the number of years of service should be taken as one.

Wage Withholding

Any amount excludable from gross income under Section 403(b) is not subject to withholding of income tax (whether or not a voluntary salary reduction agreement is involved).

Measure of Pension Benefits

An employer who maintains a qualified pension plan may define compensation covered by the plan to include elective contributions under tax-deferred annuities, as well as cash compensation paid. However, inclusion of nonelective contributions may cause the plan to be discriminatory.[29]

CONSIDERATIONS OF LOCAL LAW

Employees of Public School Systems

When the use of public funds is involved in the proposed purchase of a tax-deferred annuity, many questions of state law arise. May such funds be used to purchase a tax-deferred annuity? If so, is an incidental insurance benefit permitted or prohibited? Is a voluntary salary reduction agreement allowed? Unfortunately, these questions have not been answered in many states.

Where a voluntary salary reduction agreement is permitted, does such a reduction also require a reduction in the teacher's benefits under the state retirement system? In most states, no such reduction is required. The rulings that have dealt with this issue, expressly or by implication, were concerned with a voluntary salary reduction agreement. It may be inferred that state law may not permit the use of public funds to purchase tax-deferred annuities except on a voluntary salary reduction basis. Otherwise, there may be a violation of salary scales established by law.

State Income Taxes

No uniform pattern has as yet developed as to the tax status of tax-deferred annuities for state income tax purposes, whether they be purchased for employees of Section 501(c) (3) organizations or public school systems. Some states have ruled that the annuity premiums would be excludable from gross income under the state income tax law to the extent excludable under the federal income tax laws; other states have taken a contrary position.

---

[29]Nonelective contributions may be used to compute qualified plan benefits only if they don't cause discrimination under IRC Section 401(a)(4). See Revenue Ruling 84–74.

State Premium Taxes

A significant portion of the total tax burden imposed on life insurance companies arises out of the premium taxes imposed by the states. However, only about one half of the states impose such a tax on annuity premiums. While the majority of states that impose a tax on annuity premiums give no special relief to tax-deferred annuity premiums, some states do give them preferential treatment.

REPORTING AND DISCLOSURE REQUIREMENTS

A tax-deferred annuity plan may be an employee pension benefit plan under regulations of the Department of Labor. Accordingly, the employer must comply with the usual reporting and disclosure requirements such as completion of the summary plan description. Tax-deferred mutual fund arrangements, but not annuity plans, also must file with the IRS on the appropriate Form 5500. For 1977 and later years, annual reports otherwise due to be sent to the Department of Labor are to be sent only to the IRS. However, if the plan is completely voluntary for participation and only salary reductions are involved, the plan will not be subject to the reporting and disclosure requirements of the Department of Labor.

QUESTIONS FOR REVIEW

1. Briefly summarize the provisions of the tax code that permit one to set up a tax-deferred annuity.
2. What are the essential requirements to achieve the desired tax shelter for a tax-deferred annuity? Explain.
3. What type of contract qualifies as a tax-deferred annuity?
4. What does it mean when the IRC requires the employee's rights to be nonforfeitable? Explain.
5. Describe the exclusion allowance for an employee for the taxable year under a tax deferred annuity plan.
6. Explain how the use of the maximum exclusion in a year affects amounts of deductible contributions in future years.
7. How does the exclusion formula take into consideration what might be referred to as an allowance for past service? Explain.
8. Briefly describe the alternatives permitted for employees who have made little or no contributions under a tax-deferred annuity plan.
9. Explain the income taxation of tax-deferred annuities during one's lifetime and prior to receiving benefits if the purchased contract contains no element of insurance protection. How does the situation change if the contract does include life insurance protection?
10. Are the amounts contributed by an employer to a tax-deferred annuity subject to tax as wages for social security purposes? Are there any exceptions? Explain.

QUESTIONS FOR DISCUSSION

1. Discuss the conditions under which an employer may desire to establish a tax-deferred annuity.

2. Discuss how the new elective deferral limitations are likely to affect plan design for tax-deferred annuities.

3. Discuss how the new nondiscrimination requirements are likely to affect plan design for tax-deferred annuities.

21

Plan Installation, Administration, and Disclosure

The advantages a qualified plan provides for employers and employees have been amply noted in previous chapters. These advantages are most significant; and it is important, from the employer's viewpoint, that they be gained at minimum expense and with minimum administrative effort.

Many of the factors involved in the installation and administration of a qualified plan are interdependent, and the relative timing of certain events can be most significant. Moreover, several parties are usually involved in the installation and administration of the program, and very often these parties have differing interests. Efficient plan installation and administration requires that the efforts of these parties be coordinated and that there be complete and thorough communication among all concerned. The administrative complexities imposed by law are such that great care must be taken by all concerned to assure that the plan is installed and operated in accordance with all appropriate legal requirements.

This chapter first examines the steps involved in the installation of a qualified plan and then discusses the various administrative aspects of such a program.[1] The chapter concludes with a discussion of the reporting requirements of ERISA.

---

[1]See Revenue Procedure 80–30 for more information.

Most of these items have been discussed in other portions of this text when appropriate; however, it is important that they be consolidated and presented in a single chapter. It is also important to note that any person who has discretionary authority or control in the administration of a plan is a fiduciary under ERISA and must discharge all plan responsibilities as required under this law. Thus, a major portion of this chapter discusses these fiduciary requirements.

PLAN INSTALLATION

Preparation of Legal Documents

The first and most important step in the installation of any plan is the preparation of the necessary legal documents such as the trust agreement or the plan instrument, authorizing resolutions, enrollment forms, and so on. The employer's attorney is responsible for preparing or approving the trust agreement, the plan instrument, or both, as the case may be. If a group pension contract is involved, the insurance company prepares this document, but the employer's attorney should review the contract provisions.

Most insurers and corporate trustees have specimens of the various legal documents involved and will furnish them to the attorney who is working on a specific plan. It is particularly desirable for the attorney to have copies of these specimens (whether they are used or not), since they generally contain most of the requirements of the insurer or the trustee for the type of funding instrument involved. By giving the attorney this information, conflicts between the plan provisions and these requirements may be avoided or, at the least, these conflicts may be discussed before the instruments are finalized.

Plans That Involve a Trust Agreement.   It is possible to incorporate the plan provisions in the trust agreement, and this practice is sometimes followed in individual policy plans (particularly those that are fully insured) or where individuals are acting as trustees. It is also possible to have two separate documents—a plan instrument that establishes the details of the plan and a trust agreement that relates primarily to the duties, rights, and responsibilities of the trustee for the investment and accountability of the plan assets. This latter approach is often used if a corporate trustee is involved, since many trustees and employers prefer to limit the role of the corporate trustee in a pension or profit sharing plan to that of an investor of plan assets. Thus, they prefer that the documents clearly establish the fact that administrative duties and responsibilities are vested in the employer or in a committee appointed by the employer. Moreover, flexibility is obtained by having two instruments in that the trustee's consent is not necessary for any changes in the plan instrument alone.

If the plan is insured in any way, it is desirable to submit a draft of all documents to the insurer's home office for review prior to execution. As a matter of fact, many insurers require this step as a part of the underwriting process. It is a good practice for the parties involved to do this to avoid any possible conflicts between the plan provisions, the insurer's underwriting and administrative requirements, and the trustee's responsibilities. Similarly, if there is to be a corporate trustee, it is advisable to submit a draft of the documents to the bank or trust company for approval prior to execution.

If the employer is a corporation, its board of directors should pass a resolution or resolutions authorizing the plan and appointing the trustee. If applicable, a committee or committees should also be appointed. Also, if required by state law or the firm's charter or bylaws, it may be necessary that an authorizing resolution be passed by the firm's stockholders.

When all necessary papers have been prepared and are in acceptable form, the trust should be executed. At this time, the employer's first contribution is usually made to the trustee, although, if possible, some employers prefer not to make a contribution (or prefer to make only a token contribution) until an approval letter for the plan has been received from the Internal Revenue Service. However, if insurance is to be placed in force, a contribution of an amount necessary to pay the premiums will have to be made. Most insurers will agree to refund this premium, less a risk charge, to the trustee if the plan is disapproved by the Internal Revenue Service within some specified period of time.

In an insured plan, the trust agreement generally requires that the insurance or annuity contracts be applied for by the trustee and that the trustee pay the first premiums due on such contracts. Since the individual or corporation who is to be the trustee cannot act in this capacity until the trust is in effect, it is important to recognize that the creation of the trust is a necessary condition that must be met before the insurance may be placed in force.

If employees are to be enrolled, an enrollment form should be prepared. If the plan is contributory, this form should include an authorization for the employer to withhold any employee contributions. It is also desirable to prepare a refusal form should any employee elect not to participate. Such a refusal form, signed by the employee, would be a record that the employee had been informed of his or her rights but had declined plan participation.

Master and Prototype Arrangements.   The concept of master or prototype plans (with or without a trust) was originally developed for H.R. 10 plans. At that time, the Internal Revenue Service instituted administrative procedures under which a sponsoring institution such as an association, a bank, or an insurance company could obtain approval of a master or prototype plan. The Internal Revenue Service subsequently extended these same administrative procedures to corporate plans.

As is the case with master or prototype plans for self-employed individuals, the sponsoring organization submits the plan to the Internal Revenue

Service for approval. Any corporation wishing to avail itself of an approved master or prototype plan simply executes a joinder or affiliation agreement. The master or prototype plan sets forth the general provisions for a qualified plan. The joinder or affiliation agreement permits the corporation to select various plan features such as the benefit formula, eligibility requirements, employee contribution levels, and vesting provisions.

Adoption of such an approved plan by a corporation does not mean the corporation automatically has a qualified plan. It is still necessary that the plan be considered individually with particular reference to the individual circumstances involved. The plan may be submitted to the Internal Revenue Service for individual consideration by utilizing appropriate Treasury Department forms.

Group Pension Plans.   A trust agreement is not employed in most group pension plans. The provisions of the plan are contained either in a plan instrument or in the group contract itself. If a plan instrument is involved, the group contract is usually written by the insurer on a "reference" basis—that is, the group contract, while not spelling out the plan provisions, refers to the actual plan instrument to determine items such as eligibility, retirement benefits, vesting, and so on. If a plan instrument is not involved, the group contract itself will contain these provisions. The employer's attorney will prepare any plan instrument involved and will review the terms of the group contract prepared by the insurer.

As in the case of a plan that employs a trust, it is necessary to have the board of directors (and, where appropriate, the stockholders) pass an appropriate resolution authorizing the plan.

When an employer has decided to establish a group pension program, the first step is usually for the employer to submit a letter of application to the insurer for the group contract. This letter of application, along with a premium deposit and all pertinent information relating to the plan (including the plan instrument, if applicable), is forwarded to the insurance company. If all preliminary underwriting requirements are met, the insurer will accept the application and will then prepare the actual group contract. In many situations, particularly if the contract incorporates the actual plan provisions, a draft of the contract will be sent for the employer's approval. Once the final contract has been prepared (incorporating any changes mutually agreed upon between the insurer and the employer), the insurer generally obtains approval to issue the contract from the appropriate state insurance department, if such approval is necessary.[2]

---

[2]This is the state where the contract will be delivered and generally is the state in which the employer's principal place of business is located if that state requires that group pension contracts be approved prior to issue. It should be noted that while insurers attempt to standardize the provisions of their group contracts as much as possible, many insurers, because of variations required in a particular case, will submit each contract to the appropriate state insurance department for approval to issue the contract on a "single-case" basis. Since, in this area, insurers do not have the advantage of working with preapproved contract or policy forms, a group contract may take longer to issue than individual contracts.

After any necessary state insurance department approval has been received, the final contract will be sent for execution by the employer.

Announcing the Plan to Employees

It is necessary, with all qualified plans, that the plan be announced to employees.[3]

This announcement may take the form of a letter (usually from the president of the firm), but it is often desirable to have a brochure or booklet printed for this purpose. If desired, most insurers will supply some form of printed announcement material for a group pension program and, prior to the actual printing of this material, will usually furnish a copy to the employer for approval. The actual cost of preparing this material is usually charged to the employer through the insurer's dividend or experience rating formula. In the case of a trust fund plan or a plan funded with individual contracts, the cost of preparing announcement material is borne directly by the employer.

From the employer's viewpoint, the announcement material should be as attractive as possible since it is the first as well as the major communication employees receive concerning the plan. A well-designed brochure or booklet will do a great deal in helping to obtain maximum employee awareness of the program and appreciation of its value. Many employers find their communications program is enhanced if the preliminary announcement is followed by employee meetings and, at a later date, by more complete and permanent reference material.

The object of the announcement material is to explain the plan in clear and simple terms—but not at the price of accuracy. For this reason, it is important that this material be checked most carefully to make sure it correctly describes the plan.

Enrollment of Employees

If the plan is contributory, or if individual contracts are involved, an enrollment is always necessary. It is sometimes desirable to enroll employees under a noncontributory plan. The enrollment usually takes place at the time the plan is announced to employees or shortly thereafter. It normally involves the completion and signing of the enrollment form and, if the plan is contributory, the completion of the authorization for the employer to withhold the employee's contributions by payroll deduction. In a group program, the insurer usually supplies the enrollment and refusal

---

[3]The announcement should state that a copy of the plan document is available for inspection and where and when such inspection may take place, and must communicate all other information required by ERISA. In addition, the employees must be told of the plan's submission to the Internal Revenue Service, along with a notification that employees have the right to comment on the submission or, under specified conditions, request the secretary of labor to make such comments.

cards that should be used. In trust fund plans, the corporate trustee will often be able to supply these forms, if desired.

In an individual policy plan, the application for the employee's insurance or annuity contract will also be completed at the time of enrollment and, if necessary, a medical examination will be arranged. Many medical examiners, when there are several lives to be examined, will agree to conduct these examinations at the employer's place of business. After the enrollment has been conducted, the insurance or annuity applications, appropriately signed by the trustee, should be submitted to the insurance company for underwriting approval. If the trust agreement is satisfactory to the insurer and if all of the insurer's underwriting requirements are met, both for the plan and for individual lives, contracts will be issued for delivery to the trustee.

Medical examinations are generally not required for group pension plans, although if group permanent insurance is involved, and if the plan requires amounts of insurance in excess of the nonmedical maximum, it is possible that a few employees will have to be examined.

Other Matters

Plan Administrator.   ERISA states that unless the plan and/or the trust otherwise provides, the plan sponsor (usually the employer) will be the plan administrator for purposes of the law. Most employers prefer to designate an individual or a committee, in the plan or trust instrument, to serve in this capacity.

Evidence of Participation.   It is usually desirable that employees be given some evidence of their participation in the plan. Most insurers provide some form of certificate or statement of participation for both individual policy and group pension plans. In trust fund plans, the consultant will generally arrange to have this material prepared for the employer.

Signature Authority.   If there is more than one trustee, the trust agreement usually states whether actions taken by the trustees must be unanimous, or whether they may act by majority vote or by one of the trustees. The same is generally true for the committee of a plan with a corporate trustee. Where unanimous or majority action is required, the instruments may still permit the trustees or committee to delegate to any one of their number the authority to sign documents or to perform ministerial duties on behalf of all. When the instruments contain such a provision, most trustees and committees find it desirable that such a delegation be made for administrative convenience. The insurer, or corporate trustee, or both, requires that a copy of any such delegation be in their files if they are being asked to accept fewer than the full number of signatures otherwise required by the plan.

Checking Account.   If individual trustees are involved, it is also desirable for the trustees to open a checking account, since they have the responsibility of maintaining adequate records of money received and disbursed. Canceled checks and the accompanying statements generally are accepted as proof of payment or receipt and, for this reason, the trustee's account is most important.

Administrative Records.   In addition to the record furnished by the trustees' checking account, it is necessary that some or all of the administrative records described later in this chapter be established at the inception of the plan. Adequate administrative records, maintained from the very beginning, can prove to be a most valuable adjunct to the smooth administration of the entire program.

Tax Aspects.   To make sure an employer receives a deduction for contributions made for the fiscal year in which the plan is established, it is important that all necessary requirements be met within the time allowed under federal tax law. Thus, the plans should be adopted by the close of the employer's fiscal year. However, the contribution need not be made until the due date for filing the employer's tax return. Although not absolutely necessary, it is desirable that the plan be submitted to the Internal Revenue Service for the purpose of obtaining an advance determination letter as to the qualified status of the plan.[4]

It also is necessary that the trust obtain a taxpayer identification number even though it is tax-exempt. Treasury Department Form SS-4 is used for this purpose.

PLAN ADMINISTRATION

As a generalization, it might be said that the administration of pension and profit sharing plans is divided into two broad areas—actions that relate to the plan as a whole (such as cost calculations and tax aspects), and actions that relate to specific individuals (such as the processing of benefit payments). Actions that relate to individuals may take place at any time during the plan year and often occur without any advance notice. Actions that relate to the plan as a whole generally take place once a year, usually around the anniversary date of the plan.

While group and individual policy pension and profit sharing plans are similar in many ways, they differ considerably in plan administration—

---

[4]This information is set forth in detail in Chapter 4.

particularly in the role played by the life underwriter. Generally speaking, most insurers utilize the same administrative practices for contracts issued for individual policy plans as they do for their ordinary life business as a whole. These systems are such that only infrequently will the home office of the insurer have direct contact with the employees or the employer. Thus, most contacts with the employer and employees will be at the field level. For this reason, the role played by the life underwriter and the agency office in the administration of individual policy plans is most important.

In contrast, most insurers administer their group pension and profit sharing programs in a manner such that the home office is in direct contact with the employer, or the services of the local group field office will be utilized. The life underwriter and the agency office generally are involved only in important or unusual matters. To aid in this concept of direct administration between the employer and the home office, the insurer usually furnishes the employer with an administration manual or guide and a supply of administrative forms at the time the plan is installed. With this manual and supporting material, the employer is in a position to be in direct contact with the home office on most items of plan administration.

In trust fund plans, the plan administration is handled by the employer, frequently with the aid of the plan consultant, and the corporate trustee acts primarily as an investor of the plan assets and makes disbursements as directed by the employer or committee. Some larger employers maintain a full-time staff to administer their employee benefit plans. Consultants are also frequently involved in insured plans, particularly those that employ some form of group pension contract. Here, much of the plan administration and record-keeping normally performed by the insurer is handled by the employer or consultant, the insurer to a great extent acting within its contract terms as directed by the employer or consultant.

The following material discusses, very briefly, the major areas involved in plan administration. No attempt has been made to discuss specific administrative procedures since these vary considerably among insurers, banks and trust companies, and consultants.

Cost and Actuarial Aspects

An important aspect of the administration of any pension plan is the determination of the annual contribution to be made under the plan. For a fully insured individual policy or group permanent plan, this is a relatively simple matter, since the annual contribution is the sum of the premiums due on existing coverage plus the first premiums due on new coverage then being issued for new entrants or for benefit increases, less any employer credits.

For a group deferred annuity contract, the annual contribution will be the premiums calculated by the insurer to purchase the future service benefits accruing during the year plus, if applicable, a premium toward the liquidation of any unfunded supplemental liability, less any employer credits.

The determination of annual contributions becomes a little more complicated for those plans that employ, in whole or in part, some form of unallocated funding instrument. Here, it is necessary that some form of actuarial valuation be made. For an individual policy or group permanent combination plan, a portion of the annual contribution will consist of premiums then due. The balance will consist of the deposit that must be made to the conversion fund, and this portion must be actuarially determined. Most insurers perform the calculations necessary to determine the estimated deposits to this fund; in any event, the valuation must be performed by an enrolled actuary. Certain data must be obtained each year to perform these calculations. These data include a revised employee census that indicates new entrants, changed benefits, terminations that have occurred during the prior year, and so on.

Most insurers perform the actuarial valuations needed for unallocated group funding instruments, such as group deposit administration contracts, or will accept the actuarial valuations made for the plan by an actuarial consulting firm. In a trust fund plan, the actuarial valuations are performed by an actuarial firm. The actuary will need the employee information referred to above to perform these valuations. Usually, the consultant or the insurer will have given the employer detailed instructions as to when and how these data should be compiled. As noted above, the valuation must be made by an enrolled actuary.

Tax Aspects of Administration

Deductions. Form 5500 (or one of its variations) should be used for employers in claiming deductions for contributions made to a qualified plan.

Taxpayers need not make the actual contribution during a given taxable year and will be allowed a deduction for the contribution for such year if the actual contribution is made before the due date for filing the employer's tax return for such taxable year (including extensions) and if the contribution is designated as being on account of such taxable year.

Annual Information Returns—Forms 1099R and W-2P. Treasury Department Form 1099R is an information return that the trustee must file for each beneficiary who receives a lump-sum payment or distribution from the trust in any calendar year.[5]

Treasury Department Form W-2P is used when distribution is in the form of periodic payments. A copy must be given to the payee before January 31 of the year following the calendar year during which the payment

---

[5]If the insurer makes the payment, it must also file this information, which results in some duplication.

was made. Returns on Form 1099R are in the nature of unverified schedules showing the name and address of the payee, the amount of income paid, and the name and address of the payor. The schedules are summarized on Treasury Department Form W-3G, which must be filed by the payor with the Internal Revenue Service by February 28 of the year following the calendar year in which the payments were made.

These forms must be filed even though the payment is made in part or in whole by the cash value of an insurance or an annuity contract that is being transferred out of the trust.

In a group pension plan without a trust, it is the responsibility of the insurance company to file these forms.

Withholding.   Prior to TEFRA, withholding on distributions from qualified pension and profit sharing plans was made only at the option of the pensioner. This was accomplished by the pensioner's filing Treasury Department Form W-4P with the payor of the benefit (the trustee or the insurance company). Beginning in 1983, both periodic and nonperiodic payments from such plans, including death benefits, are subject to automatic withholding. However, the recipient of the distribution may elect not to have taxes withheld even though the benefits are, in fact, taxable.

The payor of the benefit must notify the payee of the right to elect not to have taxes withheld. In the case of periodic distributions, this notice must be given during a period that begins no more than six months before the first payment is due and ends when the first payment is made. Payors must also notify payees at least annually of their right to make and revoke withholding elections. In the case of a nonperiodic distribution, the payor must notify the payee of the right to make or revoke a withholding election at the time of distribution.

There are two methods of determining the amount to be withheld from periodic distributions. If a withholding certificate is in effect, the number of exemptions noted on the certificate should be used for this purpose. If no certificate is in effect, the amount to be withheld will be determined by treating the payee as a married individual claiming three exemptions.

The amount to be withheld for a nonperiodic distribution depends upon the nature of the distribution. Amounts withheld on lump-sum distributions will be determined by the tax on such distributions. The amount will be established under tables or other computational procedures prescribed by the Internal Revenue Service. In the case of death benefit payments, the amount to be withheld must reflect the $5,000 exclusion from gross income provided by Section 101(b) of the Internal Revenue Code, even though it may not be allowable.

In general, the payor of a distribution must withhold and is liable for payment of the required tax. However, the plan administrator of a qualified plan is also charged with the responsibility of withholding and is liable for payment of the required tax. The plan administrator may avoid this requirement by directing the payor to withhold the tax and by providing the payor with information required by Internal Revenue Service regulations.

Penalties for failing to keep necessary records have also been established beginning in 1985. A penalty will be imposed on the payor if the database necessary for reports is not maintained, regardless of whether reports are due for the period during which the record-keeping failure occurs. Each year, the penalty can be $50 for each individual for whom a failure occurs, up to a maximum of $50,000. Limited exceptions to the imposition of a penalty will be permitted for failures that result from reasonable cause, as long as willful neglect is not present.

The payor must furnish the pensioner each year with a Treasury Department Form W-2P showing the gross amount of pension paid to the pensioner during the year along with any amount of tax withheld. This form must be given to the pensioner on or before January 31 following the calendar year of payment (or within 30 days after the last payment if payments are terminated during the year). A copy of Form W-2P also must be furnished by the payor to the Internal Revenue Service.

PS 58 Costs. A participant in a qualified plan who is protected by level premium life insurance is considered, under federal tax law, to be in constructive receipt of the value of the pure insurance protection of the life insurance contract.[6]

The term cost of this pure insurance protection is, therefore, considered to be additional taxable income to the participant. This cost of insurance (often called the *PS 58 cost* because the original Treasury Department ruling on the subject was so numbered) in some cases automatically is furnished each year by the insurer or may be readily determined from tables supplied by the insurer.

It should be noted that the PS 58 costs are considered as a distribution from the trust. Failure to include these amounts as taxable income could result in the entire insurance proceeds being taxable as income to the employee's beneficiary.

Records

A pension or a profit sharing plan can be expected to exist over a considerable length of time, and it is reasonable to expect that during its existence, several different individuals will be responsible for its administration. Thus, it is most important that adequate records be established at the outset of the plan and that these records be maintained in sufficient detail to permit orderly and consistent plan administration. This is particularly so since the advent of ERISA.

---

[6]If the plan is contributory and the plan so provides, employee contributions may be first applied to meet the cost of the insurance protection, thus eliminating or minimizing the employee's current tax liability for this benefit. Most plans are written in this manner.

Records for the plan as a whole should include a list of the names, addresses, and telephone numbers of all individuals who are associated with the plan and its administration. This would include the trustees, the plan administrator, any committee members, the life underwriter, the consultant, the attorney, the accountant, and so on. These plan records should also include a complete history of all plan receipts and disbursements. A digest of the major plan provisions would be most helpful to the plan administrator in avoiding repeated reference to the legal documents constituting the plan. A major portion of the permanent plan records generally includes appropriate memoranda, letters, or minutes that support decisions made in the interpretation of the legal documents or in the exercise of discretionary powers granted to the trustee, plan administrator, or committee.

The record maintained for each employee should list such pertinent data as the employee's name, home address, social security number, date of birth, the type of proof submitted to verify this birthdate, the date of birth of the employee's joint annuitant or spouse (if applicable), the effective date of participation in the plan, the employee's hours of service and the appropriate computation periods, the employee's scheduled normal retirement date, and current beneficiary designation (if applicable). This record should show, on a cumulative basis, the employee's earnings (if benefits are related to compensation), projected benefit under the plan, and current death benefit (if any). If the plan employs individual insurance or annuity contracts, the record should also include information relating to the employee's contract or contracts such as contract numbers, dates of issue, cash values, and rating action.

If employees contribute under the plan, the employee record should include a history of these contributions. Also, if PS 58 costs are involved, a record of these should be maintained, since such costs will be part of the employee's cost basis for any future distributions under the plan.

It is also desirable to maintain, for each employee, a record of each calculation made to determine benefits. This could be most helpful in producing a consistent application of the plan's benefit formula.

Benefit Payments

Benefits are generally paid under a pension plan only upon retirement, death, termination of employment, or disability. Benefits may also be paid at other times under profit sharing and thrift and savings plans.

The trust or plan instrument often contains limitations as to what can or cannot be done in the way of benefit payments. Moreover, in an insured plan, the insurance company may impose certain limitations consistent with its underwriting and administrative systems. Any such limitations must be observed carefully in paying or providing benefits under any contingency.

Even though certain limitations may exist, the employee often will have a wide choice as to the manner in which benefits may be paid. The employee's options should be carefully and fully explained and, to the extent that the election or revocation of a spouse benefit is involved, the Code requires that the employee be given reasonable notice of the terms and conditions of the benefit and the effect of not receiving benefits under this form of payment. It also should be remembered that tax consequences frequently will play an important role in reaching a decision as to how benefits should be received. In any situation when tax consequences could be of significance, the employee should seek the guidance of tax counsel before making a decision.[7]

Employee Communications

An important part of the administration of any plan is the manner in which employees are informed initially and then reminded of their plan benefits and the value of these benefits. Full disclosure, apart from being desirable from an employee relations viewpoint, is required by ERISA. Other employer communication is required by ERISA or the tax law and described later in this chapter.

The employer's size often indicates the course of action best suited for communicating with employees. For example, if the employer is large enough to have some form of publication for employees, this is an ideal vehicle in which to point out periodically the benefits and value of the plan.

Many employers like to give each employee some type of annual report that shows the employee's accrued and projected plan benefits, as well as their value, when this can be ascertained under the funding instrument or actuarial cost method involved. (ERISA, of course, gives each employee the right, once a year, to request a statement of accrued benefits and when such benefits are or will be vested.) It is also customary for this type of annual report to include information on the employer's other employee benefit plans such as group life insurance, disability income, and medical expense. This type of report can be most effective in giving an employee a better understanding of plan benefits as well as the total value of employment.

Other techniques for publicizing the plan are bulletin board announcements, payroll envelope stuffers, personal letters, contests, preretirement counseling, and so on. The important point is that the plan should be

---

[7]Apart from the aspect of securing appropriate advice from tax counsel, there is the further consideration that any advice given to an employee should be full and complete. In *Gediman* v. *Anheuser Busch*, 299 F. 2d 537, the employer gave an employee advice concerning the various options available as to the distribution of his benefit. This advice did not make it sufficiently clear that if the employee elected one of the methods and died before receiving a distribution, his benefits would be considerably smaller than under the other methods. The court held the employer liable for negligence when the employee, in reliance on this advice, elected a method that caused his estate to lose benefits on his subsequent death. The court observed that: "[The employer,] having undertaken to advise, ... was bound to advise clearly."

publicized repeatedly by the method best suited for the particular employer, taking into account the employee relations pattern developed within the firm.

FIDUCIARY RESPONSIBILITIES

Both the tax and the labor provisions of ERISA include specific requirements concerning fiduciary responsibilities. Overall, these responsibilities can be grouped in two categories: (1) those that are positive in nature (in that they require fiduciaries to take affirmative action) and (2) those that are negative in nature (in that they prohibit certain action). The fiduciary requirements included in the tax provisions of ERISA are largely negative, although affirmative fiduciary responsibilities also exist under tax and general fiduciary laws. The labor provisions of ERISA are much more extensive and deal with both positive and negative fiduciary responsibilities. The material that follows discusses fiduciary responsibilities in general; where significant, distinctions in the tax and labor provisions of ERISA are noted.

The fiduciary provisions of ERISA were generally effective on January 1, 1975. The prohibited transactions provisions, however, did not become fully effective until June 30, 1984, in the case of investments where, on July 1, 1974, the plan was not in violation of the then applicable law and where the situation continues to be at least as favorable as an arm's-length transaction with an unrelated party.

A person (or corporation) will be considered a fiduciary under the labor provisions of ERISA if that person exercises any discretionary authority or control over the management of the plan, any authority or control over assets held under the plan or the disposition of plan assets, renders investment advice for direct or indirect compensation (or has any authority or responsibility to do so), or has any discretionary authority or responsibility in the administration of the plan.

Fiduciary Duties

A fiduciary is required to discharge all duties solely in the interest of participants and beneficiaries and for the exclusive purpose of providing plan benefits and defraying reasonable administrative expenses. In addition, a fiduciary is charged with using the care, skill, prudence, and diligence that a prudent person who is familiar with such matters would use under the circumstances then prevailing — a standard that has come to be called the *prudent expert rule*. A fiduciary is also responsible for diversifying investments so as to minimize the risk of large losses unless it is clearly prudent not to diversify. Finally, the fiduciary must conform with the documents governing the plan and must invest only in assets subject to the jurisdiction of the U.S. courts.

Liability of a Fiduciary

Under the labor provisions of ERISA, a fiduciary will be personally liable for any breach or violation of responsibilities, and will be liable to restore any profits made through the use of plan assets. Under the tax provisions, a fiduciary may also be subject to excise taxes for violation of the prohibited transaction provisions.

A fiduciary may also be liable for the violations of a cofiduciary if the fiduciary knowingly participates in or conceals a violation, has knowledge of a violation, or by the fiduciary's own violation enables the cofiduciary to commit a violation. However, if a plan uses separate trusts, a trustee of one trust is not responsible as a cotrustee of the other trust. Also, a fiduciary will not be responsible for the acts of a duly appointed investment manager (except to the extent that the fiduciary did not act prudently in selecting or continuing the use of the investment manager). A trustee also is not responsible for following the direction of named fiduciaries in making investment decisions (if the plan so provides).

Noninvestment activities can be delegated by a fiduciary if the plan so permits and the procedure for doing so is clearly spelled out; however, fiduciaries remain responsible, under the prudent expert rule, for persons delegated those responsibilities. Similarly, they remain responsible for the acts of their agents in performing ministerial duties.

Plan provisions that purport to relieve a fiduciary of responsibilities are void and of no effect. However, a plan, employer, union, or fiduciary may purchase insurance to cover the fiduciary's liability, but if the plan purchases this insurance the insurer must have subrogation rights against the fiduciary. An employer or union may also agree to indemnify a fiduciary against personal liability.

Prohibited Transactions

Both the labor and tax provisions of ERISA prohibit certain transactions between the plan and parties in interest. A party in interest is defined broadly and includes, for example, any fiduciary, a person providing services to the plan, any employer or employee organization whose employees or members are covered by the plan, a direct or indirect owner of 50 percent or more of the business interest, a relative of any of the above, and an employee, officer, director, or a person having 10 percent or more of the ownership interest in any of the above.

The following are prohibited transactions between the plan and a party of interest:

1. The sale, exchange, or leasing of property.
2. Lending money or extending credit (including the funding of the plan by contribution of debt securities).
3. Furnishing goods, services, or facilities.

4. Transfer to or use of plan assets.
5. Acquisition of qualifying employer securities and real property in excess of allowable limits.

Additionally, a fiduciary cannot deal with assets in his or her own interest or for his or her own account, act in any capacity involving the plan on behalf of anyone having an adverse interest, or receive any consideration for the fiduciary's own personal account from any party dealing with the plan.

A number of exemptions to the prohibited transaction rules are specifically provided for, and a provision for applying for additional exemptions also exists. Among the specific exemptions granted are loans to participants (if available in a nondiscriminatory fashion to all participants, if adequately secured, and if the loan bears a reasonable rate of interest), the furnishing of office space and services for reasonable compensation, the providing of ancillary banking services where this is done without interference with the interests of the plan and the plan participants and, in the case of banks and insurance companies, the utilization of their own facilities to fund their own plans.

If a qualified plan engages in a prohibited transaction, it will no longer disqualify the plan. However, an excise tax of 5 percent of the amount involved will be levied. If the situation is not corrected within the time allowed (90 days unless extended by the Internal Revenue Service), a further excise tax of 100 percent of the amount involved will be levied upon the fiduciary who participated in the prohibited transaction.

Investment in Employer Securities and Real Property

Qualifying employer securities include stock. Qualifying employer securities also include marketable obligations under specified rules relating to the source of the purchase, the establishment of the price, and the percentage of the issue held by the plan and other persons. Qualifying employer real property is real property that is dispersed geographically, is suitable for more than one use, and has been leased to the employer.

Profit sharing, stock bonus, and thrift and savings plans that specifically so provide may invest without limit in qualifying employer securities or real property.[8]

If the plan does not specifically provide for the amount of employer securities or real property to be held, the 10 percent limit described below will be applicable.

A pension plan may not acquire (by any means) employer securities and real property if the immediate effect of this would cause more than 10 percent of the fair market value of plan assets to be so held. If a plan held more than 10 percent of its assets in employer securities and real property

---

[8]This also applies to defined contribution pension plans that so provided on September 2, 1974. Other defined contribution pension plans are subject to the 10 percent limit.

on January 1, 1975, it had until December 31, 1984, to conform to the 10 percent rule; 50 percent compliance must have been achieved by December 31, 1979.

Prohibition against Holding Office

If convicted of certain specified crimes, a person cannot serve as a plan administrator, fiduciary, officer, trustee, custodian, counsel, agent, employee, or consultant for five years after conviction (or the end of imprisonment, if later). This prohibition will not apply if citizenship rights have been restored or if approved by the United States Board of Parole.

Bonding

All fiduciaries and persons who handle plan funds or other plan assets are to be bonded for 10 percent of the aggregate amount handled, with a minimum bond of $1,000 and a maximum bond of $500,000. The secretary of labor may raise the $500,000 maximum. Bonding generally is not required of corporate trustees or insurance companies with combined capital and surplus of at least $1 million, if the only assets from which benefits are paid are the general assets of the employer or a union, or if the secretary of labor finds that other bonding arrangements or the overall financial condition of the plan is adequate to protect participants.

Establishment of Plan and Trust

A pension plan must be established and maintained pursuant to a written instrument that specifically provides for one or more named fiduciaries. Each plan must provide a procedure for establishing and carrying out a funding policy and method to achieve plan objectives, and must describe any procedure for allocating operational and administrative responsibilities. There must also be a provision that sets forth the amendment procedure and identifies the persons who have authority to amend. The plan must also specify the basis on which payments are made to and from the plan.

DISCLOSURE

A major aspect of ERISA concerns the disclosure of information — to participants and their beneficiaries and to the government. While a limited amount of disclosure had been required before ERISA (under the Welfare and Pension Plans Disclosure Act and under several state laws), ERISA requires that more complete disclosure take place as a matter of course and at prescribed times. In addition, ERISA applies to a greater variety of plans and covers a much larger number of employees than did the Welfare and Pension Plans Disclosure Act (WPPDA). The disclosure requirements of

ERISA supersede those of the WPPDA, which has been repealed. ERISA also preempts state disclosure legislation.

Private employee pension and welfare plans maintained by most organizations whose employees are engaged in or affect interstate commerce are covered by ERISA. The most common plans affected are as follows:

1. Pension.
2. Profit sharing.
3. Thrift and savings.
4. ESOPs.
5. Welfare.
   a.–Life insurance.
   b.–Hospital-surgical-medical insurance.
   c.–Dental and vision care insurance.
   d.–Accident insurance.
   e.–Disability income.
   f.–Scholarship plans (which are funded).
   g.–Supplemental unemployment.
   h.–Prepaid legal services.
   i.–Some severance pay plans.
   j.–Dependent care plans.

Regardless of the number of participants in pension, profit sharing, or thrift and savings plans, such plans are subject to the disclosure requirements of ERISA. However, unfunded welfare plans, or those funded solely through insurance contracts, with fewer than 100 participants throughout a plan year, are exempt from certain filing requirements as long as employee contributions are forwarded to the insurer within three months of receipt; any rebates are returned to contributing employees within three months; and contributors are informed when they join the plan about the allocation of rebates. A number of complete or partial exemptions are provided for many different plans, including a complete exemption for unfunded pension plans and unfunded or insured welfare plans provided for a "select group of management or highly compensated employees."[9]

Certain plans are excluded from coverage under ERISA. They are government plans, church plans, plans maintained outside the United States for the benefit of nonresident aliens, excess benefit plans, and plans established only to comply with workers' compensation, unemployment compensation, or disability laws.

For a plan that must comply with ERISA's disclosure requirements, the following items must be filed with the appropriate government agencies, at required times, as well as distributed automatically to all plan participants and beneficiaries receiving benefits under pension plans:

Summary plan description — SPD (the booklet, folder, and binder that is given to employees).

---

[9]However, the Department of Labor must be notified of the existence of any such plan and the number of employees the plan covers.

Summary of material modification — SMM (a summary of any plan amendment or change in information required to be included in the SPD after the initial SPD has been issued).

Summary annual report — SAR (to participants only; need not be filed with the government except on request).

ERISA also requires the automatic distribution of the following items to plan participants when certain events occur:

Statement of benefits for all employees who terminate.

Written explanation to any plan participant or beneficiary whose claim for benefits is denied.

Individual notification of the right to elect or reject pre- and postretirement survivor benefits under pension plans

Notice to "interested parties" when application for determination of a plan's tax-qualified status is filed with the Internal Revenue Service.

Notice of intent to terminate a plan.

Notice of benefit commitment under a terminated plan.

Notification of tax treatment on rollover distribution.

Any item distributed automatically by mail must be sent by a class of mail that ensures timely delivery.

In addition, ERISA requires some items to be given to plan participants upon written request and/or to be made available for examination at the principal office of the plan administrator and at other locations convenient for participants. These items are as follows:

Supporting plan documents.

Complete application for determination of tax-qualified status (Form 5300).

Complete annual report (Form 5500 or 5500 C).

Personal pension benefits statement (on written request only and required to be furnished only once a year).

Plan termination report (Form 5310, should any pension plan wind up its affairs).

The locations in which documents must be made available include any distinct physical location where business is performed and in which at least 50 participants work. Plan materials need not be kept at each location as long as they can be provided at the location within 10 working days after a request for disclosure. The employer may charge for reproduction of all materials requested (unless the material falls in a category where it must be furnished automatically).

Table 21–1 sets forth a summary of the information that must be disclosed to the government and to plan participants and beneficiaries. This table also indicates the dates by which such information must be disclosed

TABLE 21–1: Document Summary of Disclosure Requirements

Item	To Plan Participants				To Government	
	Given Automatically	*Given on Written Request**	*Made Available for Review†*	*When*	*To Be Filed with*	*When*
1. Summary plan description.	X			Within 90 days after employees become participants, or beneficiaries start receiving benefits. Within 120 days after a new plan becomes subject to ERISA. New complete summary at least every 10 years.	Secretary of labor.	Within 120 days after a new plan becomes subject to ERISA. New complete summary at least every 10 years.
2. Plan documents (any instrument under which the plan is operated).		X	X	Within 10 days after request to review; 30 days after request for personal copies.	Secretary of labor.	"Any document relating to an employee benefit plan" at secretary of labor's request only.
3. Summary of material modification	X			Within 210 days after end of plan year in which modification is made.	Secretary of labor.	Within 210 days after end of plan year in which modification is made.
4. Annual report (Form 5500).**		X	X	As soon as report is filed with Internal Revenue Service.	Internal Revenue Service.	Within 7 months after the end of the plan year (plus any applicable extensions for income tax filing).
5. Summary annual report.	X			Within 2 months after deadline for filing annual report.		
6. Benefits statement for terminating vested employees.	X			Within 210 days after end of plan year in which termination occurs.		
7. Personal pension benefits statement.		X (not more than once a year)		Within 30 days of written request.		

			Recipient	Timing
8. Written explanation of claims denial.	X			Within 90 *days* (180 in special circumstances), whenever a claim is denied, in whole or in part.
9. Plan termination report (Form 5310).	X	X	Internal Revenue Service.	After report is filed with the IRS. / Generally 10 *days* prior to plan termination, if determination of qualified status is required.
10. Joint and survivor notification.	X			Timing requirements vary depending upon pre- or post-retirement survivor benefit elections.
11. Notification of intent to terminate a plan.	X	X	Pension Benefit Guaranty Corporation.	At least 60 *days* prior to the proposed plan termination date. This notification should be delivered to the union representative where employees are represented by a union, or may be posted in prominent locations where they are not. / As soon as possible after notice to participants. Contents and attachments are specified by regulation.
12. Notice to interested parties.	X			Between 7 and 24 *days* before application for determination of a plan's qualified status is made to the IRS.
13. Notice of benefit commitment.	X			On or before the date "notification of intent to terminate a plan" is filed with PBGC.
14. Notification of tax treatment on rollover distribution.	X			Within 60 *days* after rollover distribution is made.

*Material must be supplied within 30 days of written request; a reasonable charge may be made for all requested material.

**For applicable plans, Form 5500C is due every three years and Registration Statement R for the two intervening years and Form 5500EZ each for one participant pension plans.

†Material must be made available for examination within 10 days of a verbal request.

Source: Towers, Perrin, Forster and Crosby, Inc.

and whether it must be automatically disclosed, given on written request, or made available for review. The balance of this chapter discusses these major areas in greater detail.

Summary Plan Description

The summary plan description (SPD) is the employee booklet (or some other format) that describes the major features of each plan, positive or negative. It must do so in a "manner calculated to be understood by the average plan participant," with nothing in the format (including type size or style) that might mislead participants.

The summary plan description must be given to new employees within 90 days after becoming participants and to beneficiaries within 90 days after they start receiving benefits. For new plans, the initial summary plan description must be given to participants within 120 days after establishment of the plan, and filed with the Department of Labor at the same time. New, complete summaries must be filed and distributed at least every 10 years. Proposed regulations also give participants the right to request up-to-date information on the plan every five years if there have been material changes since the SPD was first issued. To comply with this request, plan sponsors must provide the latest SPD summaries of all pertinent changes, and an explanation of how all the information fits together to form an accurate description of the plan; for example, which changes supersede which information in the SPD.

The summary plan description must be in permanent form and must be up-to-date regarding all aspects of the plan and the information required by ERISA. The summary plan description must contain the following information:

Plan name and type of plan (e.g., for pension plans: defined contribution, defined benefit; for welfare plans: hospitalization, disability).

The type of administration of the plan (e.g., contract administration, joint board of trustees).

The name (or position title) and address of the person designated as agent for the service of legal process, as well as a statement that legal process also may be served on a plan trustee or the plan administrator.

The name and address of the employer or employee organization that maintains the plan.

The name and/or title, and business address of each trustee.

The employer identification number assigned by the Internal Revenue Service to the plan sponsor and the plan number assigned by the plan sponsor.

In the case of a collectively bargained plan maintained by at least one employer and one employee organization, or in the case of a plan maintained by two or more employers, the name and address of the most significant employer or organization plus either of the following: (1) a statement that a complete list of sponsors may be obtained on written request and is available for review or (2) a statement that, on written request, participants may receive information about whether a particular employer or organization is a sponsor and, if so, the sponsor's address.

If a collective bargaining agreement controls any duties, rights, or benefits under a plan, a statement that the plan is maintained in accordance with the agreement and that a copy of the agreement may be obtained on written request and is available for examination.

Plan requirements respecting eligibility for participation and benefits (e.g., age, service, normal retirement age).

A description of the provisions for nonforfeitable pension benefits.

Information about forfeiture of pension benefits, credited service, breaks in service, and so on.

A description of any joint and survivor benefits and any action necessary to elect or reject them.

Circumstances that may result in disqualification, ineligibility, denial, loss, forfeiture, or suspension of benefits.

A statement of the extent to which a pension plan is insured by the Pension Benefit Guaranty Corporation, where more information about this insurance is available (usually from the administrator), and the name and address of the PBGC. A summary of the pension benefit guaranty provisions of Title IV of ERISA is included in the SPD content regulations. An SPD incorporating this language will be in compliance. In addition, SPDs for any pension plans that are not insured (e.g., defined contribution plans) must note the reason for lack of insurance.

The source of contributions to the plan; the method by which the amount of contributions is calculated (for defined benefit plans, the SPD may state simply that contributions are determined actuarially); and the identity of any organization through which the plan is funded or benefits are provided.

A description and explanation of plan benefits.

The date of the end of the plan year for purposes of maintaining the plan's fiscal records.

The procedures to be followed in presenting claims for benefits under the plan and the remedies available under the plan for the redress of claims that are denied in whole or in part.

A statement of participants' rights under ERISA. This must appear as a consolidated statement; no information may be omitted. The regulations contain suggested language which, if used, will assure compliance.

When different classes of participants are covered with different benefits under the same plan, prominent notice must appear on the first page of the text listing the various classes for whom different summary plan descriptions have been prepared.

All this information must be "written in a manner calculated to be understood by the average plan participant" and should be "sufficiently accurate and comprehensive" to inform participants and beneficiaries of their rights and obligations under each plan. The explanations provided by legal plan texts and insurance contracts ordinarily will not meet these standards. The Regulations recommend the use of simple sentences, clarifying examples, clear and liberal cross-references, and a table of contents in the summary plan description. The use of type is important. Varying sizes and styles of type may not be used when they may mislead participants.

If a plan covers 500 or more people who are literate only in a language other than English, or if 10 percent or more of the participants working at "a distinct physical place of business" are literate only in a non-English language (25 percent where the plan covers fewer than 100 participants), the summary plan description must have a special feature. The booklet may still be written in English, but it must include a prominent notice in the familiar language offering assistance in understanding the plan. The procedures necessary to obtain this assistance should be explained fully in the notice. The assistance must be provided in the familiar language, but need be oral only.

Retired and terminated vested plan participants, as well as beneficiaries receiving pension plan benefits, come under ERISA's definition of participants. They must be furnished automatically copies of summary plan descriptions for all plans under which they are covered. Irrelevant plan amendments need not be communicated to retirees, terminated vested employees, or beneficiaries, although they are entitled to copies free on request. Summaries of amendments that may affect them, however, must be provided.

Annual Report (Form 5500)

The annual report Form 5500 comprises a yearly financial report on each covered pension and welfare plan. This form must be filed with the Internal Revenue Service within seven months after the close of each plan year. For employers that have received extensions from the Internal Revenue Service for income tax filings, identical extensions are automatically granted for annual reports of pension plans. At the time it is filed or within 30 days of written request, the annual report is to be made available to plan participants and beneficiaries for in-house examination.

The annual report is designed to require a complete disclosure of all financial information relevant to the operation of the plan. Thus, for example, it includes items such as a statement of assets and liabilities presented by category and valued at current value, changes in assets and liabilities during the year, and a statement of receipts and disbursements. It requests details, where applicable, for transactions with parties in interest, loans and leases in default or uncollectable, and on certain reportable transactions (e.g., transactions involving in excess of 3 percent of the current value of plan assets). The annual report also requires information on plan changes made during the reporting period, and on employees included or excluded from participation in the plan.

Certain financial statements in the annual report have to be certified by an independent qualified public accountant. Any actuarial reports included for defined benefit plans have to be certified by an enrolled actuary. In addition, insurance companies and banks are required, within 120 days after the end of each plan year (unless another date is permitted by regulations), to furnish any information necessary for the plan administrator to complete the annual report.

There are partial exemptions for unfunded or insured welfare and pension plans, regardless of the number of participants. These plans do not have to complete the financial information sections of the form, nor need they engage an accountant for an audit or include an accountant's opinion. Pension plans with fewer than 100 participants will file, every three years, a simplified Form 5500C, which does not require certification by a public accountant, and, for the intervening two years, Registration Statement R. Welfare plans with fewer than 100 participants are not required to file an annual report.

Summary Annual Report

The purpose of the summary annual report is to make information about each plan's annual financial status readily available to plan participants and beneficiaries and must be sent to them automatically within two months after the annual report (Form 5500) filing date. To relieve some of the burden on plan administrators and still meet the intent of the law, regulations governing format and content of the summary annual report have been progressively simplified. Current regulations provide prescribed language for both pension and welfare plan reports, and much of the detailed financial information earlier required to be included has been eliminated. Beginning in 1988, however, plan participants must be notified of the plan's funded status if this falls below 70 percent of the current liability (defined in Chapter 9).

OTHER DISCLOSURE ITEMS

As noted earlier, a number of other items must be disclosed to participants and their beneficiaries and to the government. The following material briefly summarizes the requirements applicable to such other items.

Summary of Material Modification

When a "material modification" is made to the plan, a summary description of that change, written in clear language, must be distributed automatically to all affected plan participants and beneficiaries and filed with the Department of Labor. The SMM should be a reasonable and adequate summary of any material modification in the terms of a plan or in the information required to be included in the summary plan description. The SMM must be furnished within 210 days after the end of the plan year in which the change is adopted.

Plan Documents

ERISA describes plan documents as "the bargaining agreement, trust agreement, contract or other instruments under which the plan is established or operated." Plan participants and beneficiaries who request any or all of these documents are entitled to receive copies within 30 days of making written request. (A reasonable charge for reproduction may be made.) Also, plan documents must be made available for review in the employer's principal offices or plants. The secretary of labor may request these documents at any time.

Benefits Statements for Terminating Employees

Each plan participant who terminates service and has a vested right in his or her accrued plan benefits should receive a clear statement of these accrued benefits and the percentage that is vested (i.e., nonforfeitable). The statement should include the nature, amount, and form of the deferred vested benefit. Any participant who has a break in service of one year (i.e., a 12-month period during which the employee has not completed more than 500 hours of service) is also automatically entitled to receive a benefits statement. Title II of ERISA (which does not directly deal with disclosure) also appears to require a statement be given to employees who terminate or incur a one-year break in service without a vested interest, thus clearly communicating the fact that any such individual is not entitled to receive benefits under the plan. The statement must be given to vested terminations within 210 days after the end of the plan year in which they terminate service.

Personal Benefits Statement

Each plan participant or beneficiary may request in writing a statement of the individual's own benefits under a pension, deferred profit sharing, or thrift and savings plan. No participant or beneficiary is entitled to receive more than one such statement in any 12-month period.

The statement should include the total benefits accrued and the portion, if any, that is vested (i.e., nonforfeitable) or, if benefits are not vested, the earliest date on which they will become vested. If an employer furnishes annual statements to individual employees, and if such statements include the above information, it is expected that such a practice will satisfy this requirement of ERISA.

Written Explanation of Claims Denial

ERISA requires that every employee benefit plan "establish and maintain a reasonable claims procedure" that is to be set forth in the summary plan description. Regulations cover what constitutes a "reasonable" procedure and specify the actions that should be taken by various parties within stated time periods. Anyone denied a claim under any plan is entitled to a written statement giving the reasons for the denial, usually within 90 days. This explanation should be a clear, comprehensible statement of the specific reasons for the denial of the claim. The explanation also must include a description of any material or information necessary for the claimant to improve the claim and the reasons why this additional material is needed. Also in the explanation should be a full description of the plan's appeal procedure for denied claims. The claimant must be given at least 60 days thereafter to appeal the claim, and is entitled to a final decision in writing within 60 days of the appeal (120 days in special circumstances).

Joint and Survivor Notifications

Under pension plans, each participant must be informed, individually and in writing, of the right to elect or reject *post-retirement* survivor benefits. Timing for notification is nine months before the earliest retirement date under the plan.

When an opportunity to elect *preretirement* survivor benefits exists, notification must be provided between the first day of the plan year in which the participant becomes age 32 and the end of the plan year in which the participant becomes age 35. If a company hires an employee who is over age 32, notification must be provided within three years after that employee becomes a plan participant. If a vested participant terminates employment before age 32, notice must be provided within one year after the termination date.

The joint and survivor notifications must include enough information about the potential financial impact on an individual's own benefit for the participant to make an informed decision. Contents are specified by regulation.

Notification of Tax Treatment on Rollover Distributions

When a distribution from a qualified plan is eligible to be rolled into an IRA or another employer's qualified plan, the plan administrator must send a notice to the participant or beneficiary explaining how taxes can be reduced or deferred (i.e., rollover or income averaging). The notice must be sent within 60 days after the distribution. If the plan administrator does not determine whether a distribution qualifies for rollover treatment, the notice must also explain how the participant or beneficiary can determine its eligibility.

ENFORCEMENT

ERISA provides for stronger enforcement than did the Welfare and Pension Plans Disclosure Act, with greater penalties for violation. Among the penalties are these:
If a plan administrator does not fill a participant's or beneficiary's written request within 30 days, the plan administrator may be personally liable to the individual who made the request for a fine of up to $100 per day.

Willful violation of any of the reporting and disclosure provisions may incur a criminal penalty of up to a $5,000 fine and/or one year in prison for an individual, and up to a $100,000 fine for a corporation.

Civil actions may be brought against the plan administrator by participants or beneficiaries to obtain information to which they are entitled under their plan, to enforce their rights under their plan, or to clarify their rights to future benefits under their plan.

Civil action may also be brought by the secretary of labor, by a participant, beneficiary, or by another fiduciary against an individual who breaches his or her fiduciary duty.

It is expected that random audits will be performed continually, and that a team of investigators will follow up on all discrepancies found and all complaints filed by plan participants or beneficiaries. Records are now required to be kept for a period of six years after the documents are due for filing, even for those plans that are exempt from filing.

QUESTIONS FOR REVIEW

1. Explain the legal documents that are important to the installation of a pension plan.
2. Describe a master or prototype pension plan.
3. Why is a trust agreement usually not used in conjunction with a group pension plan?
4. To what extent are medical examinations required in a group pension plan?
5. Outline the steps involved in the installation of a pension plan.
6. What is the purpose of obtaining an advance determination letter from the IRS?
7. Describe the nature of the withholding requirements on distributions from qualified retirement plans.
8. Why is it important to continually disclose to plan participants changes in the plan?
9. Describe the general bonding requirements for a pension plan.
10. To what extent do the statutory disclosure requirements apply to plans other than pension plans? Explain.

QUESTIONS FOR DISCUSSION

1. Discuss why it would be desirable to submit all pension plan documents to an insurer's home office prior to plan execution.
2. Discuss how a plan should be announced to employees.
3. Discuss the liability of a fiduciary under the labor provisions of ERISA.

22

Taxation of Distributions

Unquestionably, a major advantage of a qualified pension or profit sharing plan is that an employer's contributions, although currently deductible, will not be considered as taxable income to an employee until they are distributed. Moreover, when a distribution does represent taxable income to the employee or a beneficiary, it may be received under favorable tax circumstances.

Broadly speaking, distributions from a qualified plan are taxable in accordance with the annuity rules of Section 72 of the Internal Revenue Code. If a lump-sum distribution is made after the employee has attained age 59½, however, a special five-year income-averaging device will apply if certain conditions are met.[1] Although these general principles apply regardless of the contingency that gives rise to the distribution, this chapter discusses the tax aspects of a distribution in terms of the contingency that has brought it about. Thus, this chapter briefly explores the tax situation of an employee during employment, as well as the tax situation when distributions are made because of the employee's retirement, death, severance of employment, or disability.

With a view toward achieving some degree of simplicity, the discussion

---

[1] A special transitional rule applies to individuals who reached age 50 before January 1, 1986. Such an employee may elect 10-year averaging under pre-1986 tax rates. Also if the employee participated in the plan prior to 1974, a portion of the distribution may be treated as a long-term capital gain. This issue will be discussed later in this chapter.

has been confined to the federal taxation of typical forms of distribution under plans that have a qualified status when the distributions are made.

TAXATION DURING EMPLOYMENT

Even though employer contributions may be vested fully in an employee under a qualified plan, the employee will not have to report these contributions as taxable income until such time as they are distributed. Thus, employer contributions made on behalf of an employee generally will not be considered as taxable income to the employee during the period of employment.

If the plan includes a life insurance benefit for employees, however, the employee is considered to have received a distribution each year equal to the portion of the employer's contribution (or the portion of the trust earnings) that has been applied during such year to provide the pure insurance in force on the employee's life.[2] The pure insurance is considered to be the excess, if any, of the face amount of the employee's life insurance contract over its cash value. The amount that the employee must include as taxable income for each year is the one-year term insurance rate for the employee's attained age multiplied by the amount of pure insurance involved. This insurance cost often is called the PS 58 cost because the original Treasury Department ruling on the subject was so numbered.

Since the term insurance rate increases each year with the employee's increasing age, this factor tends to increase the amount the employee has to include as taxable income each year. An offsetting factor, however, is the increasing cash value of the contract, which reduces the amount of pure insurance in effect each year. For plans that employ some form of whole life insurance or its equivalent, the insurance cost will tend to rise each year, the reduction in the amount of pure insurance being insufficient to offset the increase in the term insurance rate caused by the employee's advancing age. If the plan is funded with retirement income contracts, the yearly increase in cash value is more substantial and, ultimately, the cash value will exceed the face amount of the contract. Under this type of contract, the insurance cost (after the first few years) will tend to decrease and will ultimately disappear.

Normally, the term insurance rates employed to determine the cost of the employee's insurance coverage are the rates contained in PS 58 (reissued as Revenue Ruling 55–747, as amplified by Revenue Ruling 66–1105). However, the insurer's own rates may be used if they are lower than

---

[2]Note that the amount applied during any year to provide life insurance often covers a period extending into the following year. The employee, however, will not be permitted to apportion this insurance cost between the two years and will be required to include this amount as taxable income in the year in which it is applied, even though the period of protection extends into the subsequent year.

the rates set forth in these rulings. If an employee is insurable only on an extra premium basis and the employer contributes the extra premium necessary to obtain full coverage (and follows the same practice for all employees in similar circumstances), the employee's insurance cost will be determined on the basis of the standard rates, and the extra premium paid because of the rating need not be taken into account.[3]

If employees are making contributions, the plan may provide that an employee's contribution will first be applied toward the cost of insurance coverage. This provision makes it possible to reduce or eliminate having any portion of the employer's contribution considered as taxable income to the employee during employment.

If the death benefit being provided is outside the qualified plan by a nondiscriminatory group term life insurance contract issued to the employer rather than to the trustee of the pension trust, the employee is not required to consider any part of the premium paid by the employer as taxable income, except to the extent that the employee's coverage exceeds $50,000 (or the applicable state maximum for group life insurance, if less than $50,000).[4] However, if the trustee of a qualified trust purchases the group term life insurance instead of the employer, the value of the insurance attributable to employer contributions will be considered as taxable income to the covered employees, regardless of the amounts of coverage involved.

DETERMINATION OF COST BASIS

Before discussing the taxation of benefits, it is important to have a clear idea of the elements that constitute an employee's cost basis (or "investment in the contract"), if any, since the employee's cost basis is an important factor in the taxation of distributions under the plan.

Briefly, Section 72 of the Internal Revenue Code provides that an employee's cost basis includes:

1. The aggregate of any amounts the employee contributed while employed.
2. The aggregate of the prior insurance costs the employee has reported as taxable income. (If the employee has made contributions and the plan provides that employee contributions will first be used to pay any cost of insurance, the employee's reportable income for any year is the excess,

---

[3]If the contract is issued on a graded or graduated death benefit basis, that is, a standard premium is paid but there is a reduction in the amount of insurance due to the extra mortality risk involved, the employee's insurance cost will be lower since less insurance protection is being provided.

[4]If the group term life insurance is being provided under a "discriminatory" program, then even the value of the first $50,000 of discriminatory coverage will be reportable as taxable income by highly paid employees (except to the extent the benefit is paid for with after-tax employee contributions). The definition of "highly paid employees" is the same as the one used for qualified retirement plans discussed in Chapter 4.

if any, of the insurance cost of protection over the amount of the employee's contribution for the year, and not the full cost of insurance protection.)

3. Other contributions made by the employer that already have been taxed to the employee. An example could be where the employer has maintained a nonqualified plan that was later qualified.

There also is provision for the inclusion of other items in an employee's cost basis, such as contributions made by the employer after 1950 but before 1963 while the employee was a resident of a foreign country. For the most part, however, the items listed above will constitute an employee's cost basis in the typical situation.

TAXATION OF RETIREMENT BENEFITS

This section examines the taxation of retirement benefits received in the form of lump-sum distributions as well as distributions in the form of periodic payments. In addition, the penalty tax on excess distributions is discussed.

Lump-Sum Distributions

Distributions to a Retired Employee. If an employee's benefit is paid from a qualified plan in the form of a lump-sum benefit at retirement, the employee's cost basis will be recovered free of income tax. The excess of the distribution over the employee's cost basis will qualify for favorable tax treatment if the following conditions are met:

1. The distribution is made after the employee attains age 59½.
2. The distribution represents the full amount then credited to the employee's account and the entire distribution is received within one of the employee's taxable years.

If these conditions are met, the taxable distribution may qualify for favorable tax treatment. It should be noted, however, that even though a provision exists for the favorable taxation of a lump-sum distribution to an employee who is age 59½ or over, a qualified retirement plan may not make distributions to an employee prior to his or her severance of employment.

An employee who has been a participant for at least five years may elect to treat such a lump-sum distribution under a five-year averaging rule; however, this election can be made only once by the participant. Under this rule, the tax is determined by taking one fifth of the distribution and calculating the ordinary income tax on this portion using single-taxpayer rates and assuming no other income, exemptions, or deductions. The actual tax is then determined by multiplying this amount by five. There is a minimum distribution allowance equal to the lesser of $10,000 or 50 percent of the total taxable amount, reduced by 20 percent of the amount by which the total taxable amount exceeds $20,000. If available, the minimum distribution allowance is subtracted from the total taxable distribution before calculating the tax.

If the employee participated in the plan prior to 1974 and receives a lump-sum distribution prior to 1992, a portion of the lump-sum distribution may be treated as a long-term capital gain, at the employee's discretion. Essentially, this will be determined by dividing the employee's total years of participation into the employee's years of participation prior to 1974, and applying the resulting percentage to the total lump-sum distribution. (Participation is measured in terms of months; however, any fractional year prior to 1974 will be considered a full year.) The result so obtained will be used to determine the portion of the distribution that qualifies for long-term capital gains treatment. In 1987, the entire amount attributable to pre-1974 participation will be eligible for long-term capital gains treatment. In the following years, the percentage decreases in the following manner:

In the Case of Distributions during Calendar Year	The Phase-Out Percentage
1988	95%
1989	75
1990	50
1991	25

The balance of the distribution will be treated as ordinary income under the five-year averaging rule. To determine the amount of tax under the five-year averaging rule, the tax that would be applicable to the total distribution must be calculated as if the entire amount were being taxed under that rule. The actual amount of the tax on the balance treated as ordinary income will be determined by dividing the employee's total years of participation into the employee's years of participation after 1973 and applying the resulting percentage to the tax first determined as though the total distribution were being taxed under the five-year averaging rule.

A special transition rule exists for individuals who attained age 50 before January 1, 1986. Qualifying lump-sum distributions made to these individuals, even after 1992, can continue to utilize the capital gains provisions in effect prior to the Tax Reform Act of 1986 and have the entire pre-1974 portion of the lump-sum distribution taxed as a long-term capital gain with a maximum rate of 20 percent. In addition, five-year averaging can be used on all or on the remaining portion of the lump-sum distributions and can apply to lump-sum distributions received prior to age 59½. An eligible individual making such an election may also elect to choose 10-year (as opposed to 5-year) averaging. If 10-year averaging is chosen however, the individual must use the tax rates in effect for the 1986 tax year. Not more than one election may be made under these transition provisions with respect to an employee, and five-year averaging is lost for any other distribution.

For purposes of determining whether there has been a qualifying lump-sum distribution, all plans of the same type (e.g., defined benefit or defined contribution) and all plans within a given category (pension, profit sharing, or stock bonus) are aggregated and treated as a single plan.

The value of any annuity contract distributed (including contracts distributed during the preceding five years), even though this amount is not taxable currently, must be taken into account in determining the marginal tax rate on the amount of the distribution that is being taxed under the five-year averaging rule. Community property laws are disregarded.

If any part of the distribution consists of employer securities, the employee may elect to defer taxation of any unrealized appreciation of these securities until such time as the securities are sold. Even if such an election is made, however, the net unrealized appreciation will be taken into account for purposes of the excess distribution tax.

Distributions to an Alternate Payee.   Any alternate payee who is the spouse or former spouse of the participant is treated as the distributee of any distribution or payment made to him or her under a QDRO. For purposes of computing the tax on lump-sum distributions, the balance to the credit of an employee does not include any amount payable under a QDRO.

Distributions in the Form of Periodic Payments

Distributions to a Retired Employee.   If a retiring employee receives the distribution in the form of periodic payments, these payments will be taxed to the employee as ordinary income in accordance with the annuity rules of Section 72 of the Internal Revenue Code.

Thus, in a plan where the employee has no cost basis, periodic payments will be subject to tax as ordinary income when received; otherwise the regular annuity rules of Section 72 apply.[5] First, an exclusion ratio

---

[5]For annuities whose starting date was before July 1, 1986, the exclusion ratio approach did not apply to any employee annuity under which employee contributions were recoverable within three years of the annuity starting date. Instead, all payments are excluded from taxable income until the payments received equal the employee's cost basis. Thereafter, the payments are taxed as ordinary income when received.

is determined for the employee. The exclusion ratio is the ratio of the employee's cost basis (investment in the contract) to the employee's "expected return." The resulting percentage represents the portion of each income payment that is excluded from taxable income.

For example, assume that a male employee retiring at age 65 is entitled to an annual income of $10,000 for life (with no death benefit payable in the event of his death after retirement) and that the employee has a cost basis of $50,000. The first step would be to determine the employee's expected return. This would be done by obtaining his life expectancy under the tables included in the regulations and multiplying this figure by the amount of the annual payment. In this example, the employee's life expectancy under these tables would be 20. Multiplying 20 by the annual payment of $10,000 produces an expected return of $200,000. The next step would be to divide the employee's cost basis ($50,000) by his expected return ($200,000), which yields an exclusion ratio of 25 percent. Consequently, $2,500 of each year's payment (25 percent of $10,000) would be excluded from the employee's taxable income, and the balance of $7,500 would be subject to tax as ordinary income.

The total amount excluded under the exclusion ratio is limited to the investment in the contract. If the annuitant dies before his or her entire basis is recovered, the unrecovered amount may be claimed as a deduction in the annuitant's final taxable year.[6]

If payments are made to the employee for a period certain or with a refund feature, the cost basis will be adjusted, when determining the employee's exclusion ratio, to reflect the value of the refund or period certain feature. In the example described above, if the retirement benefit of $10,000 was payable for life with a guarantee that payments would be made for at least 10 years, it would be necessary to reduce the employee's cost basis of $50,000. Under the tables included in the regulations, the value of the 10-year guarantee for a male, age 65, is 6 percent. Consequently, the $50,000 would be reduced by 6 percent ($3,000) and the employee's adjusted cost basis would be $47,000. His exclusion ratio would then be determined in the regular fashion.

If retirement payments are being made under some form of joint and survivor annuity, the expected return, rather than the cost basis, would be adjusted to reflect the value of the survivorship feature.

Distributions to an Alternate Payee. Any alternate payee who is the spouse or former spouse of the participant is treated as the distributee of

---

[6]For annuity starting dates before January 1, 1987, the exclusion ratio, once established, will apply to all future payments regardless of the length of time the employee actually lives and receives payments. If the employee lives longer than the average life expectancy assumed in the tables included in the regulations, a portion of each payment will continue to be received free of income tax, even though by that time the employee's cost basis will have been recovered.

any distribution or payment made under a QDRO.[7] Under IRS regulations to be issued, the investment in the contract must be allocated on a pro rata basis between the present value of such distribution or payment and the present value of all other benefits payable with respect to the participant to which the QDRO relates.

Tax on Excess Distributions

The Tax Reform Act of 1986 imposed a tax equal to 15 percent of the individual's "excess distributions," although the amount of the tax is reduced by the amount (if any) of the 10 percent additional tax on early distributions attributable to such excess distributions. The term *excess distributions* means the aggregate amount of the retirement distributions (including qualified pension plans, individual retirement plans, and tax-deferred annuities) with respect to an individual during a calendar year to the extent such amount exceeds the greater of $150,000 or $112,500 adjusted at the same time and in the same manner as the dollar limitations under Section 415 for defined benefit pension plans. If a distribution qualifies for favorable tax treatment, however, up to five times the normal limit (i.e., up to the greater of $750,000 or $562,500 as indexed) can be paid without imposition of the excise tax.

The following distributions will not be taken into account:

1. Any retirement distribution with respect to an individual made after his or her death.[8]
2. Any retirement distribution with respect to an individual payable to an alternate payee pursuant to a QDRO if includible in income of the alternate payee.
3. Any retirement distribution with respect to an individual that is attributable to the employee's investment in the contract
4. Any retirement distribution to the extent not included in gross income by reason of a rollover contribution (described in Chapter 19).

If, during any calendar year, retirement distributions with respect to any individual are received by the individual and at least one other person, all distributions will be aggregated for purposes of determining the amount of the excess distributions.

The tax will not apply to benefits accrued before August 1, 1986, if the employee elects grandfather protection on tax returns for 1987 or 1988. The election is available only if the accrued benefit as of August 1, 1986

---

[7]For payments prior to October 22, 1986, this treatment also applied to alternate payees other than a spouse or former spouse.

[8]However, there is a corresponding estate tax of an individual dying with "excess retirement accumulations." The details for calculating this amount are provided in IRC Section 4981(d).

exceeds $562,500. If grandfathering protection is elected, the $150,000 and $750,000 threshold amounts are not available to the individual for purposes of determining whether any non-grandfathered distributions are considered to be excess distributions. Furthermore, any grandfathered distributions will be taken into account. In effect, the 15 percent tax will apply to the amount by which the distribution exceeds the greater of: (1) the grandfathered distribution and (2) the applicable threshold amount.

TAXATION OF DEATH BENEFITS

Lump-Sum Distributions

A lump-sum distribution to the employee's beneficiary from a qualified plan made on account of the employee's death after age 59½ (either before or after severance of employment), will entitle the beneficiary to the favorable tax treatment previously described if the distribution represents the full amount then credited to the employee's account and if it is received within one taxable year of the beneficiary.

In determining the net amount of gain subject to tax, the beneficiary's cost basis will be the same as the employee's (i.e., the aggregate of the employee's contributions and any amounts, such as insurance costs, on which the employee has previously been taxed) plus, unless otherwise used, the employee death benefit exclusion provided by Section 101(b) of the Internal Revenue Code up to a maximum of $5,000. It should be noted that in the case of a lump-sum distribution that otherwise qualifies for the favorable tax treatment, this exclusion under Section 101(b) applies regardless of whether the employee's rights were forfeitable or nonforfeitable.[9]

If any portion of the distribution consists of life insurance proceeds and the employee either paid the insurance cost or reported this cost as taxable income, the pure insurance, that is, the difference between the face amount of the contract and its cash value, will pass to the beneficiary free of income tax under Section 101(a) of the Internal Revenue Code. The beneficiary will only have to treat the cash value of the contract, plus any other cash distributions from the plan, as income subject to tax.

The following example illustrates how the death benefit under a typical retirement income contract would be taxed if the employee died before retirement and the face amount of the contract were paid to the beneficiary in a lump sum.

---

[9]Briefly, Section 101(b) permits a beneficiary to exclude from gross income any payments made by the employer of a deceased employee up to a maximum of $5,000. Except as noted, this exclusion is available only to the extent the employee's rights to the amounts were forfeitable immediately prior to death.

Face amount of contract	$25,000
Cash value of contract	11,000
Amount of pure insurance excludable under Section 101(a)	$14,000
Cash value of contract	$11,000
Amount excludable under Section 101(b) (assuming not otherwise utilized)	5,000
Balance subject to income tax	$ 6,000
Beneficiary's cost basis (aggregate of prior insurance costs which employee reported as taxable income)	940
Balance taxable to beneficiary	$ 5,060

The beneficiary would, therefore, receive $19,940 of the total distribution free of income tax, and only $5,060 would be considered as being taxable.

The regulations provide that if the employee did not pay the insurance cost of his or her contract, or did not report the cost of insurance as taxable income, the portion of the insurance proceeds consisting of pure insurance will be considered as taxable income to the beneficiary.

When an employee dies after retirement and after having received periodic payments, a lump-sum death payment to the employee's beneficiary, if it meets the requirements previously noted, will qualify for the favorable tax treatment described. The beneficiary's cost basis, however, will be reduced by any amount that the employee had recovered free from income tax.

Distribution in the Form of Periodic Payments

Death before Retirement.   If death occurs before retirement and the plan provides for the distribution of the employee's death benefit over a period of years (including payments based upon the life expectancy of the beneficiary), these payments will be taxed in accordance with the annuity rules of Section 72 of the Internal Revenue Code.

The beneficiary's cost basis will consist of the amount that would have been the employee's cost basis had the employee lived and received the payments, plus, if applicable, the exclusion allowed under Section 101(b) of the Internal Revenue Code up to the maximum of $5,000. While the question of whether the employee's rights were forfeitable is immaterial for the application of Section 101(b) to a lump-sum distribution from a qualified plan on death, the same is not so when the distribution is in the form of periodic payments. Here, the exclusion under Section 101(b) is applicable only to amounts to which the employee's rights were forfeitable immediately prior to death.

If any part of the periodic payments arises from pure life insurance, the proceeds are divided into two parts:

1. The cash value of the contract immediately before death.
2. The pure insurance (the excess of the face amount of the contract over its cash value).

That portion of each periodic payment attributable to the cash value of the contract will be taxed to the beneficiary under the annuity rules. The balance of each payment that is attributable to the pure insurance element will be treated as insurance proceeds under Section 101(d) of the Internal Revenue Code.

To illustrate, if the face amount of the employee's contract were $25,000 and the proceeds were paid to the beneficiary in 10 annual payments of $3,000 each, the following would be the manner in which the payments would be taxed to the beneficiary, assuming that the contract had a cash value at death of $11,000, that the employee had forfeitable interests to the extent of $5,000, and that the aggregate of the insurance costs that the employee previously reported as taxable income was $940.

The portion of each annual payment of $3,000 attributable to the cash value is $1,320 ($^{11}/_{25}$ of $3,000). The beneficiary's cost basis for this portion would be $5,940 (the $5,000 exclusion under Section 101(b) plus the aggregate insurance costs of $940). The expected return under this portion would be $13,200 (the annual payment of $1,320 multiplied by the 10 years of payments). An exclusion ratio would be determined by dividing the cost basis ($5,940) by the expected return ($13,200). This produces an exclusion ratio of 45 percent, which would be applied to the portion of each annual payment attributable to the cash value of the contract. As a result, $594 (45 percent of $1,320) would be excluded from income each year, and the balance of $726 would be taxed to the beneficiary as ordinary income.

The portion of each annual payment of $3,000 attributable to the pure insurance is $1,680 ($^{14}/_{25}$ of $3,000). Of this amount, $1,400 ($^{1}/_{10}$ of $14,000) is excludable from gross income as Section 101 proceeds, and only the balance of $280 would be taxable as ordinary income to the beneficiary. A beneficiary of the employee would include $1,006 ($280 plus $726) as ordinary income each year, and $1,994 of each annual payment would be received free of income tax.

Death after Retirement.   The taxation of payments to the beneficiary of an employee who dies after retirement and after periodic payments have begun depends upon whether the employee had a cost basis (and if so, whether it had been recovered by the employee), as well as upon the method of payment involved. If the employee had no cost basis, each payment would be considered as taxable income to the beneficiary as received. However, where the payments are being continued under a joint and survivor annuity form, the exclusion ratio established when the annuity became effective would apply until the unrecovered investment in the contract is eliminated.[10]

Tax on Excess Accumulations.   Because payments to beneficiaries are exempt from the tax on excess distributions described earlier in this chapter, an equivalent estate tax is imposed on excess retirement accumulations.

TAXATION OF SEVERANCE-OF-EMPLOYMENT BENEFITS

For the most part, the discussion in this chapter on the taxation of distributions at retirement is equally applicable to the taxation of distributions on severance of employment. If the distribution is in the form of periodic payments, the taxation of payments to the employee will be governed by the annuity rules after taking the employee's cost basis, if any, into account. So, also, a lump-sum distribution, provided that the necessary conditions are met, may qualify for the favorable tax treatment described. However, a penalty tax on early distributions may apply.

The Tax Reform Act of 1986 added an additional 10 percent tax on any taxable amounts received before age 59½ from a qualified retirement plan. The additional tax does not apply in the case of death, disability, or early retirement under plan provisions after age 55. Exceptions are also granted for:

1. Distributions that are part of a series of substantially equal periodic payments made for the life (or life expectancy) of the employee or the joint lives (or joint life expectancies) of the employee and his or her beneficiary.
2. Distributions used to pay medical expenses to the extent the expenses exceed 7.5 percent of adjusted gross income.
3. Certain distributions made before January 1, 1990 from an ESOP.
4. Payments to alternate payees pursuant to a qualified domestic relations order (QDRO).

If the distribution is in the form of a life insurance contract, its cash value less the employee's cost basis, if any, will be considered as taxable income in the year in which the employee receives the contract, even though the contract is not then surrendered for its cash value. The distribu-

---

[10]This assumes an annuity starting date after December 31, 1986; otherwise, the tax treatment described in footnote 6 would be operative.

tion may qualify for favorable treatment if all necessary conditions are met. On the other hand, the employee may avoid any current tax liability by transferring this amount, within 60 days, to a qualified individual retirement savings plan (described in Chapter 19). The employee also may avoid any current tax liability by making an irrevocable election, within 60 days of the distribution, to convert the contract to a nontransferable annuity that contains no element of life insurance.[11] If the employee would otherwise receive a cash distribution but has the option under the plan of electing, within 60 days, to receive a nontransferable annuity in lieu of the cash payment, he or she may also avoid current tax liability by making a timely exercise of this option.

If current tax liability is avoided by such an election, the employee will not pay any tax until payments are made from the annuity contract. At that time, the payments will be considered as ordinary income under the annuity rules.

If the distribution is in the form of an annuity contract, the tax situation will be governed by the date of issue of the contract. If issued after December 31, 1962, the distribution will be treated exactly the same as the distribution of a life insurance contract unless the annuity is endorsed or rewritten on a nontransferable basis within the 60 days allowed. If issued before January 1, 1963, the employee will not have to include any amount as taxable income until payments are actually received. At that time, payments will be considered as ordinary income under the annuity rules.

TAXATION OF DISABILITY BENEFITS

Many qualified pension plans provide for a monthly benefit if an employee becomes totally and permanently disabled. Typically, the benefit is payable for life (subject to the continuance of the disability), but only for a disability that occurs after the employee has attained some minimum age such as 50 or 55, or has completed some minimum period of service such as 10 years. The benefit may or may not be related to the employee's accrued or projected pension. Frequently, the amount of the benefit will be adjusted if disability continues until the employee attains the normal retirement age specified in the plan.

---

[11]The regulations spell out what is meant by nontransferable, and the language of the regulations has been used as a guide by many insurers in endorsing their contracts. Such an endorsement might read approximately as follows:

This contract is not transferable except to the ABC Insurance Company. It may not be sold, assigned, discounted, or pledged as collateral for a loan or as security for the performance of an obligation or for any other purposes to any person other than this Company; provided, however, that notwithstanding the foregoing, the owner may designate a beneficiary to receive the proceeds payable upon death, and may elect a joint and survivor annuity.

Generally speaking, disability benefits of this type will be taxed to the employee in accordance with the annuity rules of Section 72 of the Internal Revenue Code; however, such disability benefits may qualify for the retirement income tax credit provided for in the Code.

QUESTIONS FOR REVIEW

1. What factors are included in determining an employee's cost basis in a pension plan?
2. Under what condition will a lump-sum distribution qualify for favorable tax treatment?
3. What is the five-year averaging rule?
4. How are the pension distributions in the form of periodic payments taxed when the employee has no cost basis in the plan?
5. How will the answer to the previous question change if the employee has a cost basis in the plan?
6. How are death benefits taxed for income tax purposes when paid in the form of a lump-sum distribution?
7. How are death benefits payable in the form of periodic payments taxed for income tax purposes if death takes place before retirement?
8. How will the answer to the previous question change if death takes place after retirement?
9. How are severance-of-employment benefits taxed?
10. Explain the taxation of disability benefits.

QUESTIONS FOR DISCUSSION

1. Discuss how the Tax Reform Act of 1986 changes are likely to influence employees' choices between receiving retirement distributions as a lump sum versus periodic payments.
2. Discuss the likely effect of the new excess distribution excise tax on plan design.
3. Discuss the likely effect of the new early distribution penalty tax on plan design.

23

Plan Termination Insurance

Prior to 1974, some pension plans, mostly small, had terminated, causing many participants of such plans to lose promised benefits. To correct this situation, Title IV of ERISA established a plan termination insurance program to provide insurance benefits through the establishment of the nonprofit, tax-exempt Pension Benefit Guaranty Corporation (PBGC). The basic purpose of the PBGC is to encourage the continuation and maintenance of voluntary private retirement plans to provide for the timely and uninterrupted payment of pension benefits to participants and their beneficiaries.[1]

The PBGC administers four "revolving funds" that insure the pension benefit promises made to pension plan participants in single- and multiemployer defined benefit plans under the conditions and within the limits set forth in ERISA.[2] Two of the funds are applicable to single-employer plans and two to multiemployer plans. For single-employer plans, one fund is used to assure payment of basic pension benefits, while the other is used for nonbasic benefits if any are guaranteed by the PBGC. The same arrangement applies to the two funds established to protect participants in multi-

---

[1] ERISA Sec. 4022.

[2] Robert Bildersee, *Pension Regulation Manual* (New York: Warren, Gorham & Lamont, 1979), p. 138.

employer plans.[3] Therefore, the PBGC actually is an insurance company that can intervene in the operation of retirement plans in the private sector should a major risk such as deficiencies in the funding standard account occur in plans covered by the PBGC.

PLANS COVERED

Plan termination insurance covers almost all qualified defined benefit pension plans in addition to nonqualified plans that have, in practice, met the requirements of qualified plans for five years.[4] Coverage is mandatory, as is the payment of premiums. Among the classes of plans specifically excluded from coverage are:[5]

Individual account plans (e.g., money purchase pension plans, profit sharing plans, thrift and savings plans, and stock bonus plans).

Government plans.

Certain church plans other than those that have voluntarily opted for coverage.

Certain plans established by fraternal societies to which no employer contributions are made.

Plans that do not provide for employer contributions after September 2, 1974.

Nonqualified deferred compensation plans established for select groups of management or highly compensated employees.

Plans established outside of the United States for nonresident aliens.

So-called excess benefit plans established and maintained primarily to pay benefits or accrue contributions for a limited group of highly paid employees in excess of the Section 415 limits (described in Chapter 6).

Plans established and maintained exclusively for "substantial owners," meaning proprietors, partners with a greater than 10 percent interest in the capital profits of a partnership, or shareholders of a corporation owning,

---

[3]The primary focus of this book is on single-employer pension plans. Therefore, the emphasis in this chapter is on how plan termination insurance affects single-employer pension plans. However, ERISA, and more significantly the Multiemployer Pension Plan Amendments Act (MEPPAA) of 1980, had major effects upon the Pension Benefit Guaranty Corporation's jurisdiction over multiemployer pension plans, employer liabilities, and the administrative practices of trustees. For a good discussion of MEPPAA see *The Multiemployer Pension Plan Amendments Act of 1980 Summary and Observations* (Louisville, Ky.: Meidenger, Inc., 1981). The complex law has many implications for almost all aspects of multiemployer plans, especially concerning plan termination insurance and employer liabilities.

[4]ERISA Sec. 4021(a).

[5]ERISA Sec. 4021(b).

directly or indirectly, more than 10 percent in value of either the voting stock or of all the stock of the corporation.

Plans of international organizations exempt from tax under the International Organization Immunities Act.

Plans maintained only to comply with workers' compensation, unemployment compensation, or disability insurance laws.

Plans established and maintained by labor organizations as described in Section 501(c)(5) of the Internal Revenue Code that do not provide for employer contributions after September 2, 1974.

Plans that are defined benefit plans to the extent that they are treated as individual account plans.

Any plan established and maintained by professional service employers, provided that there are not, at any time after September 2, 1974, more than 25 active participants in the plan.

The plans of trades or businesses (whether or not incorporated) that are under common control are treated as though the employees are employed by a single employer, and all such trades or businesses are treated as a single employer. This concept has great significance in determining plan termination insurance coverage, the existence of "reportable events," reporting and premium payment obligations, and liabilities on plan termination.

PLAN TERMINATION DEFINED

The termination of a pension plan should be a clearly identifiable event. Otherwise, it may be difficult to assess if a termination has occurred and, if so, when. Establishing the exact date of termination is important to all parties concerned—the plan sponsor, the plan participants and beneficiaries, and the PBGC. A plan termination can be voluntary or involuntary. However, the PBGC will not proceed with a voluntary termination of a plan if it would violate the terms and conditions of an existing collective bargaining agreement.[6]

Voluntary Plan Termination

A single-employer plan may be terminated voluntarily only in a standard termination or a distress termination.

---

[6]It should be noted that this will not limit the PBGC's authority to proceed with an involuntary termination as described later in this chapter.

Standard Termination.   A single-employer plan may terminate under a standard termination if, among other things, the plan is sufficient for benefit liabilities (determined as of the termination date) when the final distribution of assets occurs. Benefit liabilities include all fixed and contingent liabilities to plan participants and beneficiaries, including liability for benefits in effect on the date of the termination that are not protected by the anti-cutback rules.

Provided the PBGC has not issued a notice of noncompliance and the plan is sufficient for benefit liabilities when the final distribution occurs, the plan administrator must distribute the plan's assets in accordance with the requirements for allocation of assets under ERISA Section 4044 (described below).

Distress Termination.   With the exception of certain insurance contract plans, for a single-employer plan to terminate under a distress termination, the plan administrator must provide the PBGC with certification by an enrolled actuary of:

1. The amount (as of the proposed termination date) of the current value of the assets of the plan.
2. The actuarial present value of the benefit liabilities under the plan.
3. Whether the plan is sufficient for benefit liabilities.
4. The actuarial present value of guaranteed benefits.
5. Whether the plan is sufficient for guaranteed benefits.

After receiving this information, the PBGC must then determine whether the necessary distress criteria have been satisfied. Basically, these criteria are met if each person who is a contributing sponsor or a member of the sponsor's controlled group meets the requirements of any of the following:

1. Liquidation in bankruptcy or insolvency proceedings.
2. Reorganization in bankruptcy or insolvency proceedings.[7]
3. Termination required to enable payment of debts while staying in business or to avoid unreasonably burdensome pension costs caused by a declining work force.

If the PBGC determines that the requirements for a distress termination are met, it will either determine (1) that the plan is sufficient for guaranteed benefits or that it is unable to make a determination on the basis of the available information, or (2) that the plan is sufficient for benefit liabilities or that it is unable to make a determination on the basis of the available

---

[7]For this requirement to be met, a bankruptcy court must determine that, unless the plan is terminated, the sponsor will be unable to pay all its debts pursuant to a plan of reorganization and will be unable to continue in business outside the Chapter 11 reorganization process.

information. The plan administrator will be notified of the decision and one of the following types of terminations will be carried out[8]:

1. In any case in which the PBGC determines that the plan is sufficient for benefit liabilities, the plan administrator must distribute the plan's assets in the same manner as described for a standard termination.
2. In any case in which the PBGC determines that the plan is sufficient for guaranteed benefits, but is unable to determine that the plan is sufficient for benefit liabilities, the plan administrator must distribute the plan's assets in the same manner as described for a standard termination.
3. In any case in which the PBGC determines that it is unable to determine that the plan is sufficient for guaranteed benefits, PBGC will commence proceedings as though an involuntary termination (described below) were taking place.

The plan administrator must meet certain requirements during the interim period from the time the PBGC is notified to the time a sufficiency determination is made. Essentially the administrator must:

1. Refrain from distributing assets or taking any other actions to carry out the proposed termination.
2. Pay benefits attributable to employer contributions, other than death benefits, only in the form of an annuity.
3. Not use plan assets to purchase irrevocable commitments to provide benefits from an insurer.
4. Continue to pay all benefit liabilities under the plan, but, commencing on the proposed termination date, limit the payment of benefits under the plan to those benefits guaranteed by the PBGC or to which assets are required to be allocated under Section 4044 (described below).

When two organizations merge, the resulting single plan does not result in a termination if the new merged organization assumes responsibility for the plan. Also, under ERISA, a pension plan may not be merged or consolidated with another pension plan, or have its assets transferred to another plan, unless each participant in the prior plan is credited in the successor plan with a benefit at least as great as that which he or she would have received had the old plan terminated.[9]

The changing or amending of a plan from a defined benefit plan to a defined contribution plan is considered as a voluntary termination for insurance purposes. Therefore, unless the requirements for a standard termination or a distress termination are met, such conversions are not allowed.

---

[8]ERISA Section 4041(c)(3).
[9]IRC Sec. 401(a)(12)

Involuntary Plan Termination

The PBGC may institute termination proceedings in a U.S. district court in the jurisdiction where the employer does business if it finds that (a) the plan does not comply with the minimum funding standards of the Internal Revenue Code; (b) the plan is unable to pay benefits when due; (c) within the preceding 24 months, and for a reason other than death, a distribution of $10,000 or more has been made to a participant who is the substantial owner of the sponsoring firm and that following the distribution there are unfunded liabilities; or (d) the eventual loss to the PBGC for the plan may be expected to increase unreasonably if the plan is not terminated. Moreover, the PBGC is required to institute proceedings to terminate a single-employer plan whenever it determines that the plan does not have assets available to pay benefits that are currently due under the terms of the plan. The PBGC may decide not to seek involuntary termination, even if one of the conditions for action has occurred, if it deems that it would be in the best interests of those involved not to force termination of the plan.

Reportable Events

The administrator of any covered pension plan is required to report to the PBGC certain events that may indicate possible termination of a pension plan. These reportable events are: (a) inability of the plan to pay benefits when due; (b) a failure to meet the minimum funding standards; (c) determination that a complete or partial plan termination for tax purposes has occurred; (d) a merger or consolidation of the plan with another plan; (e) loss of qualified status under the Internal Revenue Code; (f) a plan amendment that decreases the benefits of the participants; (g) if the unfunded vested benefit is at least $250,000, a decrease in active participants of more than 20 percent of the number at the beginning of the plan year, or 25 percent of the number at the beginning of the previous plan year; (h) a distribution of $10,000 or more within a 24-month period to a substantial owner, for reasons other than death, that creates or increases unfunded vested liabilities; and (i) any other event the PBGC designates as reportable.[10]

Date of Termination

For purposes of Title IV of ERISA, the termination date of a single-employer plan is one of the following:

1. In the case of a plan terminated in a standard termination, the termination date proposed in the notice of intent to terminate.

---

[10]ERISA Sec. 4043 and PBGC regulations [29 CFP Part 2615].

2. In the case of a plan terminated in a distress termination, the date established by the plan administrator and agreed to by the PBGC.
3. In the case of an involuntary termination, the date established by the PBGC and agreed to by the plan administrator.
4. In the case of distress or involuntary termination in any case in which no agreement is reached between the plan administrator and the PBGC, the date established by the court.

The date on which the termination of a plan becomes effective is significant for a number of reasons. It not only establishes the date the PBGC assumes legal obligation for the plan's benefits, but also establishes the date for the determination of the employer's possible contingent liability for unfunded benefits (described below). The effective termination date also is important to the participant. It fixes the date on which benefit accruals cease, vesting schedule position is determined, and when the phase-in of insurance coverage stops.

Restoration of Plan

If it appears that the pension plan could be continued, even though plan termination proceedings have begun, the PBGC may halt the proceedings and take whatever action is necessary to restore the plan.[11]

BENEFITS INSURED

The PBGC guarantees payment of all the basic benefits of a terminated pension plan that had become nonforfeitable (or vested) by the terms of the plan up to the limits provided by the law. The limit in 1987 was $1,857.95 per month.

The PBGC can provide insurance coverage for both *basic* and *nonbasic* benefits. Coverage of basic benefits is mandatory, whereas insurance of nonbasic benefits is optional with the PBGC. The two types of coverage are to be kept separate through the use of separate trust funds discussed previously.[12]

Guaranteed versus Nonguaranteed Benefits

A guaranteed benefit is any nonforfeitable retirement benefit and any death, survivor, or disability benefit either owed or in payment status at date of plan termination.

---

[11]ERISA Section 4047.

[12]For a good discussion of basic and nonbasic benefits see Jeffrey D. Mamorsky, *Pension and Profit Sharing Plans: A Basic Guide* (New York: Executive Enterprises Publications, 1977), pp. 212–13.

A guaranteed benefit is that portion of the normal retirement benefit payable in level monthly installments for the remaining lifetime of the participant. This definition excludes lump-sum and special supplemental monthly benefits provided under some retirement plans to encourage early retirement or to ease the participant's transition from active to retired status. The PBGC only pays benefits on a monthly basis, even though the terminated plan may have provided for the participant to take some or all of the normal retirement benefit in a lump sum.[13]

The normal retirement benefit is considered the guaranteed benefit regardless of the participant's age at the time the income commences. Benefits of participants who elected early retirement prior to plan termination are insured up to the applicable limits.

Death and disability benefits not in payment status are considered nonguaranteed benefits and are not entitled to PBGC insurance protection. If, at the time of plan termination, pending death claims payable in a lump sum exist, the PBGC will honor such claims and pay them in a lump sum.

Nonguaranteed benefits include death and disability benefits not treated as guaranteed benefits, monthly retirement benefits in excess of the PBGC monthly limit, medical insurance premiums and benefits, and other more unusual benefits. Though there has been much discussion, no arrangements have been made by the PBGC to insure nonguaranteed benefits.

Limitation on Amount of Monthly Benefits

There is a limit on the amount of monthly guaranteed benefits insured by the PBGC. The amount is adjusted annually to reflect changes in the social security taxable wage base. The original limit was $750 per month, but for plans terminated in 1987 the limit increased to $1,857.95 per month. The limit is in terms of a single life annuity commencing at age 65, and without a refund feature. If the benefit is payable at a lower age, it is reduced by actuarial factors denoted by the PBGC. The benefit is not actuarially increased when the participant retires at an age later than 65.

The guaranteed monthly benefit of a participant cannot be greater than his or her average gross monthly income during the five consecutive years of highest earnings (or, if the period is shorter, the time during which he or she was an active participant in the plan).

New or Amended Plans and Benefits

To prevent possible abuses, the insurance covers guaranteed benefits, provided those benefits have been in effect under the provisions of the plan for

---

[13]However, the PBGC may pay in a lump sum or under optional annuity forms the participant's mandatory contributions under a pension plan if the participant so elects and such payment is allowed under the provisions of the plan.

60 months or longer at the time of plan termination.[14] If benefits are attributable to a plan amendment or to a new plan adopted, the benefits attributable to that amendment or new plan are guaranteed only to the extent of the greater of 20 percent of the amount of such increased or new benefit multiplied by the number of years (up to five) that the plan or amendment has been in effect, or $20 per month multiplied by the number of years (up to five) that the plan or amendment has been in effect.[15]

ALLOCATION OF ASSETS ON PLAN TERMINATION

Priority Categories

ERISA provided a procedure for allocating the assets of a terminated plan between the insured and noninsured benefits, since not all benefits are insured. On termination, the assets of a plan must be allocated in the following order of priorities:[16]

1. Employees' voluntary contributions.
2. Employees' mandatory contributions.
3. Annuity payments in pay status at least three years before the termination of the plan (including annuity payments that would have been in pay status for at least three years if the employee had retired then) based on the provisions of the plan in effect during the five years before termination of the plan under which the benefit would be the least.
4. All other insured benefits. This includes benefits that would be insured except for the special limitation with respect to a "substantial owner"; also, the aggregate benefit limitation for individuals does not apply.
5. All other vested, but uninsured, benefits.
6. All other benefits under the plan.

An allocation within a priority category that cannot be covered in full is settled on a pro rata basis, except that subpriorities within a priority category may be provided for by the plan. If there are any assets remaining after satisfaction of all liabilities for accrued benefits, they may be paid to the employer if provided for by the plan provisions.

Reversion of Residual Assets to the Employer

In general, the funds in a qualified pension plan may not be used for purposes other than the exclusive benefit of employees or their beneficiaries

---

[14]ERISA Sec. 4022(b)(8).
[15]Mamorsky, *Pension and Profit Sharing Plans*, p. 212.
[16]ERISA Sec. 4044.

prior to the termination of the plan and the satisfaction of all liabilities. However, with the exception of pension plan assets attributable to employee contributions, employers may recapture any residual assets of a terminated single-employer defined benefit pension plan if the following conditions are satisfied:

1. All liabilities of the plan to participants and their beneficiaries have been satisfied.
2. The distribution does not contravene any provision of law.
3. The plan provides for such a distribution in these circumstances

Residual assets are equal to the plan funds remaining after satisfaction of all liabilities.[17]

The Tax Reform Act of 1986 imposed a tax of 10 percent of the amount of employer reversions from a qualified plan. The tax will not be imposed on certain amounts distributed to or on behalf of employees (or their beneficiaries). An exception to the tax also exists for certain reversions transferred from a qualified plan to an ESOP prior to January 1, 1989.

The PBGC, Treasury Department, and the Department of Labor have issued the following joint implementation guidelines on asset reversions:

1. An employer may not recover any surplus assets until it has fully vested all participants' benefits and has purchased and distributed annuity contracts.
2. If employees are offered lump-sum payments in lieu of future pensions, the amount of the lump-sum distribution must fairly reflect the value of the pension to the individual.
3. An employer that terminates a sufficiently funded defined benefit pension plan may establish a new defined benefit plan covering the same group of employees, granting past service credit for the period during which an employee was covered by the terminated plan. This is known as a termination/reestablishment and the successor plan is exempt from the five-year phase-in of benefit guarantees that applies to newly established plans.
4. Spinoff/terminations[18] will not be recognized and any attempt to recover surplus assets will be treated as a diversion of assets for a purpose other than the exclusive benefit of employees and beneficiaries unless the

---

[17]Restrictions on reversions from recently amended plans are specified in ERISA Section 4044(d)(2). The allocation of residual assets attributable to employee contributions is described in ERISA Section 4044(d)(3).

[18]Under a spinoff/termination, the active participants (and their liabilities) are spun off from the original defined benefit plan. Assets are then transferred from the original plan to the new plan in an amount at least equal to the active participants' liabilities. The original plan, which at this point covers only retired and terminated employees, is then terminated and annuities are used to satisfy the plan's obligations.

employees receive timely notice of the event and the following conditions are satisfied:

   a. The benefits of all employees must be fully vested and nonforfeitable as of the date of the termination. This also applies to the benefits covered by the ongoing plan.

   b. All accrued benefits must be provided for by the purchase of annuity contracts.

5. In the case of a spinoff/termination and a termination/reestablishment, attempts to recover surplus assets will be treated as a diversion of assets for a purpose other than the exclusive benefit of employees and beneficiaries unless the funding method for the ongoing plans is to be changed by modifying the amortization bases.[19]

6. An employer may not engage in either a termination/reestablishment or spinoff/termination transaction, involving reversion of assets, any earlier than 15 years following any such transaction.

LIABILITIES ON PLAN TERMINATION

Distributee Liability-Recapture

When a plan terminates, the termination trustee is authorized to recover for the benefit of the pension plan certain payments received by a participant within the three-year period prior to plan termination. The "recoverable amount" is the sum of all payments made to the participant in excess of $10,000 made during any consecutive 12-month period within three years before termination or, if lesser, the amount he or she would have received as a monthly benefit under a single-life annuity commencing at age 65.[20] Payments to a disabled participant and payments made after or on account of the death of a participant are not subject to recovery. PBGC can totally or partially waive any amount otherwise entitled to be recaptured whenever recapture would result in substantial economic hardship to a participant or his or her beneficiaries.

Employer Liability

In any case in which a single-employer plan is terminated in a distress termination or an involuntary termination is instituted by the PBGC, any person who is, on the termination date, a contributing sponsor of the plan or a member of such a contributing sponsor's controlled group will incur a

---

[19]The modification must be in accordance with IRC Section 412(b)(4). Details of the modification are provided in PBGC News Rel. 84-23.

[20]ERISA Sec. 4045.

liability under Section 4062 of ERISA. This liability consists of two components:

1. The liability to the PBGC.
2. The liability to the Section 4042 trustee (described below).

Although special rules pertain to the case in which it is discovered that the plan is unable to pay guaranteed benefits after the authorized commencement of termination,[21] the following section defines the rules generally applying to the two components of the sponsor's liability and the required means of payment.

Liability to the PBGC.   The liability to the PBGC consists of the total amount of the unfunded benefit liabilities (as of the termination date) to all participants and beneficiaries under the plan, together with interest (at a reasonable rate) calculated from the termination date in accordance with regulations prescribed by the PBGC.

The total amount of the liability is paid to the PBGC, which, in turn, pays out a portion of unfunded benefit liabilities in excess of the unfunded guaranteed benefits based on the total value of the PBGC's recovery with respect to the total liability of the employer. Amounts paid to participants are allocated in accordance with Section 4044 as described on page 411.

The liability to the PBGC is generally due as of the termination date. The PBGC and any person liable for payment may also agree to alternative arrangements for the satisfaction of liability.

Liability to the Section 4042 Trustee.   The liability to a Section 4042 trustee for the sponsoring employer and each member of its controlled group consists of the outstanding balance (accumulated with interest from the termination date) of:

1. The accumulated funding deficiency of the plan, modified to include the amount of any increase that would result if all pending applications for waiver of the minimum funding standard account and for extension of the amortization period were denied and if no additional contributions were made.
2. The amount of waived funding deficiencies.
3. The amount of decreases in the minimum funding standard account.

Determination of Net Worth.   In general, the collective net worth, for purposes of determining the liability to the PBGC, consists of the sum of

---

[21]ERISA Sections 4062(b)(1)(B).

the individual net worths of all persons who have individual net worths greater than zero, and are contributing sponsors of the terminated plan or members of their controlled groups. The net worth of a person is determined on whatever basis best reflects, in the determination of the PBGC, the current status of the person's operations and prospects at the time chosen for determining the net worth of the person. The net worth is increased by the amount of any transfers of assets made by the pension that are determined by the PBGC to be improper under the circumstance. Determinations of net worth are made as of a day chosen by PBGC during the 120-day period ending with the termination date. Net worth is computed without regard to termination liabilities.

Liability of Substantial and Multiple Employers.   A liability applies to all employers, other than multiemployer plans terminating after April 29, 1980, who maintain a plan under which more than one employer makes contributions. The liability also attaches to all employers who, at any time within the five plan years preceding the date of plan termination, made contributions under the plan. The liability is allocated among the employers in the ratio of their required contributions for the last five years prior to termination, except that the 30 percent of net worth exposure applies separately as to each corporation.

If the withdrawing employer prefers, a bond may be furnished to the PBGC in an amount not exceeding 150 percent of its liability. The bond must be issued by a corporate surety acceptable on federal bonds on the authority granted by the secretary of the treasury.

PBGC Lien for Employer Liability.   To the extent an employer liability is not satisfied and the amount does not exceed 30 percent of the collective net worth of the sponsor and its controlled group, the amount of the liability (including interest) is a lien in favor of the PBGC upon all property and rights to property, whether real or personal, belonging to the employer. The lien is in the nature of a tax lien that supersedes the liens of other creditors of the corporation.

PREMIUMS

For plan years beginning after 1987, the single-employer flat-rate per-participant premium is $16. An additional premium of $6 per $1,000 of unfunded vested benefits, with a maximum per-participant additional premium of $34, is also required of underfunded plans.[22] If an employer made

---

[22]For purposes of determining the value of vested benefits, the interest rate is equal to 80 percent of the yield per annum on 30-year Treasury securities for the month preceding the month in which the plan year begins.

the maximum deductible contributions to the plan for one or more of the five plan years preceding the first plan year beginning after 1987, the cap on the additional premium is reduced by $3 for each plan year for which such contributions were made.[23] The contributing sponsor or plan administrator must pay the premiums imposed by the PBGC. If the contributing sponsor of any plan is a member of a controlled group, each member is jointly and severally liable for any premiums.

SECURITY RULES FOR UNDERFUNDED PLANS

If a single-employer defined benefit plan adopts an amendment which increases current liability under the plan and the funded current liability percentage of the plan in the year in which the amendment takes effect is less than 60 percent (including the amount of the unfunded current liability[24] under the plan attributable to the plan amendment), the contributing sponsor and members of the controlled group must provide security (e.g., a bond) to the plan. The amount of the security required is the excess over $10 million of the lesser of:

1. the amount of additional plan assets which would be necessary to increase the funded current liability percentage under the plan to 60 percent, including the amount of the unfunded current liability under the plan attributable to the plan amendment, or
2. the amount of the increase in current liability under the plan attributable to the plan amendment.

QUESTIONS FOR REVIEW

1. In general, what types of pension plans are covered by plan termination insurance?
2. What classes of pension plans are specifically excluded from plan termination insurance coverage?
3. How is the PBGC kept apprised of events affecting plan solvency or operations that may justify an involuntary termination?
4. Explain the significance of the date of termination for a pension plan.
5. Explain the definition of a basic benefit with respect to: (a) early retirement incentives and (b) death and disability benefits.
6. Explain how insurance coverage is phased in for benefits that have been in effect for less than five years.

---

[23] This special rule only applies for the first 5 plan years the premium is in effect.

[24] In computing unfunded current liability, the unamortized portion of the unfunded old liability amount as of the close of the plan year is not taken into account.

7. Why is it necessary to establish priority classes for pension benefits at the time of termination?

8. Is the trustee authorized to recapture benefit payments already made prior to the occurrence of the plan termination? Explain.

9. Must the sponsor of a terminated plan reimburse the PBGC for any loss that it incurs in meeting the benefit obligations of the terminated plan?

10. What condition must be satisfied before a plan sponsor is able to recapture excess assets from a pension plan?

QUESTIONS FOR DISCUSSION

1. Discuss the public policy issues involved in the termination of overfunded defined benefit pension plans.

2. In 1987, the PBGC adopted a new variable rate premium structure that would include a premium component based on the amount of a defined benefit pension plan's unfunded vested benefits. Discuss the relative merits of this approach.

3. Many people have suggested that the PBGC should switch to a risk-related premium structure in which the premium a sponsor pays for plan termination insurance is based on the relative likelihood that the plan will terminate as well as the potential magnitude of the claim. Discuss the relative merits of this approach.

24

Executive Retirement Arrangements

U p to this point, the discussion in this text has been confined, for the most part, to tax-sheltered qualified retirement plans of deferred compensation. Under the Code such plans must be nondiscriminatory in order to maintain their tax-favored status; that is, they must not discriminate in favor of highly compensated employees. Because situations arise in which an employer may wish to discriminate in favor of an executive or group of executives in their retirement benefits, executive retirement arrangements came into existence. Such plans are known as supplemental executive retirement plans (SERPs) or nonqualified deferred compensation agreements. In this chapter, the discussion of these plans is limited primarily to plans subject to the reporting and disclosure requirements of ERISA that are maintained primarily to provide deferred compensation to a select group of management or highly compensated employees.[1]

SOURCE: The authors wish to express their thanks to David L. Hewitt, F.S.A., Partner of Hay Associates. For an excellent discussion of executive retirement arrangements see David L. Hewitt, "Executive Retirement Plans," in *The Handbook of Employee Benefits*, ed. Jerry S. Rosenbloom (Homewood, Ill.: Dow Jones-Irwin, 1984), pp. 628–41, on which portions of this chapter are based.

[1] As a result of the Revenue Act of 1978, it is important to distinguish the type of employer involved in a deferred compensation plan. Different rules apply depending upon whether the employer is a private taxpayer, state or local government, or a tax-exempt organization. A private employer is one other than a state or local government or an organization exempt from tax under Code 501. This chapter is only concerned with nonqualified deferred compensation plans of private employers.

AN OVERVIEW

High taxes, inflation, and a desire to attract and retain key employees make supplemental executive retirement plans and deferred compensation/salary continuation agreements attractive to the highly compensated executive and certain employers. ERISA placed a ceiling on the amount of retirement income an individual may receive from a qualified pension plan.[2]

An executive retirement arrangement can be used to provide retirement income in excess of such limitations, or perhaps more commonly to offset the inadequacies to executives of a broad-based qualified retirement plan. Also, such an arrangement can provide for payments in the event of death or disability, in addition to retirement.

An executive retirement arrangement can be attractive to the employer as well as to the employee. It is a way for the employer to attract key people to the business. It helps to motivate and reward existing employees and ties them to the business with what has been called "golden handcuffs." It is selective and flexible — selective because the employer has the advantage of choosing those employees who will receive the benefit, and flexible because the plan can be designed to meet the needs of the parties.

Such plans are generally contractual arrangements between the employer and the employee (or independent contractor) under which the employer promises to make specific payments to the employee (or beneficiary) upon the occurrence of a specified future event such as retirement, disability, or death. Under some arrangements, the employee promises to render services to the employer in the future.

The classic plan is unfunded, so as to avoid ERISA's benefit requirements and unfavorable income tax treatment. The employee is an unsecured creditor of the employer and has no rights to any specific asset even though the employer might use a funding vehicle (such as insurance) to set aside amounts to meet its future obligation under the agreement.[3] When the plan is employee motivated, a reduction in the employee's salary is required. There is no such requirement, however, when the plan is employer motivated and set up as an additional employee benefit. In either

---

[2]The original ERISA legislation limited the maximum benefits payable under a qualified defined benefit plan to the lesser of 100 percent of an employee's three-year average pay or $75,000 (adjusted for cost-of-living changes) and an annual addition under a qualified defined contribution plan to the lesser of 25 percent or $25,000. In 1982 these adjusted figures were $136,425 and $45,475, respectively. The Tax Equity and Fiscal Responsibility Act of 1982 (TEFRA) rolled back these dollar limits to $90,000 for defined benefit plans and $30,000 for defined contribution plans beginning in 1983. Under the Tax Reform Act of 1986, the $30,000 limit will not be increased until the defined benefit limit reaches $120,000. Moreover, a new $200,000 pay limit was created. See Chapter 6 for a detailed discussion.

[3]However, the IRS has ruled in private letter rulings (8113107, 8329070, and 8325100) that under certain circumstances an employer's promise can be funded, without adverse tax consequences to the employee, by providing the employee with a nonforfeitable interest in a "rabbi trust." Under a rabbi trust, the employer creates a trust that is subject to the claims of the employer's creditors but cannot be reached by the employer.

case, a common objective is the postponement of income taxation on the benefits until they actually are received upon retirement, disability, or death.

Many practicing employee benefit specialists make a distinction between a supplemental executive retirement plan and a deferred compensation agreement on the basis of whether the executive already earned the compensation in question. If the plan really provides additional benefits, it is referred to as a supplemental executive retirement plan. If compensation already earned by the employee is merely deferred primarily to save income taxes, the arrangement is referred to as a deferred compensation agreement. This chapter focuses first on the SERP and then briefly discusses the more individualized deferred compensation agreement. Many of the considerations discussed in the first instance, however, apply to both types of plan.

Executive Retirement Arrangements under ERISA

An executive retirement plan must (1) be unfunded and (2) cover a select group of management or highly compensated employees in order to be exempt from ERISA's benefit rules. In addition to setting maximum benefit limits on qualified plans, ERISA defines "excess benefit plans" as those that pay benefits or contributions above these limits. ERISA's reporting and disclosure requirements are greatly reduced for unfunded executive retirement plans in general and do not apply at all to excess benefit plans.[4] Excess benefit plans are not covered by plan termination insurance under ERISA nor are they subject to ERISA's employer liability upon plan termination.[5]

Effect of Social Security Amendments of 1983

Because the Federal Insurance Contribution Act (FICA) was somewhat vague concerning executive retirement arrangements, benefits received under such arrangements sometimes escaped FICA taxation. The 1983 amendments to the act affected both supplemental executive retirement plans and deferred compensation agreements beginning in 1984. Under the legislation, benefits under SERPs are subject to the tax either when the service for which the benefits are payable is performed or when they are considered nonforfeitable. The law may affect an executive under a deferred compensation agreement in a number of ways. First, if the

---

[4]The ERISA exemption applies to excess plans maintained by an employer solely for the purpose of providing benefits for certain employees in excess of the limitation on contributions and benefits imposed by IRC Section 415. Therefore, the exemption does not apply to excess plans established to compensate for the $200,000 compensation limit imposed on qualified plans.

[5]For a discussion of the impact of ERISA on nonqualified plans, see Arthur H. Kroll, *The Effect of ERISA upon Nonqualified Deferred Compensation Arrangements* (Philadelphia: American Law Institute, 1978), Folio 9.

deferred benefits should become nonforfeitable after the executive's retirement, and social security taxes up to the taxable wage base have not been paid, in the year earned or the year the benefits become nonforfeitable, the benefits will be taxed. Secondly, if the benefits are contingent upon postretirement services that the executive will perform for the employer, the executive could be considered to be self-employed and thereby subject to the FICA self-employment tax upon receipt of the benefits. Finally, depending upon the extent of any postretirement services, the benefits could be counted toward the amount the executive is permitted to earn under the social security earnings test before Social Security benefits are reduced. In most cases, however, the benefits will vest when the executive is working and earning in excess of the social security taxable wage base.

SUPPLEMENTAL EXECUTIVE RETIREMENT PLANS

Before questions of design, costing, and funding of SERPs can be considered, it is necessary to establish clearly the plan's objectives. The design of a SERP must be responsive to the basic objectives to be served by the program. For this reason, it is important to identify the various objectives and to establish their relative importance. The objectives most frequently set forth for implementing a SERP are as follows:[6]

Recruiting an executive in mid- or late-career whose combined pension, from current and prior employers, falls short of reasonable retirement income objectives, since only his or her current period of service reflects the compensation levels he or she achieves before retiring.

Providing retirement income in excess of that permitted from qualified retirement plans under ERISA.

Establishing an additional element of executive compensation that will attract and motivate qualified executives.

Discouraging certain executives from terminating employment prior to qualifying for early retirement benefits.

Encouraging the early retirement of some executives by providing unreduced benefits at an earlier age.

Design Considerations

A number of factors influence the ultimate design of a SERP.[7] The primary consideration is, of course, the objectives of the plan. For example, if

---

[6]For a discussion of objectives, see Edward J. Emering, "Top Hat Pension Plans," *Journal of Pension Planning and Compliance*, May 1980, p. 168.

[7]Emering, "Top Hat Pension Plans," p. 168.

the problem of mid-career recruiting is of major importance, the SERP probably should have a relatively short service requirement to achieve full benefits.

An important factor in the design of a SERP is the question of equity. Most SERPs provide the same level of benefits as a percentage of pay for all eligible executives. Frequently, only a relatively short period of service, such as 10 or 15 years, is required to achieve these benefits. It is possible that a long-service executive might perceive such a plan as being inequitable since his or her benefit will be no greater than the benefit provided for shorter-service executives. It should be noted that this problem is not prevalent under deferred compensation agreements since their emphasis is more on the idea of an individual arrangement than on a plan covering more than one executive. This is true even though deferral for individuals may be done under the umbrella of a master agreement.

A SERP should be designed with specific objectives and needs in mind. However, the patterns and practices that exist in other similar organizations must be recognized.

The income tax dimensions of a SERP have to be evaluated. Corporate tax deductions are allowed under an unfunded SERP only as benefits are paid.[8]

For the executive, the benefits will be taxed as ordinary income when they are paid—at a maximum marginal tax rate of 28 percent.[9] No special treatment is available for lump-sum distributions. Deferred compensation agreements involve other tax considerations and are discussed later in this chapter.

As with any other type of benefit program, the ultimate cost of a SERP will equal the sum of the benefits paid plus any expenses associated with plan administration. The amount of benefits paid, in turn, reflects elements of plan design such as eligibility requirements, benefit levels, early retirement age, the inclusion of ancillary benefits, and the like. Since benefits are not prefunded, there is no offsetting element, as there would be in a tax-qualified retirement plan for investment income on plan reserves. While costs can and should be projected and considered from the viewpoint of cash flow, they also must be considered from the viewpoint of a charge against net income in accordance with accounting requirements. Accounting requirements (described in Chapter 10) may involve the recog-

---

[8]The requirements of Statement of Financial Accounting Standards No. 87, *Employers' Accounting for Pensions,* may apply to arrangements that are similar to pension plans regardless of their form and whether written or not; for example, deferred compensation arrangements or supplemental executive retirement plans, when they are the equivalent of pension plans (i.e., benefits are based on a general formula rather than being tailored to each individual in payout terms and timing of payments). See Chapter 10 for a complete discussion of accounting for retirement plans.

[9]The maximum marginal rate of tax may be 33 percent due to the 5 percent surtax imposed to phase out personal exemptions and the 15 percent tax bracket on initial levels of taxable income.

nition of cost accruals over the period of the executive's active employment. Federal tax law requires that the cost and benefits of a SERP or other executive retirement arrangement must be "reasonable" in amount when related to the total compensation of the executives.[10]

From the executive's standpoint, after the provisions of the plan have been determined, the employer must make sure that neither the tax doctrine of constructive receipt nor the tax doctrine of economic benefit applies. Under these two doctrines, an employee can be taxed currently on income he or she is deferring. This would, in essence, defeat the purpose of such a plan. The doctrine of constructive receipt states that if a taxpayer could receive the income at any time but elects to receive it later, he or she is still taxed currently because the employee has a nonforfeitable right to the income; the doctrine of economic benefit states that if a taxpayer is receiving a current benefit, he or she should be taxed currently on the value of that benefit; this concept embodies the "payment in kind" or "cash equivalent" principle. Revenue Ruling 60–31 states that deferred compensation is not taxable before actual receipt whether it is forfeitable or nonforfeitable provided the deferral is agreed to before the compensation is earned, the deferral amount is not unconditionally placed in trust or in escrow for the benefit of the employee, and the promise to pay the deferred compensation is merely a contractual obligation not evidenced by notes or secured in any other manner. Thus, while certain assets may be earmarked and informally set aside to give some assurance that benefits will be paid, there must be no formal funding instrument and the executive must not have current access to the benefits.

The benefits of a SERP or other executive retirement arrangement, including those that might be provided on death or disability of the executive, should recognize all other company-provided benefits, including those provided only for executives. For example, the determination of whether a SERP should provide a spouse benefit could be influenced by the presence or absence of a supplemental life insurance plan for executives. Government-provided benefits, such as social security, usually are taken into account. The following discusses a variety of plan provisions that may be included in a SERP to fit the individual needs of the employer and the employees.

Eligibility for Participation.   As was stated earlier, to be exempt from ERISA's various benefit rules an executive retirement plan must be maintained primarily for a select group of management or highly compensated employees. Thus, eligibility for participation normally is limited to members of top management who make significant contributions to the organization's success. This definition is subject to wide interpretation, however, and care should be taken to restrict eligibility to those executives for whom

---

[10]Federal Tax Regs. 1.162.7. See also Jerry S. Rosenbloom, "Distinguishing between Qualified and Nonqualified Deferred Compensation," in *Deferred Compensation*, ed. Herbert Chasman (Homewood, Ill.: Dow Jones-Irwin, 1978), pp. 3–4.

the plan is really intended. Eligibility requirements that are too broad or that are established so that they automatically expand the group covered (e.g., a minimum salary requirement that is eroded by inflationary pressure) can lead to substantial cost increases for an employer.

The most frequently used criteria to establish eligibility for participation is position. For the reasons noted above, a minimum salary requirement is generally not desirable unless it is tied to some sort of price or wage index. Some organizations determine eligibility by whether the executive is eligible for the company's incentive compensation program.

Some plans avoid the use of specific eligibility requirements and require the executive to be designated for consideration by a group such as the compensation committee of the board of directors of the corporation. Even when specific eligibility requirements are used, it might be desirable to have the flexibility of permitting the designation of individual executives who might not otherwise be eligible but to whom, for unusual reasons, coverage should be extended.

No constraints are imposed by the IRC or ERISA for the selection of eligibility criteria; however, if the group covered is so large that it extends beyond a select group of management or highly compensated employees, the SERP could become a retirement plan under ERISA and subject to all its requirements.

Defined Benefit or Defined Contribution.   As with qualified plans, supplemental executive retirement plans may take the form of a defined benefit or defined contribution plan.

In a defined benefit plan, the benefit could be: (1) a flat dollar amount; (2) an indexed dollar amount; or (3) a percentage of a portion of earnings either weighted for length of service or not and indexed or not. Offsets to the benefit might come from the employer's basic plans, social security, benefits from a prior employer, and other employer incentive plans such as a profit sharing plan, stock-option plan, or deferred compensation agreement the executive has with the employer. For instance, a plan might provide a benefit based upon a certain percentage of final average earnings for each year of service, including credit for service with a previous employer, up to some combined maximum, minus any basic plan benefits from both the current and any prior employer and primary social security benefits. Or, it might combine a higher percentage of final average earnings with a smaller number of maximum years less basic employer plan benefits. Or instead, some employers might use a given percentage of total compensation and subtract from this any benefits to which the executive is entitled either from the basic plan or from a prior employer. In any case, the objectives of the plan will determine how the benefit is to be set.

In a defined contribution plan, the contribution rate is often a stated dollar or percentage-of-pay amount that may or may not be conditioned on the executive's or the employer's performance. As with a defined benefit plan, the objectives of the plan will determine the method by which the contribution is set, and although a dollar or percentage-of-pay amount commonly is used, there is no one rule for choosing the form of the contribution.

In order to maintain the unfunded status of the plan, the plan may not invest the contributions themselves, and several methods have arisen to determine the investment growth in a defined contribution plan. Earmarking and setting aside certain assets to determine investment growth and pay benefits is a frequently used approach, or the employer could make hypothetical investments and base benefits on the growth of these. A third method might base the growth on any of the following: (1) employer earnings; (2) a specified interest rate; (3) a specified index of either investment yield or asset fluctuation; or (4) a specified index of wage or cost-of-living fluctuation. It should be remembered that even though certain assets are informally set aside to provide for future benefits, the employer may not take a deduction for the contributions themselves and must pay tax on any investment earnings on these assets unless the investment is tax exempt or consists of the stock of other companies, in which case 80 percent of the dividend income is tax exempt.

In some instances, employers may purchase insurance contracts to cover the future costs of benefits. If the employee were the owner, he or she would be considered to be in constructive receipt of the benefits and incur a current tax liability. If, however, the employer is both the policyholder and the beneficiary, the income is not currently taxable to the employee. In addition, although premiums may not be deducted from the employer's taxable income, investment earnings are not currently taxable to the employer and policy dividends and death benefits are not taxable when received.[11]

As mentioned earlier, the use of a defined benefit or a defined contribution plan will be determined by the objectives of the employer and of the executive or executives to be covered. In some instances, when the plan covers only one executive or a group of executives with similar characteristics, the choice may be purely one of preference in approach. The defined benefit approach is perhaps a better way to achieve a given level of retirement income. The defined contribution method, on the other hand, may prove more useful in situations where the employer wishes to base the benefit on criteria of performance. The many variables that must be considered in determining how a plan should be constructed, and that will influence the decision on whether to use a defined benefit or a defined contribution approach as well, follow.

Retirement Benefits.   In determining the level of retirement benefits to be provided by a SERP, a number of elements must be considered.

---

[11]If a corporation or partnership owns a deferred *annuity* contract, the annual increase in value of the contract is includable in the owner's gross income. Moreover, 50 percent of the inside buildup in value of company-held insurance and annuity policies and policy proceeds will be subject to the corporate alternative minimum tax; after 1989, 75 percent will be subject to the tax.

These include the compensation base to be used to determine benefits; the basic income level, as a percentage of compensation, to be provided; and the service necessary for full benefits. Also evaluated should be the sources of benefit considered in arriving at the amount of the supplemental benefit, the earliest age at which full, unreduced benefits will be payable, and the conditions, if any, under which benefits might be forfeited.

Income Objectives.   The setting of income objectives for a SERP is approached in the same way as these objectives are set for basic qualified retirement plans. SERPs generally establish an income replacement target for executives of from 50 to 55 percent of gross pay. A higher replacement objective might draw criticism from shareholders, and raise issues about the reasonableness of an executive's compensation from the viewpoint of the tax deductibility of corporate contributions.

Compensation Base.   The benefits of a SERP should be related as a minimum to the executive's basic salary. Since incentive compensation normally constitutes a significant part of an executive's total compensation, and since such incentive compensation influences the executive's standard of living, it is reasonable to include at least part of such incentive pay in the compensation base of benefits.

Once the elements of compensation have been identified, it is necessary to establish the period over which this compensation base will be determined. The most common provision is to average pay over a period of time, such as three or five years (i.e., highest three- or five-year average during the last 10 years of employment)—particularly when incentive pay is included as part of the base.

Service.   To make sure the executive has made a significant contribution to the organization before retirement, some minimum service requirement is appropriate. If a major plan objective of a SERP is to assist in mid- or late-career recruiting, the plan probably should limit the service needed to achieve the full level of benefits. For this purpose, service periods of 10 or 15 years are common. The plan may exclude any executive who does not meet this minimum service requirement or it may provide such an individual with only proportionate benefits.

Where mid- or late-career recruiting is not a major plan objective, longer service periods may be required. However, many SERPs use a service period somewhat shorter than the service period required to accrue full benefits under the company's basic qualified retirement plan. Also, when longer service is required, it is more likely that shorter service executives receive proportionately reduced benefits rather than being excluded completely.

A commonly found variation in SERPs is to tie the service requirement to the income objective of the plan on a weighted basis so that a relatively large portion of the benefit is accrued in a short period of time. A formula that produces 5 percent of pay for each of the first 5 years of service and 2.5 percent for each of the next 10 years, thus producing 25 percent of pay in 5 years, 37.5 percent in 10 years, and 50 percent in 15 years would be an example.

Benefit Sources.   The basic concept of a SERP is that it provides a layer of benefit which, when added to other benefits, brings an executive's total retirement income to a predetermined level. The two major sources recognized for this purpose are the company's basic qualified retirement plan and social security. Any other company-provided retirement benefits should also be recognized, but voluntary plans such as savings plans and elective contributions to CODAs normally are not taken into account even though they represent a potential source of retirement income. Another possible source of benefit that should be considered is the amount of any vested benefits the executive might have by reason of prior employment. In a SERP designed with liberal benefits and short-service requirements, it would be reasonable to take such benefits into account. However, only a few plans make provision for this type of offset.

Age at Retirement.   A major objective of many SERPs is to permit and/ or encourage certain executives to retire prior to the company's normal retirement age. The SERP usually follows the pattern of the company's basic qualified retirement plan and sets age 65 as the normal retirement age. However, it is also common for the executive to be able to retire with full unreduced benefits as early as age 60 or 62 if any required service has been completed. Typically, although not necessarily, the age chosen for early retirement on this basis ties in with the age at which unreduced benefits are available under the company's basic qualified retirement plan.

The extent to which full unreduced benefits are made available and the establishment of age and/or service requirements that must be met reflect the degree to which the company wishes, from a personnel viewpoint, to encourage the early retirement of executives. If the primary interest is in encouraging early retirement on a selective basis, it might be appropriate to provide full, unreduced benefits only in company-initiated retirements.

When full, unreduced benefits are not available, for example, for retirement after age 55 but before age 60, with less than the full amount of required service, or without necessary company consent, the company may provide a reduced benefit such as the benefit otherwise available reduced by 5 percent per year for each year that retirement precedes age 60. Generally, early retirement would not be made available, even on a reduced basis, before the employee also would be eligible to retire under the company's basic qualified retirement plan, for example, age 55 with 10 years of service.

Forfeitures.   The forfeiture of retirement benefits when an employee goes to work for a competitor has never been very common in qualified retirement plans, and is prohibited by ERISA. However, such a prohibition does not apply to unfunded SERP benefits. In view of the executive levels and the amount of benefits involved, particularly in SERPs that include lib-eral early retirement provisions, such forfeiture provisions are frequently found in SERPs and provide some degree of protection for the company.

Forms of Payment.   Generally, retirement benefits are paid in monthly installments for the lifetime of the executive. Because of the tie-in with the company's basic qualified retirement plan, the executive is usually given the right to elect optional forms of payment on the same terms, conditions, and actuarial bases available for basic retirement benefits.

The option of providing the SERP benefit in a lump sum is rarely made available to the executive. The primary reason is that no tax advantages exist with such a distribution and the entire amount would be treated as taxable income in one year. A second reason for not allowing this option is that the company would lose control over the executive's ability to enter into competitive employment after retirement. The issue of constructive receipt may also be a problem if this option is provided.

Death Benefits.   It is possible to provide preretirement and/or postre-tirement death benefits under a SERP. Such benefits might take the form of providing or continuing a percentage of the retirement benefit the exec-utive was entitled to receive or was receiving in the event of his or her death while eligible to retire or after having retired. Such a benefit is nor-mally payable to the executive's spouse but could be paid to any one of a group of survivors, such as dependent children, brothers, and sisters. If paid to a spouse, such a benefit could be paid for life or for a fixed period such as 10 years. Benefits to children or other survivors could be paid for a fixed number of years or, in the case of children, until they reach a certain age, such as 21. Lump-sum death benefits are rarely paid as part of a SERP; as a rule, such benefits are more tax effective if provided under group life insurance programs.

Death benefits under a SERP can be provided at company cost or can be provided on a basis that requires some contribution by the executive. Typically, any cost to the executive is established by reducing the benefit otherwise payable by the use of option factors in the case of postretirement benefits, or by a straight percentage reduction in the case of preretirement benefits.

Disability Benefits.   Many organizations maintain long-term disability income programs that provide disability income payments until an employee is age 65. During the period of disability, the employee gener-ally continues to accrue pension credits based on his or her last rate of pay and, at age 65, is considered as retired under the basic retirement plan. If a SERP is adopted, it is necessary to coordinate the SERP benefits with the long-term disability income program. One common approach is to provide the regular SERP benefits when the disabled executive reaches age 65.

Another approach is to provide all or part of the SERP benefits immediately upon disability, offsetting any disability income benefits payable to the executive until his or her basic retirement benefits begin.

If SERP benefits are provided under either approach, an important question to resolve is whether SERP benefits will be provided if the executive had not met the SERP service requirement prior to becoming disabled.

Vesting.   If an executive terminates employment prior to the earliest retirement age possible, it is not customary to provide him or her with a vested interest in an unfunded SERP. An exception might be when a major objective of the SERP is to assist in mid- or late-career recruiting. In this situation, it may be necessary to offer some degree of protection to the executive. If vesting is desired, one approach is to provide an accrued benefit once the basic service requirement for SERP benefits has been attained.

Funding Considerations

A SERP of the type described in this chapter is generally funded on a current disbursement basis; that is, company contributions are made as benefit payments come due. Such a plan is considered an "unfunded" plan because of the absence of any prefunding of obligations.

Funding such a plan could cause serious consequences. First, the plan would lose its exemption from ERISA compliance. More important, however, are the tax considerations applicable to a funded plan. Company contributions to a funded plan would not be deductible unless and until the executive achieves a nonforfeitable interest. And, as soon as the executive's rights become nonforfeitable, he or she could be considered in constructive receipt of the value of the then accrued benefit even if the funds were not then available to the executive. Further, once his or her rights become nonforfeitable, all future company contributions could be taxable to the executive as they are made, even though not then paid to the executive. Since ERISA requires vested interests be created under funded plans, even if not tax qualified, the issue of nonforfeitable rights with attendant tax consequences cannot be avoided. Even though not funded, certain accounting considerations must be observed.

For the previously mentioned reasons, it is obvious that SERPs cannot be funded with the advantages of a qualified plan. As was discussed earlier, there exist ways in which an employer may set aside assets to pay the benefits when they come due.

Benefit and Cost Information

Once a preliminary decision is made concerning the major provisions of a SERP, it is important that benefit illustrations and cost projections be made for the eligible participants. Such information enables the employer to test the operation of the tentative plan provisions and determine whether estimated costs are within acceptable parameters.

ERISA compliance for plans covering a select group of management or highly compensated employees is minimal. Unfunded plans covering such employees are only subject to Part 1 (reporting and disclosure) and Part 5 (administration and enforcement) of subtitle B of Title I of ERISA. The reporting and disclosure rules can be met by complying with the regulation requiring the forwarding of a statement to the Department of Labor. The administration and enforcement requirements under ERISA are satisfied with a claims procedure statement.

DEFERRED COMPENSATION AGREEMENTS

While the main purpose of supplemental executive retirement plans is to provide the executive with an additional layer of retirement benefits over and above those provided by the employer's basic plan, deferred compensation agreements deal primarily with earnings deferral, usually to gain tax advantages, with retirement income as a secondary consideration. Postponing the receipt of current income not only reduces executives' current taxable income, but puts them in receipt of the funds after retirement when they may be in a lower tax bracket. However, any deferral of income to a future date must take into consideration the potential effects of increased interest and inflation rates as well as current tax considerations, all of which have cast some doubt upon the effectiveness of such deferral. These combined factors have led some to believe that the executive would be better off receiving the income as it is earned, paying the taxes due, and investing the remainder.

Other reasons for deferring current income from both the executive's and the employer's viewpoints are: (1) extending the executive's income beyond normal working years into retirement; (2) spreading bonuses over a wider span of years; (3) tying the executive to the employer by stipulating conditions on the receipt of deferred amounts; and (4) adding to the executive's retirement income.

The factors to be considered in drawing up the agreement are much the same as those that were discussed for supplemental executive retirement plans and include how much compensation will be deferred, whether investment growth will be added to such amounts, whether there will be conditions on receiving the funds, and what the various benefit options will be.

In order to avoid the possibility of the executive's being judged to be in constructive receipt of the deferred funds, three rules contained in Revenue Ruling 60–31 must be followed in drawing up a deferred compensation agreement. They are: (1) the deferral must be irrevocable; (2) the deferral should be agreed to before the compensation is earned; and (3) the deferral must be for a specified length of time. The agreement must also serve a business purpose.

SUMMARY

Because of their nonqualified status, executive retirement arrangements permit a degree of flexibility unavailable in the more restricted qualified plans. When properly designed and administered, executive retirement arrangements can serve a number of needs that exist in the relationship between an employer and the executive that do not apply to the rest of the work force. From the employer's point of view, such arrangements can help attract and keep qualified executives, reward such executives for productivity and loyalty, and encourage the early retirement of certain executives. The executive, on the other hand, may look forward to retirement income higher than that provided by the employer's regular plan, or at least to full pension benefits in the case of a short-service executive; certain tax advantages; additional insurance coverage and dependent coverage; early retirement with full benefits; and the extension of income into retirement.

QUESTIONS FOR REVIEW

1. What are the typical objectives of an employer in establishing a SERP? Explain.
2. What is the ultimate cost of a SERP for an employer? Explain.
3. Describe the eligibility requirements typically used under a SERP.
4. Identify the considerations typically used to establish the level of retirement benefits and income objectives available under a SERP.
5. Describe how the compensation base applicable to benefits under a SERP usually is established.
6. Explain the reasons for including service requirements in SERPs and the types of service requirements used.
7. How can a SERP be used to encourage early retirement? Explain.
8. Are lump-sum options normally made available under SERPs? Explain.
9. Why would an employer choose not to fund a SERP? Explain.
10. Describe the advantages of deferred compensation arrangements.

QUESTIONS FOR DISCUSSION

1. Discuss the likely impact of the Tax Reform Act of 1986 on executive retirement arrangements.
2. Discuss the conditions under which an employer may desire to establish an executive retirement arrangement.

Index